A Guide To STARTING A BUSINESS IN MINNESOTA

Thirty-ninth Edition, January 2021

Charles A. Schaffer
Madeline Harris
Mark Simmer

ISBN 978-1-888404-85-2

PREFACE

This thirty-ninth edition of A Guide to Starting a Business in Minnesota, like its predecessors, is intended to provide a concise, summary discussion of the major issues faced by those starting a business in Minnesota. This edition of the Guide contains three major sections: the narrative text; a Resource Directory, which provides addresses, telephone numbers, and website addresses of organizations referenced in the text; and the Directory of Licenses and Permits, which lists all business licenses and permits required by the State of Minnesota, the state agency which issues or administers the license or permit, and contact information. Topics presented in the narrative text are presented in the order in which the new business owner typically must address them. Note that a business that will have operations or a physical presence (with the possible inclusion of an Internet presence) in another state should check with the government authorities in that state to obtain information on licensing, tax and other issues. We hope this organization is useful.

While no one publication can answer every question for every kind of proposed business, this Guide does respond to the questions and concerns most frequently raised. While it tries to be both timely and comprehensive, this Guide is not intended as a final statement on any one subject. In particular, users should be aware that the formal legal requirements for business start-up and operations may change from time to time. Specific updates and additional information may be obtained from the many sources listed.

Before engaging in any business venture, it is advisable to seek both legal counsel and advice from an accountant. Both professionals can advise you as to the best course you might take in establishing your business. The information provided in this Guide is not intended to replace that kind of advice and assistance.

Charles A. Schaffer
Madeline Harris
Mark Simmer

TABLE OF CONTENTS

CHOOSING THE FORM OF BUSINESS ORGANIZATION

TAX AND NON-TAX CONSIDERATIONS

INTRODUCTION

One of the fundamental initial decisions a new business owner faces is choosing the form of organization for the business. Generally speaking, a person should consider himself or herself to be "in business" once they have begun the operation of an activity for which they expect to be paid. This is true whether or not that person terminates other employment (such as a job that brings a paycheck), or intends to operate that business on a seasonal or short-term basis. For most businesses, the choices are:

Sole Proprietorship. In a **sole proprietorship**, the business is owned and controlled by one individual. This person alone receives the profits and bears the losses from the business, and this person alone is responsible for the debts and obligations of the business. Income and expenses of the business are reported on the proprietor's individual income tax return, and profits are taxed at the proprietor's individual income tax rate. If a husband and wife wish to own a business together, they must either form a partnership, corporation or limited liability company (in order to have each of them be an owner of the business) or a sole proprietorship (in which case only one of them will be an owner of the business).

Partnership. A **general partnership** is a business owned by two or more persons who associate to carry on the business as a partnership. Partnerships have specific attributes, which are defined by statute. All partners in a general partnership share equally in the right, and responsibility, to manage the business, and each partner is responsible for all the debts and obligations of the business. Distribution of profits and losses, allocation of management responsibilities, and other issues affecting the partnership usually are defined in a written partnership agreement. Income and expenses of the partnership are reported on federal and state "information" tax returns, which are filed by the partnership. These include Schedules K-1 which are used to report to the partner's respective shares of partnership taxable income. The partners then report this income on their separate tax returns along with their other income and pay tax at their applicable income tax rates.

A married couple who jointly operate an unincorporated business and who file a joint federal income tax return can elect not to be treated as a partnership for federal tax purposes provided that the husband and wife are the only members of the joint venture and materially participate in the running of the business. For more information refer to the Business Income Tax Returns section of this Guide.

A **limited partnership** is a type of partnership in which the limited partners share in the partnership's liability only up to the amount of their investment in the limited partnership. By statute, the limited partnership must have at least one general partner and one limited partner. The general partner has the right and responsibility to control the limited partnership, and is responsible for the debts and obligations of the limited partnership. In Minnesota, a limited partner may participate in the management and control of the limited partnership without losing limited liability protection but does not have the power to act for or bind the limited partnership (unless this is provided for in a separate agreement). Limited partnerships must be established in compliance with statutory requirements, including requirements of tax and securities laws. Because of their complex nature, limited partnerships should not be undertaken without competent professional advice.

Limited Liability Partnership and Limited Liability Limited Partnership. A general partnership may register as a **limited liability partnership (LLP)** by filing a limited liability partnership registration. In limited liability partnerships, the personal assets of the partners are shielded against liabilities incurred by the partnership in tort or contract situations. This is different from a non-LLP general partnership, in which partners may be personally liable to an unlimited extent for the debts and obligations of the partnership. It should be noted that limited liability partnerships are a relatively new type of entity and certain aspects, such as tax aspects, of such entities are not yet fully developed or understood.

Limited liability partnership status affords protection to the individual partner from liability for partnership obligations in tort and contract. An LLP files with the Secretary of State an annual report. There is a one-year grace period for retroactive reinstatement after revocation of LLP status for failure to file the annual report.

Limited liability partnerships must have a name that includes one of the following: "Registered Limited Liability Partnership," "Limited Liability Partnership," "R.L.L.P.," "L.L.P.," "RLLP," or "LLP. This should be used by the partnership in transactions with third parties so that they are aware of the partnership's status.

Minnesota law also allows a limited partnership to elect limited liability status under Minn. Stat. Chapter 321 by so designating this status in its certificate of limited partnership. This extends limited liability protection to both general and limited partners. This type of limited partnership is called a limited liability limited partnership. Limited liability limited partnerships are discussed below.

Care should be taken in naming a limited liability limited partnership; the name must contain the phrase "limited liability limited partnership" or the abbreviation "LLLP" or "L.L.L.P.", which must be part of the name, and must not otherwise contain the abbreviation "L.P." or "LP."

Corporation. A corporation is a separate legal entity. It is owned by one or more shareholders. The corporation must be established in compliance with the statutory requirements of the state of incorporation. The shareholders elect a board of directors which has responsibility for management and control of the corporation. Because the corporation is a separate legal entity, the corporation is responsible for the debts and obligations of the business. In most cases, shareholders are insulated from claims against the corporation.

It is worth noting here that because a corporation is an entity separate from its owners, if the owner (and/or members of the owner's family) performs services for the corporation, these persons are considered to be employees of the corporation. Thus, the corporation will be required to comply with most of the laws and regulations and reporting requirements applicable to employers.

The corporation may be taxed under Subchapter C of the Internal Revenue Code (a "C corporation") or the provisions of Subchapter S of the Code (an "S corporation"). Minnesota tax laws provide for comparable treatment.

A C corporation reports its income and expenses on a corporation income tax return and is taxed on its profits at corporate income tax rates. The Minnesota corporate franchise tax, sometimes called an income tax, is based on the portion of a C corporation's income that is allocated to Minnesota. Profits are taxed without regard to payment of dividends, which generally are not deductible. Dividends paid to shareholders are taxable income to them. This is sometimes referred to as "double taxation" because this effectively taxes operating income twice, once to the corporation and then again when distributed to the owners, although it actually is two separate taxpayers being taxed on their separate income.

An S corporation election may be made by the shareholders of the corporation if the corporation meets the statutory requirements for S corporation status. An S corporation that has not previously been taxed as a C corporation is taxed in much the same manner as a partnership, i.e., the S corporation files an information return to report its income and expenses, but it generally is not separately taxed. Income and expenses of the S corporation "pass through" to the shareholders in proportion to their shareholdings, and then are taxed to them at their individual rates. Under the Internal Revenue Code, an S corporation may have only one class of stock (i.e., "common" stock, although voting differences are permitted), no more than 100 shareholders, and no shareholders that are nonresident aliens or non-individuals (e.g., corporations, partnerships, limited liability companies) except for certain estates, trusts, and certain tax exempt entities. The federal 2004 American Jobs Creation act allows an S corporation to treat shareholders within six generations of one family as one shareholder thus allowing family business S corporations to distribute shares to family members of existing shareholders without those new shareholders being counted as new shareholders against the 100 shareholder limit. S corporations are described in more detail in later sections of this Guide. (If the shareholders of an existing C corporation elect to have it taxed as an S corporation additional rules as well as corporate level taxes may come into play. Any such change in tax status should be discussed in advance with a competent tax advisor.)

A **closely held corporation** is any corporation whose shares are held by a relatively small number of shareholders. The Minnesota Business Corporation Act defines a closely held corporation as one which does not have more than 35 shareholders. Most closely held corporations are relatively small business enterprises, in which all shareholders tend to be active in the management of the business. Some states provide a separate, less formal, less restrictive set of laws for closely-held corporations. Minnesota does not. In Minnesota, the business corporation law is geared to small corporations, so a separate law is not necessary, and all corporations operate under one law.

Limited Liability Company. A Minnesota business also may organize as a limited liability company. A limited liability company may have one or more members. As described further in the section on tax considerations in choosing the form of organization, under Treasury Regulations regarding entity classification the members of limited liability companies have some flexibility with respect to the federal income tax treatment of their entities. Under these rules a limited liability company with more than one member will be taxed as a partnership unless it elects to be taxed as a corporation and a limited liability company with only one member will be taxed as a sole proprietorship (a "disregarded entity") unless it elects to be taxed as a corporation. The applicable Regulations appear in 26 C.F.R. § 301.7701-1, et. seq.

A limited liability company that is taxed as a partnership or as a corporation must obtain its own tax ID numbers. A limited liability company with only one member that is taxed as a sole proprietorship generally does not need to obtain separate federal or state tax identification numbers unless it has employees or pays federal excise taxes, in which case it will obtain tax ID numbers and use them to remit employment taxes or pay excise taxes.

Business income and losses of a limited liability company that is taxed as a partnership or as a sole proprietorship are passed through to the members, included in their taxable income, and taxed at each member's income tax rate. As with a corporation, liability for business debts and obligations generally rests with the entity rather than with the individual owners. A limited liability company is not subject to many of the restrictions that apply to S corporations (unless it elects to be taxed as a corporation and wishes to be taxed as an S corporation). All members of a limited liability company may participate in the active management of the company without risking loss of limited personal liability. Minnesota adopted a new Limited Liability Company Act (Minn. Stat. Chapter 322C) that became effective August 1, 2015. Minnesota limited liability companies formed on or after that date are subject to the new act, and may be managed by the members, by a board of governors, or by a manager.

Other Forms of Organization. Other forms of organization available to Minnesota businesses include professional organizations, cooperative associations, business trusts, and certain variations of these forms of organization. These types of organizations are established and regulated by statute and involve complex legal, financial and accounting issues. Organizing under any of these forms should not be attempted without competent professional advice. Because of their highly specialized nature, these forms of organization are not addressed in detail in this Guide.

Changing the Form of Organization. Note that although the discussion in the above paragraphs is also applicable when changing the form of business organization, (e.g., when converting a sole proprietorship to a corporation), a business owner is strongly urged to seek professional assistance when doing so, because unintended consequences may result, often including significant tax consequences. For example, contracts entered into by the business may or may not be assignable to the new entity. Also, there may be tax costs to changing the form of organization, such as when an S corporation becomes a C corporation. Minnesota law also authorizes conversions in either direction between corporations and limited liability companies (including with organizations from other states that permit conversion from or into a Minnesota entity). The converting organization must adopt a plan of conversion that must be approved governors in accordance with the entity's governing statute. Upon approval, articles of conversion are drafted and filed with the Secretary of State who then will issue a certificate of conversion and a certificate of incorporation or certificate of organization if the resulting organization is a Minnesota corporation or limited liability company. Again, these changes can produce significant tax consequences and should be undertaken only when these are fully understood. For example, a conversion of a corporation into a limited liability company that is taxed as a partnership is treated for income tax purposes as a taxable liquidation of the corporation, which can produce taxable gain to both the corporation and its shareholders.

NON-TAX FACTORS IN CHOOSING THE FORM OF ORGANIZATION

In choosing the most appropriate form of organization, the business owner will want to consider a variety of factors, including: complexity and expense of organizing the business; liability of the business owner; distribution of profits and losses; management control and decision making; financing startup and operation of the business; transferability of ownership interest; continuity of the business entity following withdrawal or death of an owner; complexity and expense of terminating or reorganizing the business; extent of governmental regulation, as well as tax considerations.

These factors should be examined carefully in light of the objectives of the business owner. Competent legal, accounting and tax professionals can provide valuable advice and assistance in selecting the most appropriate form of organization.

As with many business decisions, choosing a form of organization involves weighing the advantages and disadvantages of each alternative before selecting the form most appropriate to the business owner's situation. No one form of organization will be appropriate to all situations, and as the business expands a change in the form of organization may be necessary. The discussion which follows examines the differences in each of the above factors for proprietorships, partnerships, corporations, and limited liability companies.

Complexity and Expense of Organizing the Business

All businesses, regardless of their form, will encounter certain organizational costs. These costs can include developing a business plan, obtaining necessary licenses and permits, conducting market research studies, acquiring equipment, obtaining the advice of counsel, and other costs.

Sole Proprietorship. The sole proprietorship is the simplest form of organization, and the least expensive to establish. There are no statutory requirements unique to this form of organization. From a regulatory standpoint, the business owner only needs to obtain the necessary business licenses and tax identification numbers, register the business name, and begin operations. Many individuals begin their business as a sole proprietorship. As the business expands or more owners are needed for financial or other reasons, a partnership or corporation may be formed.

Partnership. A **general partnership** is more complex to organize than a sole proprietorship, but involves fewer formalities and legal restrictions than a limited partnership, corporation, or limited liability company. Basic elements of partnership law are established by statute, but most issues can be determined by agreement of the partners. A written partnership agreement is highly recommended, but is not legally required. Factors to consider in a partnership agreement are listed in a later section of this Guide. The partnership agreement is not required to be filed with any governmental entity. Note that under the Revised Uniform Partnership Act (RUPA) of 1997, Minn. Stat. Chapter 323A, partnerships have the option of filing with the Secretary of State certain statements regarding the authority and liability of partners as well as the status of the partnership.

A **limited partnership** must meet specific statutory requirements at the time of organization, and the offering of ownership interests in the limited partnership is subject to securities laws. Accordingly, the limited partnership often is more complex and expensive to organize than a general partnership.

Limited Liability Partnership and Limited Liability Limited Partnership. An existing general partnership may elect limited liability partnership status by filing a limited liability partnership registration with the Secretary of State. Such registration is effective for an indefinite period of time. Limited liability limited partnerships are also permitted. Anyone interested in forming an LLP or an LLLP is advised to seek the advice of counsel. Note also under applicable statutes, limited liability status has an indefinite term, although the Secretary of State will revoke LLP or LLLP status if the required annual registration is not filed. Limited liability partnerships and limited liability limited partnerships generally follow the basic partnership or limited partnership law with specific exceptions as provided by law.

Corporation. The corporation is a formal and complex form of organization, and accordingly can be expensive to organize. Procedures and criteria for forming the corporation and for its governance are established by statute. **FAILURE TO FOLLOW THE STATUTORY FORMALITIES CAN RESULT IN LOSS OF CORPORATE STATUS AND IMPOSITION OF PERSONAL LIABILITY ON THE INCORPORATORS OR SHAREHOLDERS.** The S corporation faces further complexity in that an election to be taxed as an S corporation for federal tax purposes must be filed with the Internal Revenue Service in a timely fashion. In addition, care must be taken in the transfer of shares not to inadvertently lose S corporation status.

Because of the complexities involved in incorporating, corporations often will make greater use of professional advisors, which will increase costs. Other costs associated with incorporating include filing fees, which are greater for corporations, and the costs associated with tax compliance and preparing various government reports. If the corporation does business in other states, it generally will be required to register to do business in those states, thus further increasing the cost and complexity of incorporation. And, if the corporation will raise capital by selling securities, the compliance costs involved will be substantial.

Minnesota has attempted to simplify the incorporation process by including in the Minnesota Business Corporation Act all of the rules pertaining to the internal governance of the corporation. A corporation that agrees to be governed as specified in the statute need only file standard form articles of incorporation with the Secretary of State. The corporation that wishes to vary the statutory requirements generally must do so in its articles of incorporation. Prior consultation with legal counsel can assist the incorporators in determining which approach is most appropriate for the corporation. Further information on incorporating appears in the section of this Guide titled "Forming a Minnesota Business Corporation".

Limited Liability Company. The new Minnesota Revised Uniform Limited Liability Company Act takes a more partnership-like approach to these entities than did the prior Act. Nevertheless a limited liability company often will combine aspects of both partnerships and corporations. In many cases where the governance and economic rights are simple and allocated among the members equally, one can expect formation to be similar to a corporation in complexity and cost to organize. As with a corporation, the procedures and criteria for forming a limited liability company are specified by statute. **FAILURE TO FOLLOW THE STATUTORY REQUIREMENTS CAN RESULT IN LOSS OF LIMITED LIABILITY COMPANY STATUS AND IMPOSITION OF PERSONAL LIABILITY ON THE ORGANIZERS AND MEMBERS OF THE COMPANY**. There is very little case law to guide organizational and operational decisions, although Minnesota's current limited liability company law is modeled on the Revised Uniform Limited Liability Company Act, and the commentary to that may be helpful and can be found at Uniform Law Commission, https://bit.ly/2F0nK5A.

In addition, the Minnesota Revised Uniform Limited Liability Company Act contains default rules that will apply in the absence of an agreement by the member (for example, each member has equal management rights and the right to an equal percentage of nonliquidating distributions made by the limited liability company. Members of limited liability companies need to be familiar with these rules. They often will want a formal written agreement where their intentions differ from the law's default rules. For these and many other reasons, owners of a limited liability company may need to consult often with their professional advisors, increasing their costs.

Under the Treasury Regulations dealing with the federal income tax classification of business entities, the members of a limited liability company have some flexibility in choosing the tax status of their entity. Professional advice in this area is strongly encouraged.

As is the case for Minnesota corporations, members of a limited liability company may agree to have the company governed by the default provisions of the governing statute – Minn. Stat. Chapter 322C. In that case, standard form articles of organization may be used to organize the company. The law, however, permits the members of these entities to vary many of the default provisions of Minn. Stat. Chapter 322C through agreements called "operating agreements". While it is advisable in most instances to reduce an operating agreement to writing, that is not required. Like a partnership agreement, an operating agreement may be oral, in a record (e.g., in written or electronic format), implied by conduct, or in any combination thereof, as long as it is the agreement of all persons who are members when the agreement is entered into.

Further information on forming a limited liability company appears in the section of this Guide on Forming a Minnesota Limited Liability Company.

Liability of the Business Owners

Sole Proprietorship. The sole proprietor is personally liable for the debts of the business, even if those debts exceed the owner's investment in the business. All of the owner's assets – both those used in the business and personal property (subject to certain exemptions) – can be attached by creditors and sold to pay business debts. The sole proprietor may be able to minimize certain risks such as property loss, personal injury or product liability by obtaining adequate insurance.

Partnership. In a non-LLP **general partnership**, each partner may be personally liable for up to the full amount of the debts of the business, even if the debts exceed the owners' investment in the business. The partner with greater personal assets thus risks losing more than a partner with fewer personal assets. As with a sole proprietorship, many business risks can be lessened by obtaining adequate insurance.

However, in a Minnesota **limited liability partnership,** partners are not personally liable for the wrongful acts or omissions in the ordinary course of business of other partners, for the misuse of money or property of a non-partner by another partner, or for the debts or obligations of the partnership, subject to certain exceptions. It is uncertain how this kind of partnership will be treated in other states, although most states have adopted some form of limited liability partnership legislation.

In a **limited partnership**, so long as the statutory formalities are met and the limited partner is not relied upon by others as a general partner, the limited partner generally is not liable for the obligations of the limited partnership. Thus the limited partner risks loss only up to the amount of his or her investment. The general partner retains full liability as in any other partnership. In **limited liability limited partnerships** general partners will enjoy the same protections from liability enjoyed by limited partners or partners of an LLP.

Corporation. The corporation is a separate legal entity, and in most cases is the entity that is liable for the debts of the business. The shareholders generally are exempt from personal liability for those debts and thus risk loss only up to the amount of their investment in the corporation. This is true for both C corporations and the S corporations. It should be noted, however, that in a small, closely held or newly created corporation without an established credit history, some or all of the shareholders may be expected to personally guarantee repayment of certain corporate debts as a condition of obtaining a loan or credit.

Also, under certain circumstances such as fraud or personal wrongdoing, a court may "pierce" the liability shield and hold shareholders personally liable for wrongful acts. Finally, it is possible for courts to "disregard" the corporate entity and make shareholders liable under certain circumstances, especially where the corporation and the shareholders themselves have not respected the corporate entity by commingling corporate funds with those of other persons or having the corporation pay shareholder personal expenses out of corporate assets.

Limited Liability Company. Liability of the owners of a limited liability company generally is the same as for shareholders of a corporation; that is, absent fraud, personal wrongdoing or disregard of the entity, they generally are not held personally liable for the debts and obligations of the business. They therefore risk loss only up to the amount of their investment. As is the case for corporations, owners of small, closely held, or newly organized limited liability companies may be required to give personal guarantees of repayment to secure financing or credit.

No Liability Protection for Personal Act. It is important to note that no entity structure will insulate the owner from liability for his or her own personal acts.

Personal Liability for Payment of Employment Taxes. To encourage prompt payment of withheld income and employment taxes, including Social Security taxes, railroad retirement taxes, or collected excise taxes, Congress passed a law that provides for the TFRP (Trust Fund Recovery Penalty). These taxes are called trust fund taxes because you actually hold the employee's money in trust until you make a federal tax deposit in that amount. In the event that an employer fails to pay its employment taxes, its individual officers, members, directors, owners or others, who are responsible for collecting or paying withheld income and employment taxes and willfully fail to collect or pay them may be held personally liable for unpaid taxes. See the IRS Employment Taxes and the Trust Fund Recovery Penalty (TFRP) information at https://www.irs.gov/businesses/small-businesses-self-employed/employment-taxes-and-the-trust-fund-recovery-penalty-tfrp.

Distribution of Profits and Losses

Sole Proprietorship. The sole proprietor receives all the profits from the business, and bears all the losses, which may exceed the proprietor's investment in the business.

Partnership. In the general partnership, the limited liability partnership, the limited liability limited partnership and the limited partnership, profits and losses are passed through to the partners as specified in the partnership agreement. If left unspecified, profits and losses are shared equally among the partners.

Corporation. In a C corporation, profits and losses belong to the corporation. Profits may be distributed to shareholders in the form of dividends, or they may be reinvested or retained (within limits) by the corporation. Losses by the corporation are not claimed by individual shareholders. Shareholders include dividends and the gain or loss on the sale of stock or liquidation of stock in the corporation as income.

S corporation. In an S corporation, corporate income and losses flow through and are taxed to the shareholders in proportion to their shareholdings. Shareholders also include their gain or loss on the sale of stock or liquidation of stock as income. Generally cash distributions (dividends) received from the S corporation are not included in income to the extent the shareholder has basis in his or her stock.

Limited Liability Company. Profits and losses of a limited liability company flow are taxed in the same manner as those of a sole proprietorship, partnership, S corporation, or C corporation depending on how the entity has chosen to be treated for federal income tax purposes. The governing statute, articles of organization, or the operating agreement will specify how these are allocated among the members.

Management Control and Decision Making

Sole Proprietorship. The sole proprietor has full and complete authority to manage and control the business. There are no partners or shareholders to consult before making decisions. This form of organization gives the proprietor maximum freedom to run the business and respond quickly to day-to-day business needs. The disadvantage of this form is that the sole proprietor, as just one person, will have limited time, energy and expertise to devote to the business. His or her experiences may not provide the breadth of skills and knowledge necessary to deal with all phases of the business. Further, because the sole proprietor is the only person authorized to act on behalf of the business, he or she may be unable to leave the business for extended periods of time without jeopardizing its operations. As the business expands, the proprietor may be able to hire managers to perform some of these functions and provide additional expertise, but in the early years of the business, the sole proprietor often will perform many of these tasks alone.

Partnership. The general rule of management is that in both a **general partnership** and a **limited liability partnership**, all partners share equally in the right, and responsibility, to manage and control the business. The partnership agreement may centralize some management decisions in a smaller group of partners, but all partners continue to share ultimate responsibility for these decisions. By statute, unless a partnership agreement provides otherwise, certain management decisions require unanimous consent of the partners. Other decisions may be made by consent of a majority of the partners. The right to share equally in decisions can make the decision-making process cumbersome, and the risk of major disagreements can impair effective operation of the business. An advantage of the partnership that is not present in a sole proprietorship is that the partnership, with its several owners, can bring a broader range of skills, abilities and resources to the business. The owners' combined experiences also can promote more informed decision making. In addition, the workload can be shared to lessen the physical and other demands on the individual owners.

In addition, under the Revised Uniform Partnership Act (RUPA), a system of formal filings has been established that allows partnerships to limit the authority of certain partners to third parties as well as to limit the liability of partners for partnership obligations purportedly incurred by a partner after the partner has left the firm. In order to use this system, the partnership must first file with the Secretary of State an assumed name certificate or limited liability partnership statement of qualification. After that filing has been made, the partnership may again file any of the following statements with the Secretary of State:

- **Statement of Partnership Authority.** This allows the partnership to either restrict or specifically expand the authority of particular partners to conduct various transactions, particularly real estate transactions.
- **Statement of Denial.** This allows a partner to deny partnership status or the conferral of authority upon the partners by a Statement of Partnership Authority.
- **Statement of Dissociation.** This allows a partner who is withdrawing from the partnership to avoid liability for obligations for the partnership incurred after the partner has withdrawn, and also allows the partnership to eliminate the authority of that partner to bind the partnership.
- **Statement of Dissolution.** This allows the partnership to notify the world that it is dissolving and that partners will no longer have authority to act on behalf of the partnership.

The following are also permitted:

- **Statement of Merger.** This allows partnerships and limited partnerships to merge with each other.
- **Statement of Qualification.** This statement establishes a Minnesota limited liability partnership under Minn. Stat. Chapter 323A.
- **Statement of Foreign Qualification.** This statement registers a non-Minnesota limited liability partnership.

Any of these seven statements may also be amended or cancelled.

In order for any Statement to have an effect on real property transactions, a certified copy of the Statement, obtained from the Secretary of State, must be recorded in the office where land records for the county in which the real property is located, and, if applicable, has been memorialized on the certificate of title for that real property.

In a **limited partnership** in Minnesota, limited partners may participate in the management and control of the partnership but may not act for or bind the partnership (unless this is provided for in the limited partnership agreement or another agreement between the limited partner and the limited partnership). Those functions generally are performed by general partners.

Corporation. The rules for corporate decision making are established by statute, but many rules may be modified by the articles of incorporation or bylaws. Shareholders elect the board of directors, which in turn manages the operation of the business. The corporation also must have one or more natural persons exercising the functions of chief executive officer and chief financial officer. Except in very small corporations in which the shareholders are also the directors, shareholders as a group generally will not directly participate in management decisions. This concentration of decision making in a relatively few individuals promotes flexibility in decision making, but also can result in overruling of minority interests or in some cases manipulation or exploitation of minority shareholders. To resolve this problem, corporations may adopt provisions in the articles of incorporation or bylaws to give minority shareholders a stronger voice in management decisions. Decision-making authority also may be delegated by the shareholders and/or directors to hired managers, who may or may not be shareholders. This delegation further removes decision-making authority from the shareholders. Like a partnership, the corporation can draw on the skills and expertise of more than one individual in running the business. This can broaden the base of information for decision making and reduce workload demands on individual managers.

The articles of incorporation, bylaws or state business corporation act establish procedures and criteria for decision making, such as meeting and quorum requirements, voting margins, and the like, which may make decision making in the corporation more cumbersome than in a sole proprietorship or partnership.

Limited Liability Company. Minn. Stat. Chapter 322C, which governs limited liability companies takes more of a partnership approach to limited liability companies than did the older law, which was based on Minnesota's Business Corporation Act. Minn. Stat. Chapter 322C permits management by the members, management by one or more managers, and management by a board (Minn. Stat. § 322C.0407). The default structure is member management. Unless the operating agreement provides otherwise, each member has equal rights in the management and conduct of the limited liability company's activities – i.e., per capita, not in proportion to their capital contributions. Differences as to matters in the ordinary course of the limited liability company's activities may be decided by a majority of the members, while acts outside the ordinary course may be undertaken only with the consent of all members. Additional agents (who can be referred to as officers) may be appointed by the members, managers, or board. As with a corporation, the rules governing the management of a limited liability company are often specified in a written operating agreement. If not otherwise specified in an operating agreement, the default rules of the limited liability company statute will control.

In addition, the Revised Uniform Limited Liability Act as adopted in Minnesota (Minn. Stat. Chapter 322C), provides for a system of formal filings similar to those under the Minnesota Revised Uniform Partnership Act. These allow limited liability companies to put of record the authority or limitations on authority of persons holding any position that exists in or with respect to the company to execute an instrument transferring real property held in the name of the company or enter into other transactions on behalf of, or otherwise act for or bind, the limited liability company. Such statements affect only the power of a person to bind a limited liability company to persons that are not members. Any such statement also may be amended or cancelled. Filing a statement of dissolution automatically cancels all previously filed statements. The types of statements and their effects may be found in the statute (Minn. Stat. § 322C.0302.)

In the case of real property transactions, if an effective statement containing a limitation on the authority to transfer real property held in the name of a limited liability company is certified by the Secretary of State and is recorded in the real property records, all persons are deemed to know of the limitation. An effective statement of authority that grants authority to transfer real property held in the name of the limited liability company, is conclusive in favor of a person that gives value in reliance on the grant without knowledge to the contrary, whether or not a certified copy of the statement was recorded in the real property records, unless, when the person gave value, (a) the statement had been canceled or restrictively amended under and a certified copy of the cancellation or restrictive amendment had been recorded in the real property records, or (b) a limitation on the grant was contained in another statement of authority that became effective after the statement containing the grant became effective and a certified copy of the later-effective statement was recorded in the real property records.

Financing Startup and Operation of the Business

A startup business, regardless of form, generally will find it difficult to obtain outside financing. The statistical failure rate for new businesses is high, and many lenders view financing the startup business venture as extremely risky. Banks and other creditors generally will require a significant capital investment by the business owner, and a personal guarantee that the owner will repay the loan. Corporations may issue securities to pool capital from a large number of investors; however, the costs of complying with complex federal and state securities laws may be prohibitive, and there is no guarantee that a market will exist for the securities of a new firm. Likewise, limited liability companies may increase capital by admitting more members, but will need to offer prospective members some likelihood of return on their investment. Thus as a practical matter, startup financing for the new venture – whether it is a sole proprietorship, a partnership, a corporation or a limited liability company – often is limited to what the owner and others closely associated with the venture are able to raise.

The discussion which follows addresses the relative ease with which firms with established credit histories may be able to attract financing.

Sole Proprietorship. The sole proprietor's ability to raise capital generally is limited to the amount of debt he or she can personally secure. Accordingly, the sole proprietorship ordinarily will have less capital available to finance operations or expansion than will other forms of organization that may be able to attract outside investors.

Partnership. In most cases, a partnership will be able to raise capital more easily than a sole proprietorship, but not as easily as a corporation. The borrowing power of each partner may be pooled to raise debt capital, or additional partners may be admitted to increase this pooled borrowing power. Or, if the partnership does not wish to distort the ownership position of the original partners, a limited partnership may be established to raise capital. While partnership assets may be accepted as collateral by a lender, the separate assets of individual partners are often needed to secure loans, either through loans made to the partners in their individual capacity or loans to the partnership that are guaranteed by individual partners, often with pledges of individual assets as security.

Corporation. The corporation generally is the easiest form of organization for raising capital from outside investors. Equity capital may be raised by selling stock to investors. As noted in the section of this Guide on securities registration, the sale of securities is regulated by federal and state laws. Due to the complexity of these laws, the sale of securities is expensive, and the cost may be prohibitive for startup firms. Long-term financing by lending institutions is easier for a corporation to structure because corporate assets may be used to secure the financing. Personal assets of the principals of the corporation and its shareholders also may be used to guarantee loans to the corporation.

The number of shares of stock a corporation may issue must be authorized by the articles of incorporation. If a corporation has issued all of its authorized shares, it is necessary to amend the articles of incorporation to authorize additional shares. The amended articles of incorporation must be filed with the Secretary of State, and a filing fee paid. The corporation can avoid these additional costs by authorizing a large number of shares at the time of incorporation.

S Corporation. An S corporation is limited by restrictions on who can be owners as well as the single class of stock rule which requires it to allocate profits and losses proportionately. This may limit the financing alternatives available to the S corporation.

Limited Liability Company. The limited liability company is financed by contributions from members. The limited liability company offers more flexibility in structuring outside financing than does the S corporation. The limited liability company may create multiple classes and series of membership interests, and may provide in its operating agreement (or its articles of organization) that profits and losses may be allocated other than under the default rule of per capita among the members. Unless the operating agreement provides differently, distributions by limited liability companies formed under Minn. Stat. Chapter 322C that are made before dissolution and winding up are to be in equal shares among members (i.e., per capita), and upon dissolution and winding up are to be made first to return prior contributions that have not been previously returned and then in equal shares among members and dissociated members. (Tax counsel should be consulted on the tax consequences of a disproportionate allocation.)

The ability of a limited liability company to create additional membership classes or series of membership interests is typically governed by the operating agreement.

Transferability of Ownership Interests

Sole Proprietorship. A sole proprietor transfers ownership of the business by transferring the assets of the business to the new owner. The prior proprietorship is terminated and a new proprietorship is established under the new owner.

Partnership. The transfer of a partner's economic interest in a partnership is determined by the partnership agreement, or by statute if there is no partnership agreement. Unless permitted by the partnership agreement, no person may become a partner without the consent of all the other partners. If a partner attempts to transfer his or her interest in the partnership without such an agreement, the transferee does not become a partner but instead becomes entitled to receive the allocations of profit and loss and the distributions that the transferring partner otherwise would receive. A properly drawn partnership agreement will address the conditions under which an ownership interest may be transferred, and the consequences to the transferee and to the partnership.

Corporation. Ownership in a corporation is transferred by the sale of stock. A change in ownership does not affect the existence of the corporate entity. Technically, shares of stock in a corporation are freely transferable. As a practical matter, however, the market may be limited for shares of stock in a small corporation that is not publicly traded. In addition, shareholders in a new venture often will want to restrict the transfer of shares and thus may provide for transfer restrictions in the articles of incorporation, bylaws, or a buy-sell or redemption agreement. In an S corporation, shares of stock are also freely transferable, in theory. However, the S corporation election may be inadvertently terminated if the entity to which the shares are transferred does not qualify as an S corporation shareholder, so a buy-sell agreement or other form of transfer restriction is even more important in these situations.

Limited Liability Company. Membership rights in a limited liability company generally can be viewed as consisting of financial rights (referred to as the "transferable interest") – the right to share in the profits, losses and distributions of the limited liability company and other rights (rights to vote and to manage the business, information rights, etc.) Unless the operating agreement (or articles of organization) provides otherwise, a member may assign or transfer financial rights that comprise the transferable interest. Such a transfer gives the transferee all the rights to profits and distributions previously held by the transferor. Unless the operating agreement (or articles of organization) provides otherwise, a transfer does not create other membership rights in the transferee, nor can the transfer allow the transferee to directly or indirectly exercise governance rights, unless all other members give their consent. The operating agreement (or articles of organization) may provide for less-than unanimous consent.

Continuity of the Business Following Withdrawal or Death of an Owner

Sole Proprietorship. The business entity terminates at the death of the proprietor or if the proprietor becomes unable to manage it.

Partnership. General partnerships and **limited liability partnerships** under the Revised Uniform Partnership Act (RUPA) do **NOT** automatically cease to exist when a partner dies or otherwise withdraws from a partnership. The partnership continues, unless certain other events occur. A **limited partnership** does not terminate when a limited partner dies or becomes disabled. The limited partner's interest may be assigned, and if the limited partner dies, his or her legal representative may exercise all the partner's rights for purposes of settling the estate.

Corporation. A corporation is a separate legal entity, and therefore the death, disability or withdrawal of an owner has no legal effect on the business entity's existence. As a practical matter, however, many small businesses depend heavily on the efforts of one or two individuals, and the death or disability of one of those key individuals can seriously impair the economic viability of the business. For this reason, a small business corporation, like a partnership, often will obtain life insurance on key shareholder-employees. The articles of incorporation or a buy-sell or shareholder agreement may restrict the transferability of stock in order to retain control of the firm by the remaining key individuals.

Limited Liability Company. Limited liability companies governed by the new Minnesota Revised Uniform Limited Liability Company Act will not dissolve upon the termination of membership of a particular member unless specified in the operating agreement (or articles of organization) or, once a member has been admitted 90 consecutive days pass during which the limited liability company has no members. Otherwise, the termination of a member's interest does not affect the existence of the limited liability company.

Complexity and Expense of Terminating the Business

Sole Proprietorship. There are no federal or state regulations governing termination of the sole proprietorship itself. The sole proprietor simply winds up the affairs of the business and discontinues operations. If the business had employees, the owner must notify federal and state taxing authorities that the proprietor is no longer operating the business and paying employees.

See also the section of this Guide entitled "Business Taxes – Income Tax Withholding – Withholding Tax Penalties and Interest". The final report of income and expenses attributable to the business is included in the proprietor's individual income tax return, which is filed at the usual time. No final return or early filing is required. Tax consequences may flow from the sale or other disposition of assets used in the business.

Partnership. The partnership, because it is a more formal structure than a sole proprietorship, is more complex to terminate. RUPA identifies several ways in which dissolution may occur, but the partners may provide for continuation of the partnership even if an act of dissolution occurs. The consequences of causing the dissolution of a partnership also are specified in RUPA. The statute addresses the allocation and distribution of partnership property upon dissolution, liability of persons continuing the business, and other rights and liabilities of the partners. However, the statute does not address procedural matters such as filing final tax returns, notifying taxing authorities of the termination for employment tax purposes, notification of creditors and similar matters involved in winding up the affairs of the partnership. Assistance with these matters may be obtained from legal counsel. Tax consequences may apply to the disposition of partnership assets, and those tax consequences will flow through to the partners. The **general partnership** may file a Statement of Dissolution with the Secretary of State but generally otherwise need not file notice of dissolution or termination of the partnership with any governmental entity. The **limited partnership** must formally cancel the certificate of limited partnership and file the cancellation with the Secretary of State. A **limited liability partnership** will revert to a general partnership upon voluntarily terminating limited liability partnership status, which is done by filing a withdrawal or termination statement with the Secretary of State. Limited liability partnerships do not expire unless the partnership fails to file the annual registration, in which case the limited liability partnership status is terminated and the partnership reverts to general or limited partnership status.

Note that the Revised Uniform Partnership Act (RUPA) also allows for mergers of partnerships which terminate all but the surviving partnership.

Corporation. The corporation is the most complex business form to terminate. Formal dissolution procedures, both before and after the issuance of shares, are specified by statute, and include, for example, filing notice of intent to dissolve the corporation and articles of dissolution with the Secretary of State, notification of creditors, disposition of assets, and distribution of the proceeds to shareholders. Tax consequences will affect both the corporation and its shareholders. Because of the complexity of the statutory procedures and tax implications, professional legal and accounting advice is highly recommended.

Corporations may end their separate existence by merging into another corporation or into a limited liability company.

Limited Liability Company. As is the case with partnerships, limited partnerships, and corporations, the procedures for dissolving a limited liability company, both before and after accepting contributions, are spelled out in the governing legislation. Different procedures apply, depending on when the limited liability company is dissolved and who dissolves it. The law specifies the notices to be given (e.g., to members and creditors), filings with the Secretary of State and procedures for winding up the business of the limited liability company.

Limited liability companies may end their separate existence by merging into another limited liability company or into a corporation.

Subsequent Reorganization or Change in the Tax Status of the Business. If the business is being terminated because the owner wishes to do business under a different type of entity (such as converting a sole proprietorship to an S corporation), special issues might need to be addressed. For instance, when an S corporation terminates its election and becomes a C corporation, adverse tax consequences often result. Likewise if the shareholders of a C corporation elect to have it taxed as an S corporation, it may be subject to adverse tax consequences requiring the corporation to be subject to various entity level taxes that can be significant. Also, certain assets of the business may not be transferable; for example, a contract that the business has entered into might or might not be transferable if the business is terminated and reorganized. Many other issues could arise when a business is terminated and begun again under a different form of organization. Although generally speaking an owner is permitted to change the form of his or her business at any time, a business owner is advised to seek professional assistance when considering changing the form of his or her business to avoid unintended consequences.

Extent of Government Regulation

Certain types of government regulation will apply to the business regardless of the form of organization. Licenses or permits will be required of all business entities conducting the regulated activity. Note that businesses operating in multiple jurisdictions (whether cities, states or counties) should inquire about licensing requirements imposed by each of those jurisdictions. This is equally true of businesses using the Internet. Federal, state and local consumer protection laws regulate business relationships with the public, without regard to the form of organization. Every business that hires employees will be required to comply with certain federal and state labor and tax laws governing the employment relationship. The following paragraphs identify the major differences in the extent of regulation for each type of business organization.

Sole Proprietorship. The sole proprietorship, as a form of business organization, is not generally regulated by the state. Other than tax filings and specialized reports applicable to certain kinds of businesses (e.g., hazardous waste generators), no special governmental filings or reports are required, making the sole proprietorship the least restrictive, most private form of organization.

Partnership. A **general partnership,** like a sole proprietorship, operates with relatively few governmental controls. RUPA provides statutory rules for basic questions of partnership management and relationships between the partners and third persons, but most issues are determined by the partnership agreement. No special partnership reports or filings with government entities are required, but an assumed name certificate may be required, depending upon the partnership name.

Limited partnerships, limited liability partnerships and **limited liability limited partnerships** must file with the Secretary of State on a yearly basis in order to retain their special status.

Corporation. Rules governing the corporation are established by laws of the state of incorporation and the corporation's articles of incorporation. These rules are more formal and complex than those governing partnerships and limited partnerships. In addition to complying with laws and regulations applicable to similarly situated businesses, any corporation that issues registered securities will be required to make periodic filings with state and federal regulators and must comply with other reporting requirements. Tax laws applicable to corporations generally are more complex than those applicable to proprietorships or partnerships and specific statutory procedures apply to dissolving the corporate entity. Most governmental filings are public documents, making the corporation the least private form of organization. An S corporation must meet specific requirements to qualify for S corporation tax treatment, and this status may be terminated when these requirements are not met.

Minnesota corporations must file an annual corporate registration with the Secretary of State which will provide corporations with a reminder-to-file notice. Failure to file an annual registration for two years will trigger administrative dissolution of the corporation.

Limited Liability Company. Rules governing the limited liability company are established by statute as well as the limited liability company's operating agreement and its articles of organization. These rules are similar in complexity to those governing partnerships and corporations.

TAX CONSIDERATIONS IN CHOOSING THE FORM OF ORGANIZATION

This section discusses the major tax considerations for the sole proprietorship, partnership, and corporation. For limited liability companies, the Internal Revenue Service has adopted rules (which appear in 26 C.F.R. 301.7701-1 et. seq.) that allow the organizer(s) to select the federal tax treatment for the LLC: either as a sole proprietorship or a corporation, (in the case of LLCs with only one member); or as a partnership or a corporation, (in the case of LLCs with at least two members). (The Minnesota Department of Revenue, in Revenue Notice 13-08, has stated that the Department of Revenue will for Minnesota tax purposes respect the choice made under the Federal Regulations). Because LLCs are treated as sole proprietorships, corporations, or partnerships, they are not specifically described in the following text. How a business is treated for federal tax purposes, is how it will be treated for Minnesota state tax purposes. Detailed advice on specific situations should be obtained from a competent tax advisor.

Considerations addressed in this section include:

- Who is the Taxpayer?
- What Tax Forms Are Used?
- Tax Rates
- Tax Impact
- Selection of the Tax Year
- Compensation for Services
- Employment Taxes and Workers' Compensation Insurance
- Employee Retirement Benefit Plans
- Fringe Benefits
- Capital Gains and Losses
- Net Operating Loss
- Estimated Tax Payments
- Disposition of Ownership Interest

Who Is the Taxpayer?

Sole Proprietorship. In a sole proprietorship, the taxpayer is the individual business owner. The proprietor is taxed on the entire net income from the business, regardless of whether the income is withdrawn for personal use or retained in the business. This is the case for both federal and Minnesota tax purposes.

Partnership. The partnership itself is not a taxable entity. The partnership serves as a conduit through which income, deductions and credits are passed through to the individual partners. Each partner is taxed on his or her share as defined in the partnership agreement. All income of the partnership is taxed to the partners, whether or not it is actually distributed. The partnership itself files an information return which reports partnership income and distributions to the partners. This is the case for both federal and Minnesota tax purposes.

Corporation. A corporation is a separate legal and taxable entity. For tax purposes, the corporation may be a "C corporation" (taxed under Subchapter C of the Internal Revenue Code and corresponding sections of Minn. Stat.) or it may elect to be treated as an "S corporation" (taxed under Subchapter S of the Internal Revenue Code and corresponding sections of Minn. Stat.). Both C corporations and S corporations file federal and Minnesota tax returns. In the case of a C corporation, the corporation itself is the taxpayer and pays tax on corporate profits. After taxes are paid any remaining corporate profits may be distributed to shareholders in the form of dividends. The shareholders are then taxed on the dividends they receive from the corporation. In general, an S corporation is taxed in a manner similar to a partnership; that is, the income, deductions and credits of the corporation are passed through to shareholders and are taxed to shareholders at their individual tax rates. These rules become more complicated in the case of an S corporation that was taxed as a C corporation at some time prior to electing to be taxed as an S corporation.

It is worth noting here that because a corporation is an entity separate from its owners, if the owner (and/or members of the owner's family) performs services for the corporation, these persons are considered to be employees of the corporation. Thus, the corporation will be required to comply with most of the laws and regulations and reporting requirements applicable to employers, including filing employment tax forms.

Limited Liability Company. Both multi-member and single member limited liability companies have the option of being taxed as a corporation (where the LLC pays taxes on its income) or as a pass-through entity (where income passes through to the owner or owners to be reported on personal income tax returns). A multi-member LLC files an election to be taxed as a corporation or pass-through by checking the appropriate box on IRS Form 8832. A single member LLC desiring to be taxed as a "disregarded entity" (like a sole proprietorship) does not need to file Form 8832 but does need to file Form 8832 if it wishes to be taxed as a corporation.

What Tax Forms Are Used?

Note: Income tax forms identified here apply to the 2020 tax year. Amendments to the Minnesota tax laws and federal Internal Revenue Code may change these requirements.

Sole Proprietorship. Federal: The sole proprietor reports income and expenses from the business on Schedule C and any related forms and schedules. The net income or loss from the business is then transferred to the proprietor's individual Form 1040. The sole proprietor uses Schedule SE to report net self-employment income for purposes of computing Social Security, Medicare and self-employment tax. **Minnesota:** There is no separate form for reporting proprietorship income. To compute Minnesota income tax, the proprietor uses Form M1 - Individual Income Tax Form. A copy of the federal Form 1040, including a copy of Schedule C (Form 1040), plus Schedule SE, if appropriate, must be attached to Minnesota Form M1. Minnesota does not impose a self-employment tax.

Partnership. Federal: The partnership files Form 1065, U.S. Return of Partnership Income, which is an information return. No tax is paid by the partnership with this return. Other forms and schedules may be required, including Schedules K (Form 990) and K-1 (Form 1041). Individual partners use Schedule E (Form 1040), Supplemental Income and Loss which is prepared with information from their Schedule K-1 of Form 1065, to report their distributive share of partnership income, deductions, credits and losses on their individual Form 1040. Schedule SE (Form 1040) is used to compute Social Security and Medicare self-employment tax. **Minnesota:** The partnership files Form M3, Partnership Return and taxes paid by the partnership with this return include: Minnesota Minimum Fee, Minnesota Composite Income Tax, and Withholding for Nonresident Partners (described in the Tax Rates section of this Guide). Schedules KPI and KPC are supplemental K-1 type schedules used to report modifications to federal tax computations of partnership income and the other information a partner needs to complete the Minnesota individual income tax return, Form M1. Schedule KC is used for computing the Minnesota Composite Income Tax (when the partnership pays the Minnesota income tax on behalf of nonresident partners). Schedule M3 is used for reporting the_Nonresident Withholding for Partnerships. Minnesota does not impose a self-employment tax.

C Corporation. Federal: The C corporation reports its income, deductions and credits, and computes its tax, on Form 1120 or Form 1120-A. Supporting forms and schedules may be required. If the corporation issues dividends, it must annually send its shareholders Form 1099-DIV, Dividends and Distributions, stating the amount of dividends paid. A copy also is filed with the Internal Revenue Service and the Minnesota Department of Revenue. The shareholder reports dividends received from the corporation on his or her individual Form 1040. **Minnesota:** The corporation files Minnesota Form M4. Dividends paid to shareholders are included in the shareholders federal taxable income reported to the Department of Revenue, Form M1.

S Corporation. Federal: The S corporation files Form 1120-S and supporting forms and schedules, including Schedules K and K-1 (Form 1120-S). The S corporation generally is not separately taxed. Individual shareholders report their share of the S corporation's income, deductions and credits on their individual Form 1040, using information contained on the Schedule K-1. **Minnesota:** For Minnesota income tax purposes, the S corporation files Form M8. Taxes paid by the S corporation include: Minnesota S Corporation Taxes, (which apply only if the S corporation is paying federal income tax), Minnesota Minimum Fee; Minnesota Composite Income Tax; and Withholding for Nonresident Shareholders (see discussion in the Tax Rates section of this Guide). Schedule KS is a supplemental K-1 type schedule used for reporting modifications to federal income tax computations of S corporation income and the other information a shareholder needs to complete the Minnesota individual income tax return, Form M1. Schedule KC is used for computing the Minnesota Composite Income Tax (when the S corporation pays the Minnesota tax on behalf of the nonresident shareholder). Schedule MW3NR is used to report the Withholding for Nonresident shareholders.

Limited Liability Companies. A multi-member limited liability company electing to be taxed as a partnership reports its income on IRS Form 1065, U.S. Partnership Return of Income. Each owner shows their share of partnership income, credits, and deductions on Schedule K-1 (1065). A multi-member limited liability company electing to be taxed as a C corporation reports its income on Form 1120, U.S. Corporation Income Tax Return. A multi-member limited liability company electing to be taxed as an S corporation files IRS Form 1120S, Income Tax Return for an S Corporation. Each owner shows their share of corporate income, credits, and deductions on Schedule K-1 (Form 1120S). A single member limited liability company electing to be taxed as a disregarded entity does not file a return and its owner reports all income on Form 1040 and appropriate schedules.

Tax Rates

The rate of tax paid on income from the business activity depends on how the business is organized. Income from a sole proprietorship, S corporation, partnership, or limited liability company is taxed to the owner at federal and state individual rates. A C corporation's income is taxed to the corporation at the federal and state corporate rates.

Federal Corporate Income Tax rates. Corporate tax rates. For tax years beginning after December 31, 2017, the graduated corporate tax structure is no longer applicable. Corporations, including qualified personal service corporations and members of a controlled group, are taxed at a flat rate of 21 percent of taxable income.

Federal Individual Income Tax Rates. For tax years beginning with 2020 the federal individual tax rate applicable to pass through income for owners of sole proprietorships, S corporations, and limited liability companies taxed as pass through entities depends on income:

Tax Rate	Individuals	Married Filing Jointly
10%	Up to $9,700	Up to $19,400
12%	$9,701 to $39,475	$19,401 to $78,950
22%	$39,476 to $84,200	$78,951 to $168,400
24%	$84,201 to $160,725	$168,401 to $321,450
32%	$160,726 to $204,100	$321,451 to $408,200
35%	$204,101 to $510,300	$408,201 to $612,350
37%	$510,301 or more	$612,351 or more

The individual income tax rates and brackets for 2021 have not yet been published.

Net Investment Income Tax. A Net Investment Income Tax of 3.8 percent is imposed on unearned income of individuals whose adjusted gross income exceeds $200,000 ($250,000 for joint filers). For purposes of the tax unearned income includes interest, dividends, most capital gains, and income from passive business activities.

Federal Deduction for Qualified Business Income of Individuals. The 2017 Tax Cuts and Jobs Act added a new section 199A to the Internal Revenue Code providing that non-corporate pass-through taxpayers may deduct up to 20 percent of qualified business income from gross income from a partnership, S corporation, or sole proprietorship or deduct up to 50 percent of the greater of W-2 wages paid by the qualified business or the sum of 25 percent of W-2 wages plus 2.5 percent of the basis of all qualified property. Qualified business income is defined as the net amount of income, gain, deductions, and loss. A qualified business is a trade or business (not being an employee) that is not a specified service business to include professional practices (e.g., doctors, dentists, accountants), consulting activities, athletes and athletic performances, brokers and financial services, investments and investment managers.

Refer to IRS information:

- Qualified Business Income Deduction at https://www.irs.gov/newsroom/qualified-business-income-deduction
- Qualified Business Income Deduction FAQs at https://www.irs.gov/newsroom/tax-cuts-and-jobs-act-provision-11011-section-199a-qualified-business-income-deduction-faqs

Limitation on Deductibility of Business Interest. The 2017 Tax Cuts and Jobs Act also added new language limiting the deductibility of interest paid by the business to 30 percent of the business's adjusted taxable income. This would include, for example, interest paid to a commercial lender on a business loan. For S corporations and partnerships the limitation is applied at the partner or shareholder level. **But taxpayers that have annual gross receipts of $25 million or less during the preceding three years are exempt from this provision.**

Refer to IRS information:

- Basic questions and answers about the limitation on the deduction for business interest expense at https://www.irs.gov/newsroom/basic-questions-and-answers-about-the-limitation-on-the-deduction-for-business-interest-expense
- Business Expenses, Publication 535 at https://www.irs.gov/pub/irs-pdf/p535.pdf

Minnesota Corporate (Franchise) Tax Rates. The Minnesota corporate income tax rate is 9.8 percent. Corporations are subject to an alternative minimum tax based on Minnesota alternative minimum taxable income at the 5.8 percent. The amount due is the excess of the alternative minimum tax liability over business' regular franchise liability.

Minnesota Minimum Fee Rates. A graduated minimum fee is imposed on Minnesota entities filing as corporations, S corporations, and partnerships. The fee is indexed annually for inflation. The 2020 brackets are:

Minnesota property, payroll, and sales	Fee
Less than $1,040,000	$0
$1,040,000 to $2,069,999	$210
$2,070,000 to $10,379,999	$620
$10,380,000 to $20,749,999	$2,070
$20,750,000 to $41,499,999	$4,160
$41,500,000 or more	$10,380

Minnesota Single Factor Apportionment Formula. Businesses that operate both within and outside of Minnesota are required to calculate the amount of income subject to Minnesota tax by allocating the business income to Minnesota based on the percentage of sales to Minnesota customers compared to total sales.

Minnesota Individual Income Tax Rates. The Minnesota individual income tax rates for 2019 are 5.35 percent, 6.80 percent, 7.85 percent, and 9.85 percent depending on income and filing status. Partnerships and S corporations that have nonresident individual partners or shareholders are allowed to file and pay using a composite income tax, on behalf of their nonresident partners or shareholders who do not have other Minnesota income, on the partnership's or S corporation's return. In this situation, the nonresident partners or shareholders do not have to file separate Minnesota individual income tax returns. The tax rate for the Minnesota Composite Income Tax is 7.85 percent of the individual's "Minnesota source" income. If a partnership or S corporation does not pay a composite income tax on behalf of nonresident individual partners or shareholders withholding tax at a rate of 7.85 percent must be paid from that individual's "Minnesota source" income, and submitted with the partnership's or S corporation's return. The partner or shareholder then files an individual income tax return claiming the tax paid by the entity on line 3 of schedule M1W.

Tax Impact

Many factors determine the full tax burden on a business. Some of these factors – such as treatment of capital gains, deductibility of certain items, and the availability of certain credits – will vary depending on the form of organization. Other factors, such as employment taxes attributable to non-owner employees or property taxes, will apply regardless of the form of organization. For detailed analysis of these factors in the context of the specific business, a competent tax advisor should be consulted. The following paragraphs describe the major differences in tax impact attributable to the form of organization.

Sole Proprietorship. A sole proprietorship business in itself is not subject to tax. Instead the net income or loss from the business is combined with the proprietor's income and losses from other sources to determine the proprietor's income for tax purposes. The proprietor is taxed on the net income of the business, regardless of whether the income is withdrawn for personal purposes or retained in the business. Because income or loss from the business is combined for tax purposes with income and losses from other sources, the tax impact on income from the business may be different than if the business were taxed as a separate entity. However, because only the proprietor is taxed and not the business entity, distribution of the business profits to the owner are not subject to tax. Another consideration of the sole proprietorship compared with a C corporation is that not only the amount but also the character of various income items, deductions, and credits may be claimed by the business owner. In a C corporation, items are claimed by the corporation on its tax return and are not passed through to shareholders.

Partnership. Partnership income is taxable to the partners regardless of whether it is actually distributed or retained in the business. The partners report their distributive share of partnership income, deductions and credits on their individual income tax returns, where these items will be combined with income and losses from other sources. This income is taxed at the individual income tax rate applicable to that partner's tax bracket. The partners may allocate their distributive share of partnership income, deductions and credits for tax purposes in the partnership agreement. As long as there is "substantial economic effect" to the allocation (as defined by tax laws and Internal Revenue Service regulations), the partnership may offer greater opportunity for tax planning than the proprietorship or corporate form of organization. By "substantial economic effect" the Internal Revenue Service essentially means that the allocation made in the partnership agreement may actually affect the dollar amount of the partner's share of the partnership income or loss independently of any tax consequences. As with the proprietorship, both the amount and character of various income and deduction items are passed through to shareholders. However, certain deductions may not be permitted, certain items must be separately stated, and a partner's ability to claim his or her share of partnership losses generally is limited to the partner's adjusted basis in the partnership interest. (Basis is a way of measuring an individual's investment in property.) In the case of a partnership interest it generally starts with the amount of cash or basis of property contributed for the partnership interest (or the amount paid in the case of a purchase from another partner) and is increased by later contributions and income allocated to the interest and decreased by losses allocated to the interest and distributions. Basis also can be affected by the amount of partnership debt allocated to a partner for tax purposes. These rules can be quite complex and often should be discussed with competent advisors when a partner's tax basis is relevant.

C Corporation. C corporations are legal entities and taxed separately from their owners. The C corporation's taxable income, and tax, are determined prior to distribution of profits to shareholders. Profits which are distributed to shareholders in the form of dividends are then taxable to the shareholders. Thus both the C corporation and the shareholder are subject to tax on their respective incomes. The dividends are taxed to the shareholder as ordinary income. The attributes of capital gains, charitable contributions and other income and deduction items end at the C corporation and do not retain their character when passed to shareholders in the form of dividends. Similarly, individual shareholders do not share a corporation's losses for tax purposes.

C corporations offer some opportunity for tax planning in that dividends may be accumulated by the corporation rather than distributed to shareholders. However, Internal Revenue Service regulations limit the amount of accumulated earnings that may be retained by the corporation. An accumulated earnings tax may be imposed on excessive accumulated earnings. Because all income of the sole proprietorship, partnership, and S corporation is taxable to the owners whether or not it is distributed, these entities are not subject to the accumulated earnings tax. The C corporation also may pay a salary to owner-employees. Salaries are deductible by the corporation and thus are not included in the corporation's taxable income. However, the Internal Revenue Service may treat excessive salaries as dividends and disallow that portion of the salary expense.

S Corporation. Like a partnership, the S corporation is a conduit through which the firm's income and deductions flow to the shareholders. Income items (including capital gains) and deductions generally retain their character when passed through to shareholders. Special reporting rules apply and the opportunity to fully claim a share of the S corporation's losses may be limited by passive activity or other tax rules as well as by the shareholder's tax basis in stock and in loans made by the shareholder to the S corporation. Unlike a partnership, allocations to S corporation shareholders must be in proportion to their shareholdings. Thus this form of organization may offer less attractive tax planning opportunities.

A shareholder's pro rata share of S corporation income and deductions is combined with income and losses from other sources and reported on the shareholder's individual income tax return. The total taxable income is taxed at individual income tax rates applicable to the shareholder's tax bracket.

Limited Liability Company. Both multi-member and single member limited liability companies have the option of being taxed as a corporation (where the LLC pays taxes on its income) or as a pass-through entity (where income passes through to the owner or owners to be reported on personal income tax returns). A multi-member LLC files an election to be taxed as a corporation or pass-through by checking the appropriate box on IRS Form 8832. A single member LLC desiring to be taxed as a "disregarded entity" (like a sole proprietorship) does not need to file Form 8832 but does need to file Form 8832 if it wishes to be taxed as a corporation.

Selection of the Tax Year

The business figures its taxable income and files a tax return on the basis of an accounting period called a tax year. A tax year usually is 12 consecutive months, although in some cases a 52-53 week year or a short tax year may be permitted. A **calendar** tax year is 12 consecutive months ending December 31. A **fiscal** tax year is either 12 consecutive months ending on the last day of any month other than December, or a 52-53 week year. To use a fiscal tax year, the business must keep its books on that basis. Once a tax year is established, the business generally may not change it without Internal Revenue Service approval. The application to change the tax year must show a substantial business purpose for the change, and that no significant tax advantage will result.

Sole Proprietorship. Like most individual taxpayers, sole proprietors generally use the calendar year as their federal and Minnesota tax year. The sole proprietor must report income from all sources on the basis of the same tax year.

Partnership. In general, the partnership must use the same tax year as the partners who own a majority interest in partnership profits and capital. If those partners have different tax years, the partnership must use the same tax year as its principal partners. Principal partners are defined by the Internal Revenue Service as those having an interest of five percent or more in partnership profits or capital. If the principal partners have different tax years, the partnership generally must use the calendar tax year. However, a partnership may adopt a fiscal tax year if it can establish to the satisfaction of the Internal Revenue Service that it has a business purpose for using a fiscal tax year. If a business purpose for using a fiscal tax year cannot be shown, a partnership that would otherwise be required to use a calendar tax year may in some cases elect a fiscal tax year by filing with the Internal Revenue Service Form 8716, Election to Have a Tax Year Other than a Required Tax Year. This election is called a "Section 444 election." A partnership that makes the Section 444 election must in some cases make a payment to the government that reflects the value of the tax deferral obtained by the partners as a result of the partnership's use of a fiscal tax year. A partnership uses the same tax year for both federal and Minnesota income tax purposes.

C Corporation. A C corporation establishes its tax year when it files its first income tax return. The first tax year must end not more than 12 months after the date of incorporation. A C corporation that is not a personal service corporation may choose a calendar tax year or a fiscal tax year, so long as the tax year selected does not distort income. This allows the corporation to establish a tax year in conformity with its natural business cycle. C corporations that are personal service corporations must use a calendar tax year unless the corporation establishes to the satisfaction of the Internal Revenue Service that it has a business purpose for using a fiscal tax year, or makes a Section 444 election.

S Corporation. S corporations must use a calendar tax year unless there is a business purpose for using a fiscal tax year and the Internal Revenue Service approves. If the S corporation cannot establish a business purpose for using a fiscal tax year, it may be eligible to make the Section 444 election described above. The corporation uses the same tax year for both federal and Minnesota tax purposes.

Compensation for Services

A business may use a variety of methods to compensate persons who provide services to it. Some of these methods include salaries or wages, personal draw, cash for services, and property for services. This section discusses the tax consequences of compensation for services provided by the owner of the business. Compensation to non-owner third parties, including the spouse or children of a sole proprietor, generally will be a deductible expense so long as compensation is reasonable and the services are necessary to the business.

Sole Proprietorship. A sole proprietor is not considered an employee of the business and does not receive wages or salary for tax purposes. A sole proprietor is subject to tax on the net income of the business as it is earned, regardless of whether it is withdrawn. Compensation for services or other amounts withdrawn from the business thus are considered withdrawals of income and are not again taxed at the time of withdrawal.

Partnerships. Like sole proprietors, partners of a partnership are considered to be "self-employed" and, as such, are not considered employees of the business and do not receive wages or salary for tax purposes. Amounts paid for services in a manner similar to salary or in the form of benefits that are not determined with respect to partnership income are taxed as "guaranteed payments" – ordinary income to the partner and deductible or capitalizable by the partnership depending on the nature of the payment. The partners also are subject to tax on their share of partnership income as it is earned, regardless of whether it is withdrawn. In the case of partners treated as "general partners" for federal income tax purposes, these amounts may be considered income from self-employment and may be subject to the tax on self-employment income. Typically distributions made to partners are not taxable unless they exceed the partner's basis in his or her partnership interest.

C Corporations. Payments to owners: Payments to shareholder-employees in the form of salary or wages are deductible by the corporation in determining taxable income. As with other wages and salaries, these payments are taxed to the recipient as wage or salary income. Payments must be reasonable and the services must be necessary to the business. Compensation to shareholder-employees which is found by the Internal Revenue Service to be unreasonable may be reclassified as a dividend. This is to prevent using salary payments as a device to reduce corporate profits subject to tax.

S Corporations. Payments to owners: The payment of wages or salary to S corporation employees, including owner-employees, is deductible by the corporation in determining taxable income. These payments are then taxed to the recipient as wage or salary income. Payments must be reasonable and the services must be necessary to the business. The question of unreasonably large salaries to shareholder-employees of S corporations is not as important as it is in C corporations, because the S corporation generally pays no taxes at corporate rates. However, the Internal Revenue Service may challenge salaries which are used as a device to shift income to shareholders in lower income tax brackets. In addition, the cost of fringe benefits paid for employee shareholders who own more than two percent of the company's stock must be included in the income of the shareholder.

Note: Special rules apply to tax treatment of property, such as stock, received for services. Business owners contemplating such transfers should consult with their tax advisor prior to the transfer.

Employment Taxes and Workers' Compensation Insurance

Employment taxes include income tax withholding, Social Security and Medicare taxes and federal and state unemployment insurance taxes. Although workers' compensation insurance technically is not a tax, coverage is required for most employees. Employment taxes and workers' compensation insurance are deductible business expenses in determining net income.

Note: The following information on employment taxes and workers' compensation insurance applies only to businesses that have employees. Sole proprietors and partners that provide services to the business are not considered employees for purposes of paying unemployment taxes or obtaining workers' compensation insurance coverage for themselves. They may, however, be liable for Social Security and Medicare self-employment tax. (See the discussion of the self-employment tax below.) Shareholders in a C corporation or an S corporation who perform services for the corporation generally will be considered employees of the corporation and therefore will be subject to employment taxes. In most situations, workers' compensation coverage for these shareholders also will be required.

Self-Employment Tax. The self-employment tax (SE tax) is a Social Security and Medicare tax primarily for individuals who work for themselves. It is similar to the Social Security and Medicare taxes withheld from the pay of most wage earners.

You figure SE tax yourself using Schedule SE (Form 1040). Social Security and Medicare taxes of most wage earners are figured by their employers, also, you can deduct half of your SE tax in figuring out your adjusted gross income. Wage earners cannot deduct Social Security and Medicare Taxes.

SE tax rate. The self-employment tax rate is 15.3 percent. The rate consists of two parts: 12.4 percent for Social Security and 2.9 percent for Medicare. An additional 0.9 percent is imposed on earnings from self-employment above a threshold amount of $200,000 for single and head of household filers; $250,000 for joint filers; $125,000 for a married person filing separately.

Maximum earning subject to SE tax. For 2021 only the first $142,800 of combined wages, tips and net earnings are subject to any combination of the 12.4 percent Social Security tax. All combined income is subject to the 2.9 percent Medicare part of the SE tax or Social Security tax.

SE tax deduction. Half of the SE tax (excluding the additional 0.9 percent described above) can be deducted in figuring the adjusted gross income. The deduction only affects your income tax. It does not affect your net earnings from self-employment or your SE tax.

Social Security and Medicare Tax. The Social Security tax and Medicare tax are collected from both employers and employees. For 2021 the combined total Social Security and Medicare tax rate will be 15.3 percent of the first $142,800 of wages paid. Additional Medicare Tax of 0.9 percent is imposed on earnings above a threshold amount of $200,000 for single and head of household filers; $250,000 for joint filers; $125,000 for a married person filing separately.

Social Security and Medicare taxes other than the additional 0.9 percent Medicare Tax are paid by both the employer and the employee. The additional 0.9 percent Medicare Tax is paid solely by the employee. Social Security and Medicare taxes are not required for a sole proprietor's children under age 18 who work in the sole proprietorship.

Federal Unemployment Tax. Employers generally are liable for both federal and Minnesota unemployment taxes. The federal unemployment tax rate is 6.0 percent of the first $7,000 in wages paid each employee. A credit of up to 5.4 percent may be allowed for state unemployment taxes paid for a normal net tax of 0.6 percent. This credit is reduced during periods where the state unemployment insurance trust fund has borrowed from the federal treasury and has not fully repaid the loan. Wages paid to a spouse or child under age 21 who works in a sole proprietorship owned by the spouse or parent are not subject to federal unemployment taxes; other exceptions also may apply.

Editor's note: changes in state unemployment tax law may change your FUTA liability. Timely payment of state unemployment tax creates an offset credit on FUTA tax liability. Contact a tax advisor for more information.

Minnesota Unemployment Tax. State unemployment tax rates are discussed in the business tax section of this Guide. Different rates apply to new businesses and experience rated businesses. Wages paid by a sole proprietor for services performed by their parent, spouse or child under the age of 18 are not subject to Minnesota unemployment taxes. Wages paid to corporate officers or members of an LLC who own 25 percent or more of the corporation or LLC are not subject to Minnesota unemployment tax. Other exceptions also may apply.

Workers' Compensation Insurance. Workers' compensation insurance rates depend on the nature of the work performed by the employee and the employer's experience rating. A sole proprietor or partner may elect to obtain workers' compensation coverage for an employee who is a spouse, parent or child of the owner, but coverage for these family employees is not required. In addition, certain closely held corporations may elect coverage for executive officers who own at least 25 percent of the stock of the corporation.

Retirement Benefit Plans

Retirement benefit plans include qualified employee benefit plans, nonexempt trusts and annuity plans, self-employed retirement plans, individual retirement arrangements, and simplified employee pension plans. The tax treatment of contributions to these plans is highly technical; also there are frequent changes in tax laws that affect the treatment of those contributions. A business owner contemplating such a plan or making deductions for contributions to the plan should obtain the advice of competent counsel.

Note: Whenever the term "IRA" is used in the following paragraphs, generally speaking the discussion applies to both conventional IRAs and Roth IRAs.

Sole Proprietorship. A sole proprietor may establish and contribute to a Keogh retirement plan. Depending on the proprietor's adjusted gross income and net earnings from self-employment, he or she may open and contribute to an individual retirement account (IRA) in addition to or in place of the Keogh plan. Qualified contributions to the sole proprietor's own Keogh plan or IRA are deductible (with some exceptions) in determining the proprietor's adjusted gross income on Form 1040. Those contributions are not considered expenses of the business, however, and therefore are not deductible in computing net income from the business on Schedule C. Minnesota generally follows IRS rules in the tax treatment of Keogh and IRA contributions. A sole proprietor who has employees may establish a qualified retirement plan for the employees. Contributions to the plan, if they meet IRS requirements, are deductible from business income reported on Schedule C.

Partnership. Like sole proprietors, working partners in a partnership may contribute to a Keogh plan established by the partnership. They also may open and contribute to an IRA if they meet income limitations for such contributions. Qualified contributions by each partner may be deducted (with some exceptions) in computing their individual adjusted gross income on Form 1040. Contributions by or on behalf of partners to their own retirement plans are not deductible from partnership income. Minnesota generally follows IRS rules. Retirement plans which are established for employees must comply with Internal Revenue Service requirements. Contributions to qualified plans on behalf of employees are deductible business expenses.

Corporation. Generally, contributions by the corporation to qualified pension plans and qualified profit sharing plans will be deductible by the corporation. The plan must be approved by the Internal Revenue Service.

Note: Master and prototype retirement plans may be available to the business. In many cases, it will be easier to use these samples rather than setting up a new plan. Master and prototype plans may be sponsored by trade or professional organizations, banks, insurance companies, or regulated investment companies. These entities usually will have applied for, and received, an IRS opinion letter on the plan. Using one of these master or prototype plans does not mean that the plan is automatically qualified. The plan still must meet all IRS requirements. However, the master or prototype may offer a firm some guidance in developing its own plan.

Fringe Benefits

Fringe benefits include items such as accident and health insurance, medical savings accounts, group term life insurance, salary continuation plans, reimbursements for educational expenses, dental insurance, death benefits, day care programs, supplemental unemployment benefits, "cafeteria plan" programs, and others. As with employee retirement benefit plans, the tax treatment of fringe benefits is a highly technical area. Accordingly, it is recommended that the advice of competent counsel be obtained prior to structuring such plans.

The following paragraphs discuss the tax treatment of providing fringe benefits to owners of the business. The cost of providing fringe benefits to employees generally will be a deductible business expense if reasonable in amount and in compliance with federal and state tax codes and other statutory requirements. In some cases the benefits may be taxable to the employee and subject to income tax withholding.

Sole Proprietorship. Sole proprietors generally may not deduct as a business expense the cost of obtaining fringe benefit items for themselves, although items such as day care for the proprietor's children may be eligible for a tax credit if they otherwise meet IRS requirements. For federal tax purposes sole proprietors may deduct up to 100 percent of the cost of medical insurance premiums paid for themselves, assuming IRS requirements are met. Note that this issue is frequently the subject of legislation in Congress, so anyone affected should monitor developments.

Partnership. Partners of a partnership (including members of a limited liability company that is taxed as a partnership) are considered self-employed individuals, and are subject to the same rules on deductibility of fringe benefits as sole proprietors.

C Corporation. The C corporation may deduct the cost of providing fringe benefits to employees, including shareholder employees. To be deductible, the fringe benefit plan must meet requirements of the federal and state tax laws, including nondiscrimination in favor of executive or highly compensated employees. Employee health plans also must comply with applicable state statutory requirements to be deductible for Minnesota income tax purposes.

S Corporation. An S corporation may deduct the cost of providing fringe benefits that it pays to all employees, including shareholder employees. However, the cost of fringe benefits paid for employee shareholders who own more than two percent of the company's stock must be included in the income of the shareholder. Typically, this is reported on the shareholder employees' Form W-2 in addition to their normal salary.

Capital Gains and Losses

A business that sells or otherwise disposes of capital assets will have a capital gain or capital loss from the transaction. Capital assets are defined by Internal Revenue Service regulations and generally include everything a business owns except property held for sale to customers, most accounts or notes receivable, real and depreciable personal property used in the business, copyrights and similar intellectual property, and certain government publications.

Sole Proprietorships, Partnerships, and S Corporations. Capital gains realized by these entities are taxed to the owners at the rate applicable to the owner. In the case of an individual the maximum federal income tax rate applicable to long term capital gains (on capital assets held more than one year) is 20 percent for 2020. Individuals with an adjusted gross income in excess of $200,000 and married couples with an adjusted gross income in excess of $250,000 and filing jointly will also pay a 3.8 percent Net Investment Income tax on most capital gains.

Federal long-term capital gains tax rates for 2020 are as follows:

The tax rate on most net capital gain is no higher than 15 percent for most taxpayers. Some or all net capital gain may be taxed at 0 percent if you're in the 10 percent or 12 percent ordinary income tax brackets. However, a 20 percent tax rate on net capital gain applies to the extent that a taxpayer's taxable income exceeds the thresholds set for the 37 percent ordinary tax rate ($518,401 for single; $622,051 for married filing jointly or qualifying widow(er); $518,401 for head of household.

C Corporation. A corporation's capital gains are taxed at the corporation's regular tax rate. Thus the maximum federal tax rate on a corporation's capital gain is 21 percent. A corporation may deduct capital losses only up to the amount of its capital gains. If a corporation has a net capital loss, the loss cannot be deducted in the current tax year but instead must be carried to other tax years and deducted from capital gains that occur in those years. This is the case for both federal and Minnesota tax purposes.

Net Operating Loss

If the taxpayer's deductions for the year exceed gross income, the taxpayer may have a net operating loss (NOL). The NOL is used to reduce taxable income in other years. There are limits on the kinds of deductions, and the amounts, that can be used in computing an NOL. These limits are different for individuals and for corporations and for federal and Minnesota returns. For C corporations, if the NOL is attributable to business carried on both in and outside Minnesota, a computation allocating a portion of the NOL may be required on the Minnesota return.

Federal tax law changes in the 2020 CARES Act made several important changes in how to treat a federal NOL. These changes include the requirement to carryback a NOL five years and it may offset up to 100 percent of federal taxable income. Minnesota tax law does not currently recognize those changes. For Minnesota, the provisions in the 2017 Tax Cuts and Jobs Act determine the Minnesota treatment of a NOL:

- The carryback of a NOL was eliminated except for losses resulting from the business of farming.
- The deduction that may be claimed with respect to a NOL is limited to 80 percent of taxable income.
- A NOL may now be carried forward for an indefinite period of time rather than the previous 20 year carry forward period.

Sole Proprietorship. The NOL is determined on the proprietor's gross income from all sources as reported on the Form 1040, not just on the income or loss from the business reported on Schedule C. In general, an NOL is computed in the same way taxable income is computed: deductions are subtracted from gross income, and if deductions exceed gross income there is a net operating loss. However, there are rules that limit what deductions may be taken in computing an NOL. In general, these rules do not permit a deduction for net capital losses, nonbusiness losses, nonbusiness deductions, personal exemptions and NOL carryovers or carrybacks from previous years. Some deductions also must be modified in taking the NOL. Internal Revenue Service regulations and those of the Minnesota Department of Revenue determine the years to which the NOL is carried, and the order in which NOLs are deducted.

Partnership. A partnership is not allowed to take an NOL deduction. All losses to the partnership for tax purposes are passed through to the partners each year. The partners may use their separate shares of the partnership's loss to compute their individual NOL. The rules for sole proprietors discussed above apply.

C Corporation. For federal tax purposes, a C corporation determines and deducts an NOL in much the same way an individual does. The same carryback and carryover periods apply and the same rules apply when two or more NOLs are carried to the same year. A corporation's NOL differs from an individual's NOL in three ways. First, a corporation is allowed to take different deductions in figuring an NOL. Second, a corporation must make different modifications to its taxable income in the carryback or carry forward year when figuring how much of the NOL may be deducted. Third, Minnesota does not permit carryback of an NOL. (An NOL may be carried forward 15 years.) Because the corporation is a separate taxable entity, the NOL is deducted by the corporation and is not passed through to shareholders. Minnesota's tax laws must be followed in taking the NOL deduction for Minnesota income tax purposes.

S Corporation. The S corporation, like a partnership, is not allowed to take an NOL deduction. If the S corporation incurs a loss for the year, it is passed through to shareholders in proportion to their shareholdings. The shareholders of the S corporation may use their share of the corporation's loss to compute their individual NOL.

Estimated Tax Payments

Sole Proprietorship. The sole proprietor generally will be required to make federal and Minnesota estimated tax payments if his or her income tax and (for federal purposes) self-employment tax will exceed taxes paid through withholding and credits by $500 or more ($1,000 for federal individual income tax purposes). The tax is determined on income from all sources, including income from the business. A penalty may be imposed on underpaid estimates.

Sole proprietors who receive salaries and wages can avoid having to pay estimated tax by asking their employer(s) to withhold more tax from their earnings. A new Form W-4 would need to be filed with their employer. A special line on Form W-4 is where the sole proprietor would enter the additional amount they want their employer to withhold. Review IRS Estimated Taxes information at https://www.irs.gov/businesses/small-businesses-self-employed/estimated-taxes.

Partnership. The partnership itself is not required to make estimated tax payments. However, for Minnesota tax purposes, a partnership is required to pay quarterly estimated tax if its Minnesota minimum fee is $500 or more or if it has a nonresident partner whose share of the composite income tax is $500 or more. As with the sole proprietorship, individual partners generally will be required to make estimated tax payments if their income tax and self-employment tax will exceed taxes paid through withholding and credits by $1,000 or more. The tax is based on taxable income from all sources, not just the income from the partnership. If the tax is underpaid, a penalty may be imposed on the partner. As with the sole proprietorship, both federal and Minnesota estimates generally will be required.

C Corporation. Federal: A C corporation whose estimated tax is expected to be $500 or more is required to make estimated tax payments using the Electronic Federal Tax Payment System (EFTPS). **Minnesota:** A corporation with an estimated tax of $500 or more must make Minnesota quarterly estimated tax payments. In addition, a C corporation with more than $10,000 in tax liability must make all its tax payments via electronic funds transfer. These payments are filed with the Minnesota Department of Revenue. For both federal and Minnesota purposes, a penalty may be imposed for failure to pay the correct estimated tax on or before its due date.

S Corporation. The S corporation is not subject to estimated tax on income which passes through to shareholders. For Minnesota tax purposes, an S corporation is required to pay quarterly estimated tax if its S corporation taxes and minimum fee is $500 or more or if it has a nonresident shareholder whose share of the composite income tax is $500 or more. A penalty may be applied if the estimated taxes are underpaid.

Disposition of Ownership Interest

Sole Proprietorship. The sole proprietor who sells the business is treated as selling the individual assets of the business. The income tax treatment of the sale will depend on whether or not the property is a capital asset, and the length of time the property has been held. The assets may also be subject to state sales tax. A sole proprietor also may change the form of the business without selling its assets, such as by joining with one or more persons to form a partnership or a corporation, and then transferring the assets of the sole proprietorship to the new organization. The tax consequences of such a transfer should be discussed in advance with a competent tax advisor.

Partnership. The sale or exchange of a partner's interest in a partnership ordinarily results in capital gain or loss on the difference between the amount realized and the adjusted basis of the partner's interest in the partnership. **The partner's share of partnership debt is taken into account as well. If a partner sells or exchanges the partner's entire interest in a partnership, the partner generally is treated as if the partner received a cash distribution in an amount equal to the partnership debt allocable to the interest**. Special rules apply to exchanges of an interest in one partnership for an interest in another, liquidation of a partner's interest, and the treatment of unrealized receivables and inventory items. Tangible assets sold as part of the transaction also may be subject to state sales tax. Because of the complexity of the tax laws affecting the disposition of a partnership interest, the tax consequences of such a disposition should be thoroughly explored in advance with a competent tax advisor.

Note also that under the Revised Uniform Partnership Act (RUPA), mergers of partnerships are allowed. Again, because of the complexity of tax laws, a competent tax advisor should be consulted when considering a merger of partnerships.

Corporation. Disposition of an ownership interest (shares of stock) in a corporation must be distinguished from liquidation of the corporation. Individual shareholders who sell their stock generally will recognize capital gain or capital loss on the sale of their shares. The gain or loss will be long term or short term, depending on the length of time the shares were held. An interest in a corporation also may be disposed of by complete or partial liquidation of the corporation. In liquidation, the corporation may either dispose of its property for cash, and distribute the cash to its shareholders, or it may distribute its property to the shareholders in exchange for the corporation's capital stock held by those shareholders. In either case, the distribution generally will result in capital gain or capital loss to the shareholders. Tangible assets sold as part of the transaction also may be subject to state sales tax. In some cases, the timing of the transaction may affect the tax consequences. The tax consequences of corporate liquidations and stock redemptions for both C corporations and S corporations and their shareholders can be complex. For this reason, it is advisable to consult with a competent tax advisor prior to attempting to liquidate the corporation or dispose of corporate assets.

NAMING THE BUSINESS ENTITY

CERTIFICATE OF ASSUMED NAME

When Filing is Required

An individual or partnership that conducts or transacts business in Minnesota under a name that is different from the full, true name of each business owner must register the name of the business by filing a certificate of assumed name with the Minnesota Secretary of State Office. A corporation, limited partnership, limited liability partnership or limited liability company that conducts business under a name that is different from the exact, legal name likewise must file a certificate of assumed name for the business name.

An assumed name filing is also required when a general or limited partnership that is not also a limited liability partnership (or its partners) wishes to file statements of partnership authority, statement of denial, statements of merger, statements of dissociation, statements of dissolution or amendments or cancellations of those statements. (Note that such a partnership is not "assuming" a business name by making these filings; instead, the reason for making the certificate of assumed name filing is that the Secretary of State requires it to be filed before any such statements may be filed.)

For example, if John Smith, a sole proprietor, does business under "Smith's Realty," he must file a certificate of assumed name. Filing is not required, however, if John Smith, a sole proprietor, does business as "John Smith Realty." Likewise, if Able Building Company, a corporation, does business as "ABC Construction," it must register the assumed name "ABC Construction." If, however, Able Building Company does business under the name Able Building Company, it is not required to file a certificate of assumed name.

Restrictions on Assumed Names

An assumed name may include a designation required to be in the name of a business entity only if the business owner using the assumed name is that type of entity. For example, ABC Incorporated, a corporation, may file the assumed name XYZ Limited, because Limited is a corporate designation and the business owner is a corporation. If, however, John Smith is an individual in the realty business, the assumed name cannot be registered as "Smith Realty, Inc." Also, assumed names may not include in their names a geographic reference to a place or community if the business is not located in that community. Finally, financial institutions wishing to use an assumed name must first receive approval from the commissioner of the Minnesota Department of Commerce.

Reason for Filing

The reason for filing a certificate of assumed name is to provide information to the consumer on the identity of the business owner. **Registration of the assumed name does not protect the name against use by other persons.** It is up to the individual to decide whether to take legal action to prevent use of the name. An attorney can provide advice on the likelihood of success and potential costs of such a lawsuit. **Note also that registering a domain name or Federal trademark is a process completely separate from making any filing with the Secretary of State.**

Determining Whether an Assumed Name is Available

An assumed name will not be accepted for filing if it is the same as, or is not distinguishable from, the name of a corporation, limited liability company, limited partnership, limited liability partnership or state trademark on file with the Secretary of State. (See the section titled "Determining Whether A Name is Distinguishable" later in this chapter.)

Business owners may call the general information line of the Secretary of State 651-296-2803, or access the Secretary of State website at https://www.sos.state.mn.us, prior to registration to determine whether a name is available. The Secretary of State will perform a preliminary check but does not guarantee that the name will be available at the time of filing. There is no procedure for reserving an assumed name. A sole proprietorship or partnership that intends to incorporate at a later date may, however, reserve the corporate name by filing a reservation of corporate name with the Secretary of State. This procedure is described in the section of this Guide on forming a corporation.

Upon the dissolution or termination of a business entity for failure to file an annual renewal, the Secretary of State automatically files a name reservation to hold the name of the dissolved or terminated entity for a period of one year from the date of dissolution or termination. This is to prevent a party from "name squatting" on the name of a business that has forgotten to file its yearly renewal and then demanding payment from the business to get the name back.

Filing Procedure

Assumed names can be filed with the Secretary of State online at https://mblsportal.sos.state.mn.us. Alternatively, a simple, one-page Certificate of Assumed Name form can be downloaded from the Secretary of State at https://www.sos.state.mn.us/business-liens/business-forms-fees/assumed-namedba. Also available by mail from that office. The business owner completes and signs the form and files it with the Secretary of State, along with a filing fee. The Secretary of State then processes the form. After the Secretary of State notifies the business owner that the filing is accepted, the business owner must have the certificate published for two consecutive issues in a newspaper qualified to print legal notices (sometimes called a "legal newspaper") in the county where the registered office or principal place of business is located. A qualified newspaper is one which meets the statutory standards established by Minn. Stat. Chapter 331A. The cost of publishing this notice is set by the newspaper and paid for by the person or entity making the assumed name filing. The Secretary of State maintains a list of "legal newspapers."

Failure to publish the notice renders the assumed name filing invalid. A business that fails to file its assumed name as required by law will be assessed $250 in costs at the time of any subsequent lawsuit by or against the business.

Duration of Filing Period; Filing Amendments

A certificate of assumed name is valid as long as an annual renewal is filed, unless there are changes in the information provided on the certificate. The Secretary of State mails the business a renewal form six months prior to expiration of the certificate. For this reason, it is important to file an amendment to the assumed name certificate each time the address information on the certificate becomes outdated.

If other information provided on the certificate of assumed name changes, the business must also file an amendment with the Secretary of State. Any amendments must be filed within sixty days after the change takes place.

See the Secretary of State Fee Schedule later in this Guide for filing fees.

NAMING A CORPORATION, LIMITED PARTNERSHIP, LIMITED LIABILITY PARTNERSHIP OR LIMITED LIABILITY COMPANY

Statutory Requirements

Name requirements for corporations, limited liability partnerships and limited liability companies are established by statute.

The name of a corporation must:

- Be in the English language or any other language expressed in English characters;
- Contain the words "corporation", "incorporated", or "limited", or an abbreviation of one or more of these words, or the word "company" or the abbreviation "Co." if that word or abbreviation is not preceded by "and" or "&" or in the case of a professional corporation, the words "professional association," or "chartered," or the abbreviation "P.A.";
- Not contain a word or phrase indicating that the corporation conducts a business that is not a legal business purpose; and
- Be distinguishable from the name of each domestic or foreign corporation, limited liability company, limited partnership, limited liability partnership or any reserved name, assumed name, trademark or service mark on file with the Secretary of State at the time of the filing.

The name of a limited partnership that is not a limited liability partnership must:

- Contain the phrase "limited partnership" or the abbreviation "L.P." and may not contain the phrase "limited liability limited partnership" or the abbreviation "LLLP" or "L.L.L.P."

The name of a limited liability partnership must:

- Be in the English language or any other language expressed in English characters;
- Contain the words "limited liability partnership" or the abbreviation "L.L.P." or in the case of a professional limited liability partnership the choices already stated or the words "professional limited liability partnership" or the abbreviation "P.L.L.P.";

- Not contain a word or phrase indicating that the limited liability partnership conducts a business that does not constitute a legal business purpose;
- Be distinguishable from the name of each domestic or foreign corporation, limited liability company, limited partnership, limited liability partnership or any reserved name, assumed name, trademark or service mark on file with the Secretary of State at the time of the filing; and
- If the limited liability partnership is also a limited partnership, contain the phrase "limited liability limited partnership or the abbreviation "LLLP," or "L.L.L.P.," and must not otherwise contain the abbreviation "LP" or "L.P."

The name of a limited liability company must:

- Be in the English language or any other language expressed in English characters;
- Contain the words "limited liability company" or the abbreviation "LLC" (in the case of a professional limited liability company the words "professional limited liability company" or the abbreviations "PLC" or "PLLC" also may be used);
- Not contain the words "corporation" or "incorporated" or the abbreviations of either or both words;
- Not contain a word or phrase that indicates or implies that the limited liability company is organized for a purpose other than a permitted purpose; and
- Be distinguishable from the name of each domestic or foreign limited liability company, corporation, limited partnership, limited liability partnership or any reserved name, assumed name, trademark or service mark on file with the Secretary of State.

Determining the Availability of a Corporate Name or Limited Liability Company Name

The Secretary of State will not accept for filing articles of incorporation for a corporation, articles of registration for a limited liability partnership or articles of organization for a limited liability company if the name of the corporation, limited liability partnership or limited liability company is the same as, or not distinguishable from, the name of a Minnesota or foreign corporation, limited liability company, limited partnership, limited liability partnership or reserved name or trademark. (See the section titled "Determining Whether A Name is Distinguishable" later in this chapter.)

The Secretary of State will perform a preliminary check to determine the availability of a corporation, limited liability partnership or limited liability company name before the articles of incorporation, registration or organization are filed. Business owners may call the Secretary of State, or access the Secretary of State website at https://www.sos.state.mn.us/business-liens/business-help/how-to-check-business-name-availability/?searchTerm=name%20availability, prior to filing to determine whether the name is available. The telephone number is 651-296-2803. The Secretary of State does not guarantee that the name will be available at the time of filing, however incorporators or organizers who wish to place a hold on a name before proceeding with formation of a corporation or limited liability company may file a name reservation with the Secretary of State. (See the section of this chapter below on "Reserving a Corporate Name or Limited Liability Company Name.")

Warning

As is the case with filing a certificate of assumed name, the registration of a corporate name or limited liability partnership or limited liability company name does not necessarily mean that the name can be used without penalty. There may be existing users of that name who have perfected a prior federal trademark or common law right to the name without filing with the Secretary of State.

Note also that registering an Internet domain name is a process completely separate from making a filing with the Secretary of State. These users may be able to use the courts to prevent the incorporators, organizers, or business entity from actually using the name even though it may be available for registration with the Secretary of State.

Reserving a Corporate Name or Limited Liability Company Name

A corporate name or limited liability company name may be reserved by an individual or entity in one of the eligible categories listed below. The reservation is made on a form available from the Secretary of State, and is effective for 12 months. The reservation may be renewed for an unlimited number of 12-month periods. The fee for reserving the name appears in the Secretary of State Fee Schedule later in this Guide.

Eligible categories are:

- A person doing business in this state under the desired name (the term "person" includes a corporation or unincorporated association);
- A person intending to incorporate under Minn. Stat. Chapter 302A or form a limited liability company under Minn. Stat. Chapter 322C;
- A domestic corporation or domestic limited liability company intending to change its name;
- A foreign corporation or foreign limited liability company intending to apply for a certificate of authority to transact business in Minnesota;
- A foreign corporation or foreign limited liability company authorized to transact business in Minnesota and intending to change its name;
- A person intending to incorporate a foreign corporation or foreign limited liability company and tending to have that entity apply for a certificate of authority to transact business in Minnesota; or
- A foreign corporation or foreign limited liability company doing business under that name or a name deceptively similar to that name in one or more states other than Minnesota and not described above.

DETERMINING WHETHER A NAME IS DISTINGUISHABLE

General Rule

In general, any name which contains a different word from existing names on file with the Secretary of State is distinguishable and the name is acceptable for filing as an assumed name or as the name of a corporation or limited liability partnership or limited liability company. Exceptions to this general rule are stated in the following section.

Exceptions

Names which are identical except for the following are not distinguishable and will not be accepted for filing:

- Entity designations regardless of where they appear in the name. These include Incorporated, Corporation, Company, Limited, Limited Liability Company, Limited Liability Limited Partnership, Professional Limited Liability Company, Limited Liability Partnership, Professional Limited Liability Partnership, Professional Association, Limited Partnership and their abbreviations, and Chartered.
- The inclusion or omission of articles of speech, conjunctions, contractions, prepositions or punctuation. An article of speech is any one of the words "a," "an," or "the." A conjunction is a word or symbol that joins clauses, phrases or words together. Examples include "and," "or," "as," "because," "but," "+," "–," "&." A contraction is the shortened form of a word such as assn. for association and dept. for department. A preposition is a word which expresses the relationship between a noun and another word. Examples are "at," "by," "in," "up," "of," "to."
- The abbreviation versus the spelling out of a word or different tenses of the same word. An abbreviation is the shortened form of a word or a recognized shortening of a word to an unrelated combination of letters, e.g., "Mister" to "Mr.," "pound" to "lb.," "Brothers" to "Bros."
- The spacing of words, the combination of commonly used two-word terms or the splitting of words usually found in compound form.
- An obvious misspelling or alternative spelling or homonym.
- The use of the word or numerals (including Roman) for the same number, e.g., "two," "2," or "II."

Options for Dealing with Names Which are Not Distinguishable

A business that wishes to use a name that is not distinguishable from a name that is already on file with the Secretary of State has several options. These include changing the name, obtaining and filing consent to use the name, filing a court order, and filing a statement of dormant business. A fee is charged for each filing.

Changing the Applied-For Name. The name may be changed by adding or deleting words to distinguish the name.

Filing Consent to Use the Name. Written consent may be obtained from the holder of the conflicting name and filed with the Secretary of State. A form for this purpose is available from the Secretary of State's office. Applicants for a trademark may not obtain consents, but they may submit affidavits from themselves and from holders of conflicting names describing the nature of the businesses and the geographic and market area served as evidence that the marks will not be confusingly similar. There is no fee for filing these affidavits, although a fee is charged for filing a consent.

Filing a Court Order. An applicant for a name who obtains a court order establishing a prior right to use of that name may file the name. The court order must be attached to the filing.

Filing a Statement of Dormant Business. To use this method, the applicant must file a signed affidavit stating that: the existing corporation or business has been in existence for three years or more and is on file with the Secretary of State; the existing corporation has not filed anything with the Secretary of State in the past three years; the applicant mailed a written notice by certified mail return receipt requested, to the registered office of the existing corporation or business, and the notice has been returned as undeliverable; the applicant has made a diligent inquiry and has been unable to find a telephone listing for the existing corporation or business in the county of its registered office; and the applicant has no knowledge that the existing corporation or business is still operating.

FORMING A SOLE PROPRIETORSHIP

As noted in the section on choosing the form of organization, a sole proprietorship is the simplest form of business organization. There are no statutory requirements unique to this form of organization. From a regulatory standpoint, the business owner only needs to register the business name as an assumed name (if it does not contain the business owner's first and last names), obtain business licenses and tax identification numbers if necessary, and begin operations.

A list of business licenses required by the state of Minnesota appears in the Directory of Licenses and Permits section of this Guide. Procedures for registering the business name as an assumed name are discussed in the previous section of this Guide.

The sole proprietor must obtain federal and state tax identification numbers if the business has employees even if those employees are members of the sole proprietor's immediate family. A sole proprietor who will hire employees also will need an unemployment insurance employer account number and must secure workers' compensation insurance for employees. A sole proprietor who will be selling a product or service that is subject to sales tax will need to register for sales and use tax purposes. These taxes and procedures for obtaining tax numbers are discussed in the section of this Guide on business taxes.

Sole proprietors who will be hiring employees also should review the section of this Guide on Issues for Employers.

FORMING A PARTNERSHIP

There are two types of partnerships: general partnerships and limited partnerships. Both general and limited partnerships can elect certain legal rules that give partners in these partnerships greater protection against personal liability. A general partnership that makes this election is called a "limited liability partnership"; a limited partnership that makes this election is called a "limited liability limited partnership."

A general partnership that is formed in a state other than Minnesota, or in a foreign country, is called a foreign general partnership. A limited partnership that is formed in a state other than Minnesota, or in a foreign country, is called a foreign limited partnership and is subject to additional regulatory requirements. A limited liability partnership (or limited liability limited partnership) formed in a state other than Minnesota, or in a foreign country, is called a foreign limited liability partnership (or foreign limited liability limited partnership) and is subject to additional regulatory requirements.

GENERAL PARTNERSHIPS

A general partnership is a business that is owned by two or more persons who associate to carry on the business of the partnership for profit. General partnerships have specific attributes, which are defined by Minn. Stat. Chapter 323A. The general rule is that in a general partnership all partners share equally in the right, and responsibility, to manage the business, and each partner is responsible for all the debts and obligations of the business. General partnerships that have elected limited liability partnership status operate much like general partnerships, but generally partners in limited liability partnerships are not personally liable for the wrongful acts of other partners or for the debts or obligations of the partnership.

Regulatory Requirements

From a regulatory standpoint, a partnership must obtain business licenses if necessary, obtain federal and state tax identification numbers and an unemployment insurance employer account number and will need to register the business name as an assumed name, unless the first and last name of each partner is included in the name of the partnership. Note that, as explained below, it is also strongly recommended that the partnership (no matter what type) draw up a written agreement addressing key issues like the allocation of management responsibilities, the distribution of profits and losses, and rights upon termination. The partnership agreement is not filed with the state, however. Issues commonly addressed in a partnership agreement are discussed in the next section.

A list of business licenses required by the state of Minnesota appears in the section of this Guide titled "Directory of Licenses and Permits". Procedures for registering the business name as an assumed name are discussed in the previous section of this Guide.

Note that any partner of a general partnership that has elected limited liability partnership status, or professional limited liability partnership status, is jointly and severally liable for contributions or reimbursement, including interest, penalties and costs with respect to unemployment insurance benefits if the partnership, as an employer, fails to pay any amounts with respect to unemployment insurance benefits due to the Minnesota Unemployment Insurance (UI) Program.

Although the partnership itself is not a taxable entity, it must file an annual federal and state "information" return with the Internal Revenue Service and the Minnesota Department of Revenue. For this reason, both federal and state tax identification numbers must be obtained by the partnership. A partnership that will be selling a product or service that is subject to sales tax also will need to register for purposes of Minnesota sales and use tax. A partnership that will hire employees, even if those employees are members of a partner's family, must secure workers' compensation insurance covering employees. These taxes and procedures for obtaining tax numbers are discussed in the section of this Guide on business taxes.

Partnerships that will be hiring employees also should review the section of this Guide on issues for employers.

Registration of Domestic and Foreign Limited Liability Partnerships

In order to become a limited liability partnership, a Minnesota general partnership must file a registration to that effect. A form, Minnesota Limited Liability Partnership Statement of Qualification, that includes the specifically required language is available from the Secretary of State at Minnesota Limited Liability Partnership Forms, https://www.sos.state.mn.us/business-liens/business-forms-fees/minnesota-limited-liability-partnership-forms/. Also available by mail from that office. The partnership is subject to limited liability partnership rules of law on and after the date the registration is filed. That registration is valid indefinitely as long as the annual registration for the partnership is filed on a calendar year basis.

Non-Minnesota limited liability partnerships must similarly register with the Secretary of State a Foreign Limited Liability Partnership Statement of Qualification, available at Foreign Limited Liability Partnership Forms, https://www.sos.state.mn.us/business-liens/business-forms-fees/foreign-limited-liability-partnership-forms/, and must attach to the registration a certificate of good standing or status from the state or province where the foreign limited liability partnership is formed.

The Partnership Agreement

The partnership agreement addresses a number of issues relating to the management and operation of the partnership. In drawing up the partnership agreement, the prospective partners should consult with legal counsel to assure that the needs and desires of the partners and relevant legal issues are addressed. Some of the issues typically addressed in a partnership agreement include:

- Name of the partnership.
- Duration of the partnership.
- Location of its place of business.
- Capital contribution of each partner.
- Whether partners may make additional contributions.
- The level at which capital accounts of the partners must be maintained.
- Participation of each partner in profits and losses.

- The amounts of any regular drawings against profits.
- Responsibilities and authority of each partner.
- Amount of time to be contributed by each partner.
- Prohibition of partners' outside business activities which would compete with the partnership business.
- Name of the managing partner and method for resolving management disputes.
- Procedure for admitting new partners.
- Method of determining the value of goodwill in the business, in case of death, incompetence, or withdrawal of a partner or dissolution of the partnership for any other reason.
- Method of liquidating the interest of a deceased or retiring partner.
- Circumstances under which a partner must withdraw from active participation, and arrangements for adjusting the partner's salary and equity.
- Whether or not surviving partners have the right to continue using the name of a deceased partner in the partnership name.
- Basis for expulsion of a partner, method of notification of expulsion, and the disposition of any losses that arise from the delinquency of such a partner.
- Period of time in which retiring or withdrawing partners may not engage in a competing business.
- Procedures for handling the protracted disability of a partner.
- How partnership accounts are to be kept.
- The fiscal year of the partnership.
- Whether or not interest is to be paid on the debit and credit balances in the partners' accounts.
- Where the partnership cash is to be deposited and who may sign checks.
- Under what conditions limited partners may be accepted into the firm, and, if so, who shall be designated as the general partner.
- Prohibition of the partners' pledging, selling, hypothecating, or in any manner transferring their interest in the partnership except to other partners.
- Identification of material contracts or agreements affecting the liability or operation of the partnership.

LIMITED PARTNERSHIPS

A limited partnership is a type of partnership in which the limited partners share in the partnership's liability only up to the amount of their investment in the limited partnership. By statute, the limited partnership must have at least one general partner and one limited partner. The general partner has the right and responsibility to control the limited partnership, and is responsible for the debts and obligations of the limited partnership. The limited partner, in exchange for limited liability, generally does not participate in the day-to-day management and control of the business.

Regulatory Requirements

As is the case with general partnerships, a limited partnership will need to obtain business licenses if necessary, obtain federal and state tax identification numbers and may need to register the business name as an assumed name. A limited partnership that will hire employees, even if those employees are members of a partner's immediate family, must obtain an unemployment insurance employer account number and worker's compensation insurance for those employees. The limited partnership must file a certificate of limited partnership with the Secretary of State before commencing business. The filing requirements are discussed in the next section.

A limited partnership that will be selling shares in the limited partnership to the public likely will be required to register with the federal Securities and Exchange Commission and the Minnesota Department of Commerce. Persons contemplating such an offer or sale should consult with legal counsel well in advance of the offering to assure that it complies with federal and state securities laws.

Certificate of Limited Partnership

A limited partnership must file a Certificate of Limited Partnership with the Secretary of State. Minn. Stat. § 322A.11 sets forth the minimum content requirements of the certificate. A form containing these requirements is available from the Secretary of State at https://www.sos.state.mn.us/business-liens/business-forms-fees/minnesota-limited-partnership-forms/. Also available by mail from that office. A limited partnership is formed at the time the certificate of limited partnership is filed with the Secretary of State or at a later time specified in the certificate.

In addition to the Certificate of Limited Partnership, the limited partnership may also adopt a limited partnership agreement. As is the case with a general partnership agreement, the limited partnership agreement governs the details of the partnership and the management arrangement between the general partners and the limited partnership. Issues and concerns to be addressed in the limited partnership agreement as well as consideration of securities law requirements and tax consequences should be discussed with legal counsel.

In order to become a limited liability limited partnership, the first step is to establish the limited partnership, second, it is necessary to follow the procedures required for creating a limited liability partnership described in the preceding sections of this Guide. It is recommended that the name of the limited partnership and the name on the limited liability limited partnership registration match so that there is no question whether the limited partnership entity has elected limited liability partnership status.

FOREIGN LIMITED PARTNERSHIPS

A limited partnership that does business in Minnesota and is formed in another state or country must register with the Secretary of State as a foreign limited partnership. Filing requirements are established by Minn. Stat. § 322A.70. A registration form, Foreign Limited Partnership Certificate of Authority, containing the required information is available from the Secretary of State at Foreign Limited Partnership Forms, https://www.sos.state.mn.us/business-liens/business-forms-fees/foreign-limited-partnership-forms/. Also available by mail from that office. The foreign limited partnership must attach to its registration a certificate of good standing (sometimes called a certificate of status) from the state or province where the foreign limited partnership is formed.

A foreign limited partnership also must obtain a Minnesota tax identification number. If the foreign limited partnership has employees, even if those employees are members of a partner's immediate family, it must obtain an unemployment insurance employer account number and workers' compensation insurance covering its employees.

FORMING A MINNESOTA BUSINESS CORPORATION

A corporation is a separate legal entity that is owned by one or more shareholders. The shareholders elect a board of directors which is responsible for the management and control of the corporation. As a separate legal entity, the corporation is responsible for the debts and obligations of the business. In most cases the shareholders are insulated from personal liability for claims against the corporation.

A corporation is formed according to the laws of the state in which it is organized. In Minnesota the business corporation statute is Minn. Stat. Chapter 302A. The following material describes the process for incorporating a business in Minnesota and some of the post-incorporation issues faced by new corporations. The formation of a state bank or trust company with the Minnesota Department of Commerce is beyond the scope of this publication. Other issues are described in the sections of this Guide on choosing the form of business organization, business taxes, and issues for employers.

ARTICLES OF INCORPORATION

A corporation is formed by one or more incorporators filing articles of incorporation with the Secretary of State and paying the filing fee. Incorporators must be at least 18 years of age. Minimum requirements are satisfied by filing an Articles of Incorporation for a Minnesota Business Corporation. The articles are available from the Secretary of State at https://www.sos.state.mn.us/media/1388/domesticbusinesscorparticlesofinc.pdf. Also available by mail from that office. Incorporators may, in the articles of incorporation, add to or modify many of the basic statutory provisions set forth in the Minnesota Business Corporation Act. If the incorporators choose to modify the statutory provisions, they must draft their own articles of incorporation; they cannot use the form provided by the Secretary of State. An attorney can assist in determining whether modifications are needed and in drafting articles of incorporation.

Corporate Name

Requirements for the corporate name are discussed in the section on naming the business entity, earlier in this Guide.

Registered Office

A corporation must maintain a registered office located in the state of Minnesota. The address of a registered office must set forth the complete office address (**not a post-office box**). This address may be a street address, a rural route **and** rural route box or fire number, or directions from a landmark. If directions are given, a mailing address in the same town or in an adjacent area must also be given. All addresses **must** have a zip code.

Registered Agent

The corporation is not required to name a registered agent in the articles of incorporation, but if the corporation decides to name an agent, the articles must list the name of the agent and the agent must be located at the registered office.

Corporate Seal

The corporation is no longer required to have a corporate seal.

Number of Authorized Shares of Stock

A corporation may authorize any number of shares of stock. The articles of incorporation require only the total number of shares authorized. Neither a par value nor a stated value is required, although the articles may include par value if shares are to have a par value. Corporations that plan to do business in another state should consider including a provision specifically stating that shares have a par value of one cent per share for franchise fee purposes. This is a restatement of Minn. Stat. § 302A.401, subd. 2(c) and may enable the corporation to avoid paying excess franchise fees in other states.

Note: While the number of authorized shares is fixed in the articles, the decision to issue shares is up to the directors, who may reserve shares for later issuance. The board must approve each issuance and ensure that the corporation receives fair value for its shares.

Names, Addresses and Signatures of Incorporators

The articles must list the names and complete mailing addresses, including zip codes, of each of the incorporators. There must be at least one incorporator. Each incorporator must be a natural person of at least 18 years of age and must sign the articles.

Other Provisions

There is no publication (i.e., no "legal advertisement") requirement for corporations incorporated under Minn. Stat. Chapter 302A. There is also no statutory minimum capital requirement for these corporations.

There are a number of provisions of Minn. Stat. Chapter 302A that may be altered or adopted in the articles of incorporation, but that need not appear in the articles in order to properly form a corporation. A brief description of each of these provisions appears in Minn. Stat. § 302A.111, subdivisions 2, 3 and 4. Some of these provisions include:

- The power to adopt, amend, or repeal the bylaws is vested in the board of directors (Minn. Stat. § 302A.181);
- Directors serve for an indefinite term that expires at the next regular meeting of shareholders (Minn. Stat. § 302A.207);
- A corporation must allow cumulative voting for directors (Minn. Stat. § 302A.215);
- Absent directors may be permitted to give written consent or opposition to a proposal (Minn. Stat. § 302A.233);
- A larger than majority vote may be required for board action (Minn. Stat. § 302A.237);
- The affirmative vote of a majority of directors present is required for an action of the board (Minn. Stat. § 302A.237);
- A written action by the board taken without a meeting must be signed by all directors (Minn. Stat. § 302A.239);
- All shares have equal rights and preferences in all matters not otherwise provided by the board (Minn. Stat. § 302A.401);
- A shareholder has certain preemptive rights, unless otherwise provided by the board (Minn. Stat. § 302A.413);
- The transfer or registration of transfer of securities may be restricted (Minn. Stat. § 302A.429);
- Regular meetings of shareholders need not be held, unless demanded by a shareholder under certain conditions (Minn. Stat. § 302A.431);
- Unless otherwise provided by law not less than ten days' notice is required for a meeting of shareholders (Minn. Stat. § 302A.435, subd. 2);
- The affirmative vote of the holders of a majority of the voting power of the shares represented and voting at a duly held meeting is required for an action of the shareholders, except where this chapter requires the affirmative vote of a majority of the voting power of all voting shares (Minn. Stat. § 302A.437, subd. 1);
- A larger than majority vote may be required for shareholder action (Minn. Stat. § 302A.437);
- The number of shares required for a quorum at a shareholders meeting is a majority of the voting power of the shares entitled to vote (Minn. Stat. § 302A.443);

- A corporation may agree to submit a matter to its shareholders whether or not the board of directors determines, at any time after approving the matter, that the matter is no longer advisable and recommends that shareholders reject it (Minn. Stat. § 302A.439);
- Indemnification of certain persons is required (Minn. Stat. § 302A.521).

Amending the Articles of Incorporation

A corporation may amend its articles of incorporation to include or modify any provision that is required or permitted to appear in the articles or to omit any provision not required to be included in the articles. Amendments are required when any changes are made in the articles of incorporation. Common reasons for amending the articles include: changing the corporate name or registered address; increasing the number of authorized shares; and changing other provisions affecting the rights of shares and shareholders.

A corporation amends its articles of incorporation by submitting the amendment to the shareholders at a regular or special meeting called with proper notice and having the amendment approved by the required number of votes. Proper notice means the corporation mailed information on the meeting time and other agenda items and a brief description of the amendment to each shareholder entitled to vote at least ten days before the meeting, unless other laws or the articles or bylaws permit a shorter time for notice.

Electronic meetings and participation by electronic means are permitted in Minnesota. Consult your attorney for further information on how to properly set up a virtual meeting, do corporate business by electronic mail, or allow electronic participation in physical meetings.

The amendment may be approved by the holders of a majority of the voting power unless the articles require a larger majority or the amendment will either increase or reduce a majority already required in the articles or required by Minn. Stat. Chapter 302A. In that case the amendment must receive the approval of the higher of the two, if the corporation is not publicly held. A publicly held company requires the approval of a simple majority.

The articles of amendment must include the name of the corporation (which must be identical to the name on file with the Secretary of State), the text of the amendment, and a statement that the amendment was adopted pursuant to Minn. Stat. Chapter 302A. There is a filing fee. Amendment to Articles of Incorporation forms are available from the Secretary of State at https://www.sos.state.mn.us/media/1387/dcnpamendment.pdf. Also available by mail from that office.

A corporation may also restate its articles of incorporation in their entirety. In addition to stating the name of the corporation and reciting that the restatement was approved pursuant to Minn. Stat. Chapter 302A, all articles are presented in the language as amended. In other words, all changes are combined in one document. A restatement that includes substantive amendments must be approved by the shareholders in the same way any other amendment is approved. If the purpose of the restatement is only to combine all previous changes into one document, only the board of directors need approve it.

Articles of amendment must also be signed by a person who has been authorized by the corporation to sign corporate documents.

Change of Registered Office or Registered Agent

The registered office or registered agent may be changed by amending the articles of incorporation that sets forth the registered office or registered agent. To do this, the corporation must follow the procedure for amending articles of incorporation.

Every time a corporation moves or changes its registered office or agent it must file a Notice of Change of Registered Office/Registered Agent with the Secretary of State. The Notice of Change of Registered Office/Registered Agent must state the name of the corporation; the new address of the registered office, if the registered office is being moved; the name of the new registered agent, if a new agent is being appointed; and that the change of office or agent was approved by the board of directors. Notice of Change of Registered Office/Registered Agent forms are available from the Secretary of State at https://www.sos.state.mn.us/media/1382/changeofregisteredofficeagent.pdf. Also available by mail from that office.

The statement must be signed by an authorized representative of the corporation. There is a filing fee.

POST-INCORPORATION ISSUES

General Considerations

When a corporation is formed, it becomes a legal entity that is separate from the owners or shareholders. The corporation can only act, however, through the individuals who are the incorporators, officers, directors, or shareholders. As part of the process of organizing the corporation, those individuals address a number of organizational matters, such as planning the capitalization, choosing the state of incorporation, selecting and reserving the corporate name, and drafting articles of incorporation and bylaws. Once the corporation is formed, those individuals will need to start up and operate the corporation. Specific guidance may be obtained from the firm's legal and tax advisors. In general, start-up and maintenance tasks include:

- Obtaining federal and state tax identification numbers and an unemployment insurance employer account number for the corporation.
- Issuing shares of stock in conformity with the articles of incorporation; note also that federal and state securities laws apply to the issuance of corporate shares. Corporate shares may be represented by share certificates or may be "uncertificated." Uncertificated shares do not have certificates but are still reflected on the records of the corporation. As stated elsewhere in this Guide, these laws are complex, and the advice of knowledgeable professionals should be obtained before attempting to issue corporate securities.
- Setting up and maintaining corporate books and records, including books of account, shareholder records, and corporate minute books.
- Calling and conducting the initial meeting of the board of directors or shareholders in conformity with the articles of incorporation and applicable laws.
- Assuring that all actions taken and decisions made by the corporation through its directors, officers and shareholders conform with the articles of incorporation, bylaws, and applicable law. All actions and decisions should be recorded in the corporation's minute book.

Annual Registration

Minnesota corporations must file an annual corporate registration with the Secretary of State which will provide corporations with a reminder-to-file notice. Failure to file an annual registration for any calendar year will trigger an administrative dissolution of the corporation.

Business Activities Report

Every corporation that does business in Minnesota must annually file with the Minnesota Department of Revenue a business activities report. Corporations are exempt from this requirement if they:

- File a Minnesota corporate income tax return on time;
- Possess a certificate of authority to do business in Minnesota;
- Are a tax-exempt corporation;
- Are engaged solely in secondary market activity in Minnesota; or
- Are financial institutions that annually conduct business with fewer than 20 persons, and have total assets and deposits of less than $5 million.

A corporation that is required to file a business activities report and fails to do so is prohibited from prosecuting any cause of action upon which it may bring suit under Minnesota law. In addition, those corporations generally are barred from using Minnesota courts for contracts executed and causes of action arising during the violation period. The Commissioner of Revenue may disclose to litigants whether a business activities report has been filed by a party to a lawsuit.

Copies of Form M4R Minnesota Business Activity Report, may be obtained from the Minnesota Department of Revenue at the contact information listed in the Resource Directory section of this Guide.

SUBSIDIARIES

When a corporation extends into a new product line or a new geographic area, it frequently establishes a "subsidiary" corporation. A subsidiary corporation is a separate legal entity which happens to be controlled by another corporation (its "parent") that owns enough shares of the subsidiary's stock to dictate policy. Some subsidiaries are wholly-owned, some are not. As a separate entity, separate records and management are required, although consolidated financial and tax reporting may be possible under certain circumstances. Subsidiaries may also serve to insulate the parent corporation from liability for the action of the subsidiary under certain circumstances.

PUBLIC BENEFIT CORPORATIONS

Public Benefit Corporations, a new legal corporate form, are like traditional for-profit business corporations in most ways except that they choose to make social commitments a part of their business plan. Primarily, a public benefit corporation declares a legally binding social purpose, in addition to its general business purpose, which its directors and officers must consider when making strategic decisions for the business. A public benefits corporation publicly reports its progress toward its social purpose each year by filing an annual benefit report with the Minnesota Secretary of State.

Minn. Stat. Chapter 304A creates two different types of public benefit corporations, a general business corporation (GBC) and specific benefit corporation (SBC). The corporation must elect one of these two types in Minnesota and use the name of the type of entity in its legal name. A GBC always has a purpose to pursue a general public benefit, and may have an additional purpose to pursue a specific public benefit, while an SBC has a purpose to pursue only a specific public benefit and not any general public benefit. The distinctions between a GBC and an SBC effect the scope of the fiduciary duties of the directors.

The Public Benefit Corporation Act does not create a new corporate tax status, nor does election to be a PBC confer tax-exempt status or transform a for-profit enterprise into a nonprofit organization. A PBC is taxed as a regular business corporation – either as a C corporation under the Internal Revenue Code or, if it qualifies and makes an election, as a Subchapter S corporation. A nonprofit corporation cannot become a PBC, but it can create a subsidiary PBC. Under Minnesota law enacted in 2016, an LLC is prohibited from converting directly to a Public Benefit Corporation.

FOREIGN CORPORATIONS DOING BUSINESS IN MINNESOTA

A corporation that is organized under the laws of a state other than Minnesota that transacts business in Minnesota must register a Certificate of Authority to Transact Business in MN before doing business in Minnesota. The requirements for obtaining the Certificate of Authority are specified by Minn. Stat. Chapter 303, and are set forth on a required form available from the Secretary of State's website at https://www.sos.state.mn.us/media/1559/foreigncorpregistration.pdf, which is also available by mail from that office. A recently-issued (within the past 90 days) certificate of existence from the state of incorporation must accompany the application.

The term "transacting business" is not clearly defined in statute, but the standard used in making the determination is the "minimum contacts" standard used in determining jurisdiction. Under this standard the facts are analyzed to determine whether the business or its local agents have conducted a continuous course of business in Minnesota or with Minnesotans sufficient to justify being governed by Minnesota law. This analysis will not be performed by the Secretary of State or any other state executive agency; each business is responsible for performing its own analysis on the topic.

Neither the Secretary of State nor any other state agency will make a determination as to whether a particular organization should register as a foreign corporation. As a general rule, doubts should be resolved in favor of registering the organization. Minn. Stat. § 303.03 establishes certain activities as exceptions to the registration requirement. Corporations organized outside Minnesota should consult with their legal counsel to determine whether any of the exceptions apply.

A foreign corporation also must file with the Secretary of State an Foreign Corporation Annual Renewal and pay the fee. Annual renewal forms are sent by the Secretary of State to the registered agent and office address of the corporation in Minnesota. The forms are also available at https://www.sos.state.mn.us/media/1560/foreigncorprenewal.pdf, which is also available by mail from that office. Failure to file the annual registration in a calendar year will result in revocation. Foreign nonprofit corporations are exempt from this requirement.

In addition to obtaining the certificate of authority, a foreign corporation must obtain a Minnesota tax identification number from the Department of Revenue. If the corporation will have employees in Minnesota, it also must obtain a Minnesota employer withholding tax number and an unemployment insurance employer account number and arrange for workers' compensation insurance. The procedure for obtaining these numbers is described in the section of this Guide on business taxes and the Checklist for Hiring an Employee.

Foreign corporations also must obtain any state and local business licenses necessary to conduct business operations. Information on business license requirements may be obtained from the Small Business Assistance Office at the address and telephone number provided in the Resource Directory section of this Guide.

Finally, the Minnesota Department of Revenue has the power to order the Secretary of State to revoke a foreign corporation's certificate of authority to do business in Minnesota if that corporation "fails to comply with any tax laws" administered by the Department of Revenue.

FORMING A MINNESOTA LIMITED LIABILITY COMPANY

A limited liability company is a form of business organization with limited liability characteristics of a corporation and the ability to be treated for tax purposes as a sole proprietorship (or disregarded entity), partnership or corporation. (It will be treated for tax purposes as a sole proprietorship (or disregarded entity), if there is a single member, or as a partnership, if there are multiple members, unless it affirmatively elects to be taxed as a corporation.) The formation and operation of a Minnesota limited liability company is governed by Minn. Stat. Chapter 322C.

In the case of a limited liability company that is taxed as a partnership or disregarded entity, business income and losses of the limited liability company are passed through to the owners of the business and are taxed to the owner's individual tax rate. As with a corporation, liability for business debts and obligations generally rests with the entity rather than with individual owners.

A limited liability company that is taxed as a pass-through entity is not subject to many of the restrictions that apply to S corporations, such as a maximum of 100 shareholders, a single class of stock, and limited types of non-individual shareholders. All members of a limited liability company may participate in the active management of the company without risking loss of limited personal liability.

For a limited liability company that elects to be taxed as a corporation, it will be taxed as a C corporation unless it qualifies and elects to be taxed as an S corporation. As of 2009, when a single-member limited liability company that is taxed as a disregarded entity fails to pay federal unemployment taxes, the limited liability company, not the owner is now liable.

ARTICLES OF ORGANIZATION

A limited liability company is formed by filing Minnesota Limited Liability Company Articles of Organization with the Secretary of State and paying the filing fee. Minimum requirements for the articles of organization are provided on an articles of organization form is available from the Secretary of State at https://www.sos.state.mn.us/media/1824/llcarticlesoforganization.pdf. Also available by mail from that office. The articles of organization may add to or modify many of the basic statutory provisions set forth in the Minnesota Revised Uniform Limited Liability Company Act. Many of these also may be, and typically are, modified in an operating agreement. An attorney can assist in drafting articles of organization to assure that the needs and desires of the members, as well as legal requirements, are met. An organizer of a limited liability company must be at least 18 years of age.

Limited Liability Company Name

Requirements for the limited liability company name are discussed in the section on Naming the Business Entity, earlier in this Guide.

Registered Office

A limited liability company must have a registered office located in the state of Minnesota. The registered office may be the place where the business is located or it may be in a different location. The registered office address must be a street address – the address of a physical location where a person who represents the limited liability company can be found. A registered office address cannot be a post office box. Acceptable registered office addresses include a complete street address, a rural route and rural route box or fire number or directions from a landmark to the office location. If directions are given, a mailing address in the same or an adjacent town must be given. All addresses must have a zip code.

Registered Agent

The limited liability company is not required to name a registered agent in the articles of organization, but if the limited liability company decides to name an agent, the articles must list the name of the agent and the agent must be located at the registered office.

Names, Addresses and Signatures of Organizers

The articles of organization must list the names and complete mailing addresses, including zip codes, of each organizer. There must be at least one organizer. Each organizer must be a natural person who is at least 18 years old. Each organizer must sign the articles.

Other Provisions

Under Minn. Stat. § 322C.0201, subd. 3, the articles of organization may contain other provisions, but they will be effective only if they would be effective in a valid operating agreement.

Amending Articles of Organization

A limited liability company may amend its articles of organization at any time to include or modify any provision that is required or permitted to appear in the articles or to omit any provision not required to be included. Amendments are required if any provision contained in the articles of organization is, or becomes, inaccurate. The Minnesota Limited Liability Amendment to Articles of Organization form is available from the Secretary of State at https://www.sos.state.mn.us/media/1568/llcamendment.pdf. Also available by mail from that office.

Articles of organization may be amended in the manner provided in the operating agreement.

The articles of amendment must include the following provisions: the name of the limited liability company as it appears in the records of the Secretary of State; the changes the amendment makes to the articles of organization as most recently amended or restated; and a statement that the amendment was adopted pursuant to Minn. Stat. Chapter 322C. There is a filing fee.

A limited liability company also may restate its articles of organization in their entirety at any time. In addition to stating the name of the limited liability company and reciting that the restatement was approved pursuant to Minn. Stat. Chapter 322C, all articles are presented in the language which the limited liability company now wishes to use. In other words, all changes are combined in one document. A restatement that includes substantive amendments must be approved by the members in the same way as any other amendment is approved.

Articles of amendment must be signed by a person who has been authorized by the limited liability company to sign such documents.

Change of Registered Office or Registered Agent

Every time a limited liability company moves or changes its registered agent (if it has one), it must report the new information to the Secretary of State on Notice of Change of Registered Office/Registered Agent form available at https://www.sos.state.mn.us/media/1382/changeofregisteredofficeagent.pdf. Also available by mail from that office. The form states the name of the limited liability company, the new address of the registered office, the name of the new registered agent, if one is being appointed, and that the change was approved by the board of governors.

As noted earlier, if a registered agent is appointed, the registered agent must be physically located at the registered office address. The statement must be signed by an authorized representative of the limited liability company. There is a filing fee.

The registered office address and agent information can also be changed using the amendment procedure described above.

POST-ORGANIZATION ISSUES

General Considerations

Until a limited liability company that has been formed has at least one member, it lacks capacity to do any act or carry on any activity except (1) delivering to the Secretary of State for filing a statement of change, an amendment to the certificate, a statement of correction, an annual report, and a statement of termination; (2) admitting a member; and (3) dissolving. Once the limited liability company has at least one member, the member(s) may ratify prior actions that occurred when the limited liability company lacked capacity.

A newly formed limited liability company must perform certain start-up tasks, such as obtaining federal and state tax identification numbers, obtaining an unemployment insurance employer account number, setting up and maintaining the books and records of the business, and taking other actions to organize itself. All actions taken and decisions made by the limited liability company through its members, governors and/or managers must conform with the provisions of the articles of organization, the operating agreement, and applicable law. While not necessary, it is advisable and helpful to record all actions and decisions in a minute book or record book maintained for the company. Specific guidance on post-organization issues may be obtained from the company's legal and tax advisors.

Annual Registration

Both Minnesota and non-Minnesota limited liability companies must register with the Secretary of State once every year. The Secretary of State will send a Limited Liability Company Annual Renewal form to the limited liability company at its registered office. The form is also available from the Secretary of State at https://www.sos.state.mn.us/media/1569/llcdomesticforeignrenewal.pdf. Also available by mail from that office. The registration is due before the end of the calendar year. Failure to file will result in administrative termination. Reinstatement may occur within one year of the date of the administrative termination by filing the registration form and paying a reinstatement fee.

Operating Agreements

The operating agreement is the most important contract among the members of a limited liability company. Many aspects of the members' relationship and the limited liability company's business can be controlled by the operating agreement, which is similar in function to a partnership agreement. Operating agreements are specific to the circumstances of each limited liability company. While operating agreements need not be in writing, and may be oral or implied by conduct, it is almost always advisable to reduce an operating agreement to writing, as it greatly increases the likelihood that the members are acting with a common understanding and minimizes the risk of disputes arising later on.

Generally an operating agreement will spell out how the limited liability company's rules differ from the default rules that would otherwise apply under Minn. Stat. Chapter 322C. Rules that members may wish to change may include:

- Acts outside the ordinary course of the limited liability company's business require the consent of all members. (Minn. Stat. § 322C.0407, subds. 2, 3(4)(iii), 4(16));

- All members have an equal vote and an equal say in management matters, rather than voting rights in proportion to the value of their contributions. (e.g., Minn. Stat. § 322C.0407, subds. 2(2), 4(17));
- Each member has a right to participate equally in current distributions and, upon dissolution, in residual distributions after contributions have been returned. (Minn. Stat. §§ 322C.0404; 322C.0707);
- The consent of all members is required to admit a new member (Minn. Stat. § 322C.0401, subd. 4(3));
- The consent of all members is required to: (i) sell, lease, exchange, or otherwise dispose of all, or substantially all, of the limited liability company's property, with or without the good will, outside the ordinary course of the company's activities. (Minn. Stat. § 322C.0407, subds. 2, 3(4)(i), 4(16)(i)). Member consent, however, is not required for a grant of a security interest in all or substantially all of the company's property and assets, whether or not in the usual course of business; nor is member consent required for the transfer of any or all of the company's property to an organization all the ownership interests of which are owned directly or indirectly by the company through the wholly owned organization.;
- The consent of all members is required to amend the operating agreement. (Minn. Stat. § 322C.0407, subds. 2, 3(4)(iv), 4(16)(iii));
- The consent of all members is required to approve a merger, conversion, or domestication. (Minn. Stat. § 322C.0407, subds. 2, 3(4)(iv), 4(16)(ii)).

Limited liability company members should consult with legal counsel in creating or signing such agreements.

FOREIGN LIMITED LIABILITY COMPANIES DOING BUSINESS IN MINNESOTA

A limited liability company that is organized under the laws of a state other than Minnesota and transacts business in Minnesota must register a Certificate of Authority to Transact Business in Minnesota before doing business in Minnesota. The requirements for a foreign limited liability company obtaining an initial certificate of authority are specified by Minn. Stat. §§ 322C.0801 to 322C.0809, and are set forth on Foreign Limited Liability Company Certificate of Authority available from the Secretary of State at https://www.sos.state.mn.us/media/1580/foreignllccertificateofauthority.pdf. Also available by mail from that office. A certificate of status or certificate of good standing from the state or province of organization must accompany the registration form.

The term "transacting business" is not clearly defined in the law, but the standard used in making the determination is the "minimum contacts" standard used in determining jurisdiction. Under this standard the facts are analyzed to determine whether the limited liability company business or its local agents have conducted a continuous course of business in Minnesota or with Minnesotans sufficient to justify being subjected to Minnesota law.

Neither the Secretary of State nor any other state agency will make a determination as to whether a particular limited liability company should register as a foreign limited liability company. As a general rule, doubts should be resolved in favor of registering the organization.

Minn. Stat. § 322C.0803 establishes certain activities as exceptions to the registration requirement. Limited liability companies organized under the laws of a state other than Minnesota should consult with their legal counsel to determine whether any of the exceptions apply.

In addition to obtaining the certificate of authority, a foreign limited liability company must obtain a Minnesota tax identification number from the Minnesota Department of Revenue. If the company will have employees in Minnesota, it also must complete the Minnesota Department of Revenue's withholding tax forms and arrange for workers' compensation insurance. The procedure for obtaining these numbers and forms is described in the section of this Guide on business taxes and the Checklist for Hiring an Employee. If the foreign limited liability company changes the name or address of its registered agent or other statements made in the application for the certificate of authority become inaccurate, the foreign limited liability company must file an amended certificate of authority with the Secretary of State. A foreign limited liability company also must obtain any state and local business licenses necessary to conduct business operations. Information on business license requirements may be obtained from the Small Business Assistance Office at the address and telephone number provided in the Resource Directory section of this Guide.

SPECIAL TYPES OF BUSINESS ORGANIZATIONS

S CORPORATIONS

Both "S" and "C" corporations are created by filing articles of incorporation with the Secretary of State, after which the shareholders must decide whether to treat the corporation as an S corporation or as a C corporation for tax purposes. An S corporation is a corporation which meets Internal Revenue Service criteria for tax treatment as an S corporation rather than as a C corporation, and whose shareholders unanimously choose to be treated as an S corporation. An S corporation is subject to the provisions of Subchapter S of the Internal Revenue Code, whereas C corporations are taxed under Subchapter C of the Internal Revenue Code. A corporation that has a valid election to be taxed as an S corporation for federal purposes is also an S corporation for Minnesota tax purposes.

The S corporation is subject to the taxing provisions in much the same manner as a partnership, i.e., the S corporation files an information tax return, Form 1120S, to report its income and expenses, but it is not separately taxed. Income (including, if certain requirements are met, capital gains) and expenses of the S corporation flow through to the shareholders in proportion to their shareholdings, and profits are taxed to the shareholders at the shareholders' individual tax rates. For Minnesota purposes, the S corporation also pays a minimum fee, based on its Minnesota-sourced property, payroll and sales. See the Tax Rates section of this Guide.

By contrast, the C corporation is a separate taxable entity. The C corporation reports its income and expenses on a corporation income tax return and is taxed on its profits at corporation income tax rates. Dividends distributed to the shareholders is taxable income to the shareholders. In contrast, all the income of an S corporation is taxable income to the shareholders whether or not the income is distributed to the shareholders as dividends.

An S corporation is defined by statute as a domestic corporation (i.e., a corporation organized under the law of one of the states of the United States) which:

- Does not have more than 100 shareholders;
- Does not have any non-individual shareholders (other than estates, certain trusts, and certain tax exempt entities);
- Does not have a nonresident alien as a shareholder, and
- Does not have more than one class of stock.

Certain corporations by statute are ineligible for S corporation status. If the corporation qualifies for S corporation status, the shareholders must formally choose to be so treated for tax purposes. This is accomplished by filing Form 2553 with the Internal Revenue Service on which all shareholders consent in writing to have the corporation treated as an S corporation. The election must be made in a timely manner, as prescribed by the Internal Revenue Service.

The election is valid for the taxable year for which it is made, and for all succeeding taxable years of the corporation, until the election is terminated. Statutory procedures determine how the termination is accomplished. In general, S corporation status is terminated when it is revoked by vote of the shareholders, or when the corporation no longer meets the statutory criteria for S corporation status. S corporation status also may be terminated when passive investment income (income from interest, rents, royalties, dividends and the like) exceeds a certain statutorily defined threshold).

Because of the possibility that S corporation status may be inadvertently terminated, persons planning to establish an S corporation are strongly encouraged to consult in advance with legal and tax counsel in order to properly structure the corporation and its capitalization. In some cases, forming a limited liability company, rather than an S corporation, may better suit the owners' business and tax objectives. See the discussion of limited liability companies in the sections of this Guide titled Choosing the Form of Business Organization and Forming a Minnesota Limited Liability Company.

PROFESSIONAL ENTITIES

The Minnesota Professional Firms Act, Minn. Stat. Chapter 319B, authorizes practitioners of certain licensed professions to elect to be professional firms under any one of three different forms of organization: corporations (either for-profit or nonprofit); limited liability companies; and limited liability partnerships. In the absence of the Minnesota Professional Firms Act and its predecessors, members of such professions would not be able to practice under these forms of organization because the ethics rules of their respective licensing boards prohibit organizing in a way that limits the professional practitioner's professional liability towards clients. The Minnesota Professional Firms Act does not affect a practitioner's liability for her or his own malpractice or other wrongful conduct directly arising from the rendering of professional services, but permits the professional to have limited liability for debts or obligations of the business itself to the extent that the generally applicable governing law for the chosen form of organization permits.

Professional firms are subject to the law under which the entity has been formed as well as the Professional Firms Act which contains additional restrictions; where the two conflict, the Professional Firms Act will control. Members of the professional firm are also subject to the laws, regulations and licensing requirements of their respective licensing boards.

In order to practice a profession in any form other than sole proprietorship or general partnership, professionals must comply with the Professional Firms Act, except as the rules of the respective licensing board provide otherwise.

Members of the following professions may elect to be professional firms: medicine and surgery; chiropractic; registered nursing; optometry; psychology; social work; marriage and family therapy; dentistry and dental hygiene; pharmacy; podiatric medicine; veterinary medicine; physician's assistants; architecture; engineering; surveying; landscape architecture; geoscience; certified interior design; accountancy; and law.

In order to operate as a professional firm, a Minnesota entity must first be formed under the chosen statute: the Minnesota Business Corporation Act (Minn. Stat. Chapter 302A); the Minnesota Nonprofit Corporation Act (Minn. Stat. Chapter 317A); the Minnesota Revised Uniform Limited Liability Company Act (Minn. Stat. Chapter 322C); or the Minnesota Limited Liability Partnership Act (Minn. Stat. Chapter 323A). An existing non-Minnesota entity wishing to practice a profession in Minnesota should register under the Minnesota Foreign Corporation Act (Minn. Stat. Chapter 303) or the foreign registration provisions of the Limited Liability Company or Limited Liability Partnership Acts.

Then, either as an addendum to the original documents of formation for the entity or as a later amendment or update to those documents, the firm must file with the Secretary of State language stating:

- that the firm elects to be covered by the Minnesota Professional Firms Act (Minn. Stats. §§, 319B.01 to 319B.012);
- that the firm acknowledges that it is subject to those sections; and
- specifying from the list of professions set forth above the profession or professions to be practiced by the firm.

A non-Minnesota firm must state in addition to the above that to the extent that it's generally applicable governing law differs from or conflicts with Minn. Stats. §§ 319B.01 to 319B.12, that it has made the necessary changes to the agreements and other documents controlling its structure, governance, operations and internal affairs so as to comply with those sections.

Such a filing constitutes an election to be a professional firm. These entities may rescind such elections, may again elect professional status, and may change the designated practiced profession freely, subject to the regulations of the appropriate governing board(s).

Health professionals (including medicine and surgery; chiropractic; registered nursing; optometry; psychology; dentistry and dental hygiene; pharmacy and podiatric medicine) are specifically authorized to practice in the same professional firm; others should consult their licensing boards for further information on whether joint practices are permitted. Where they are not, a professional firm can provide only those professional services listed in the election described above.

The name of a professional firm which is a corporation must include one of the following designations or abbreviations; Professional Corporation, Professional Service Corporation, Service Corporation, Professional Association, Chartered, Limited, P.C., P.S.C., S.C., P.A., or Ltd.

The name of a professional firm which is an LLC must include Professional Limited Liability Company, Limited Liability Company, P.L.L.C., P.L.C., or L.L.C.

The name of a professional firm which is an LLP must include Professional Limited Liability Partnership, Limited Liability Partnership, P.L.L.P. or L.L.P.

The internal governance of professional firms is governed by the same statutes that apply to non-professional firms. For example, a professional LLP and a non-professional LLP are bound in virtually all respects by the same statutes. The only difference is that the professional LLP may provide professional services as listed above and the non-professional LLP may not.

NONPROFIT CORPORATIONS

A Minnesota nonprofit corporation is defined by statute as a corporation which:

- Is formed for a purpose not involving pecuniary gain to its members (other than members that are nonprofit organizations or governmental units), and
- Pays no dividends or other pecuniary remuneration, directly or indirectly, to its members as such (other than to members that are nonprofit organizations or governmental units).

Thus, a business corporation (regardless of whether it actually makes a profit) cannot be a nonprofit corporation because a primary purpose of every business corporation is to remunerate its shareholders.

A nonprofit corporation may be formed under the Minnesota Nonprofit Corporation Act, Minn. Stat. Chapter 317A, for any lawful purpose, unless another statute requires incorporation for a different or specific purpose. The nonprofit corporation is managed by a board of directors, which must consist of at least three individuals. The nonprofit corporation must have at least two officers, a president and a treasurer. One person may perform both of these functions. The Minnesota Nonprofit Corporation Act does not apply to cooperative associations, public cemetery corporations and associations, and private cemeteries. Religious corporations may be formed under the Minnesota Nonprofit Corporation Act or under the Minnesota religious corporation statute, Minn. Stat. Chapter 315. Nonprofit corporations are required to file an annual registration with the Secretary of State once each calendar year, on a registration form mailed to the corporation's registered office address. Failure to file in a calendar year will result in statutory dissolution, but nonprofit corporations may be reinstated at any time upon filing the annual registration. The registered office address may be updated without charge.

Minnesota Nonprofit Corporation Articles of Incorporation and Minnesota Nonprofit Corporation Annual Renewal forms are available from the Secretary of State at https://www.sos.state.mn.us/business-liens/business-forms-fees/minnesota-non-profit-corporation-forms/. Also available by mail from that office.

A nonprofit corporation may qualify for tax exempt status for some or all of its income, for federal or state tax purposes, or both. Donors to the tax exempt organization may qualify for a tax deduction on their contributions to the organization. Application for tax exempt status must be made with the Internal Revenue Service and the exemption must subsequently be established with the Minnesota Department of Revenue. Additional specific language may be required in the articles of incorporation by the Internal Revenue Service before an application will be granted. Annual federal and state informational filings also are required, and if the organization solicits funds in Minnesota, it also must register with the Charities Division of the Minnesota Attorney General's office. The formation and tax treatment of nonprofit corporations are highly technical areas which should not be attempted without competent advice from qualified professionals. Review the IRS information: Tax Information for Charities & Other Non-Profits at https://www.irs.gov/charities-non-profits; Before Applying for Tax Exempt Status at https://www.irs.gov/charities-non-profits/before-applying-for-tax-exempt-status; Applying for Tax Exempt Status at https://www.irs.gov/charities-non-profits/applying-for-tax-exempt-status; Publication 557, Tax Exempt Status for Your Organization at https://www.irs.gov/pub/irs-pdf/p557.pdf. IRS contact information for charities and non-profit organizations is available at https://www.irs.gov/charities-non-profits/about-irs-exempt-organizations.

Unrelated Business Income Tax

Tax-exempt organizations may be subject to Unrelated Business Income Tax (UBIT) on income made from regularly conducted trade or business activities not substantially related to the organizations' tax exemption.

Organizations with $1,000 or more of unrelated business income must file two forms:

- Federal Form 990-T, Exempt Organization Business Income Tax Return
- Minnesota Form M4NP, Unrelated Business Income Tax (UBIT) Return

COOPERATIVES

A cooperative is a form of business organization in which the business is owned and controlled by those who use its services. A cooperative may be organized as a legal entity or it may be an unincorporated association. Cooperative associations are organized as legal entities under and governed by Minn. Stat. Chapter 308A. Non-Minnesota cooperatives that wish to do business in Minnesota register under Minn. Stat. Chapter 303.

Cooperatives are organized primarily for the purpose of providing service to their user-owners, rather than to generate profit for investors. Although cooperatives had their origins in Minnesota in the agricultural sector, in recent years many consumer cooperatives have been established. Some of the more common purposes for which cooperatives are formed are:

- To supply members with agricultural production components such as fuels, fertilizers, feed and chemicals;
- To provide members with an organizational structure for jointly handling and marketing their products;
- To provide services to members, like housing, electricity, telephone, insurance, and health care.

Cooperatives have several features that distinguish them from for-profit business corporations. These include control of the cooperative by user-owners, services provided at cost, and limited return on equity capital.

Cooperatives are required to file an annual renewal once each calendar year. Failure to file this registration will result in dissolution. The cooperative will have one year to reinstate by filing the registration and paying the fee.

User-owner Control

Cooperatives are owned and controlled by their members. By statute in Minnesota, members each have one vote, rather than multiple votes based on their capital investment in the cooperative. In some other states, proportional voting based on a member's volume of business with the cooperative is allowed. Operations generally are conducted by a board of directors elected by members, and by management hired and supervised by the board.

Service at Cost

Cooperatives stress providing services to members at the lowest responsible cost. After setting aside reserves to protect the cooperative's financial security and growth, any remaining net margin is distributed to members as a patronage refund, according to the business volume each has done with the cooperative during the year.

Limited Return on Equity Investment

Cooperatives are designed primarily to provide services to members, rather than to produce a profit for investors. Accordingly, the return on investment in the form of dividends is limited. Minnesota Statutes permit, but do not require, the payment of dividends on capital stock. Dividends may be paid only when the net income of the cooperative for the previous fiscal year is sufficient, and dividends may not be cumulative.

New Investors

In an effort to encourage capital investment, all forms of cooperatives in Minnesota are allowed to take on investor-members in addition to the traditional patron-members. Investor members may not necessarily purchase products from the cooperative but join the cooperative to earn a profit from an investment and to provide capital funds for cooperative expansion. In allowing for investor-members, the law largely combines portions of the traditional cooperative statute with portions of the limited liability statute.

FRANCHISES

A franchise is an agreement or contract between two or more persons by which the franchisor, for a fee, gives the franchisee the right to engage in the business of offering or distributing goods or services using the franchisor's trade name, trademark, service mark, logotype, advertising, or other commercial symbol. Both the franchisor and the franchisee must have a community of interest in the marketing of the goods or services.

Franchising is a method of distributing and marketing goods or services. It is not a separate form of business organization. The franchisor's business and the franchisee's business each will take one of the forms of organization previously discussed.

Franchises are regulated in Minnesota by the Minnesota Department of Commerce, and anyone contemplating the sale of a franchise should check with that office for registration and filing requirements and exemptions that may apply. Regulatory requirements applicable to franchises are discussed further in the section of this Guide on Franchise Registration.

FILING DOCUMENTS WITH THE OFFICE OF THE MINNESOTA SECRETARY OF STATE

DRAFTING THE DOCUMENT

Standard forms are available without charge from the Secretary of State, Business Forms & Fees at https://www.sos.state.mn.us/business-liens/business-forms-fees/, and also available by mail from that office. While these forms are designed to meet minimum requirements of the law, they are not intended to address every possible situation. Consultation with an attorney can help the business owner draft a document that reflects the needs and desires of the parties and understand the legal effects of the filing.

Documents must be legible. The Secretary of State permanently records all documents; this process demands a legible copy. Thus, documents that are illegible are not accepted for filing. Copies and legible fax transmissions are acceptable. Original signatures are acceptable if legible, but are not required; in most cases a copy will suffice.

The proper fee must accompany the document. A current fee schedule appears at the end of this section. Information regarding online payments is available from the Secretary of State at https://www.sos.state.mn.us/business-liens/business-help/how-to-make-a-payment/.

TIME REQUIRED FOR FILING AND PROCESSING DOCUMENTS

Documents are usually reviewed the day they are received by the Secretary of State. In cases of complex documents or heavy seasonal workloads, review may take place the day following receipt. Non-expedited drop-offs are reviewed the business day following drop off.

COMMON REASONS WHY DOCUMENTS ARE NOT ACCEPTED FOR FILING

A document may be returned unapproved and not accepted for filing by the Secretary of State for a number of reasons. Some of these include:

- An incomplete address is submitted. Documents must state the full street address, city or town and zip code number.
- The filing fee submitted is not correct.
- The signatures of the required parties are incorrect or incomplete. All incorporators of a corporation or organizers of a limited liability company must sign the original articles. Other filings must be signed by a person who is authorized by the business entity to sign those documents. The business entity's attorney can assist in determining who is authorized to sign documents.
- The name referred to in an amendment or subsequent filing is incorrect. In submitting amendments or any other subsequent filings the name of the corporation or other business entity must be identical (in spelling and punctuation) to the legal name on file with the Secretary of State.
- The name submitted for a corporation, limited liability company or limited liability partnership is not distinguishable from an existing corporate or assumed name, trademark or servicemark, limited liability company, limited partnership or limited liability partnership name.

ELECTRONIC ACKNOWLEDGEMENTS AND ONLINE SIGNATURES

The Secretary of State is authorized to receive documents and issue acknowledgements electronically.

Any document submitted to the Secretary of State online may be signed by any person as agent of the person whose signature is required by law. The signing party must indicate on the application that they are acting as agent of the person whose signature would be required and that they have been authorized to sign on behalf of the applicant. The name of the person signing, entered on the online application, constitutes a valid signature by such an agent.

OFFICE OF THE MINNESOTA SECRETARY OF STATE
FEE SCHEDULE FOR BUSINESS ENTITY FILINGS

The following fees are effective as of the date this Guide was printed. Questions may be directed to the Office of the Minnesota Secretary of State at the address and telephone number provided in the Resource Directory section of this Guide.

Business Services Filings Fees

Filing Type	Mail Filings	In-Person & Online Filings
Assumed Name ***Minn. Stat. Chapter 333***		
Certificate of Assumed Name -Original Filing	$30	$50
Amendment	$30	$50
Annual Renewal	$0	$0
Annual Renewal Reinstatement	$25	$45
Cancellation	$0	$0
Limited Liability Partnership (Domestic) / Foreign) ***Minn. Stat. Chapter 323A***		
Statement of Qualification -Original Filing	$135	$155
Statement of Amendment/Cancellation	$135	$155
Annual Renewal	$135	$155
Annual Renewal Reinstatement	$160	$180
Statement of Denial / Dissociation / Dissolution / Merger	$135	$155
Statement of Partnership Authority	$135	$155
Resignation of Agent	$135	$155
Limited Partnership (Domestic) / (Foreign) ***Minn. Stat. Chapter 321***		
Certificate of Limited Partnership / Certificate of Authority -Original Filing	$100	$120
Amendment	$50	$70
Annual Renewal	$0	$0
Annual Renewal Reinstatement	$25	$45
Cancellation / Conversion / Merger	$50	$70
Resignation of Agent	$50	$70

Business Services Filings Fees

Filing Type	Mail Filings	In-Person & Online Filings
Business Corporation (Domestic)		
Minn. Stat. Chapter 302A		
Articles of Incorporation -Original Filing	$135	$155
Amendment / Dissolution Filings	$35	$55
Annual Renewal	$0	$0
Annual Renewal Reinstatement	$25	$45
Conversion to Limited Liability Company	$35	$55
Merger	$60	$80
Resignation of Agent	$35	$55
Business Corporation (Foreign)		
Minn. Stat. Chapter 303		
Certificate of Authority -Original Filing	$200	$220
Amendment / Merger / Withdrawal Filings	$50	$70
Annual Renewal	$115	$135
Annual Renewal Reinstatement	$500	$520
Conversion	$35	$50
Dissolution	$50	$70
Resignation of Agent	$50	$70
Nonprofit Corporation (Domestic)		
Minn. Stat. Chapter 317A		
Articles of Incorporation -Original Filing	$70	$90
Amendment / Merger / Dissolution Filings	$35	$55
Resignation of Agent	$35	$55
Annual Renewal / Reinstatement	$0	$0
Change of Registered Agent and Office	$35	$55
Change of Registered Office only	$0	$0
Resignation of Agent	$35	$55
Nonprofit Corporation (Foreign)		
Minn. Stat. Chapter 303		
Certificate of Authority -Original Filing	$50	$70
Amendment / Merger / Withdrawal Filings	$50	$70
Dissolution	$50	$70
Resignation of Agent	$50	$70

Business Services Filings Fees

Filing Type	Mail Filings	In-Person & Online Filings
Limited Liability Company (Domestic)		
Minn. Stat. Chapter 322C		
Articles of Organization	$135	$155
Amendment	$35	$55
Annual Renewal	$0	$0
Annual Renewal Reinstatement	$25	$45
Conversion Filings	$60	$80
Domestication Filings	$60	$80
Statement of Dissolution	$35	$55
Statement of Termination	$35	$55
Merger	$60	$80
Resignation of Agent	$35	$55
Statement of Authority / Authority /Amendment	$35	$55
Cancellation	$35	$55
Limited Liability Company (Foreign)		
Minn. Stat. Chapter 322C		
Certificate of Authority	$185	$205
Amendments	$35	$55
Annual Renewal	$0	$0
Annual Renewal Reinstatement	$25	$45
Conversion Filings	$60	$80
Domestication Filings	$60	$80
Resignation of Agent	$35	$55
Withdrawal	$35	$55
Termination	$35	$55
Cooperative (Domestic)		
Minn. Stats. Chapters 308A & 308B		
Articles of Incorporation/Organization - Original Filing	$60	$80
Amendment	$35	$55
Annual Renewal	$0	$0
Annual Renewal Reinstatement	$25	$45
Conversion / Dissolution	$35	$55
Merger	$60	$80
Resignation of Agent	$35	$55

Business Services Filings Fees

Filing Type	Mail Filings	In-Person & Online Filings
Cooperative (Foreign) *Minn. Stat. Chapter 303*		
Certificate of Authority -Original Filing	$200	$220
Amendment / Merger / Withdrawal Filings	$50	$70
Annual Renewal	$115	$135
Annual Renewal Reinstatement	$500	$520
Dissolution		
Resignation of Agent	$50	$70
Reservation of Name		
Name Reservation - Original Filing	$35	$55
Name Reservation Renewal	$35	$55
Cancellation	$0	$0
Trademarks *Minn. Stat. Chapter 333*		
Certificate of Registration -Original Filing	$50	$70
Renewal	$25	$45
Cancellation	$0	$0
Assignment	$15	$35
Legal Newspapers		
Legal Newspaper Registration -Original Filing	$25	$25
Legal Newspaper Renewal	$25	$25
Miscellaneous Business Filings		
Abandoned Name Affidavit	$35	$55
Articles of Correction	$35	$55
Consent to Use of Name	$35	$55
Pre-Clearance Filings	$250	$250
Service of Process		
Minnesota Entities	$35	$55
Non-Minnesota Entities	$50	$70

Business Services Filings Fees

Filing Type	Mail & In-Person Orders	In-Person & Online Filings
Business Copy & Certification Schedule		
Copy of Original Filing	$3	$13
Copy of Amendments	$3 per Filing	$3 per Filing plus $10 Online Fee
Certification of Filing(s)	Additional $5 per Certification	Additional $5 per Certification
Certified Copy of All / Specify Amendments	$8	$18
Copy of Specific Amendment	$3	$13
Business Certificate		
Certificate of Good Standing or Certificate of Existence & Registration (Certificate issued depends on business types)	$5	$15
No Record Certificate	$5	N/A

REGULATORY CONSIDERATIONS

SECURITIES REGISTRATION

Broadly defined, a security is an interest in, or an obligation of, the business entity that issues the security. Examples of securities are corporate stock, interests in a limited partnership, and corporate bonds and debentures. Note that the label assigned to an interest in a business is not necessarily determinative, and that the definition of a security is a very broad one; note that many seemingly innocent activities, such as the use of a website can constitute the "offer" of securities.

A business owner who is giving or selling ownership interests in a business to other persons, even to friends and family members, is strongly advised to seek the advice of counsel. This is true whether the ownership interests are transferred when the business is organized or later in its life. In general, securities must be registered with the federal Securities and Exchange Commission (SEC) and/or the Minnesota Department of Commerce before they legally can be advertised or sold to investors unless the security or transaction qualifies for an exemption under state or federal laws. A security or transaction may qualify for a federal exemption but not a state exemption or vice versa. Again, given the highly technical laws, regulations, and judicial decisions in this area, as well as guidance from the SEC (such as that issued on the use of electronic media), the advice of counsel is very important.

The basic purpose of both state and federal securities laws is to protect the investor. Therefore, sales in violation of these laws, even if done through inadvertence or in good faith reliance, can create civil and criminal penalties on both the state and the federal level. If interstate sales are involved, civil and criminal penalties in multiple states may apply. The anti-fraud provisions of these laws apply even if the securities or the transaction are exempt from registration.

Securities registration is a sophisticated area requiring the services of experienced professionals. In some cases these professionals may be able to assist in structuring the offering and sale to qualify for an exemption. In other cases their services may be necessary to register and to sell the securities. In all cases involving the offer or sale of securities, discussing the matter with legal counsel is the best starting point.

The JOBS Act of 2012 made substantial changes to federal securities law in three areas: raising the dollar limit for securities offered under Regulation A; removing the general solicitation prohibition on offerings to accredited investors Under Regulation D Rule 506; authorizing a crowdfunding exemption to registration. As noted in the sections below, rules implementing and expanding operation of Regulation A were added in 2015; rules implementing the changes to Regulation D Rule 506 were added in 2013. Final rules implementing the federal crowdfunding exemption were adopted by the Securities and Exchange Commission on October 30, 2015 with an effective date of 180 days after publication in the Federal Register.

In June, 2019, the U.S. Securities and Exchange Commission published its "Concept Release on Harmonization of Securities Offerings Exemptions." That lengthy release discussed potential changes to the exemptions from federal securities registration for the types offerings described below. It also discussed the possibility of changes to the definition of "accredited investor" that would not be tied to an investor's net worth but could involve other standards such as permitting individuals with certain professional credentials, or individuals who passed an accredited investor examination, to qualify as accredited investors.

A rule adopted August 26th, 2020, keeps in place the current assets and income limits for an "accredited investor": net worth exceeding $1 million jointly or with spouse and not including the primary residence, or income exceeding $200,000 ($300,000 with spouse) in each of the last two years with reasonable expectation of the same level of income in the current year. That new rule did add to the definition individuals holding certain securities licenses: Series 7 (licensed general securities representative; Series 65 (licensed investment advisor representative), and Series 82 (licensed private securities offerings representative).

On November 2nd, 2020, the Securities and Ecchange Commission published a final rule implementing many of the conceppts of the June 29th release. Those final rule changes are reflected in the material below.

Registered Offerings Under 2015 Regulation A Plus

The JOBS Act of 2012 raised the limit for offerings of securities under Regulation A from $5 million to $50 million. In March 2015 the Securities and Exchange Commission adopted rules now known as Regulation A Plus to address what was seen as an impediment to the expanded use of Regulation A; that is the requirement that issuers had to register with both federal regulators and state regulators in every state where the securities would be sold. Regulation A Plus creates two tiers of offerings: Tier 1 with offerings up to $20 million in a 12 month period, and Tier 2 with offerings up to $75 million in a 12 month period. The rule preempts state regulation for Tier 2 offerings but keeps in place coordinated review by both federal and state regulators for Tier 1 offerings.

Regulation A Plus has several other substantial elements:

- No limit on investors. Offerings may be made to both accredited and non-accredited investors subject to the investment limits noted below.
- Investment limits. There are no limits to how much any investor may invest in a Tier 1 offering. In a Tier 2 offering investors may invest a maximum of the greater of 10 percent of their net worth or 10 percent of their net income.
- Investors can self-certify income or net worth. No documentation is required.
- SEC approval of the offering circular is required. The issuer must file a disclosure document and financials with the SEC. This must be approved by the SEC prior to any sales. For Tier 1 offerings reviewed financials are sufficient but for Tier 2 offerings audited financials are required.
- Ongoing disclosure requirements. There are no ongoing disclosure requirements for Tier 1 offerings. Tier 2 issuers must provide an annual disclosure, a semi-annual report, and current reports which will be equivalent to, but less expensive than, current Form 10-K, Form 10-Q, and Form 8-K.

- Securities offered will be unrestricted and transferable assuming a secondary market for these securities develops.

Federal Private Placement Exemption Under Regulation D

The Regulation D exemptions authorize the offer and sale of securities through certain private placement transactions. There are restrictions on the number and amount of sales, and on advertising or solicitation, and resale. Notice of Regulation D offerings must be filed with the Securities and Exchange Commission, but the full registration and disclosure requirements of a public offering need not be met.

Regulation D includes four exemptions:

- **Rule 504** provides an exemption for offerings up to $10 million during the twelve months before the start of and until the completion of the offering. Purchasers need not meet any suitability test and there is no limit on the number of purchasers to whom the offeror can sell.
- **Rule 505** provides an exemption for offerings up to $5 million during the twelve months before the start of and until the completion of the offering. Sales may be made to an unlimited number of accredited investors (defined below), but may not be made to more than 35 non-accredited investors.
- **Rule 506(b)** permits a company to sell an unlimited dollar amount of securities. Sales may be made to an unlimited number of accredited investors, but may not be made to more than 35 non-accredited investors, each of whom must be a "sophisticated investor."
- **Rule 506(c)** added by the Jobs Act of 2012 allows for general solicitation and advertising in Rule 506 private placements where all purchasers are accredited investors and the issuer has taken reasonable steps to verify that the purchasers are accredited investors.

The term "accredited investor" as applied to natural persons means any individual natural person whose net worth (alone or jointly with spouse) exceeds $1 million not including the value of the person's primary residence; or, a natural person whose income exceeded $200,000 ($300,000 with spouse) in each of the two most recent years with a reasonable expectation of the same level of income in the current year. A rule adopted by the Securities and Exchange Commission on August 26, 2020, adds to that definition individuals holding Series 7, Series 65, and Series 82 securities licenses.

Note that the prohibition on general solicitation and advertising remains in Rule 506 offerings where not all investors are accredited investors.

The Intrastate Exemption

The intrastate exemption applies to securities offerings which are confined to a single state and which are purely local in nature. The scope of the intrastate exemption is extremely narrow, and even though the offering is exempt from federal regulation, it is subject to state law requirements. To qualify for the intrastate exemption, the securities must be part of an issue that is offered and sold only to residents of a single state. The issuer must be a resident of the same state and must have its principal place of business there. If the issuer is a corporation it also must be incorporated in that state. There are restrictions on subsequent sales of the securities, and the issuer must take certain precautions against interstate offers and sales.

The Federal Equity Crowdfunding Exemption

The federal JOBS Act of 2012 provides an exemption from federal securities registration for securities sold through "crowdfunding," the process by which a company solicits smaller dollar amount investments from a large number of non-accredited investors using social media and other online platforms. Several conditions apply:

- The offering must be conducted by an SEC registered broker or an SEC registered funding portal. The offeror cannot advertise the terms of the offering except for notices which direct the investor to the broker or portal.
- Investments collected by a portal must be held by an escrow agent separate from the portal.
- The aggregate amount of investment offerings by a company cannot exceed $5 million in any 12 month period.
- There are no investment limits for accredited investors. Investors who are not accredited may use the greater of their income or net woth to compute the maximum investment of $107,000.
- The offeror must file with the Securities and Exchange Commission, and provide to investors, disclosures to be determined by Securities and Exchange Commission rules. The disclosures will address the nature of the company, its business plan, its financial condition, and the risks associated with investment. Depending on the size of the offering the offeror will also be required to provide tax returns and certified, reviewed, or audited financial statements.

The Act provides that this kind of offering will be exempt from state registration or regulation.

NOTE: in May 2020 the Securities and Exchange Commission published a final temporary rule allowing issuers to solicit statements of interest from potential investors in advance of the offering.

MINNESOTA BLUE SKY LAWS

A company selling securities to residents of the state of Minnesota must comply with federal and state securities laws. State securities laws are collectively and individually referred to as "Blue Sky Laws." These Blue Sky Laws vary among the states, sometimes to a significant degree. It is important to note that the Minnesota Legislature recently enacted a version of the Uniform Securities Act, which provides for substantial revisions to the current version of the Minnesota Securities Act. The Minnesota Uniform Securities Act ("MUSA") became effective in August 2007. This section highlights the most frequently used exemptions from the securities laws of the state of Minnesota and summarizes certain changes that will result from the enactment of MUSA, where applicable.

The securities laws of Minnesota require registration with the Minnesota Department of Commerce of all offers and sales of securities made to residents of Minnesota unless a particular exemption is available. If registration is required, it should be noted that, prior to the passage of MUSA, Minnesota was a "merit" review state, Minnesota is now a "disclosure" only state. Generally, this means that as long as the issuer satisfies the information disclosure requirements under MUSA, the Minnesota Department of Commerce cannot prohibit the issuer from selling its securities within the state.

Minnesota Equity Crowdfunding Legislation

In 2015 Minnesota enacted its own equity crowdfunding legislation, MNvest (refer to The Law section of the MNvest website at http://mnvest.org/the-law/), which provides an exemption from registration for offering of equity securities via an online portal which can be a broker dealer, the issuer itself, or another entity approved for that purpose by the Minnesota Department of Commerce. Some important elements of the law are:

- The offering must meet the requirement for the federal exemption for intrastate offerings.
- The sale of the securities must be conducted *exclusively* through an online MNvest portal (emphasis added).
- The issuer can raise no more than $2 million in a twelve month period if it has audited or reviewed financial statements, and no more than $1 million if it does not have audited or reviewed financials.
- At least 80 percent of the proceeds of the offering must be used in connection with operation of the issuer's business within Minnesota.
- No single purchaser may purchase more than $10,000 in securities in connection with the MNvest offering unless the investor is an accredited investor.
- All funds for purchase must be held in escrow until the minimum amount stated in the offering is reached. The escrow agent must be a bank, trust company, savings bank, savings association or credit union authorized to do business in Minnesota. Portal operators are explicitly prohibited from serving as escrow agents.
- The MNvest issuer and the portal operator may engage in solicitation and advertising of the offering provided the advertisement is clear that it is not the offering and is for informational purposes only and that the offering and sale are made through a portal to Minnesota residents only. The advertisement may contain other information like anticipated uses of funds to be raised and a link to the issuer's website.
- The portal must conspicuously display a statement whose exact wording is contained in the statute and which makes clear that no agency of government has made any determination of the merits and risks of the investment. The portal must obtain a written or electronic certification from a potential investor that the investor is a Minnesota resident who understands and can bear the risk of loss in the securities and also understands that there is at time offering no market for the secondary sale of the securities.

The legislation also contains procedures for application to become a portal, details on portal operator's responsibility to keep purchaser information private, and a "bad actor" disqualification which disqualifies from a MNvest offering any issuer having any director or executive officer who has been subject to listed disqualifying events.

Amendments in 2017 to the crowdfunding statute enabled issuers to avoid the problem of integration of offering amounts where a company makes more than one offering in a given period of time and the amounts of the offerings are summed together providing the possibility of exceeding the statutory limit on offering amounts.

The amendments effectively follow the new integration exemptions for federal crowdfunding offerings found in U.S. Securities and Exchange Commission Rule 147. Offers or sales made in reliance on the MNvest crowdfunding statute will not be integrated with:

1. Offers or sales of securities made prior to commencement of a MNvest offering or
2. Offers or sales of securities made after completion of a MNvest offering that are:
   A. Registered offerings under the Securities Act of 1933 ; or
   B. Exempt from registration under SEC Regulation A;
   C. Exempt from registration under SEC Rule 701 (dealing with equity offered to employees as compensation);
   D. Made pursuant to an employee benefit plan;
   E. Exempt from registration under SEC Regulation S (dealing with equity offerings outside the United States;
   F. Exempt from registration under the federal crowdfunding securities exemption;
   G. Made more than six months after completion of a MNvest offering.

The amendment notes also that "for purposes of clarity" the new section does not permit a MNvest issuer to conduct simultaneous securities offerings.

Isolated Sales

Sales by a nonissuer of securities to no more than ten purchasers in Minnesota during any period of twelve consecutive months are exempt from registration as are nonissuer transactions by or through a broker dealer where the security has been in the hands of the public for at least 90 days. The exemption covers sales or offers to sell to an institutional investor; an accredited investor; a federal covered investment advisor, or any other person exempted by rule promulgated by the Commissioner of the Minnesota Department of Commerce.

Limited Offerings

Sales by a company to no more than 35 persons in Minnesota during any consecutive twelve month period are exempt from registration if the following conditions are met:

- the company reasonably believes that all the buyers in Minnesota (other than institutional investors) are purchasing for investment;
- no commission or remuneration is paid or given directly or indirectly to a person other than a broker-dealer or a registered agent for soliciting a prospective purchaser in Minnesota;
- no general solicitation or general advertising is made in connection with the sale or offer to sell the security; and
- notice has been filed with the Minnesota Department of Commerce at least ten days in advance of any sale or such a shorter period as permitted by the Department. However, an issuer who makes sales to ten or fewer purchasers in Minnesota during any twelve consecutive months is not required to provide this.

SCOR (SMALL CORPORATE OFFERING REGISTRATION)

The Small Corporate Offering Registration (SCOR) is a simplified procedure for registering stock offerings which enables small, start-up companies to raise up to $5 million in a 12-month period.

SCOR: Access to Capital for Small Businesses

Increased Access to Capital

A SCOR offering is a tool for small businesses to raise capital without the prohibitive costs involved in traditional stock offerings.

Regulatory Relief and Streamlining

Because the offering is registered solely with the state, multiple reporting requirements are eliminated. In addition, the enhanced form U7 disclosure document is simply formatted into 50 detailed questions designed to satisfy the necessary disclosures without burdensome requirements.

Completing the Form U7

The process of completing a SCOR offering is centered around the form U7. The Form U7 is less complex than traditional stock prospectuses. The Form U7 consists of 50 detailed questions designed to provide the state and the investor with important information regarding the company's operations. The questions in the U7 form consist of items such as the company's history; its business and properties; risk factors facing the company; use of the offering proceeds; description of the securities being offered; dividend history; key personnel; principal stockholders; and pending or threatened litigation.

Answering the Form U7 questions adequately and completely will satisfy the required disclosures in law.

Once the Form U7 is completed, it is submitted, along with reviewed or audited financial reports, and the required fee to the Minnesota Department of Commerce Registration Division. The Department reviews and provides comments on the documents. So long as no stop order is in effect and no proceeding is pending under Minn. Stat. § 80A.13 a SCOR registration statement becomes effective automatically at 5:00 p.m. on the twentieth full business day after the filing of the registration statement, or the last amendment of it, or at some earlier time determined (by order) by the Commissioner of the Minnesota Department of Commerce.

For purposes of a nonissuer transaction, other than a transaction by an affiliate of the issuer, all outstanding securities of the same class identified in the small corporate offering registration statement as a security registered under Minn. Stat. Chapter 80A are considered to be registered while the small corporate offering registration statement is effective. The registration statement is effective for one year after its effective date or for a longer period designated by an order of the Commissioner of Commerce. The registration statement may be withdrawn only with the approval of the Commissioner of Commerce.

An issuer can raise up to $5 million in a 12 month period, and offerings must sell for at least $1 per share.

FRANCHISE REGISTRATION

DEFINITION OF FRANCHISING

Franchising is a method of marketing and distributing goods and services. Franchises are offered and sold for many types of businesses, including services, retail trade, finance, real estate, transportation, and communications.

A franchise is broadly defined as a contract or agreement between two or more persons by which the franchisor (the seller), for a fee, gives the franchisee (the buyer) the right to engage in the business of offering or distributing goods or services using the franchisor's trade name, trademark, servicemark, logotype, advertising or other commercial symbol. Both the franchisor and the franchisee must have a community of interest in the marketing of the goods or services.

Under the Minnesota franchising statute, a franchise also includes business opportunities in which the seller sells or leases products or services to the purchaser **and** represents that the seller will find or assist in finding locations; or represents that the seller will purchase the products made; or guarantees that the purchaser will make a profit.

FRANCHISE REGISTRATION AND REGULATION

Any proposed offer or sale of a franchise that meets the above definition may be subject to the registration and other requirements of the Minnesota Franchise Act (Minn. Stat. Chapter 80C) and rules of the Minnesota Department of Commerce, Minnesota Rules 2860.0100-2860.9930. Unless there is a specific statutory exemption, a proposed franchise must be registered with the Department of Commerce and must be effective before any offers or sales are made.

The Minnesota Franchise Act and rules define franchises and exemptions; establish registration criteria, procedures, and fees; set requirements for public offering statements; define unfair and prohibited practices; mandate the keeping of books and records; establish enforcement standards, and provide for imposition of civil liability for violations. The Act and rules also address issues like termination and notice periods for non-renewal of franchises, liquidated damages, termination penalties, arbitration, security deposits and governing law.

Minnesota accepts franchise applications which comply with the Uniform Franchise Offering Circular (UFOC) Guidelines of the North American Securities Administrators Association. The UFOC Guidelines prescribe disclosures that a franchisor must make available to prospective franchisees, and require that franchisors supply prospective franchisees with audited financial statements and copies of all proposed contracts and agreements pertaining to the proposed franchise relationship.

MINNESOTA DEPARTMENT OF COMMERCE ENFORCEMENT ACTIONS

The Enforcement Division of the Minnesota Department of Commerce investigates complaints against companies selling franchises and business opportunities. Action can be taken only when a violation of the Minnesota Franchise Law has occurred. Enforcement actions can be viewed on the Minnesota Department of Commerce website. Contact information is the Resource Directory section of this Guide.

OTHER ENFORCEMENT AND INFORMATION ASSISTANCE

In addition to the regulation done by the State of Minnesota, the United States Federal Trade Commission (FTC) has regulatory authority over the sellers of franchises and business opportunities. Pursuant to Section 5 of the Federal Trade Commission Act, the FTC has issued its filing complaints about franchises and business opportunities. The National Fraud Information Center (NFIC) assists the FTC and state Attorneys General by entering complaints into a computerized database to help track and identify operators of frauds.

Along with its enforcement activities, the FTC issues a number of articles and publications designed to educate potential buyers and sellers of franchises and business opportunities. Examples are: *A Consumer's Guide to Buying a Franchise,* explains how to shop for a franchise opportunity, the obligations of a franchise owner, and questions to ask before investing*; Advertising FAQs: A Guide for Small Business,* an A-Z primer focusing on the federal truth-in advertising standards: *Work-at-Home Businesses:* and *Complying with the Telemarketing Sales Rule.* Articles and publications are available at FTC Business Center at https://www.ftc.gov/tips-advice/business-center. Also available on the FTC website is information regarding Case Highlights; Compliance Documents; Laws, Rules, Reports, and Guides.

EXEMPTIONS

There are eight registration exemptions available under Minn. Stat. § 80C.03. These include sale of a franchise by a franchisee-owner; sales by an executor, administrator, sheriff, trustee in bankruptcy, guardian or conservator; sales to a bank or insurance company; sales of registered securities; a single isolated sale of a franchise under specified conditions; the sale of a franchise to a franchisee with specified experience in the business and who derives 80 percent or more of its sales from other sources; sale of a foreign franchise to a nonresident of Minnesota under specified conditions; and sales exempted by order of the Commissioner of the Minnesota Department of Commerce. It is strongly recommended that anyone considering the offer or sale of a franchise consult a knowledgeable attorney before relying on an exemption.

FRANCHISING IN OTHER STATES

Although many states regulate franchises in a manner similar to Minnesota, each state's laws are different. Accordingly, franchisors who plan to offer or sell franchises in other states should check with appropriate officials in those states regarding their franchising laws and requirements.

INTERPRETIVE OPINIONS

Under Minn. Stat. § 80C.18, subd. 2, a company may request an interpretive opinion from the Minnesota Department of Commerce on whether a business being offered is a franchise, whether registration is required, and whether an exemption is available. An opinion fee is required.

FEES

Fees charged by the Department of Commerce for franchise-related transactions are: initial application fee, $400; annual report (renewal) fee, $200; amendment fee, $100; and opinion fee, $50.

QUESTIONS AND FURTHER INFORMATION

Questions concerning franchise registration should be directed to the Minnesota Department of Commerce at the address and telephone number provided in the Resource Directory section of this Guide.

The Minnesota Franchise Act is available at https://www.revisor.mn.gov/statutes/cite/80C. The Minn. Rules are available at https://www.revisor.mn.gov/rules/2860/. The North American Securities Administrators Association, Inc. (NASSA) UFOC Guidelines (including forms) can be downloaded from a link on the Minnesota Department of Commerce at https://mn.gov/commerce/industries/securities/franchises/.

EVALUATING A BUSINESS OPPORTUNITY

SOME GENERAL CONSIDERATIONS

When buying an existing business, investing in a franchise, or beginning a new business, the entrepreneur should thoroughly evaluate the business opportunity he or she is considering. This step is very important but often overlooked; many times, a person's hopes for a business cloud his or her judgment. It is not uncommon for an entrepreneur to invest a substantial sum in a business without analyzing whether the business opportunity is a viable one. In addition, it is not uncommon for an unscrupulous business promoter to take advantage of such an entrepreneur.

Although there are no foolproof steps to take in evaluating a business, this section of this Guide will offer guidance on the types of questions to ask, and sources of information to review, before investing in a new business (whether or not it is a franchise) or buying an existing business. Assuming that after evaluating the opportunity the entrepreneur still wants to proceed, the sections of this Guide on Accounting for the New Business – Income Forecasting Techniques, and on Business Plans, should be consulted.

It is worth emphasizing here that an entrepreneur's analysis and evaluation should occur before he or she makes any kind of commitment (even oral), whether contractual or financial, to the business, or makes any payment, of any size, in connection with the business. In any event, a potential entrepreneur should carefully avoid obligating himself or herself to participating in any business opportunity, in any way, without first evaluating that opportunity.

SOURCES OF INFORMATION

One source of information is the Minnesota Attorney General, at 651-296-3353, online at https://www.ag.state.mn.us and the Better Business Bureau, at 651-699-1111, online at https://www.bbb.org/local-bbb/bbb-of-minnesota-and-north-dakota to determine if any complaints have been filed in connection with that business. Also, the National Consumer League's (NCL), Fraud Center is a private, nonprofit organization that operates a consumer hotline to provide service and assistance in filing complaints against unscrupulous business operators. The NCL helps the FTC and state Attorneys General by entering complaints into a computerized database to help track and identify operators of business frauds. Contact the Fraud Center online at https://www.fraud.org. These are prudent, but not foolproof, steps in evaluating any business opportunity.

Note that the FTC is another potential source of information about the offeror. The FTC's website, https://www.ftc.gov, contains a summary of each of the FTC's legal actions against offerors of franchises and business opportunities, along with information on specific types of fraudulent business opportunities that the FTC has become familiar with. Also, the website contains a copy of the FTC's brochure, Franchise and Business Opportunities, which summarizes the types of protections provided to entrepreneurs by the FTC's *Franchise Rule Compliance Guide,* 16 C.F.R. section 436 (the FTC Franchise Rule). Remember that, as discussed in more detail in the Franchise Registration section of this Guide, the Minnesota Department of Commerce also will have copies of the registration statement made by the offeror of any franchise or business opportunity that is a franchise within the meaning of the Minnesota Franchise Act, Minn. Stat. Chapter 80C.

SPECIFIC INFORMATION TO SEEK FROM THE OFFEROR

If the franchise or business opportunity is a franchise under the Minnesota Franchise Act, the offeror is required to make certain filings, including the Uniform Franchise Offering Circular (UFOC) with the Minnesota Department of Commerce, before offering that franchise or business opportunity to anyone. See the section of this Guide on Franchise Registrations. Note that although the UFOC will contain certain detailed information on the business opportunity or franchise, including audited financial statements, it is not the job of the Minnesota Department of Commerce, or any other government agency, to assess the merits, completeness, or even accuracy of any of the information contained in a UFOC. That work is for the entrepreneur.

Similarly, if a franchise or business opportunity does not meet the definition of a "franchise" for Minnesota state law purposes, it nevertheless may be subject to the FTC Rule. Similar to the Minnesota regulation of franchises and business opportunities, the offeror of a business venture covered by the FTC Rule must provide certain information to the prospective offeree. Also, and again similar to the Minnesota system of regulation, it is not the job of the FTC to assess the merits, completeness, or even accuracy of the information mandated by the FTC Rule.

Even for ventures not regulated by the Minnesota Department of Commerce or the FTC, the FTC in its *A Consumer's Guide to Buying a Franchise* brochure recommends that an entrepreneur seek the following information before investing or committing to a franchise or business opportunity:

- Talk to any persons named as owners or investors in the opportunity. Don't rely on persons listed as "references", unless it is clear that they are truly owners or investors.
- Carefully and thoroughly investigate any claims made about potential earnings. Seek written information on this topic, not just oral statements, and seek the most detailed information available (i.e., do not rely on broad claims such as "we are a ten billion dollar industry"). Independently analyze, if possible, the written basis for those claims. For example, the entrepreneur could hire his or her own CPA to independently audit that information.
- Seek similar information from the business competitors of the offeror. For instance, seek the UFOCs from other offerors of similar franchises or business opportunities.
- Be aware of high pressure sales tactics, and consider why they are being used; if the offeror does not have any other way to sell the franchise or business opportunity, do you really want it? Be wary of any oral statement that differs from any statement made in writing. Also be wary of any presentation that promises "easy money". Successful entrepreneurs almost always agree that there is no "easy money", and that owning one's own business, while rewarding, takes a great deal of time and energy.

USING PROFESSIONAL ADVISORS

Before beginning any evaluation of a business opportunity, the entrepreneur should decide whether to perform that evaluation himself or herself, or engage an accountant or attorney to assist him or her. Professional advisors, such as attorneys and accountants, can greatly enhance an entrepreneur's review of a potential business. This is true for at least two reasons. First, those professionals will have no emotional attachment or stake in that review process; their objectivity may serve as an important counterbalance to an entrepreneur's enthusiasm. Second, those professionals should be able to provide thorough review of financial or intellectual property information provided, and should be knowledgeable of any potential obstacles to the success of the business (such as the need for licenses or permits). For instance, it is important that someone thoroughly evaluate financial information supplied by a seller or offeror, or pro forma information prepared by the entrepreneur, and in many cases a professional is best suited to that task.

BUSINESS LICENSES AND PERMITS

IN GENERAL

The startup, operation or expansion of a business in Minnesota may involve securing one or more business, occupational or environmental licenses or permits. Those licenses and permits fall into a number of categorical groupings according to purpose:

- Licenses and permits to ensure the competency of practitioners of a business, trade or profession.
- Licenses and permits to ensure the safety and efficacy of a product or process.
- Licenses and permits to prevent fraud or ensure the financial solvency of parties to a business transaction.
- Licenses and permits to control access to markets or to encourage or restrict competition in a specific industry.
- Licenses and permits to regulate activities in pursuit of broad social goals like clean air, clean water.
- Licenses and permits to ensure the appropriate and responsible use of natural resources, Minnesota Dept. of.
- Licenses and permits to control the development and implementation of new technology.
- Licenses and permits to authorize a business to serve as the state's agent for collection of revenue.

The Bureau of Business Licenses provides information about federal, state and local licenses and assistance in securing them. The Bureau also publishes, free of charge, the State of Minnesota Directory of Licenses and Permits which contains a complete list of regulated activities, licenses and permits, and the appropriate state agency contact. It is reprinted at the end of this Guide.

A list of licenses and permits with more extensive information on state requirements, schedules, fees is available at Minnesota ELicensing, https://mn.gov/elicense/.

From the Minnesota ELicensing website, a business can access licensing information on over 750 licenses administered by state agencies in Minnesota. This includes information on permits, registrations, certifications, credentialing and other forms of approval granted by state agencies and boards as a condition of doing business: conducting a trade, profession or occupation, or pursuing a recreational activity in Minnesota. This includes equipment and vehicles and the right to operate them. This site is easy to use and conveniently lets you access licensing information by activity, administering agency, name of license, or with a keyword search.

Note that Minn. Stat. § 645.44, subd. 19 makes explicit that monies paid to a government entity for a business or individual to engage in trade, profession, or business or to improve private property are a tax not a fee.

LOCAL LICENSURE

In addition to the licensing requirements imposed by the state, some local governments also require certain kinds of business activity to be licensed on the local level. In some cases this local licensure may take the form of a general business license involving no more than registration and payment of a fee. In other cases it may involve compliance with local ordinances specific to a particular type of business. For example, current state law imposes no license requirements on commercial building contractors. Many municipalities, however, require registration and bonding of these contractors before the municipalities will issue necessary building permits or conduct necessary inspections.

Larger cities like Minneapolis and St. Paul have licensing departments. Smaller municipalities usually rely on the city clerk to direct licensing activities. A call to either of these early in your business planning will help avoid confusion and delay later. In addition, the city clerk can in most cases give you information on local zoning requirements. Refer to the County and City Licensing Contact information in the Resource Directory of this Guide.

LOCAL ZONING

Zoning is the process by which a local community enacts ordinances to regulate and control the uses of privately owned land and structures within the community. In practice this process involves the creation of districts or zones within the community and restriction on the use of land, and the use, height and area of buildings within these districts. Zoning serves to promote and conserve the health, safety, convenience and general welfare of the community.

The local zoning board or planning commission should be contacted early in your business planning to determine the regulations regarding any space in which you plan to operate your business. This is true especially if you plan to operate your business out of your home.

The zoning ordinances of each local community detail the procedure for establishment of zones and the procedures for petition for variances.

Note that the Legislature enacted modifications to certain statutes that, speaking generally, prohibit counties and municipalities from using “amortization” to eliminate or terminate a particular use of land. In this context, the term “amortization” occurs when a local government asserts that a once-lawful use of land is no longer allowed, so that the unit of government can take or condemn that land under the theory that it has no value.

BONDING

A bond is a contract, similar to an insurance policy, between a bonding company (called a "surety") and the business that purchases the bond. The bond runs in favor of a third person to protect that person against financial loss caused by the act or default of the business. Surety bonds guarantee the performance of various types of obligations assumed by contract or imposed by law. Fidelity bonds guarantee against loss (e.g. theft of money or property) due to the dishonesty of employees.

Performance Bonds

Performance bonds provide financial guarantees that contracts and other business deals will be completed according to mutual terms. When a principal breaks a bond's terms, the harmed party can make a claim on the bond to recover losses.

Each performance bond that's issued operates among the "obligee", the "principal", and the "surety".

- The obligee (the entity for whom the work is being performed) requires the principal (the entity performing the work) to purchase a bond to avoid potential financial loss to the obligee.
- The principal purchases the bond to guarantee the performance and quality of work to be done.
- The surety issues the bond and financially guarantees the principal's capacity to perform a specific task.

Before contacting a surety provider, professionals should check all federal, state and local regulations regarding performance bonds in their respective industries. Regulations regarding a specific performance bond in one state will vary from those that apply to a performance bond in another.

Businesses that contract to provide goods or services to the state or other public agencies within the state generally have performance bonds. These bonding requirements are established by statute. Note that some public and private contracts can require the "fidelity bonding" of individual employees of the principal to protect against loss caused by employee dishonesty.

Bonds are obtained through insurance agents or through a bonding company. The cost of a bond is a portion of the face amount of the bond and will depend in part on the risk to the bonding company in covering the potential loss.

See the information regarding the Minnesota Federal Bonding Service in the Sources of Information, State Programs section of this Guide.

ENVIRONMENTAL PROTECTION PROGRAMS

The Legislature has declared in statute that each person in Minnesota has a right to the protection, preservation and enhancement of air, water, land and other natural resources, and that each person also has the responsibility to contribute to the protection, preservation and enhancement of those resources. To secure and advance that right a number of state agencies have responsibility and authority for policy development, standard setting, permitting and enforcement in environmental areas. These agencies include the Minnesota Environmental Quality Board (EQB), the Minnesota Pollution Control Agency (MPCA), the Minnesota Department of Natural Resources (DNR), the Minnesota Department of Agriculture (MDA), the Minnesota Department of Health (MDH), and others. The Directory of Licenses and Permits at the back of this Guide lists the appropriate regulatory agency by regulated activity.

ENVIRONMENTAL REVIEW AND PERMITTING

Certain projects (for example, the construction or expansion of commercial or industrial facilities) can trigger specialized environmental review intended to prevent damage to environmental resources as a result of private or public development projects. This preventive planning approach helps identify and mitigate possible environmental problems while the project is still in the planning stages before permits are issued and construction or operation begins.

Those reviews are conducted by a legally defined "responsible governmental unit" and are of two types: an Environmental Assessment Worksheet and an Environmental Impact Statement. An Environmental Assessment Worksheet is a preliminary review to evaluate the potential for significant environmental effects from a project. An Environmental Impact Statement is a more comprehensive environmental review. The size and nature of certain projects trigger a mandatory Environmental Assessment Worksheet and/or an Environmental Impact Statement while in other cases the nature of review is at the discretion of the responsible governmental unit. For more information, contact the Minnesota Environmental Quality Board or the Minnesota Pollution Control Agency at the address and telephone numbers listed in the Resource Directory section of this Guide.

Once environmental review is complete, or in cases where no environmental review is required, the project proposer may proceed to submission of an application for permit. It is the goal of the state that environmental or resource management permits be issued or denied within 150 days of application.

The legislature created the Minnesota Business First Stop program to ensure the coordination and implementation of state environmental permits. A project proposer may apply to the program for assistance in obtaining necessary state permits and approvals. That assistance shall include: providing a list of all federal, state, and local permits required; providing a timeline for issuance of permits; coordinating the drafting any memoranda of understanding among permitting agencies; coordinating all federal, state, and local comment periods and hearings; providing such other assistance requested to facilitate final approval and issuance of permits. For more information contact Minnesota Business First Stop at the address and telephone number listed in the Resource Directory section of this Guide.

THE MINNESOTA POLLUTION CONTROL AGENCY

As noted above, several state agencies have responsibilities for environmental protection. The Minnesota Pollution Control Agency (MPCA) is the agency specifically charged with efforts to eliminate, reduce or control the levels of pollution in the environment. It is the principal agency for permitting associated with air quality and water quality, for the management of hazardous and solid waste, and for the enforcement of pollution control rules, statutes, and regulations.

Permit requirements, application procedures, schedules and other procedural requirements vary with the facility or activity involved. Most permits require a 30-day public notice. If members of the public object to issuance of the permit, and/or ask for a public hearing before a state administrative law judge, there may be further evaluation of the application and delay in issuance of the permit. The MPCA always has the option of denying a permit if the proposed facility or activity may result in some significant potential for pollution that cannot be corrected.

Non-compliance with MPCA rules or permit requirements could result in MPCA enforcement action involving administrative penalties, stipulated damages, civil or criminal legal action, and revocation of the MPCA permit. As a practical matter, MPCA permit holders should ensure that they have adequate and appropriate operating practices and qualified personnel in place to meet permit requirements and avoid enforcement action.

HAZARDOUS WASTE

Minnesota has an extensive program for the "cradle-to-grave" management of hazardous waste. Every business in Minnesota is responsible for determining if the waste it produces is hazardous. Many types of businesses, organizations, nonprofit groups and governments generate hazardous waste in the course of providing their products or services, including but not limited to the following: cleaning and maintenance; chemical manufacturing and formulating; construction; equipment repair; health care providers; furniture manufacturing and refinishing; wood preservation; laboratories; laundries and dry cleaning; metal manufacturing; electroplating; transportation; electronics; textile, plastics, and leather manufacturing; pesticide manufacture and application; printing and photography; painting, schools and colleges; vehicle repair and auto body shops; and utilities.

Wastes may be hazardous by either exhibiting a hazardous-waste characteristic or by being listed as a hazardous waste.

Characteristic wastes include:

Ignitable waste. A liquid is ignitable if it has a flash point less than 140 degrees Fahrenheit. Check the product's label or Safety Data Sheet (SDS) for this information. A non-liquid waste is ignitable if, at a standard temperature and pressure, it can cause a fire through friction, absorption of moisture, or spontaneous chemical changes, and burns so persistently that it creates a hazard.

Oxidizing waste. An oxidizer adds oxygen to a reaction or fire in the absence of air. Oxidizing wastes often have chemical names beginning with "per..." or ending with "...oxide" or "...ate" (for example: persulfate and chlorate). Many oxidizing wastes also contain nitrogen or halogens such as fluoride, chlorine, bromine, and iodine.

Corrosive waste. Any water-based waste having a pH of 2 or less (an acid) or 12.5 or more (a base) is corrosive. Check the product's label or SDS for this information. A corrosive waste may also be a liquid that is able to corrode greater than one-fourth of an inch of steel per year at 130 degrees Fahrenheit.

Reactive waste. Unstable or explosive wastes, wastes that react violently when brought in contact with water, and wastes that release toxic vapors (such as hydrogen cyanide or hydrogen sulfide) are considered reactive and hazardous (example of reactive waste: unspent lithium batteries greater than 9 volts).

Lethal waste. Lethal wastes exhibit oral and dermal values or inhalation values below a certain lethal threshold. If the health hazard data on the MSDS or other information leads you to suspect a waste may be lethal, contact your metropolitan county (Anoka, Carver, Dakota, Hennepin, Ramsey, Scott or Washington) or MPCA district office hazardous waste staff for assistance.

Toxic waste. Wastes are considered toxic if when using the Toxicity Characteristic Leaching Procedure (TCLP), they leach metals or organics at or above certain threshold values. A list of toxic chemicals and their maximum allowable concentrations is available from the MPCA at Waste Publications, https://www.pca.state.mn.us/waste/waste-publications.

Listed hazardous wastes are printed in the Code of Federal regulations, title 40, part 261, subpart D and include the following:

- Many spent chlorinated solvents used for degreasing (carbon tetrachloride, methylene chloride, trichloroethane, trichloroethylene, and others);
- Many other waste solvents, cleaners and strippers (acetone, butyl alcohol, carbon disulfide, cresol, ethyl acetate, methyl ethyl ketone (MEK), methyl isobutyl ketone (MIBK), methyl or wood alcohol, toluene, xylene, and others);
- Certain wastes derived from products containing ten percent or more of the above solvents;
- Residues from distillation units (or other similar systems) used to recover the above solvents;
- Most wastes from electroplating operations (cleaning and stripping tank solutions, plating bath solutions and sludges, and sludges from pre-treatment of wastewater);
- Certain wastes from the heat treatment of metals;
- Wastes produced during specific manufacturing processes (certain chemicals, explosives, inks, and pigments), petroleum refining and steel finishing (pickle liquor);
- Many unusable or off-specification commercial products: aniline, certain antibiotics, arsenic compounds, benzenes, chloroform, creosote, cyanide compounds, formaldehyde, hydrofluoric acid, hydrogen sulfide, lead compounds, mercury compounds, naphthalene, many nitrogen compounds, many pesticides, and pentachlorophenol (penta);
- Phenols and pyradine; and
- Polychlorinated biphenyls (PCBs) at concentrations greater than 50 parts per million.

The four lists of hazardous waste (F, K, P and U) are available from MPCA at Hazardous waste documents and forms, https://www.pca.state.mn.us/waste/hazardous-waste-documents-and-forms.

Hazardous waste must be managed in accordance with Minnesota Hazardous Waste Rules. The generator requirements are summarized as follows:

- Obtain a Hazardous Waste Identification (HWID) Number (formerly called an EPA identification number) (at no cost) by using the MPCA's online e-Services Notification of Regulated Waste Activity, https://rsp.pca.state.mn.us/TEMPO_RSP/Orchestrate.do?initiate=true. Review Notification of Regulated Waste Activity e-Service Instructions at https://www.pca.state.mn.us/sites/default/files/w-hw5-12.pdf. There is no fee to obtain an HWID. Obtaining an HWID will not make your site liable for any additional regulation it is not already required to comply with. If you cannot use the online tool, you may contact the MPCA to request a paper form be mailed to you. In an emergency situation, contact the MPCA to request an expedited HWID issuance.
- Next, a company may have to apply for a hazardous waste generator license from the MPCA (for businesses located in greater Minnesota) or from the appropriate metropolitan county (for businesses located in the seven-county metropolitan area).
- Hazardous waste containers must be properly marked and labeled. As soon as a waste is put in a container, it must be marked with the words "hazardous waste," an accumulation start date, and an easily understood description of the waste.
- Prior to off-site shipment, most hazardous wastes must be placed in specific Minnesota Department of Transportation (DOT) containers and labeled with a DOT hazard label and hazardous waste label. For more information, contact the MPCA or your metropolitan county office.
- Store hazardous waste properly and restrict its accumulation time and amounts to specified limits as noted below.

Indoor storage of hazardous waste is regulated by fire prevention and building codes, in addition to hazardous waste rules. Containers must be stored closed, with adequate aisle space between them for easy access and inspection. Floor drains must not allow waste to escape.

Hazardous waste stored outdoors must be in an area where access is restricted. The waste must be stored on a curbed, impermeable surface, and, if ignitable, must also be protected from direct sunlight.

Very Small Quantity Generators (VSQG)

If less than 220 pounds (or 100 kilograms) of hazardous waste is generated each month, the generator can accumulate up to 2,200 pounds (1,000 kg) indefinitely. Once this amount (about four drums of liquid) has accumulated, the generator has 180 days to have it transported off-site to a storage, treatment, or disposal facility within 200 miles. If the designated facility is farther away than 200 miles, the generator has an additional 90 days to ship the waste.

Minimal Quantity Generator (MQG)

A sub-classification of VSQGs is MiniQGs, which generate 100 pounds (about 10 gallons liquid) or less of hazardous waste per year. However, if any acute hazardous waste is generated, the MiniQG classification can not be applied. The generator can accumulate up to 550 pounds indefinitely. Once this amount (about one 55 gallon container) has accumulated, the generator has 75 days to have it transported off-site. The MPCA does not require MiniQGs to apply for a license, however metropolitan counties may. Some counties do not recognize the MiniQG classification.

Small Quantity Generators (SQG)

If between 220 and 2,200 pounds (or 100 to 1,000 kilograms) of hazardous waste is generated each month, the generator must ship the waste to a storage, treatment, or disposal facility within 180 days of the accumulation start date, provided the receiving facility is within 200 miles. If the facility is farther away than 200 miles, the generator has 270 days to ship the waste.

Large Quantity Generators (LQG)

If more than 2,200 pounds (1,000 kg) of hazardous waste is generated each month, the generator must ship all accumulated hazardous waste off-site to a storage, treatment, or disposal facility within 90 days of the accumulation start date. If the 90-day deadline is not met, the generator must obtain a hazardous-waste storage facility permit.

Licenses

Licenses must be renewed annually and fees are based on the amount of hazardous waste generated and the disposal method. Permit fees are also assessed if generators need an MPCA permit for their waste treatment, storage or disposal activities. For more information contact the MPCA or the metropolitan county hazardous-waste office.

It is the generator's responsibility to know the rules that apply to the management of a particular hazardous waste. Copies of the hazardous-waste rules can be obtained from the Minnesota Bookstore at the address and telephone number listed in the Resource Directory section of this Guide.

STORAGE TANKS

Most underground storage tanks (UST's) are regulated by the MPCA under Minnesota Rules, Chapter 7150. Examples of UST's not regulated are tanks with a capacity of 110 gallons or less and heating fuel tanks of 1100 gallons or less (used exclusively on the premises where stored). Most aboveground storage tanks (AST's) with a capacity greater than 1100 gallons are regulated by the MPCA under Minnesota Rules, Chapter 7151. A detailed list of tanks exempted from regulation can be found in the Minnesota Rules.

Tank owners of regulated tanks, either UST's or AST's, must register their tanks with the MPCA within 30 days of installation, discovery or a change in ownership, contents, or use. Tanking a tank out of service is an example of a change in use. The agency provides forms for this purpose.

The MPCA must receive 10 days advance notice prior to the installation or removal of any UST system. A UST system includes tanks, piping, dispensers and any pertinent equipment. Some UST system repairs and upgrades also require a 10 day advance notification prior to any work. The MPCA provides forms for this purpose. Any UST system activities (installs, removals or repairs/ upgrades) requiring a 10 day advance notice must be conducted only by an MPCA certified contractor. The agency provides a list of these certified contractors. Certified contractors, generally, will assist you in filling out and submitting tank registrations and advance notices.

At this time, the MPCA does not require AST owners to use MPCA certified contractors for the installation, removal, repair or upgrade of AST systems, or to submit advance notification of such activities. However, individuals and companies doing AST work must follow applicable standards outlined in Minn. Rules, Chapter 7151.

For information regarding the operation of tanks, either USTs or ASTs, call the MPCA or visit the MPCA website to view Minnesota Rules, notifications, guidance documents or publications at Storage Tanks, https://www.pca.state.mn.us/waste/storage-tanks.

Underground Storage Tanks (USTs)

According to Minnesota Rules, Chapter 7150, most new and existing regulated USTs must have spill, overfill and corrosion protection and leak detection. USTs that do not have these safeguards must immediately be upgraded or taken out of service, by a MPCA certified tank contractor. In the case of corrosion protection upgrades or repairs, industry standards must be followed or the work must be certified by a corrosion protection expert.

New UST systems installed after December 2007, must have liquid tight secondary containment on the tank and piping, as well as containment under submersible pumps and dispensers. Existing UST systems do not have to be upgraded with secondary containment provided that submersible pumps and piping are not replaced or disturbed.

All regulated USTs and associated piping must have leak detection. Tanks and piping installed after December 2007 must use interstitial monitoring as the primary form of leak detection. Other forms of tank leak detection include Automatic Tank Gauges (ATGs) and Statistical Inventory Reconciliation (SIR). Additionally, pressurized product lines are required to have automatic line leak detectors (LLDs) that continuously monitor for leaks.

Other items that are required on UST systems include drop tubes, also known as fill pipes, that extend to within 6 inches of the bottom of the tank, tank overfill protection devices, and properly operating and secured shear valves under dispensers. Shear valves are also known as breakaway valves and as fire valves.

Metal components of UST systems, tanks and piping, that are routinely contain fuel and are in contact with soil must be protected from corrosion. There are two primary types of corrosion protection (CP). Sacrificial Anode has special anodes attached to the tanks and piping that prevent corrosion. Impressed Current systems prevent corrosion by placing an electrical charge on the metal components. Impressed Current systems are recognizable because they will have a large electric box, called a rectifier, somewhere near the main power source or outside near the tanks. Tanks that have been lined with an approve lining suitable for the product stored do not require CP on the tank.

Monthly Checks

- Tank Leak detection – One “PASSING” test result per tank per month is required
- Site inspections – looking for leaks and equipment deficiencies.
    - Tank/pump sumps – Sump must be inspected monthly unless the sump is equipped with a sump sensor that it is function tested annually. Keep contained sumps free or liquids and debris.

o Spill buckets at fills – Keep spill buckets free or liquids and debris. Look for cracks or damage to spill buckets.

o Under dispensers – Look for leaks under dispensers and at any pipe joints or unions. Check boots where pipes and electrical conduits enter sumps for damage. Keep contained sumps free of liquid and debris.

60 Day Check

- Inspect rectifiers on impressed current corrosion protection systems to make sure they are functioning. Record "Volts" and "Ampere" readings. (Note: Most people do this monthly during the site inspection)

Annually Check

- Function testing of all interstitial monitors on the USTs and in containment systems.
- Line tightness testing of all pressurized and non-safe suction piping.
- Function testing of line leak detectors (LLDs)
- Function Testing of Impressed Current CP systems.

3 Year Check

- Sacrificial Anode CP systems by be function tested to assure the UST systems are properly protected from corrosion.

5 Year Check

- For those tanks with an internal lining, the tank must be emptied, cleaned and inspected every 5 years to assure that the lining has not failed. Some minor repairs are allowed, but if the lining has failed, the tank must be taken out of service.

The monthly leak tests, checks and inspections can be conducted by yourself, although many operators are hiring contractors to do the tank sump, dispenser sump and spill bucket checks. Testing of any sensors, leak detectors, line testing or corrosion protection must be conducted by MPCA certified tank contractors or certified corrosion protection testers. All repairs to UST systems must be conducted by MPCA certified tank contractors following industry standards.

Be sure to keep good records and documentation of all inspections, testing and repairs conducted on any UST system.

If a UST is out of service for more than 90 days, the tank must be put into temporary closure. This means that the tank is emptied (less than 1 inch of product left in tank) and a notification form must be filed with the MPCA. Corrosion protection must be maintained on the UST. On sites with impressed current CP system, the power must remain on! If CP is not maintained the UST cannot be placed back into service unless a CP expert inspects the CP system and certifies that the CP has been restored and that the UST has not degraded due to lack of CP. After one year of inactivity, the tank owner must request and receive written approval to extend the temporary closure period, otherwise the tanks must be permanently closed. This means closed in-place (filled with an inert substance) or removed from the ground. After five years of inactivity, all tanks must be permanently closed.

Anyone that owns, leases or operates must be certified by the MPCA. For more information on becoming a certified tank owner/operator, or for any information regarding the operation of UST system please call the MPCA or visit the MPCA's website.

Above Ground Storage Tanks (ASTs)

Most aboveground storage tanks (ASTs) are regulated according to Minnesota Rules, Chapter 7151. Some tanks excluded from these regulations include ASTs used for farming activities provide the material stored is not distributed for commercial purposes, heating oil ASTs less than 1,500 gallons, used on premises where stored, and other ASTs less than 1,500 gallons, provided that they are not located within 500 feet of surface water.

Regulated ASTs are required to have the following safeguards;

- Secondary containment capable of containing 110 percent of the capacity of the largest tank in the containment.
- Corrosion protection for any AST not in an impermeable containment area.
- Substance transfer areas designed to contain releases.
- AST overfill protection, which in most cases is a product lever gauge visible to the person transferring product.
- Emergency information, which include;
    - o Labeling tanks to identify product stored, tank capacity and a unique tank number.
    - o Labeling of product piping, valves and transfer connections.
    - o Site diagram with tanks, secondary containment, drains, waterways and any other information that might be pertinent in an emergency. This sign must be posted outside the containment area.
    - o Owner information, including a 24 hour contact phone number in the event of an emergency.
    - o A spill response plan that outlines the action to be taken to stop, confine and clean up releases, or to respond to other emergencies.
- Monthly leak detection and site inspections to check for leaks or other deficiencies in the tank systems. Log all inspections (dated, who conducted it and results).

Tank owners and operators can participate in an environmental audit program. This program allows tank owners to make improvements to their site before fines or violation notices are issued or enforcement action is taken. The environmental audit cannot be used at facilities where serious and repeat violations have occurred.

More information regarding AST's is available by contacting the MPCA or by visiting the MPCA's website.

WATER QUALITY REQUIREMENTS

Businesses may need a permit or certificate from the MPCA if they:

1. Discharge any wastewater into surface waters (including storm sewers);
2. Operate an agricultural feedlot;
3. Operate a disposal system which land-applies wastewater, or by product;
4. Operate a large on-site drain field; or
5. Operate any one of a class of categorical industries.
6. Discharge storm-water from an industrial or construction site.
7. Plan to dredge, fill, inundate or drain a wetland to the extent that a United States Army Corps of Engineers permit would be required. The MPCA must then certify that permit.

Businesses requiring an extension of a sanitary sewer system will be affected by the MPCA requirement that any municipality must have a Sewer Extension Permit before extending its sanitary sewer lines. For more details, see Water permits and forms at https://www.pca.state.mn.us/water/water-permits-and-forms. There is a sewer extension permit application fee.

Feedlot Permits

The Minnesota Pollution Control Agency regulates the collection, transportation, storage, processing and disposal of animal manure. The Feedlot Program implements rules governing these activities. MPCA is the principal agency for regulating feedlots in Minnesota. In addition, many counties administer the program for feedlots under 1,000 animal units. A National Pollution Discharge Elimination System (NPDES) permit is required for all feedlots that meet or exceed the threshold for large Concentrated Animal Feeding Operations (CAFO) under the Code of Federal Regulations, or with 1,000 animal units or more.

The feedlot rules apply to all aspects of livestock manure and process wastewater management including the location, design, construction, operation and management of feedlots and manure handling facilities and the land application of manure and process wastewater.

Information on feedlot permits, regulations and related issues is available at Feedlots, https://www.pca.state.mn.us/water/feedlots, and at the address and telephone number listed in the Resource Directory section of this Guide.

National Pollutant Discharge Elimination System (NPDES) Permits

NPDES permits are required for any discharge of wastewater into surface waters, including non-contact cooling water and air-conditioning or heat-pump water. NPDES permits are not required if the discharge is to a publicly-owned sanitary sewer system. However, local and State Disposal System (SDS) permits may be required – check with your local municipality and the PCA.

NPDES permits are required for feedlots that either exceed the large Concentrated Animal Feeding Operations (CAFO) threshold (i.e. 700 dairy cows, 2,500 swine, 1,000 beef, etc.) or have a capacity of 1,000 animal units or more.

Permit applications are available from the MPCA at the address and telephone number listed in the Resource Directory section of this Guide. Applications must be submitted 180 days before the planned activity commences. There is an application fee, and an annual permit fee. Except for the categorical industries listed below, there are no such fees if the discharge goes to a sanitary sewer. Applicants should be prepared to provide information on the location, quantity and quality of the proposed discharge. NPDES permits are issued for a period of up to five years.

Stormwater Discharge Permits

Certain types of industrial facilities must apply for a storm-water discharge permit from the MPCA. In addition, stormwater permits may be required for certain construction activities. Minnesota's stormwater permitting program is designed to help improve the quality of the state's waters by reducing or eliminating the chemicals, sediments, and other pollutants carried into surface waters with storm-water runoff.

All required industrial facilities must apply for a general storm-water discharge permit from the MPCA. In addition, an industry-specific permit may be required depending on the environmental risk of storm-water runoff from the facility. Construction projects disturbing one or more acres must apply for a general NPDES stormwater permit from the MPCA. Stormwater permits may require the preparation of a plan for managing stormwater runoff, potentially including construction of holding basins or diversion structures.

If you have potential discharges find out if your industrial facility requires a stormwater permit. The MPCA and EPA have websites with information on the storm water permit programs. See Stormwater at https://www.pca.state.mn.us/water/stormwater, and EPA NPDES Stormwater Program at https://www.epa.gov/npdes/npdes-stormwater-program for information.

State Disposal System (SDS) Permits

National Pollutant Discharge Elimination System (NPDES) or State Disposal System (SDS) permits (see https://www.pca.state.mn.us/water/npdes-and-sds-permits) are required for disposal of wastewater other than to surface waters, including large septic tank and drainfield systems and spray irrigation of wastewater. The need for an SDS permit may be satisfied by certain construction or operating practices; these must be evaluated on a case-by-case basis. Only domestic sewage should be discharged to drainfields.

Process wastewater, washwater and other wastewater should be discharged to a city sewer system unless a separate NPDES permit is obtained to discharge to a surface water. This may be a major consideration when siting a new industry.

Application forms are available from the MPCA at the address and telephone number listed in the Resource Directory section of this Guide. Applications should be submitted 180 days ahead of the anticipated beginning of construction. SDS permits are issued for a period of up to five years. There is an application fee and annual fees, which depend on the size of the facility.

Permits for Categorical Industries

Certain types of industries are required to be regulated under the Clean Water Act even if they discharge their wastewater to a municipal sanitary system. Examples of these industries are: pulp and paper mills; most food processing plants; textile mills; chemical manufacturing plants; electroplating companies; plastics and other synthetics manufacturers; fertilizer plants; metal manufacturing plants; steam power plants; companies producing leather, glass, asbestos, rubber, and timber products.

Requirements for categorical industries are set by the U.S. Environmental Protection Agency. In most cases, a prospective permit holder cannot contest these requirements. Categorical industries are subject to U.S. EPA pretreatment regulations.

A number of large sanitary districts and cities have been delegated authority to issue categorical-industry permits. Delegated cities include the Metropolitan Council, Environmental Services, the Western Lake Superior Sanitary District, Albert Lea, Austin, Faribault, Hutchinson, Mankato, New Ulm, Northfield, Owatonna, Red Wing, Rochester, St. Cloud, and Winona.

Categorical-industry permits are issued for other cities by the MPCA for a period of up to five years. Application forms may be obtained from the MPCA. There is an application fee and an annual fee for categorical industry permits. Permit applications should be submitted 180 days ahead of the commencement of the proposed activity. Questions about water quality permits should be directed to the MPCA. Addresses and telephone numbers are listed in the Resource Directory section of this Guide.

Underground Disposal Control

Disposal of industrial wastewater in underground sewage treatment systems is not allowed.

AIR POLLUTION CONTROL REQUIREMENTS

Minnesota businesses must comply with MPCA rules to protect air quality. Some rules apply even though the business will not have air emissions requiring permits.

Motor Vehicle Emission Controls

Owners of businesses that operate motor vehicle fleets should be aware that it is contrary to state rules and federal regulations to remove or disable the air pollution control equipment on motor vehicles, and it is illegal to operate motor vehicles unless the pollution control equipment is in place and is in operating condition.

Notification of Emergency Air Releases

The MPCA must be notified immediately of any releases to the air that might endanger human health, damage property or create a public nuisance. The business must take the steps necessary to prevent such releases.

Air Emissions Facility Permits

An air-emissions facility permit will be required if the business has the potential to emit more than the following airborne pollutants in a single year (in tons/year): lead 0.5; fine particulate matter < 10 microns, 25; single hazardous air pollutant 10; two or more hazardous air pollutants 25; sulfur dioxide 50; nitrous oxides, 100; carbon monoxide 100; particulate matter 100; volatile organic compounds 100. There is an application fee and an annual permit fee. Under certain circumstances, local health and welfare problems have to be addressed through an air emission facility permit even though the business would otherwise be exempt under Minnesota rules. This may be because of toxic air emissions or dust from the proposed business.

Although not all will require air-emissions permits, business operators who should be aware of MPCA air quality rules are those whose businesses include the use of boilers, incinerators, electrical generators and solvent-borne coatings. Other businesses whose operations fall under air quality rules are those that create emissions such as dust, including grain elevators, concrete batch plants, sand and gravel operations and building demolition operations.

Permits should be obtained before construction is to begin. Applicants will need to know the characteristics of the exhaust gas stream before and after, any emission control equipment, type and design of emission control equipment, the relation of emission points to nearby structures and other information. The permitting process may be delayed if information is inadequate, if the facility is proposed in an area where the air quality is already below standards, or if public demands result in scheduling public hearings.

Business operators in doubt about the need for a permit should call the MPCA. Businesses that have fewer than 100 employees and are independently owned and operated may call the MPCA's Small Business Environmental Assistance Program at the telephone number listed in the Resource Directory section of this Guide.

Green House Gas Emissions

Information about Greenhouse gas emissions calculations may be found at https://www.pca.state.mn.us/air/greenhouse-gas-emissions-calculations.

Asbestos Removal

Prior to any renovation or demolition work in a commercial space, a survey for the presence of asbestos is required. This survey must be conducted by an inspector that is certified by the Minnesota Department of Health. An asbestos abatement contractor licensed by the Minnesota Department of Health may be required for removal depending on the type and quantity of asbestos affected by the project. Notifications must be submitted to the MPCA 10 working days prior to all demolition and most asbestos abatement projects. Business owners should be aware that asbestos removal is also regulated by the Asbestos and Lead Compliance Unit of the Minnesota Department of Health and the Occupational Safety and Health Division of the Minnesota Department of Labor and Industry. The respective addresses and telephone numbers for information on these requirements is listed in the Resource Directory section of this Guide. For further information, contact the MPCA.

Lead Paint

Contractors performing renovation, repair and painting projects that disturb lead-based paint in homes, child care facilities, and schools built before 1978 must be EPA certified and must follow specific work practices to prevent lead contamination. Contractors can find the closest EPA training course at Locate an RRP Training Class or Provider in your area, https://cfpub.epa.gov/flpp/pub/index.cfm?do=main.trainingSearch, or contact the Minnesota Department of Health at the number listed in the Resource Directory of this Guide. MPCA information for the disposal of lead paint can be found at https://www.pca.state.mn.us/sites/default/files/w-hw4-23.pdf.

SOLID WASTE MANAGEMENT

County Solid Waste Management Plans

The Minnesota Legislature gave primary responsibility for solid waste management to the state's 87 counties. Contact the county solid waste officer for details about the county solid waste management plan, which outlines waste disposal options for businesses and for information about relevant ordinances. This plan, developed by the county and approved by the MPCA, may have specific business-related requirements. Cities may also have local solid waste ordinances, and those plans should be reviewed as well.

The Legislature also gave direction to counties about the most preferred methods of waste management, a hierarchy from the most to the least environmentally beneficial. Since waste generation has increased one to two percent each year for more than 30 years, it pays for government and businesses to reduce wastes as much as possible, thereby reducing garbage bills, specific business solid waste fees, and the percentage of taxes going toward waste disposal costs.

The waste management hierarchy is:

- **Reduce** – the best waste is, of course, none at all, so it is prudent to reduce waste by wise purchasing and good inventory management.
- **Reuse** – Reuse provides opportunities for materials to be reused in their current form, for their original intended use. An opportunity for business to business material reuse can be found on the Minnesota Materials Exchange website at https://www.mnexchange.org.
- **Recycling** – by separating materials with intrinsic value, disposal costs can often be reduced. While availability of collection may vary by location and hauler, materials which are frequently collected for recycling include: glass, aluminum, tin, plastics, white office paper, mixed paper, cardboard, paperboard, Tyvek envelopes, newsprint, printer cartridges, carpet, and more. Also, by establishing business policies that promote recycling, such as separating white office paper, and purchasing recycled paper and packaging, markets are created for those materials that otherwise might be discarded. The Minnesota Pollution Control Agency and some counties have new information helpful towards the deconstruction of a building; this can help towards LEED credits as well.
- **Organics Recycling (Composting)** – yard wastes, food waste, nonrecyclable paper, and certified compostable plastics can be composted into beneficial soil amendments. Check with your county environmental office or your waste contractor for current options to divert source separated organics from landfills.

- **Waste-to-Energy (Incineration)** – a permitted waste-to-energy incinerator consumes solid waste and produces energy, but has possible air-quality impacts, costs more than landfilling and produces its own waste – ash.
- **Landfilling** – landfilling is the least preferable waste management method because it creates the highest potential for environmental and human health impacts without reducing solid-waste volume. While shipping wastes to a permitted landfill does isolate waste, and provide protections to groundwater and soil, there are no secondary benefits, except in rare cases where methane is recovered for energy use.

Counties' integrated waste-management systems use a combination of these waste-management techniques. By considering these various options along with the county's plan, a business can demonstrate concern for community needs and enhance its reputation as a business that cares about the environment.

Solid Waste Taxes for Business Wastes

Businesses pay different solid waste taxes from households in the same area. The tax rate is 9.75 percent on residential garbage service and 17 percent on commercial garbage service. Several counties have additional solid waste taxes. Businesses that produce construction, demolition debris, medical waste, or nonhazardous industrial waste will pay a tax of 60 cents per cubic yard of collection capacity. The Department of Revenue collects the taxes, which are used to support cleanup of old landfills and grants for waste-reduction and recycling programs. Taxes are also collected when a business or individual applies and utilized a Demolition Permit By Rule Permit. The rate is also 60 cents per cubic yard of demolition debris material that is going to be buried. In addition, we have a General Solid Waste Concrete Burial Permit which if utilized there is also a tax that is assessed at 60 cents per cubic yard.

Solid-Waste Permits and Enforcement

The Minnesota Pollution Control Agency permits and regulates solid waste facilities, including landfills (mixed municipal solid waste, demolition debris, and industrial types), transfer stations, recycling facilities, incinerators, composting facilities and more. In addition to state permits, local units of government (such as counties, cities or townships) may also have ordinances or licenses required for certain activities or facility types. These requirements attempt to assure that any solid wastes disposed of in Minnesota facilities will not become a source of liability later. If your wastes go to other states, it makes sense to find out whether you could be held liable for cleanup of those wastes later.

The MPCA has permit application processes to build or operate a solid-waste facility as part of a business, or to dispose of nonhazardous industrial wastes by land application (lime residues applied to agricultural land, for example). Concerns about illegal dumping, burying, or burning of solid waste on a property can be directed to the county solid waste officer, the MPCA or the Minnesota Department of Natural Resources (DNR), all of which have certain authorities that may be of assistance.

Specific Materials Banned From the Waste Stream or Requiring Specific Disposal

Some wastes are banned or must be disposed of according to state laws or MPCA rules. Among those things that are banned from normal disposal are: waste tires; yard and tree waste; motor oil and filters, as well as other vehicle fluids; lead-acid batteries; nickel-cadmium batteries or other rechargeable or nonremovable battery packs; major appliances, including removal of items containing polychlorinated biphenyls (PCBs), such as old transformers; computer monitors; telephone books; all mercury including fluorescent and high-intensity discharge lamps and mercury switches (building, automotive); lead paint waste; chlorofluorocarbon (CFC) refrigerants; and petroleum-based sweeping compound. To find out more about disposal or recycling options for these materials, contact your solid-waste officer. Contact information listed in the Resource Directory Section of this Guide.

Electronic Waste

Electronic waste, or E-waste, is any waste that has a circuit board or cathode ray tube (CRT). This includes items that businesses use every day, such as computers, televisions, telephones and fax machines. Because of their potential lead content, when these items become a waste a business must then to be hazardous unless supporting test data is available proving otherwise. Businesses can either have the e-waste recycled or handled as a hazardous waste.

Minn. Stats. §§ 115A.1310 to 115A.1330 impacts retailers, collectors, recyclers, and manufacturers of video display devices sold to households (for example, televisions and computer monitors, including laptops). Among its requirements, this law requires retailers to only sell products of registered manufacturers. Registration and reporting requirements also apply to businesses that collect, recycle, or manufacture video display devices. For more information on these requirements, call the MPCA or review Managing Electronic Wastes, https://www.pca.state.mn.us/sites/default/files/w-hw4-15.pdf.

Heavy Metals in Products

Minnesota law prohibits the use of heavy metals (lead, cadmium, mercury and hexavalent chromium) in all packaging and certain products. If the business produces, purchases, uses or distributes a product or packaging using these metals, contact the MPCA to determine whether the business is in compliance with regulations. Certain legal products containing mercury, such as thermometers, thermostats, and automobile switches, are among the materials with restricted distribution or disposal. Contact the MPCA if you have questions about heavy metals in products or packaging.

Buying Environmentally Preferable Products

Businesses that buy environmentally preferable products help to reduce the environmental impacts of procurement. Through responsible purchasing of more sustainable products, a business makes a statement about its commitment to the environment. Resources for implementing Environmentally Preferable Purchasing (EPP) programs can be found at Sustainable government purchasing, https://www.pca.state.mn.us/waste/sustainable-government-purchasing.

Recycling Space Requirements for Building Owners

Minnesota state law requires new or significantly remodeled commercial buildings of 1,000 square feet or more to provide "suitable space" for the separation, collection, and temporary storage of recyclable materials (Minn. Stat. § 16B.61). In addition, the 2014 legislature added metro county commercial recycling requirements to Minn. Stat. § 115A.151, effective January 1, 2016. Any commercial building that contains "a business classified in sectors 42 to 81 under the North American Industrial Classification System," and which "contracts for four cubic yards or more per week of solid waste collection" must collect at least three recyclable materials (e.g. paper, glass, metal, plastics, organics). Contact the MPCA for additional information and assistance.

Labeling and Purchasing Recycled Products

The recycling logo is one way to signal that the business produces a product that contains recycled materials or is packaged in recycled materials to the consumer. While there are no specific regulations governing use of the recycling logo, the preferred practice is to use the logo, percent of recycled content, and percent of recycled content made up of post-consumer waste (i.e., materials recycled by consumers).

Food Wastes

The MPCA and other organizations can assist businesses seeking to reduce or recycle food wastes. If a business produces food wastes and other compostable materials, there are several cost-saving, environmentally sound methods of reuse or recycling including food to people, food to livestock, and composting. Contact the MPCA for more information.

COMPLIANCE ASSISTANCE

MPCA Publications

The MPCA offers free fact sheets to assist the regulated community. See MPCA publications, https://www.pca.state.mn.us/about-mpca/mpca-publications, within the program pages and also do a Search Box keyword search. In addition, the MPCA publishes an "Environmental Guide for Small Business in Minnesota", https://www.pca.state.mn.us/sites/default/files/p-sbap1-00.pdf, created to give small businesses a user-friendly guide to Minnesota's environmental regulations. The publication addresses air quality, hazardous waste, water quality, emergency response, storage tanks, cleanup and remediation, pollution prevention, OSHA, and agriculture issues. Copies are available by contacting the MPCA's Small Business Environmental Assistance Program, https://www.pca.state.mn.us/smallbizhelp, and at the address and telephone number listed in the Resource Directory section of this Guide. A free quarterly newsletter, the Small Business Enterprise, provides updated information on compliance, training and pollution prevention and is available on the website or contact the MPCA.

Minnesota Technical Assistance Program (MnTAP)

This business assistance program helps industrial-waste generators improve process and efficiency while minimizing impacts on human health and the environment. MnTAP, http://bced.umn.edu/MTAP-Consulting, is a nonregulatory program that offers free, confidential assistance to help business comply with environmental regulations by evaluating pollution prevention strategies before offering other waste management suggestions. Contact information is listed in the Management Assistance, General section of the Resource Directory section of this Guide.

Superfund and Voluntary Investigation and Cleanup (VIC)

The federal and state Superfund programs deal with hazardous-waste sites where contamination threatens public health and the environment. The Minnesota Environmental Response and Liability Act (MERLA), Minnesota's Superfund law, gives the MPCA the authority to require those responsible for the contamination to undertake investigation and cleanup.

The Voluntary Investigation and Cleanup program provides guidance and technical assistance to parties who want to voluntarily clean up a property contaminated with hazardous substances. For more information about the state or federal Superfund programs or the VIC program, contact the MPCA. Contact information listed in the Resource Directory of this Guide.

Small Business Environmental Assistance Program (SBEAP)

SBEAP, https://www.pca.state.mn.us/smallbizhelp, provides small business owners and managers with practical advice and tools to implement sustainable and environmentally preferable business practices that go beyond compliance.

SBEAP will help the business:

- Identify any regulatory requirements, including site visits upon request;
- Understand the impact the business has on the environment;
- Develop and implement a strategy to minimize this impact; and
- Explore the opportunities to become more sustainable.

Businesses requesting this confidential service should contact SBEAP at 651-282-6143 or 800-657-3938.

Small Business Ombudsman

The Small Business Ombudsman, https://www.pca.state.mn.us/regulations/small-business-ombudsman serves as a representative, or a liaison, for small businesses in their interactions with the MPCA. The Ombudsman offers the following services: confidential assistance to small businesses involving resolution of complaints or disputes involving regulations; help in identifying funding sources to purchase equipment that meets or exceeds environmental regulations; and coordination of small business input during rule development. The Ombudsman also solicits feedback from small businesses and trade associations for the development of assistance activities tailored to small business needs. Contact information is listed in the Resource Directory section of this Guide.

Small Business Environmental Assistance -Low-interest Environmental Loans

For existing businesses, the Small Business Environmental Assistance Low-interest environmental loans offers low interest loans of up to $50,000 for financing environmental projects such as equipment or process upgrades and costs associated with the investigation and clean-up of hazardous materials. More information is available by calling the Small Business Environmental Assistance Program at MPCA at the address and telephone number listed in the Financing, State Sources section of the Resource Directory of this Guide.

Potential Environmental Problems with Property

Real-estate transactions have consequences for property buyers, sellers, developers, lenders, insurance companies, landlords and tenants. These parties have an interest in limiting the potential liability involved with the transfer of land that has been affected by hazardous substances, pollutants or contaminants. As a result, the MPCA receives requests from many businesses for assistance with evaluating and dealing with known or suspected land contamination.

The state has a range of services to assist those involved in land transfers in dealing with potential problems. In most cases, potential land buyers or developers will request or be willing to perform an environmental assessment of the property before sale. If contamination is discovered, then decisions need to be made about who will pay for further investigation or cleanup and how health or environmental risks will be minimized or eliminated. The following programs can be helpful to those involved with land transactions, including environmental consulting firms hired to help businesses assess or clean up property.

Properties Where Environmental Assessments Have Not Been Completed

Over the past few years, it has become standard practice for those involved in land transfers to perform an environmental assessment of the property before sale. Buying or developing land, particularly in former or current industrial-use areas, can pose problems if all parties involved do not know whether the property has been affected by its former use. Past disposal practices did not take into account what we now know are the problems posed by hazardous substances. It pays to follow the general rule "buyer beware." A business owner might wish to initially do a review of the information provided in the Minnesota Pollution Control Agency's, *What's In My Neighborhood?* website at https://www.pca.state.mn.us/data/whats-my-neighborhood. This is a searchable inventory of cleanup sites and of environmental permits issued to businesses that are proximate to a property of interest.

The first step in performing a more formal assessment is usually hiring an environmental consulting firm with the expertise to conduct an environmental assessment of the property. While the MPCA does not recommend specific consulting firms, the agency does have lists of environmental consultants who can be hired to assess property. The agency's Voluntary Investigation and Cleanup (VIC) Program also has a series of fact sheets which outline the features of a good environmental assessment. These can be accessed at Cleanup guidance, https://www.pca.state.mn.us/waste/cleanup-guidance. If the business performing the assessment wants legal assurances that the property poses no or limited liability, the business can sign up for the VIC Programs. The staff will oversee the environmental investigation and cleanup, if needed, and work to provide the necessary assurances. Voluntary parties pay the cost of MPCA review, oversight and preparation of assurances of the assessment.

If petroleum chemicals are the contaminants most likely to be found on site, the MPCA Petroleum Brownfields Program can assist with review and oversight and provide closure letters. If agricultural chemicals are involved, the Minnesota Department of Agriculture provides similar review and oversight services.

The environmental assessment involves seeking existing information about the property, its past uses, and its enforcement or permitting history, if any. It also includes an inspection of the site, noting areas where further testing is needed.

The environmental investigation involves actual testing of soil, ground water, surface water, tank contents or other possible contamination areas. The results of the testing may indicate the need for another round of testing or may be sufficient to make a determination about whether the site is contaminated and, if so, where and with what substances at what levels. If the assessment indicates site contamination, the business and/or consultant performing the assessment has the duty to notify the MPCA (through the Minnesota Duty officer), no matter whether the land transfer takes place or not. The land owner may also have the responsibility of filing an affidavit with the county where the property is located prior to a transfer of ownership. However, the business discovering environmental problems is not necessarily the party who is required to perform further work to clean up the site.

"Brownfields" Sites

"Brownfield" is a term for industrial or commercial properties that are candidates for redevelopment but sit idle due to actual or suspected contamination. Cities, development agencies, counties and other groups have identified land that would be attractive to developers if information about environmental status of these sites were available. For sites where no voluntary party has come forward, the state and federal governments have developed several initiatives that will allow interested parties to obtain environmental information about sites. The MN Department of Employment and Economic Development (DEED), the U.S. Environmental Protection Agency (EPA), and the MPCA (see https://www.pca.state.mn.us/waste/brownfields) all are involved in various efforts to assess and, if needed, clean up brownfield sites. Contact the MPCA or DEED to find out more information about brownfields initiatives.

Superfund: Sites Posing Imminent Risks, Abandoned Sites, and Enforcement Approaches

There are certain sites that are not good candidates for voluntary approaches, and the state and federal Superfund programs are designed to handle these problem sites. Among the types of sites most appropriate for Superfund:

- Sites that pose an imminent risk to public health or the environment, where the state must act quickly to assure that the public or environment is protected;
- Sites that pose risks, and have no responsible parties that can fund investigation and cleanup activities; and
- Sites where responsible parties are known, but are unable or unwilling to undertake necessary investigation and cleanup actions.

Under Superfund law, responsible parties are defined, in part, as site owners, facility operators who handled wastes on the site, transporters who brought wastes to the site, and generators whose wastes end up on the site. If a risk to public health or the environment is identified, a site can be assessed by the MPCA and placed on the state Superfund list. Listed sites are eligible for use of the funds appropriated for site investigations and cleanups under the state Superfund law. The MPCA can also utilize these funds to perform removal work or emergency actions if an imminent risk to public health or the environment does exist.

If responsible parties are known but refuse to undertake cleanup, both state and federal laws can be used to enforce action. Usually, this non-cooperative approach is more expensive, time-consuming and difficult for both the regulatory agency and the responsible party.

Other Land Contamination Programs

The state has other special programs or laws dealing with contaminated land, a few of which are listed below:

- Contamination Tax: The Minnesota Legislature has established a contamination tax on properties affected by hazardous substances to allow for a deduction in the value of the property based on contamination present. The tax ratio varies depending on whether the tax payer is a responsible party and has a MPCA approved Response Action Plan. This law is designed to provide a tax incentive to landowners who clean up contaminated property. Contact the Minnesota Department of Revenue for more information.

- Contamination Cleanup Grants: The Legislature provides money for Contamination Cleanup Grants for cities, housing and redevelopment authorities, economic development authorities and port authorities. To qualify for a grant, the applicant must provide the Commissioner of DEED with a site description, approved response action plan, detailed estimate of cleanup costs, appraisal of the market value of the property, description of planned land use, and explanation of how the applicant plans to pay for its share of the project. The applicant must be willing to pay at least 25 percent of the project cost. Review Contamination Cleanup and Investigation Grants at https://mn.gov/deed/government/financial-assistance/cleanup/contamination.jsp.

- Dry cleaner Legislation: A special fund has been established to deal with land contamination from former dry-cleaning operations. Funds for investigation and cleanup activities come from annual registration fees and fees on some dry cleaning chemicals. Contact the MPCA for more information.

- Guidance Documents and Technical Assistance: The MPCA provides guidance documents for investigation and cleanup of contaminated land, fact sheets on state and federal Superfund programs, site-specific fact sheets on some sites, and other brochures and newsletters on contaminated property issues. Contact the MPCA for more information.

Environmental Audit Program

Environmental auditing is a process of examining a facility to determine how well its operations are complying with all applicable environmental regulations and to think about pollution prevention opportunities. This program encourages businesses and other organizations to conduct their own environmental audits and correct any problems they may discover in addition to going beyond compliance. It allows businesses to discover and correct minor problems before they become major liabilities, and, in most cases, to avoid enforcement penalties that might otherwise be assessed.

Any business or governmental unit that is regulated by an environmental law or rule in Minnesota can conduct an environmental audit, using either on-site personnel or an outside firm if desired. The MPCA provides some assistance and checklists to assist organizations in conducting their audits. After the audit, the organization must submit a report that includes a summary of the results, a schedule for any corrective actions that must be taken (subject to MPCA approval if greater than 90 days), and either a statement that pollution-prevention opportunities have been examined (for smaller facilities) or a certification that pollution-prevention requirements have been met (for larger facilities).

Audit forms need not be submitted to the MPCA (although they may be requested by the agency if there is probable cause to believe that a crime occurred), but participants should be aware that their summary reports are considered public documents and will be placed in the agency's files, subject to public review under Minnesota's Data Practices Act.

When a participant successfully meets the requirements of the program, that facility can display a "Minnesota Green Star" award for a period of two years after completing the audit and any required corrective or cleanup work.

INTELLECTUAL PROPERTY PROTECTION*

Intellectual property protection is an area regularly overlooked; however, this is a pivotal area of law, especially for entrepreneurs and small and medium sized businesses.

Most people, when they think about intellectual property, assume it pertains just to tech-based innovations. However, at some level, every company has intellectual property rights to protect. In today's world, fewer companies have tangible assets such as equipment, manufacturing facilities or real estate. Instead, the vast majority of companies today have most of their assets based on intellectual property rights. This includes the yoga studio that needs to protect its name, all the way to the biotech company that has inventions to protect. No matter what size or type company you have, there are aspects of intellectual property law that touch your company and those rights need to be managed and protected.

The intellectual property of a business is a valuable asset. Securing and protecting it is essential to a business' future success, so it is vital for a business to understand its rights and how intellectual property law can help.

A separate publication, *A Guide to Intellectual Property Protection,* available free from the Small Business Assistance Office, sets out different types of legal protection available for intellectual property (including patents, trademarks and copyrights) and explains the range of things a business can do to protect and manage these rights.

*A comprehensive discussion of intellectual property protection issues is provided in the publication, ***A Guide to Intellectual Property Protection***. The publication is available without charge from the Small Business Assistance Office, 1st National Bank Building, 332 Minnesota Street, Suite E200, St. Paul, MN 55101. Telephone: 651-556-8425 or 800-310-8323
Email: deed.mnsbao@state.mn.us Website: https://mn.gov/deed/business/help/sbao/

BUSINESS PLAN

One of the first steps in a new venture is the development of a business plan. The business plan describes the business: its product or service, market, people and financing needs. A well-prepared business plan serves several purposes:

- For the new business, it helps the owner determine the feasibility and desirability of pursuing the steps necessary to start a business.
- For the company seeking financing, it is an important sales tool for raising capital from outside investors.
- For an existing company, the business plan forms the basis of a more detailed operational plan and thus becomes an important management tool for monitoring the growth of the firm and charting future directions.

This outline represents a generalized approach. Business plans always should be tailored to the specific circumstances of the business and should emphasize the strengths of the proposed venture and address the potential problems and challenges to be faced. Although it is possible to prepare a business plan by merely "filling in the blanks" from a template (such as those available on the Internet), the likelihood of achieving desired results from doing so is small (e.g., how often do you respond to form letters?). Business plans prepared in connection with a loan application or for the purpose of obtaining venture capital financing will emphasize financial data and characteristics of the management team. The business plan should comply with the format requirements of the lender or venture capitalist.

Several organizations offer assistance in preparing business plans. These include Minnesota Small Business Development Centers, SCORE organizations, Small Business Management programs and others described in the section of the Guide, titled Sources of Information and Assistance. Addresses and telephone numbers of these organizations are provided in the Resource Directory section of the Guide.

SAMPLE BUSINESS PLAN FORMAT

Summary

The summary should concisely describe the key elements of the business plan. For the firm seeking capital, the summary should convince the lender or venture capitalist that it is worthwhile to review the plan in detail. The summary should briefly cover at least the following items:

- Name of the business.
- Business location and plan description.
- Discussion of the product, market, and competition.

- Expertise of the management team.
- Summary of financial projections.
- Amount of financing requested (if applicable).
- Form of and purpose for the financing (if applicable).
- Purpose for undertaking the project (if financing is sought).
- Business goals.

The Company

This section provides background information on the company. It commonly includes a general description of the business, including the product or service and may describe the historical development of the business, legal structure, significant changes in ownership, organizational structure, products or lines, acquisitions, subsidiaries and degree of ownership, and the principals and the roles they played in the formation of the company.

The Product or Service

This is a detailed description of product or service lines, including the relative importance of each product or service to the company. Include sales projections if possible. If available, include product evaluations, comparison to competitors' products or product lines, competitive advantages over other producers, and the elasticity or inelasticity of demand for this product (i.e., does demand respond to factors other than price?). Possible sources of information for this section include competitors' websites, business directories and census data.

The Project

If financing is sought for a specific project, describe the project, the purpose for which it is undertaken, its cost, and the amount, form and use of the financing.

Management

Discuss the firm's management. Provide an organizational chart. Discuss key management and supervisory personnel having special value to the organization. Describe their responsibilities and provide resumes describing their skills and experience as they relate to activities of the business. State their present salaries, including other compensation such as stock options and bonuses. Discuss planned staff additions. Describe other employees, including the number of employees at year end, total payroll expenses for each of the previous five years (break down by wages, benefits, etc.), method of compensation, and the departmental or divisional breakdown of the workforce.

Ownership

Provide names, addresses, and business affiliations of principal holders of the firm's common stock and other types of equity securities. Discuss the degree to which principal holders are involved in management. Describe principal non-management owners. Provide the names of the board of directors, areas of expertise, and the role of the board. Specify the amount of stock currently authorized and issued.

Marketing Strategy/Market Analysis

Describe the industry and the industry outlook. Identify the principal markets (commercial/industrial, consumer, government, international). Include industry size currently as well as its anticipated size in the next ten years. Explain the sources of your projections. Describe major characteristics of the industry and the effects of major social, economic, technological or regulatory trends on the industry.

Describe major customers, including names, locations, products or services sold to each, percentage of annual sales volume for each customer over previous five years, duration and condition of contracts in place.

Describe the market and its major segments. Describe principal market participants and their performance. Identify the firm's target market. For each customer, include the requirements of each and the current ways of filling these requirements. Also include information on the buying habits of the customers and the impact on the customer of using the product or service.

Describe the companies with which the business competes and how the business compares with these competitive companies. This is a more detailed narrative than that contained in the description of the product or service, above.

Describe prospective customers and their reaction to the firm and any of the firm's products or services they have seen or tested.

Describe the firm's marketing strategy, including overall strategy; pricing policy; method of selling, distributing and servicing the product; geographic penetration, field/product support, advertising, public relations and promotion; and priorities among these activities.

Describe how the firm will identify prospective customers and how and in what order the firm will contact the relevant decision-makers. Also, describe the sales effort the firm will have (e.g., sales channels and terms, number of salespersons, number of sales contacts, anticipated time, initial order size) and estimated sales and market share.

Sources of information include census data (on both industries and on consumer demographics), business directories, specific industry reports (either from government or private sources), and competitors' websites.

Technology

Describe the technical status of your product (i.e., idea stage, development stage, prototype stage, etc.) and the relevant activities, milestones, and other steps necessary to bring the product into production. Discuss the firm's patent or copyright position. Include how much is patented and how much can be patented (i.e., how comprehensive and effective the patents or copyrights will be). Include a list of patents, copyrights, licenses or statements of proprietary interest in the product or product line.

Describe new technologies that may become practical in the next five years which may affect the product. Also describe new products the firm plans to develop to meet changing market needs. Describe regulatory or approval requirements and status, and discuss any other technical and legal considerations that may be relevant to the technological development of the product. Include a discussion of research and development efforts and future plans for research and development.

Production/Operating Plan

Explain how the firm will perform production or deliver its service. Describe capacity and status in terms of physical facilities: are they owned or leased; size and location; sales volume and unit capacity; expansion capabilities; capital equipment. Include a facilities plan and description of planned capital improvements and a timetable for those improvements.

Describe suppliers including name and location of principal suppliers; length of lead time required; usual terms of purchase; amounts, duration and conditions of contracts; and subcontractors. Also describe the current and planned labor supply, including number of employees; unionization; stability (seasonal or cyclical); and fringe benefits (insurance, profit sharing, pension, etc.).

Provide a profile of key patents and describe technologies and skills required to develop and manufacture the products. Provide a cost breakdown for material, labor, and manufacturing overhead for each product, plus cost vs. volume curves for each product. Provide block and workflow diagrams of the manufacturing process where appropriate, and provide a schedule of work for the next one to two years. Describe the production or operating advantages of the firm. Discuss whether they are expected to continue.

Financial/Administrative

Provide name and address of key advisors, including auditor, legal counsel, and banker.

Describe financial controls including the cost system and budgets used. Describe cash requirements, now and over the next five years, and how these funds will be used. Specify financial needs to be raised from debt and from equity. Discuss plans to "go public." Relate this to future value and liquidity of investments.

Provide financial statements and projections for next five years. These should include profit and loss or income statements by month at least until break-even and then by quarter; balance sheets as of the end of each year; cash budgets and cash flow projections; capital budgets for equipment and other capital acquisitions; include key assumptions you have made in your *pro formas* and how these assumptions reflect industry performance.

If financing is sought, most lenders and venture capitalists will require a funding request indicating the desired financing, capitalization, use of funds, and future financing; a financial statement for the past three years; current financial statements; monthly cash flow financial projections including the proposed financing for two years, and projected balance sheets, income statement, and statement of changes in financial position for two years including the proposed financing.

ACCOUNTING FOR THE NEW BUSINESS

BASIC ACCOUNTING PRINCIPLES

Accounting is the process of collecting, organizing, maintaining, reporting and interpreting financial data about a business.

That financial information is useful both to the business owners and managers in operating a business in a profitable and efficient way, and to outsiders like investors or creditors who require a picture of the business' financial position and performance. In both cases the information is intended to make decision making easier: decisions inside the business about the use of resources and structuring transactions for the lowest tax liability, and decisions by outsiders about subjects like the granting or continuing of credit to the business.

The information collection, organization and maintenance parts of accounting are called bookkeeping. The reporting and interpreting parts are called statement preparation. The complexity and sophistication of bookkeeping and statement preparation depend on the size and nature of a business and the size and nature of its markets and are beyond the scope of this publication. It is valuable here, however, to understand the way in which any accounting system, small or large, handles financial information.

Accounting is the formal process performed according to a set of generally accepted accounting principles. In many cases the business can choose the principles to be used as long as they are consistently applied and any changes in the principles used are disclosed to users of the business' financial statements. Certain industries have specialized accounting principles specific to businesses in those industries.

Because both internal and external users will rely on accounting information, accounting systems contain definitional concepts and principles which both define and limit the nature and use of the information they contain.

The business entity concept provides that for accounting purposes every business is separate and distinct from both its owners and from other businesses. Defining the business entity that way prevents distortion of the financial position of the business which might occur if information on the business owners or other related businesses were included.

The going concern concept assumes that a business on which accounting information is being prepared will continue in existence and is not about to be liquidated. As a result the financial information provided offers only a snapshot of the business based on historical data and ongoing reporting rather than reflecting current market values.

The stable dollar concept requires reporting of accounting information in dollar units which remain stable in value with no adjustment for inflation or the purchasing power of money.

The accounting period concept requires that financial reports showing changes in financial position be produced at fixed annual reporting periods.

The cost principle requires that all costs be recorded at the actual acquisition cost regardless of what the asset acquired might be perceived as being "worth." The cost recorded is the actual exchange price.

The objectivity principle requires that costs be objectively established and verifiable: guesses or estimates are not acceptable.

The revenue recognition principle requires that revenue be entered in the accounting records only at the time it is earned and not before.

The matching principle requires that expenses be matched with the revenue they produced.

The full disclosure principle requires that no significant information be omitted or concealed and that statements be prepared in accordance with generally accepted accounting principles.

The materiality principle provides for an exception from full disclosure for transactions with insignificant economic effect.

The consistency principle requires that the same accounting principles be followed from period to period to allow for comparison of financial performance.

The conservative principle requires that in presenting financial information, accounting procedures should be used which present the least favorable view of the firm's owners' equity.

These concepts and principles taken together produce a periodic picture of the financial position of the business expressed in constant dollars. While all the information which goes into the system is "real," the accounting principles used can change the way transactions are structured and reported and the effects – like tax consequences – of the transaction.

In addition, an accounting system imposes a set of internal controls on the business to ensure appropriate and consistent control of financial operations.

As noted above, the substance of any accounting system will vary with the size, complexity and sophistication of the business. The choice of an accounting system, the use of bookkeeping services or broader accounting services, and the use of mechanical or computerized systems or recordkeeping aids are best discussed with an accounting professional.

INCOME FORECASTING TECHNIQUES

One of the most important steps in the construction of a written plan for your proposed business is the development of meaningful financial projections. No business enterprise should be undertaken without a clear plan of profit potential and an understanding of the sales volume needed to achieve this profit. Experienced entrepreneurs recognize such projections as necessary for the success of any new business, and potential investment and lending sources will insist upon reviewing your financial projections before any serious discussion can take place. To be of maximum value in the planning process, your projections should accurately reflect the potential of your business and must not be influenced by wishful thinking.

Maintaining a high level of objectivity while researching the potential for a new business can be difficult. The difficulty results from the fact that many prospective business owners select the type of business to enter for a variety of quite personal reasons. They may choose a type of operation because the very nature of the work involved appeals to them. Others may work for someone else in a similar business and now would like to be their own boss. Some may have spent time acquiring the necessary technical skills or may have simply observed that a particular enterprise appears enjoyable or profitable. When combining any of these personal reasons for entering business with the complex task of analyzing the market, it is not uncommon for a prospective business owner to start up an operation with unrealistic expectations of the potential returns.

It is suggested that in your planning efforts you use the desired income approach to help determine the feasibility of your idea. This approach recognizes that, for the investment of time and effort and the assumption of risk, you are entitled to a fair monetary return. If this business were not started, your money could be invested to earn a return elsewhere and your time and effort could be devoted to working for someone else. The desired income approach allows you to select the minimum desired return and build on this to determine the level of sales required to achieve this return. If this sales level cannot be reasonably supported by market analysis, you would probably be better off working for someone else or investigating a different business opportunity.

To begin, you must first ascertain the minimum acceptable level of profit. To do this, it is necessary to explore the uses of profit. Profit can be used to support personal living needs, to pay back borrowed funds, or to reinvest in the company. Since we are attempting to determine the minimum level of profit, we will not be concerned with reinvestment which involves a use of profit over this minimum.

To determine personal living requirements, you must consider the minimum amount you will need to withdraw from the proposed business. If there is substantial personal income available from other sources, the amount required from the proposed business may be reduced. If there is no other source for personal income, then the proposed business should be recognized as the sole source for providing a living. Obviously, this desired draw will vary by individual needs and must be arrived at by thoughtful personal planning.

If it is necessary to borrow funds to begin the proposed enterprise, it must be realized that these borrowed dollars will have to be repaid from earnings of the business. This is of special importance to prospective lenders. It is the reason why a presentation of a projected income statement is required when seeking outside financing for a business. To determine the level of profit necessary to repay a loan, you need to determine the dollar amount to be borrowed, the term of the loan and the percentage of interest likely to be charged.

The loan amount usually is the total amount of money needed to begin the business less the amount supplied by you in the form of equity. The term of the loan is based on the use of the proceeds and the percent of interest reflects the general risk involved. It is advisable to speak with lenders and those offering business advice to help determine realistic terms and current interest rates for your situation.

For our example, we will use $30,000 as the amount of the loan requested and a term of five years at 15 percent annual interest rate.

The calculation of the annual payment is as follows:

$30,000 over five years at 15 percent
$30,000 / .023790* = $713.70/month
$713.70 x 12 months = $8,564.40/year
*(.023790 comes from loan amortization tables which are available at local bookstores or in most finance textbooks.)

This $8,564.40 represents the total interest and principal repaid on the loan the first year of operation. If we round this figure to $8,600 and estimate personal living expenses to be withdrawn from this business at $15,000, we have a total of $23,600 which must be generated to sustain our personal needs and keep current with the lender.

The next step is to determine the level of sales necessary to earn the $23,600. From industry statistics, we can ascertain average performance data for various types of business operations. One of the most commonly used sources for this information is ***Annual Statement Studies***, published by The Risk Management Association, https://www.rmahq.org/Default.aspx. Other sources can be found in the library and include Dun and Bradstreet, Industry Norms and Key Business Ratios™, the Almanac of Business and Industrial Financial Ratios (CCH) and local and national trade associations. Be sure to determine that the industry standard being applied includes the owner's draw as a part of profit. If it does not, this withdrawal amount will have been deducted as a salary expense in the operating statement and will have to be added to the stated profit to get an accurate indication of the total percent of sales available as profit to the business owner. For our example we will assume the industry sources show that, for the type of business under consideration, the average profit, including the owner's draw or salary, is 11 percent of sales.

To determine required annual sales volume:

$23,600 is 11 percent of X
X = minimum required annual sales
.11 X = $23,600
X = $214,500

We have now determined that, if our proposed business is assumed to be average, we will need to sell $214,500 of our products or services to cover expenses, keep our loan current through the first year and withdraw the desired $15,000. This in no way implies that we will sell $214,500, of products or services, but this dollar amount serves as a goal that must be met. We now have available a minimum target sales figure to test and verify through the techniques of market analysis. For some, it will be readily apparent that the required sales target is not realistic. For others, careful market research will be necessary before any conclusion can be drawn.

The desired income approach of determining required sales can help us answer the question of whether we would start a particular business, begin the business as we have it conceptualized or whether the idea we have is likely not to grant the desired return. It gives a benchmark that must be met. It provides a realistic financial goal that must be achieved. If our research shows that this goal is attainable and that estimated sales are likely to meet or surpass this level, we can enter business with that much more confidence. If our market investigation does not thoroughly support the minimum required sales level, we can rethink our position. We can consider changes to our business plan which will make the concept more realistic or we can search for another, potentially more profitable business opportunity. The desired income approach allows us to start up a business operation with knowledge of what must be achieved and the level of return we can expect for our efforts.

To verify whether your target minimum sales are attainable, it is necessary to thoroughly investigate your potential market. Market research is an imprecise science, but basic research can be performed by most prospective entrepreneurs. Stated simply, market research is the orderly and objective gathering of facts about your market. It involves finding out how things are, not how you think they are or would like them to be. Much raw data already exists, but before this data will be of use to you, it is necessary to develop some basic definitions regarding your proposed business.

The first of these definitions involves describing in detail the business you wish to establish and the industry it will operate within. Concerns here relate to the image you wish to project and the products and services to be offered. Your business image is the single most important factor in achieving target sales. Be careful to design an image that addresses a perceived market need, and do not select an image that appeals solely to you. Industry influences are also important and involve an assessment of firms currently operating within your industry and major historical trends. In addition, you should examine and define significant outside influences on your business such as government regulation, energy concerns, inflation and other economic factors. Many of these forces will be beyond your control, but they must be recognized and planned for.

A full and complete analysis of your production capabilities should be developed. Your ability to satisfy market demand will be directly limited by your ability to produce, finance, sell and service. It is of little value to determine from the market that potential revenues can meet or exceed your target minimum sales volume if your production cannot match this needed output. Similarly, sales revenues are limited by the availability of working capital and by your ability to negotiate sufficient sales transactions. Indeed, you may determine that a substantial market potential exists, but you will need to consider the restricting impact of these internal factors.

Next, you will need to define the actual market segment you wish to enter. Attempt to describe in detail the target customer most likely to be interested in your product or service. There is a definable portion of the population to whom the output of your business will be of special interest. This is your target customer and the focus of your market analysis. Target customers can be defined in terms of some demographic descriptor. Examples could include income level, home ownership, sex, marital status, age, occupation, education or any of a host of market-related characteristics. You will need to spend considerable time researching and defining a target customer profile, but this process is critical to further market analysis.

Once you have arrived at a definite category of customer, you can begin investigating where your potential customers are and in what numbers. Basic demographic data outlining population size, density, distribution and other vital statistics is readily available from a variety of sources. A list of such sources would include the following: U.S. Bureau of Census, Chambers of Commerce, colleges and universities, and your local library, which contains sources for locating trade journals, directories and local and national trade associations. You will also need to develop a trade area based on geographic considerations. Defining your trade area involves making a determination of how far you can reasonably and profitably take your product or service out into the marketplace or how far you can expect to draw customers to your place of business. This trade area is related to the type of business you are investigating and can range from a segment of a community to international dimensions. Within this trade area you will need to examine the population data you have researched to determine how many target customers are available. Of course, not all these potential customers will do business with you. The market deals with people and their constantly changing likes and dislikes which are affected by hundreds of influences.

Competition within and adjacent to your trade area should be thoroughly examined. Attempt to describe who your competitors are and compare strengths and weaknesses with the business you want to operate. Become familiar with your competitors' pricing policies and overall method of operation. You will be competing head-on for the limited number of opportunities within your selected trade area and you must have as much knowledge of your competition as possible. Do not neglect to analyze future competition. Market dynamics are not static and freely allow others to enter your market and to change and improve on products or services you will be offering.

Keep in mind throughout all of your research efforts that verification of your target minimum sales is your goal. Ask basic questions about your business. How much does the average customer spend in a typical sales transaction? How many sales transactions are required to meet your target minimum sales? Does your knowledge of the market indicate that there is a sufficient customer base to generate the needed sales revenue? As mentioned previously, market research is an inexact process, but, with a desired income as your target and an orderly approach to gathering data, you can become aware of the magnitude of market opportunities. This knowledge will then assist you in making rational and intelligent decisions regarding your proposed business.

BUSINESS GRANTS

SMALL BUSINESS GRANTS IN MINNESOTA

The number of companies and outright scams—all selling information about "government grants" or guides to government grants—is growing through Internet spam and telemarketing. All of these offers are built on the false idea that individuals are eligible to receive thousands of "unclaimed" dollars from the government—money that can be used for almost anything, including personal expenses or starting a business.

Television ads and Internet sites use the word "grant" to describe any kind of payment from the government. Most of the "hidden government money" comes from public assistance for low-income families, the elderly or the disabled. These are largely entitlement programs—not competitive grants. For individual benefit programs, the federal government provides comprehensive information at Benefits.gov, https://www.benefits.gov; Grants.gov, https://www.grants.gov; and GovLoans.gov, https://www.govloans.gov.

In reality, both federal and state governments make their investments primarily through direct loans—not grants—to individual businesses or through grants to third-party organizations that use the funds for loan programs for end-user businesses. There are, however, a few grant programs of the Minnesota Department of Employment and Economic Development that make grants directly to businesses: the Minnesota Job Creation Fund; Launch Minnesota Program; Export Financing Programs; the State Trade and Export Promotion Program; as well as the Dairy Business Planning Grants and Specialty Crop Grants of the Minnesota Department of Agriculture; and the Environmental Assistance Grants of the Minnesota Pollution Control Agency. Information on these appears in this publication in the section on "Financing / Tax Credits, State Sources".

BUSINESS LOANS

Debt Financing

There are many sources of debt financing: banks, savings and loans, commercial finance companies and government agencies are most common. State and local government have developed many programs in recent years to encourage the growth of small businesses. Family members, friends and associates are all potential sources, especially when the capital requirements are small.

Typically, banks have been the major source of small business funding. Their principal role has been as a short-term lender offering demand loans, lines of credit, and single-purpose loans for machinery and equipment. Banks generally have been reluctant to offer long-term loans to small firms. The SBA guaranteed lending program encourages banks and non-bank lenders to make long-term loans to small firms by reducing their risk and leveraging the funds they have available.

In addition to the traditional term loans and revolving lines of credit most often provided by commercial banks, other types of debt financing arrangements, such as asset-based financing from business financing companies, lease and equipment financing and sale and leaseback arrangements, have gained popularity.

Historically, it is extremely difficult to start a business with 100 percent debt. Private lenders and government loan programs often require 20 to 50 percent equity participation by the owner. The exact percentage depends on the project, the financial resources of the owners, the type of industry the use of funds and the financial institution's general loan policy. In addition to equity considerations, lenders commonly require the borrower's personal guarantees in case of default. This ensures that the borrower has a sufficient personal interest at stake to give paramount attention to the business and satisfies requirements of regulations.

Most traditional lenders prefer manufacturing or industrial operations where funds will be used to purchase fixed assets, i.e. land, building, or production equipment. These items offer the type of collateral often required to secure the debt. Guarantee programs offered by SBA and other government entities can mitigate the reliance on collateral.

Loan Packaging

Before inquiring about debt financing, an entrepreneur should assess such things as:

Do you actually need more capital or can you manage existing cash flow more efficiently?

How do you define your need? Do you need money to expand or as a cushion against risk?

How urgent is your need? Do you want money to expand or as a cushion against risk?

How great are your risks? All businesses carry risks, and the degree of risk will affect cost and available financing alternatives.

In what stage of development is the business? Needs are most critical during transitional stages.

For what purpose will the capital be used? Any lender will require that capital be requested for very specific needs that may be part of determining loan repayment terms.

What is the state of your industry? Depressed, stable, or growth conditions require different approaches to money needs and sources. Businesses that prosper while others are in decline will often receive better funding terms.

Is the business seasonal or cyclical? Seasonal needs for financing generally are short term. Loans advanced for cyclical industries such as construction are designed to support a business through depressed periods of inadequate cash flow.

How strong is the management team? Management is one of the most important elements assessed by money sources.

Perhaps most importantly, how does the need for financing mesh with the business plan? If you don't have a business plan, make writing one your first priority. All capital sources will want to see your plan for the start-up and growth of your business.

An example of a business plan is included in this Guide. A business advisor such as a Small Business Development Center counselor can review the plan and help you determine the amount of financing your projections will likely support. The counselor can also help you identify potential sources of financing and help you prepare a loan package. You will then need to approach potential lenders to explain your project in detail and apply for the loan. It may be helpful to contact several lenders prior to preparing loan documents to learn about their lending practices and determine the feasibility of applying for financing.

Regardless of the specific type of loan or credit facility, almost every debt financing instrument will contain specific terms and conditions or "rules" relating to how the borrower uses the funds and conducts its business until the debt is repaid. These rules are contained in the credit agreement and ancillary documents, primarily in sections referring to "representations and warranties" and "covenants." The borrower's compliance with these covenants also serves as the means by which the lender monitors the loan and assures itself of a return on its investment. Compliance with covenants also serves as the means by which lenders demonstrate to federal and state regulators that they are in compliance with the rules and regulations applicable to the types of loans they are permitted to make.

The Small Business Assistance Office has a free publication, *Loan Documentation: An Introduction for Small Businesses* which provides an overview of how loan documents are structured and discusses common terms contained in most credit agreements. Representations, warranties and covenants are discussed as are security interests, guarantee agreements and other forms of collateral commonly required to secure a loan. A discussion of the consequences of failure to comply with loan covenants and a lender's rights upon borrower default is also included in the book. A free copy is available from the Small Business Assistance Office.

Past Credit Problems

In starting a business, your personal credit history is a key factor in any lender's decision to make a loan. If your credit report shows a history of late payments, judgments or tax liens, it will be very difficult to obtain a loan until the adverse entries are removed from the credit report. If you have ever declared bankruptcy or defaulted on a student loan or other federal loan, you may be permanently ineligible to obtain a federal loan such as an SBA-guaranteed loan.

PUBLIC SOURCES OF FINANCING – FEDERAL PROGRAMS

U.S. SMALL BUSINESS ADMINISTRATION (SBA)

Small Business Administration (SBA)
330 2nd Ave. South, Suite 430
Minneapolis, MN 55401-2224
612-370-2324
https://www.sba.gov/mn

Lender Match

Free online referral tool that connects small businesses with participating SBA-approved lenders.
https://www.sba.gov/lendermatch

The Small Business Administration (SBA) has financial assistance programs which provide access to debt and equity primarily from lenders and non-lender organizations. The list of participating lenders and organizations can be found at Minnesota Lenders List, https://www.sba.gov/offices/district/mn/minneapolis/resources/minnesota-lenders-list. The various types of SBA financing programs are briefly explained below. The qualifications for these programs change from time to time, and it is recommended that you check with SBA for the most recent criteria.

SBA evaluates each loan application on two levels. The first is for eligibility which varies by industry and SBA program. The second evaluation is based on the credit merits of the application. The SBA uses the North American Industry Classification System (NAICS) instead of SIC codes for this purpose. For information about the NAICS and tables see the SBA's Size Standards at https://www.sba.gov/federal-contracting/contracting-guide/size-standards.

Eligibility

Eligible Applicants-Size Standards. SBA's size standards for eligibility are based on the North American Industry Classification System (NAICS). The size standards table applies to most of SBA's programs and to many other federal government programs and actions where eligibility as a small business is a factor or consideration. SBA's Table of Size Standards can be accessed at https://www.sba.gov/document/support--table-size-standards.

Ineligible Applicants. Most small businesses in Minnesota are eligible for SBA financial assistance, provided they are independently owned and operated, are not dominant in their field and can show that they are unable to obtain private financing on reasonable terms without SBA assistance. The Small Business Act, however, does exclude certain businesses, namely the following:

- Nonprofit businesses (for-profit subsidiaries are eligible);
- Financial businesses primarily engaged in the business of lending, such as banks, finance companies, and factors (pawn shops, although engaged in lending, may qualify in some circumstances);
- Passive businesses owned by developers and landlords that do not actively use or occupy the assets acquired or improved with the loan proceeds. (Certain business that require, or renovate property that is leased to another operating company may be eligible);

- Life insurance companies;
- Businesses located in a foreign country (businesses in the U.S. owned by aliens may qualify);
- Pyramid sale distribution plans;
- Businesses deriving more than one-third of gross annual revenue from legal gambling activities;
- Businesses engaged in any illegal activity;
- Businesses that restrict patronage for any reason other than capacity;
- Government-owned entities (except for businesses owned or controlled by a Native American tribe);
- Businesses engaged in promoting religion;
- Loan packagers earning more than one third of their gross annual revenue from packaging SBA loans;
- Businesses with an associate who is incarcerated, on probation, on parole, or has been indicted for a felony or a crime of moral turpitude;
- Businesses in which the lender or any of its associates owns an equity interest;
- Businesses which present live performances of a prurient sexual nature;
- Businesses which derive directly or indirectly more than *de minimis* gross revenue through the sale of products or services, or the presentation of any depictions or displays, of a prurient sexual nature;
- Unless waived by SBA for good cause, businesses that have previously defaulted on a federal loan or federally assisted financing, resulting in the federal government or any of its agencies or departments sustaining a loss in any of its programs, and businesses owned or controlled by an applicant or any of its associates which previously owned, operated, or controlled a business which defaulted on a federal loan (or guaranteed a loan which was defaulted) and caused the federal government or any of its agencies or departments to sustain a loss in any of its programs. For purposes of this section, a compromise agreement shall also be considered a loss;
- Businesses primarily engaged in political or lobbying activities; and
- Speculative businesses (such as oil wildcatting).

Credit Merits

The SBA places its primary emphasis for loan consideration on the demonstrated ability of the business to repay all business-related debt, including the new loan obligation. Additionally, a reasonable "at stake" equity injection by the applicant is required. Each application is individually considered based on earnings potential, collateral, track record and/or projections, management, and the type of businesses in the same field. While SBA's standards are designed to be more relaxed than those of commercial lenders the SBA will not approve loans to businesses with unsatisfactory profit history, inadequate equity investment, unsupported projections, or, unacceptable credit histories.

SBA LOAN PROGRAMS

SBA's basic loan programs are as follows:

- 7(a) loan program
- Certified Development Company Loans (504 Guaranteed Loans)
- Microloans
- Small Business Investment Companies

Regular Guaranteed Loans

This is SBA's most frequently used loan program. A guaranteed loan is one made by a lender to a small business customer. The SBA provides the lender with a guarantee that will pay the lender a portion of the unpaid balance on loans that are not paid in full by the customer. Every lender has its own internal credit standard and policy for approval of its loans. The SBA's guarantee permits a lender to broaden its own criteria to accommodate additional lending because of the federally-backed assurances. While the guaranty extends the range of credit available through commercial lenders, it will not cover unsubstantiated repayment, poor collateralization, or improperly documented requests. Therefore, it is incumbent on the applicant to find out if the request has a chance and then work with the lender to submit all required documentation first, so that the lender may evaluate the proposal and make its decision. Under this program, the lender analyzes the credit and makes one of three decisions: to approve it entirely by itself; to approve subject to an SBA guaranty; or to decline the loan. Should the second method be chosen, the lender will submit the application to SBA on behalf of both the borrower and itself. Keep in mind that the applicant is the lender's customer and the lender is SBA's customer. The prospective borrower does not need to contact the SBA.

7(a) Loans

Maximum Loan Amount: $5 million gross.

Percent of Guaranty: 85 percent for loans of $150,000 or less; 75 percent guaranty loans greater than $150,000 (up to $3.75 million maximum guaranty).

Use of Proceeds: Term Loan. Expansion/renovation; new construction, purchase land or buildings; purchase equipment, fixtures, lease-hold improvements; working capital; refinance debt for qualifying reasons; seasonal line of credit, inventory.

Maturity: Depends on use of proceeds. Generally, working capital & machinery & equipment (not to exceed life of equipment) is up to 10 years; real estate is up to 25 years.

Maximum Interest Rates: Loans less than 7 years: $0 - $25,000 Prime + 4.25 percent; $25,001 - $50,000 Prime + 3.25 percent; Over $50,000 Prime + 2.25 percent. **Loans 7 years or longer:** 0 - $25,000 Prime + 4.75 percent; $25,001 - $50,000 Prime + 3.75 percent; Over $50,000 Prime + 2.75 percent.

Guaranty Fees: The upfront guaranty fee depends on the loan amount and the maturity of the loan.

For loans with a maturity that exceeds 12 months the fees are:

> For loans of $150,000 or less: 2 percent of the guaranteed portion;

> For loans of $150,001 to $700,000: 3 percent of the guaranteed portion;

> For loans of $700,001 to $5,000,000: 3.5 percent of the guaranteed portion up to $1,000,000 plus 3.75 percent of the guaranteed portion over $1,000,000.

For loans with a maturity of 12 months or less, the guarantee remains 0.25 percent of the guaranteed portion.

Who qualifies: Must be a for profit business and meet SBA size standards; show good character, credit, management, and ability to repay. Must be an eligible type of business. Prepayment penalty for loans with maturities of 15 years or more if prepaid during first 3 years. (5 percent year 1, 3 percent year 2 and 1 percent year 3).

SBA Express

The SBA Express program features an accelerated turnaround time for SBA review.

Maximum Loan Amount: $350,000.

Maximum SBA guarantee percentage: 50 percent

Interest rate: Lenders and borrowers can negotiate the interest rate, but it may not exceed the SBA maximum.

Eligibility decision: Qualified lenders are granted authorization to make eligibility determinations.

Revolving lines of credit: Up to 10 years but must be revolving and include term out periods.

Forms: Lender primarily uses own forms and procedures, plus SBA Form 1919.

Collateral: Lenders are not required to take collateral for loans up to $25,000. May use their existing collateral policy for loans over $25,000 up to $350,000.

Credit decision: By the lender.

Export Express

The Export Express program provides exporters and lenders a streamlined method to obtain SBA-backed financing for loans and lines of credit up to $500,000. Lenders use their own credit decision process and loan documentation. The SBA will respond to an application within 24 hours.

Maximum loan amount: $500,000

Maximum SBA guarantee percentage: 90 percent for loans of $350,000 or less, 75 percent for loans more than $350,000.

Interest: Lenders and borrowers can negotiate the interest rate, but it may not exceed the SBA maximum.

Eligibility decision: By the SBA

Revolving lines of credit: May not exceed 7 years

SBA response time: 24 hours

Forms: Lender primarily uses own forms and procedures, plus SBA Form 1919, Borrower Information.

Collateral: Lenders follow collateral policies and procedures that the lender has established for its non-SBA-guaranteed loans.

Credit decision: By the lender

Export Working Capital

Export Working Capital loans are for businesses that can generate export sales and need additional working capital to support these sales. Lenders review and approve applications and submit the request to the U.S. Export Assistance Center location servicing the exporter's region.

Maximum loan amount: $5 million

Maximum SBA guarantee percentage: 90 percent

Interest: No SBA maximum interest rate cap but SBA monitors for reasonableness.

Eligibility decision: By the SBA

SBA turnaround time: 5-10 business days

Forms: SBA-EIB 84-1, plus attachments.

Collateral: Export-related inventory and receivable generated by export sales financed with EWCP funds. The SBA also requires personal guarantee of owners with 20 percent or more ownership.

Credit decision: By the SBA.

Small Loan Advantage

The Small Loan Advantage program allows lenders to get a pre-qualification indication from the SBA that the business has sufficient creditworthiness to warrant giving the applicant full consideration for financing.

Maximum loan amount: $350,000

Maximum SBA guarantee percentage: 85 percent for loans up to $150,000 and 75 percent for those greater than $150,000.

Interest: Lenders and borrowers can negotiate the interest rate, but it may not exceed the SBA maximum.

Eligibility decision: By the SBA. Qualified lenders may be granted authorization to make eligibility determinations.

Revolving lines of credit: Up to 7 years with maturity extensions permitted at the outset.

SBA turnaround time: Within 36 hours.

Forms: Lender primarily uses own forms and procedures, plus SBA Form 1919, Borrower Information.

Collateral: Lenders are not required to take collateral for loans up to $25,000. May use their existing collateral policy for loans over $25,000 up to $350,000.

Credit decision: By the lender.

Purchase: Lender may request expedited SBA purchase on small loans or in situations where liquidation may be delayed.

Preferred Lenders
Under the Preferred Lenders program, the SBA gives qualifying lenders more authority to process, close, service, and liquidate SBA-guaranteed loans. An SBA field office serving the area in which a lender's office is located can nominate the lender, or the lender can ask a field office to consider it for preferred status.

In making its decision, the SBA considers whether the lender:

- Has the ability to process, close, service and liquidate loans.
- Has the ability to develop and analyze complete loan packages.
- Has satisfactory SBA performance.

CAPLines
CAPLines is an umbrella program that helps small businesses meet their short-term and cyclical working-capital needs. It features four lines.

- Seasonal line: Borrowers must use the loan proceeds solely to finance the seasonal increases of accounts receivable and inventory — or in some cases associated increased labor costs. It can be revolving or non-revolving.
- Contract line: This line finances the direct labor and material cost associated with performing assignable contracts. It can be revolving or non-revolving.
- Builders line: This line can finance direct labor and material costs for a small general contractor or builder constructing or renovating commercial or residential buildings. The building project serves as the collateral, and loans can be revolving or non-revolving.
- Working Capital: This is an asset-based revolving line of credit for businesses unable to meet credit standards associated with long-term credit. It provides financing for cyclical growth, recurring and/or short-term needs. Repayment comes from converting short-term assets into cash, which is remitted to the lender. Businesses continually draw from this line of credit, based on existing assets, and repay as their cash cycle dictates. This line generally is used by businesses that provide credit to other businesses. Because these loans require continual servicing and monitoring of collateral, additional fees may be charged by the lender.

CAPLines loans have a maximum amount of $5 million. Each of the four lines of credit has a maturity of up to 10 years, except the Builders line which has five years.

7(a) Loans (to veteran-owned small businesses)

Guaranty Fees: For Express Loans made to veteran-owned small businesses in FY2019, the guaranty fee will be zero and the ongoing fee will be .55%.

Veteran-owned businesses are one of the fastest-growing and significant segments of the U.S. economy. Veteran-owned firms comprise 7.5 percent of the nation's 5.4 million businesses with employees.

To be eligible to receive a Veterans fee relief, a small business must be at least 51 percent owned and controlled by someone in one of the following groups:

- Honorably discharged veterans.
- Active Duty Military service member eligible for the military's Transition Assistance Program (TAP).
- Active Reservists and/or active National Guard members.
- Current spouse of any veteran, active duty service member, Reservist, National Guard member, or the widowed spouse of a service member who died while in service or as a result of a service-connected disability.

Microloans

The SBA gives intermediaries the authority to issue Microloans. These loans have certain conditions between the SBA and intermediaries, and certain conditions between intermediaries and borrowers.

Generally, intermediaries should not make a Microloan of more than $10,000 to any borrower. An intermediary may not make a Microloan of more than $20,000 unless the borrower demonstrates that it is unable to obtain credit elsewhere at comparable interest rates and that it has good prospects for success.

An intermediary may not make a Microloan of more than $50,000, and no borrower may owe an intermediary more than $50,000 at any one time. Each Microloan must be repaid within six years.

Maximum Loan Amount: $50,000.

Use of Proceeds: Purchase machinery and equipment, fixtures, leasehold improvements; finance increased receivables; working capital. Cannot be used to repay existing debt or real estate purchase.

Maturity: Shortest term possible, not to exceed 6 years.

Maximum Interest Rates: More than $10,000 - the interest rate charged on the SBA loan to the Intermediary, plus 7.75 percent. $10,000 or less - the interest rate charged on the SBA loan to the Intermediary, plus 8.5 percent.

Who qualifies: Same as 7(a).

CDC Loans or 504 Loan Program
Provided through Certified Development Companies (CDCs) which are licensed by SBA.

Maximum Loan Amount: 504 CDC maxi-mum amount ranges from $5 million to $5.5 million, depending on type of business.

Project Structure: Project costs financed as follows: CDC - up to 40 percent; Non-guaranteed financing - Lender: 50 percent; Equity - 10 percent; under certain circumstances, 20 percent. Lender (non-guaranteed) financing secured by first lien on project assets. CDC loan provided from SBA 100 percent guaranteed debenture sold to investors at fixed rate secured by second lien.

Use of Proceeds: Acquisition or expansion of owner-occupied commercial real estate and/or the purchase of capital equipment and to refinance debts originally for these purposes.

Maturity: CDC Loan: 10- OR 25-year term fixed interest rate. Lender Loan: (unguaranteed) financing may have a shorter term. May be fixed or adjustable interest rate.

Maximum Interest Rates: Fixed rate on 504 Loan established when debenture backing loan is sold. Declining prepayment penalty for 1/2 of term.

FEES: SBA 504 loan fees are set by regulation and financed as part of the debenture. See the CDC for details.

Who qualifies: Alternative Size Standard: For-profit businesses that do not exceed $15 million in tangible net worth, and do not have an average two full fiscal year net income over $5 million. Owner Occupied 51 percent for existing or 60 percent for new construction.

Small Business Investment Companies

The SBA licenses, regulates and provides financial assistance to privately owned and operated Small Business Investment Companies (SBICs) whose major function is to make venture investments by supplying equity capital and extending unsecured loans and loans not fully collateralized to small enterprises which meet their investment criteria. SBICs are privately capitalized and obtain financial leverage from the SBA. The administration of the SBIC program is handled by the SBA Central Office in Washington, D.C. A list of the Minnesota SBICs can be found in the Financing Federal Sources section of Resource Directory of this Guide.

On March 27, 2020, the President signed into law the Coronavirus Aid, Relief, and Economic Security (CARES) Act, which contained $376 billion in relief for Small businesses. In addition to traditional funding programs, the Cares Act established several temporary programs to address the COVID-19 outbreak.

Among the funding options: Paycheck Protection Program (PPP) (loan program providing loan forgiveness for retaining employees by temporarily expanding the traditional SBA 7(a) loan program); Economic Injury Disaster Loan (EIDL) (a loan program to provide economic relief to small businesses and nonprofit organizations experiencing a temporary loss of revenue); SBA Express Bridge Loans (enables small businesses who currently have a business relationship with an SBA Express Lender to access up o $25,000 quickly); and SBA Debt Relief (provides a financial reprieve with SBA paying the principle, interest, and fees of current 7(a), 504, and microloans for a period of six months). The SBA will automatically pay the principle, interest, and fees of new 7(a), 504, and microloans issued prior to September 27, 2020.

U.S. DEPARTMENT OF AGRICULTURE (USDA) RURAL DEVELOPMENT

Rural Business-Cooperative Service
375 Jackson Street, Suite 410
St. Paul, Minnesota 55101-1853
651-602-7791
https://www.rd.usda.gov/mn

Programs & Services for Businesses
https://www.rd.usda.gov/programs-services/programs-services-businesses

Business & Industry Loan Guarantees
https://www.rd.usda.gov/programs-services/business-industry-loan-guarantees

The U.S. Department of Agriculture is a federal agency that creates Rural Development Programs that encourage economic development in rural areas. USDA provides funding opportunities for rural small businesses through loans, loan guarantees, and grants. A list of USDA Rural Development Field offices can be found in the Government, Federal section of the Resource Directory of this Guide.

PUBLIC SOURCES OF FINANCING / TAX CREDITS – STATE PROGRAMS

Under State legislation (Minn. Stat. §§ 116J.993 to 116J.995), business receiving a "business subsidy" will be required, among other things, to enter into a "business subsidy agreement" that will include goals for wages and jobs to be offered and paid by that business. If those goals are not met within a certain period of time, in almost all cases the business will be required to repay the amount of the subsidy, plus interest.

MINNESOTA DEPARTMENT OF AGRICULTURE

Minnesota Department of Agriculture (MDA)
625 Robert Street N.
St. Paul, MN 55155-2538
651-201-6000 | mda.info@state.mn.us
https://www.mda.state.mn.us

Loan and Grant Programs
https://www.mda.state.mn.us/funding

The MDA provides many programs to assist farmers in improving and expanding their current operations.

Agriculture Best Management Practices (BMP) Loan Program
651-201-6618

Water quality program that provides low-interest loans to farmers, rural landowners, and agriculture supply businesses.

Aggie Bond Beginning Farmer Loan
651-201-6556

Offers affordable financing for a qualified beginning farmer.

Agricultural Improvement Loan
651-201-6666

Assists eligible farmers to finance capital improvements to their farming operation.

Beginning Farm Loan
651-201-6666

Offers affordable financing, a reasonable down payment and built-in safeguards, such as farm management training and financial planning.

Farm Opportunity Loan Program
651-201-6666

Designed to finance the purchase of equipment to add value to crops or livestock, adopt best management practices, reduce agricultural inputs to improve the environment, and increase on-farm energy production.

Livestock Equipment Loan Program
651-201-6666

Designed to help finance the purchase of livestock-related equipment.

Livestock Expansion Loan Program
651-201-6666

Assists livestock and dairy producers to finance the construction of state of the art facilities.

Methane Digester Loan Program
651-201-6666

Helps supplement the funds needed for livestock producers in Minnesota to begin installing digesters on their farms.

Pilot Agricultural Microloan Program
651-201-6666

Program was established to assist non-traditional farmers by providing lending capital while developing their farm business towards traditional agricultural credit.

Restructure II Loan Program
651-201-6666

Designed to help farmers who remain in good credit standing with their local ag lender, but are having trouble with cash flow due to adverse events.

Seller Assisted Loan Participation Program
651-201-6666

A cooperative financing effort involving a buyer, a seller, a local lender, and the Minnesota Rural Finance Authority (RFA), where the seller participates in financing the sale of their farm by providing a portion of the financing.

Value Added Stock Loan Program
651-201-6666

Helps farmers finance the purchase of stock in a cooperative, limited liability company, or limited liability partnership proposing to build or purchase and operate a facility to process or produce products from ag crops.

AGRI Livestock Investment Grant
651-201-6458

Encourages long-term industry development for Minnesota livestock farmers and ranchers by helping them improve, update, and modernize their livestock operation infrastructure and equipment.

AGRI Value-Added Grant Program
651-201-6135

Helps Minnesota processors add value to Minnesota agricultural products by helping underwrite equipment purchases and physical improvements.

Dairy Business Planning Grant
651-201-6646

Grants encourage business planning and modernization activities and other improvements on Minnesota dairy farms and also help pay for stray voltage testing.

Specialty Crop Block Grant Program
651-201-6539

A grant program designed to enhance the competitiveness of specialty crops in domestic and foreign markets.

TAX CREDITS

Beginning Farmer Tax Credit
651-201-6004 | mda.bftc@state.mn.us
https://www.mda.state.mn.us/bftc

Contact Minnesota Department of Revenue 651-296-3781 | individual.incometax@state.mn.us

Credit provides tax credits for the rent or sale of farm land or a variety of farm assets to beginning farmers. This includes incentives for the sale of farm land.

A Beginning Farmer is defined as:

- A Minnesota resident who is seeking entry, or has entered into farming within the last 10 years
- A farmer who will provide the majority of the labor and management of the farm that is located in Minnesota
- Has adequate experience and knowledge of the type of farming for which they seek assistance from the Rural Finance Authority

- Can provide positive projected earnings statements
- Is not directly related to the owner of the agricultural asset. This includes parents, grandparents, brothers, sisters, spouses, children, and grandchildren. Legal adoption shall be considered in full effect.
- Has a net worth that does not exceed the limit provided under Minn. Stat. § 41B.03, subdivision 3, paragraph (a), clause (2). This limit is $851,000 in 2020.
- The beginning farmer may need to participate in an approved financial management program. Costs of financial management programs up to a maximum of $1,500 per year (for up to 3 years) may also be eligible for a tax credit. The financial management credit need not be tied to any agricultural asset sale or rental.

Definition of "Agricultural Asset": Agricultural land, livestock, facilities, buildings and machinery used for farming in Minnesota

Credit to the agricultural asset owner:

- 5 percent of the lesser of the sale price or fair market value of the agricultural asset up to a maximum of $32,000;
- 10 percent of the gross rental income in each of the 1st, 2nd, and 3rd years of the rental agreement, up to a maximum of $7,000 per year, or
- 15 percent of the cash equivalent of the gross rental income in each of the 1st, 2nd, and 3rd years of a share rent agreement, up to a maximum of $10,000 per year.

The agricultural asset owner can claim credits in one of the above categories in a given tax year on a per-owner basis up to the maximums stated.

Role of the Rural Finance Authority (RFA)

The RFA will administer the tax credits by:

- Certifying beginning farmers
- Assisting beginning farmers with locating eligible financial management program options in their area
- Certifying that owners of agricultural assets are eligible for the tax credit. This is a first come, first served initiative. The maxim amount available in 2020 is about $12 million.

The asset owner may be an individual, trust, a qualified pass-through entity. The Owner of agricultural assets cannot be an equipment dealer, livestock dealer, or comparable entity engaged in the business of selling agricultural assets for profit.

MINNESOTA DEPARTMENT OF EMPLOYMENT AND ECONOMIC DEVELOPMENT

Minnesota Department of Employment and Economic Development (DEED)
1st National Bank Building
332 Minnesota Street, Suite E200
St. Paul, MN 55101-1351
651-259-7114 800-657-3858
https://mn.gov/deed/

Minnesota Job Creation Fund
651-259-7483 800-657-3858
https://mn.gov/deed/business/financing-business/deed-programs/mn-jcf/

The Minnesota Job Creation Fund (JCF) program provides financial incentives to new and expanding businesses that meet certain job creation and capital investment targets.

Companies deemed eligible to participate may receive up to $1 million for creating or retaining high-paying jobs and for constructing or renovating facilities or making other property improvements. For extremely large projects, companies may be eligible to receive up to $2 million. The size of an award depends on variety of factors including (but not limited to) Minnesota's competitiveness, local economic conditions, job creation, wage levels and capital expenditures. Expenditures and hiring related to the JCF assistance may not occur until funding has been formally approved.

Eligibility

The program is available to businesses engaged in select industries including manufacturing, warehousing, distribution and technology-related industries, among others. Local government must support an application submitted by the expanding business. To be eligible, the business must meet requirements including:

- Invest at least $500,000 in real property improvements within one (1) year of entering the program
- Create at least 10 full-time jobs that meet wage and compensation requirements within two (2) years of entering the program
- Have other location options outside of Minnesota
- Operate in an eligible industry
- Firms that are located in Greater Minnesota or if 51 percent of the business is cumulatively owned by minorities, veterans, women or persons with a disability may qualify for the program by investing at least $250,000 and creating at least 5 full-time jobs.

Funding is provided annually once minimum thresholds are met. Actual dollars provided depend on job and eligible capital investments.

Minnesota Investment Fund
651-259-7430 800-657-3858
https://mn.gov/deed/business/financing-business/deed-programs/mif/

This Minnesota Investment Fund (MIF) provides financing to help add new workers and retain high-quality jobs. The program's focus on industrial, manufacturing and technology-related industries and aims to increase the local and state tax base and improve economic vitality.

Eligibility

Funds are awarded to local units of government that provide loans to assist expanding businesses. Cities, counties, townships, selected economic development organizations and recognized Indian tribal governments are eligible. Project requirements include:

- All projects must meet minimum criteria for private investment, number of jobs created or retained and wages paid.
- At least 50 percent of total project costs must be privately financed through owner equity and other lending sources.
- Although loan proceeds may be used to help purchase land and buildings, most MIF loans are used to finance equipment.

The size of an award depends on variety of factors including (but not limited to) Minnesota's competitiveness, local economic conditions, job creation and wage levels. All expenditures and hiring related to the MIF assistance may not occur until funding has been formally approved.

Minnesota Emerging Entrepreneur Loan Program
651-259-7450
https://mn.gov/deed/business/financing-business/deed-programs/elp/

The Minnesota Emerging Entrepreneur Loan Program (ELP) supports the growth of businesses owned and operated by minorities, low-income persons, women, veterans and/or persons with disabilities. DEED provides grant funds to a network of nonprofit lenders which use these funds for loans to start-up and expanding businesses throughout the state.

The program has additional goals of providing jobs for minority and/or low-income persons, creating and strengthening minority business enterprises, and promoting economic development in low-income areas.

Program Requirements

DEED provides ELP funding to certified nonprofit partners to make loans to Minnesota businesses that are majority-owned and operated by minorities, low-income persons, women, veterans and/or persons with disabilities. Businesses must apply directly with a certified lender, although DEED may be able to assist in identifying an appropriate lender. Once the lender approves the loan, they will forward the loan package to DEED for approval by the commissioner and disbursement of funds for the project.

Eligibility

In order to qualify for an ELP loan businesses must be based in Minnesota and majority owned and operated by one or more Minnesota residents who are minorities, low-income persons, women, veterans and/or persons with disabilities.

The program will finance a variety of start-up and expansion costs, including normal expenses such as machinery and equipment, inventory and receivables, working capital, new construction, renovation, and site acquisition. Financing of existing debt is not permitted.

Most businesses are eligible for an ELP loans but the program does not make loans to liquor stores or establishments primarily selling liquor made off site, stores primarily selling tobacco or electronic smoking products, gambling operations, or adult oriented businesses.

Certain provisions, including eligibility of retail businesses, are available only to beginning microenterprises, defined as businesses that have fewer than five employees and have generated sales revenue for two years or less.

Indian Business Loan Program
651-259-7483
https://mn.gov/deed/business/financing-business/deed-programs/indian/

The Indian Business Loan (IBL) program supports the development of Indian owned and operated businesses and promotes economic opportunities for Indian people throughout Minnesota.

Loan proceeds may cover startup and expansion costs, including normal expenses such as machinery and equipment, inventory and receivables, working capital, new construction, renovation and site acquisition.

Eligibility

Applicants must be enrolled members of a federally recognized Minnesota-based band or tribe. Businesses must be wholly owned by an enrolled member and can be located anywhere in the state, although the bulk of the loans are made to businesses on a reservation.

At least 25 percent of the project financing must be contributed from non-IBL funds and business owners must provide a portion of the financing needed to undertake the project. Financing of existing debt is not permitted.

Minnesota Reservist and Veteran Business Loan Program
651-259-7427
https://mn.gov/deed/business/financing-business/deed-programs/reservists/

This program provides loans to companies that are affected when certain employees are called to active military duty. It also gives loans to individual veterans who have returned from active duty and want to start their own business.

The program provides one-time, interest-free loans of $5,000 to $20,000.

Eligibility

Business loans are for existing small businesses that have an essential employee called to active service in the military reserves for 180 days or longer on or after September 11, 2001. The business must be injured substantially due to the employee's absence.

Startup loans are for veterans who were on active duty on or after September 11, 2001, seeking financial assistance to start their own businesses.

Export Financing Programs

https://mn.gov/deed/business/exporting/export-financing/

Programs provide grants, loans and loan guarantees, working capital, credit or insurance to help companies become export ready, help new exporters make their first foreign sales, or help current exporters expand into new markets.

STEP (State Trade & Export Promotion Program) Export Assistance for Small Business

651-259-7487
https://mn.gov/deed/business/exporting/export-financing/

The STEP program provides financial and technical assistance to qualifying Minnesota small businesses with an active interest in exporting products or services to foreign markets.

Participants may be first-time exporters or companies that are currently exporting but are interested in expanding into new international markets.

Financial Assistance Available

Small businesses may apply for reimbursement of up to $500 for export-training that will result in the development of an export strategy or up to $7,500 for approved export-development activities, including:

- Participation in trade missions
- Exhibiting at trade shows or industry-specific events
- Translation of marketing materials
- Development of foreign language websites
- Gold Key or other business matchmaking services
- Company-specific international sales activities
- Testing and certification (such as CE marking) required to sell products in foreign markets

Eligibility

Eligible companies must fit the SBA definition of a small business, based on annual sales or number of employees, and:

- Have been in operation for at least one year
- Be operating profitably, based on U.S. operations
- Have an understanding of the costs associated with exporting
- Have a strategic plan for exporting (unless applying for an export-planning grant)

Activities must be pre-approved in order to be eligible for reimbursement. Companies MAY NOT APPLY for reimbursement for activities that have already taken place.

Eligible companies must also have products or services that are appropriate for the target market, must agree to participate in surveys and provide information on program outcomes, and must apply through the Minnesota Trade Office (MTO), which administers the program in the state.

TAX CREDITS / BENEFITS /GRANTS

Greater Minnesota Job Expansion Program
651-259-7434
https://mn.gov/deed/business/financing-business/tax-credits/greater-mn-job-expansion/

Program provides tax benefits to businesses located in Greater Minnesota that increase employment. Qualifying businesses that meet job-growth goals may receive sales tax refunds for purchases made during a seven-year period.

Eligibility

Businesses must meet program requirements including:

- Have operated for at least one year in Greater Minnesota
- Meet wage and compensation requirements
- Will add at least two employees or 10 percent of current staff, whichever is greater, within three years
- Meet industry eligibility including not being engaged in retail, gambling, entertainment, among many other industries

Border Cities Enterprise Zone Program
651-259-7415 800-657-3858
https://mn.gov/deed/business/financing-business/tax-credits/border-cities/

This program provides business tax credits to qualifying businesses that are the source of investment and job creation or retention in the cities of Breckenridge, Dilworth, East Grand Forks, Moorhead, Ortonville, and Taylors Falls. Tax benefits include property tax credits, debt financing credit on new construction, sales tax credit on construction equipment and materials, and new or existing employee credits.

Eligibility

Businesses locating or existing in those cities are eligible, unless they are:

- Recreation or entertainment facilities
- Owned by a fraternal or veteran's organization
- Owned by a public utility
- Used in operation of a financial institution
- Owned by a retail food or beverage service business
- Operating under a franchise agreement requiring the business to be located in the state

Data Center Sales Tax Incentives
651-259-7415
https://mn.gov/deed/business/financing-business/tax-credits/data-center-credit/

Companies that build data or network operation centers in Minnesota may receive sales tax exemptions for 20 years on:

- Computing, network, or data storage equipment
- Software
- Electricity used to operate or maintain a qualified data center

Eligibility

Companies that build data or network operation centers of at least 25,000 square feet and invest $30 million in the first four years, as well as companies that refurbish a data or network operations center of at least 25,000 square feet and invest $50 million in the first two years.

To become a designated data center and receive the sales tax exemptions, companies must first be certified to participate in the program.

Research and Development Tax Credit
Contact Minnesota Department of Revenue 651-556-3075 | businessincome.tax@state.mn.us
https://mn.gov/deed/business/financing-business/tax-credits/research-dev-credit/

The R&D credit is equal to 10 percent of qualifying expenses up to $2 million, and 2.5 percent for expenses above that level. Qualifying expenses are the same as for the federal R&D credit - defined in Section 41 of the Internal Revenue Code - but must be for research done in Minnesota.

Examples include R&D-related wages, supplies and research contracted outside your business. Contributions to qualified nonprofit organizations that make grants to early-stage technology businesses in Minnesota also may qualify.

Angel Tax Credit
651-259-7599 | angel.credit@state.mn.us
https://mn.gov/deed/business/financing-business/tax-credits/angel-tax-credit/

The Angel Tax Credit (Small Business Investment Tax Credit, Minn. Stat. § 116J.8737) is intended to encourage equity investment in early stage, technology-based business and encourage job creation by providing tax incentives to investors making investments in start-up companies. The credit encourages start-ups that are focused on developing high technology, using new proprietary technology, or developing a proprietary product, process or service in a limited number of fields.

A comprehensive discussion of the structure and operation of the Angel Tax Credit is provided in the free publication, *Minnesota's Angel Tax Credit 2019*. This publication is available without charge from the Small Business Assistance Office, 1st National Bank Building, 332 Minnesota Street, Suite E200, St. Paul, MN 55101. Telephone: 651-259-8425 or 800-310-8323. Website: https://mn.gov/deed/business/help/sbao/.

Launch Minnesota
launchminnesota@state.mn.us

Launch Minnesota was created in 2019 to provide entrepreneurs and emerging technology companies with financial assistance in the form of grants as a spur to business growth. These grants are of three types:

- A grant of up to $35,000 for research and development expenses, direct business expenses, and the purchase of technical assistance or services from public higher education institutions and nonprofit entities. Allowable research and development expenditures may include, but are not limited to, proof of concept activities, intellectual property protection, prototype designs and production, and commercial feasibility. Direct expenses may include rent, equipment purchases, and supplier invoices. Technical assistance or services must be purchased to assist in the development or commercialization of a product or service. Each recipient business or entrepreneur may receive only one grant per biennium.
- A grant of up to $7,500 to reimburse an entrepreneur for housing or child care expenses for the entrepreneur or their spouse or children. Each recipient may receive only one grant per biennium.
- A grant of up to $50,000 to a business entrepreneur that has been awarded a phase 2 award under the federal Small Business Innovation Research (SBIR) program or the Small Business Technology Transfer (STTR) program with an award date after July 1, 2019.

As this publication went to press, Launch Minnesota is a two-year public initiative and grants will be available through June 30, 2021.

MINNESOTA POLLUTION CONTROL AGENCY (MPCA)

Minnesota Pollution Control Agency (MPCA)
Resource Management and Assistance Division
520 Lafayette Road, 2nd Floor
St. Paul, MN 55155-4100
651-296-6300 800-657-3864
https://www.pca.state.mn.us

Financial Assistance: Grants and Loans
https://www.pca.mn.us/about-mpca/financial-assistance-grants-and-loans

Environmental Assistance Grant and Loan Programs
https://www.pca.state.mn.us/about-mpca/environmental-assistance-grants-and-loans-program

The MPCA offers environmental assistance grants and loans that could help existing businesses move toward environmentally sustainable projects or practices. Projects must focus on pollution and waste prevention, recycling market development, environmental education, sustainable community development and/or resource recovery.

Environmental Assistance Grants
651-757-2459 800-657-3864
https://www.pca.state.mn.us/about-mpca/environmental-assistance-grants

Environmental Assistance grants provide financial assistance for researching, developing, or implementing projects and practices related to all aspects of waste management and prevention including hazardous substances, toxic pollutants, and problem materials. Additionally, market development and education grants are also allowed.

Eligible applicants, grant award amounts and minimum matching fund requirements will vary by Focus Areas and Preferred Proposals.

Loans awarded throughout the calendar year.

Environmental Assistance Loans
651-757-2459 800-657-3864
https://www.pca.state.mn.us/about-mpca/environmental-assistance-loans

Priority eligible projects: green chemistry, pollution prevention, source reduction, recycling, and source-separated composting.

Eligibility

Eligible loan costs limited to the capital costs of implementing waste or pollution prevention technologies in Minnesota. Capital costs are limited to the costs of acquisition of machinery and equipment, including freight and installation, and related improvements.

Small Business Environmental Assistance
https://www.pca.state.mn.us/smallbizhelp

Low-interest Environmental Loans
https://www.pca.state.mn.us/regulations/low-interest-environmental-loans

The program provides low-interest loans to small businesses to finance environmental projects such as capital equipment upgrades that meet or exceed environmental regulations, and costs associated with the investigation and cleanup of contaminated sites.

Eligibility

To qualify, a borrower must be an existing small business corporation, sole proprietorship, partnership or association with;

- fewer than 100 full-time employees
- an after-tax profit of less than $500,000
- a demonstrated ability to repay the loan

Loan terms and conditions

- loan amount between $1,000 or more than $75,000
- Interest rate at or below one-half the prime rate, not to exceed five percent
- repayment term up to seven years
- flexibility in the types of collateral accepted
- awarded throughout the year

Small Business Environmental Assistance -Funding Opportunities
https://www.pca.state.mn.us/regulations/funding-opportunities

The Small Business Grant Program provides financial assistance to businesses, organizations, and entities for the development of projects that go beyond regulatory requirements to improve their environmental stewardship. Requests for proposal are open throughout the year for a variety of projects and industries.

PUBLIC SOURCES OF FINANCING – LOCAL PROGRAMS

Various governmental units at different levels are currently providing some form of assistance to entrepreneurs. This assistance may be in the form of financial services and loan packaging or technical assistance, tax credits, and the like. To learn more about the variety of programs, contact the planning or business services unit of the county, municipality or township where the proposed business will be located.

In Minneapolis, contact the Community Planning and Economic Development Agency, Business Assistance, Crown Roller Mill, Suite 200, 105 Fifth Ave. S., Minneapolis, MN 55401, 612-673-5095 or http://www.minneapolismn.gov/cped/ba/index.htm.

In St. Paul, contact the Planning & Economic Development, Economic Development Department, City Hall Annex, 25 West Fourth Street, Suite 1300, St. Paul, MN 55102, telephone 651-266-6604 or https://www.stpaul.gov/departments/planning-economic-development/economic-development.

Note that the Financing, Local Sources section of the Resource Directory of this Guide contains information on other sources of local public financing throughout the state.

PRIVATE SOURCES OF FUNDS

VENTURE CAPITAL FIRMS

Venture capital firms provide equity capital to emerging and growth-oriented businesses that have high market potential. Their major function is to assess management ability, determine market potential and provide equity capital to businesses evidencing growth potential and anticipated high returns of venture investments. The listing of major venture capital firms in Minnesota can be found at your local business library.

MINNESOTA INITIATIVE FUNDS

Minnesota initiative funds are charitable, private nonprofit organizations funded with a McKnight Foundation allocation supplemented with funds from various public and private sources. Funds are distributed in grants and loans for human services, economic and business development, education, leadership development, health, community services and administration. The six initiative funds are separate entities and each has its own programs, funding levels and guidelines. Four of the six initiative funds (Northwest, Northeast, Central and Southwest) now refer to themselves as Foundations, which they feel more accurately describes their functions. Initiative funds, the counties they serve, and the office addresses are provided in the Resource Directory section of this Guide.

COMMUNITY/ECONOMIC DEVELOPMENT CORPORATIONS

Community Development Corporations (CDCs) are privately owned community development agencies serving a predefined geographic area. CDCs are usually organized as nonprofit corporations in order to obtain funds from sources interested in economic development such as federal or state governments. CDCs address the development needs of a geographically defined area and investment emphasis will vary by locality. The one requirement for a CDC investment is that the venture be located in the community being served. Examples of programs operated by CDCs include economic and business development programs, including programs that provide financial and other assistance to start, expand, or locate businesses in or near the areas served so as to provide employment and ownership opportunities for residents of such areas; community development and housing activities that create new training, employment and ownership opportunities and which contribute to improved living conditions; and manpower training programs. Most CDCs can assist new or expanding businesses in developing a business plan, management or financial plans including assistance in qualifying for a loan, putting the paperwork together and presenting a proposal to a financial institution.

Information on Community/Economic Development Corporations can be obtained from the Minnesota Department of Employment and Economic Development. Addresses, telephone numbers and websites for both are listed in the Resource Directory section of this Guide.

INSURANCE

Before you begin your business, you should thoroughly investigate your business insurance needs. The insurance industry today can tailor an insurance package to meet the general and specialized needs of almost every business.

Because the insurance problems and needs of each business differ, no general insurance program can be outlined to fit every business. To be completely satisfactory, it should be tailored to fit the individual needs of each business. You should consult with an experienced insurance agent or broker.

TYPES OF INSURANCE

Business insurance is a matter of good business judgment. It is difficult to conceive of a sound business not carrying insurance custom-tailored to its individual needs. Among the basic kinds of coverage you should consider are:

Property Insurance. This protects the owner of the property (or the mortgagee) against loss caused by the actual destruction of a part or all of the property by fire, windstorm, explosion, falling aircraft, riot and other perils.

Business Interruption Insurance (and Other Time Element Coverages). These protect a business against loss of earnings resulting from an interruption caused by damage to or destruction of the physical property. Business interruption insurance will pay you approximately what you normally would have earned. The premiums, especially when part of a complete insurance package, are low. There is also similar insurance which provides coverage if you are hospitalized and have to shut down business.

Liability Insurance (Including Business Automobile). This protects a business against loss arising out of legal liability for death, injury or damage to the person or property of others caused by negligence. Included are obligations to pay medical, hospital, surgical and disability benefits to injured persons, and funeral and death benefits to dependents, beneficiaries or personal representatives of persons who are killed, irrespective of legal liability.

Bonds. Fidelity bonds guarantee against loss due to the dishonesty of employees. Surety bonds guarantee the performance of various types of obligations assumed by contract or imposed by law. Surety bonds are most often used in the construction industry and are often required on public construction projects.

Workers' Compensation Insurance. This provides for payment of compensation benefits, as established by state law, to injured employees of a business. See the section in this Guide on Workers' Compensation for additional information.

Group Insurance for Employees. Group life insurance and group health insurance provided as employee benefits must conform to standards established by state and federal statute. These requirements are described in greater detail in the section of this Guide on Employee Benefits.

Product Liability. This refers to insurance coverage for any product manufactured by the insured. Coverage applies to the product once it leaves the manufacturer's hands and covers the manufacturer in case the ultimate user of the product sues for bodily injury or property damage.

E-INSURANCE FOR COMPANIES WITH AN ONLINE PRESENCE

With the growth of the Internet and e-commerce, the law regarding business insurance is evolving as coverage is being extended to new areas. Both the insurance industry and the courts are starting to sort out how existing insurance products apply to e-commerce.

Businesses that operate on the Internet face the possibility that their activities may subject them to liability in other jurisdictions. Since the Internet transcends geographical boundaries, one may be subject to a lawsuit in another state or even another country. It is fair to say that any company doing business on the Internet should consider that it is essentially a global business that might be sued in any court and in any territory where its business presence becomes known.

Companies with operations on the Internet are in the business of information publishing, vulnerable to liabilities that typically plague media companies such as defamation, invasion of privacy and intellectual property infringement claims. While these causes of action are not new, an Internet company's assets are more vulnerable to theft or business interruption. Damages associated with intangible assets, such as data theft or loss of business capability, pose risks unique to Internet companies.

As with all insurance, a business must make sure of what is and is not covered by their current insurance before investigating the variety of Internet-specific policies.

HELP FOR BUSINESSES UNABLE TO OBTAIN LIABILITY INSURANCE

The Joint Underwriting Association (JUA) was created to provide liability insurance coverage only to persons or entities unable to obtain insurance through ordinary methods if the insurance is required by statute, ordinance or otherwise required by law, or is necessary to earn a livelihood or conduct a business and serves a public purpose. The legislature specifically authorized the JUA to provide insurance coverage to day care providers, foster parents, foster homes, developmental achievement centers, group homes, sheltered workshops for mentally, emotionally, or physically disabled persons and certain citizen participation groups. The JUA is also authorized to provide liquor liability and certain medical malpractice coverages. The eligibility of other classes of business for JUA coverage is determined on a class by class basis.

The JUA is specifically prohibited by statute from issuing either product liability coverage or environmental impairment coverage. Further, the JUA cannot issue coverage to any business which is conducted substantially outside the state of Minnesota unless the insurance is required by statute, ordinance, or otherwise required by law. The JUA may reject high risk clients and risks it deems hazardous.

After having been unable to find an insurer willing to write the coverage sought, application may be made to the JUA. Upon receipt of an application, the JUA will make a determination whether the risk falls within a class for which the Association has already been activated to provide assistance. The Commissioner of the Minnesota Department of Commerce may publish notices of activation of the JUA for specified new classes of business each week in the *State Register.* The JUA has the authority to insure classes of business for 180 days from the time the notice is published. A public hearing may be held with each notice of activation in order to receive testimony from a class of business to determine whether statutory requirements for JUA coverage have been met.

The actual time frame for issuing a policy is dependent on several factors including whether:

- The appropriate policy form has been approved for use by the JUA Board of Directors;
- A rate schedule has been adopted for that class;
- The class or particular applicant requires committee or Board review prior to quoting;
- The 30-day MMAP period has expired and no quote for coverage has been offered;
- The applicant's current coverage has expired; and
- No market can be found; or
- The applicant is quoted by MMAP a premium rate ten percent or more in excess of the JUA's rates for similar coverage.

ISSUES FOR EMPLOYERS*

WHO IS AN EMPLOYEE?

IN GENERAL

Many laws affecting the worker/employment relationship will require the business owner to first determine whether an individual who performs services for the business is an "employee" for purposes of the particular law. **Business owners who use "independent contractors" may think they do not have employees and, therefore, employment laws do not apply to them. An individual's status as an independent contractor, however, is not determined by agreement or by what he or she is called; the individual's status is determined by what he or she does, and their relationship to the business.**

The relationship between the business and the individual may be that of:

- A common law employee.
- A statutory employee.
- An independent contractor.

If the individual is a common law employee, the business by law must obtain workers' compensation coverage, withhold FICA (Social Security and Medicare) and income taxes, pay the employer's share of the FICA tax and pay federal and state unemployment taxes. Fair labor standards laws, occupational safety and health requirements and a variety of other federal and state laws also may apply.

If the individual is a statutory employee, the business does not withhold federal or state income tax. The employer should consult with an attorney or other competent tax advisor with respect to withholding Social Security and Medicare taxes and paying unemployment tax. Fair labor standards laws will probably apply.

An independent contractor is himself or herself a sole proprietor of a business, and not an employee of the firm who contracts with them. The tax requirements for sole proprietorships are discussed in the Choosing the Form of Business Organization – Tax and Non-Tax Considerations section of this Guide.

---

*A comprehensive discussion of employment issues is provided in the publication, *An Employer's Guide to Employment Law Issues in Minnesota.* The publication is available without charge from the Small Business Assistance Office, 1st National Bank Building, 332 Minnesota Street, Suite E200, St. Paul, MN 55101-1351. Telephone: 651-556-8425 or 800-310-8323
Email: deed.mnsbao@state.mn.us | Website: https://mn.gov/deed/business/help/sbao/

The question of whether a worker is an independent contractor or an employee may be determined by common law rules (definitions fashioned by the courts based on specific cases) or by statute. A person may be an employee for certain purposes but not for others. If a question arises, the employer is strongly urged to seek professional advice.

COMMON LAW EMPLOYEES

Under common law rules, courts balance a number of factors to determine whether an employer-employee relationship exists. The employer's right to control the manner and means of performing the work is the most important factor distinguishing an employer-employee relationship. It does not matter that the employer gives the employee substantial discretion and freedom to act, so long as the employer has the legal right to control both the method and result of the service.

Some of the other factors examined by the courts in determining whether an employment relationship exists include:

- **Mode of payment**. Workers who are paid on a regular basis, e.g., hourly or biweekly, are more likely to be considered employees than are persons who are paid a fixed amount for a specific service, regardless of the amount of time taken to complete the task. Withholding for taxes and providing fringe benefits such as medical insurance are considered typical of an employer-employee relationship.
- **Materials and tools**. A person who furnishes his or her own materials and tools and equipment and has a significant investment in the tools and equipment used in connection with providing the service is less likely to be considered an employee than is a person who uses tools, equipment, and materials furnished by the hiring entity.
- **Control of the premises.** An employer-employee relationship is more likely to be found where the hiring entity owns or controls the premises where the work is performed. Premises controlled by the service provider or by a third person are considered more characteristic of an independent contractor relationship.
- **Right of discharge.** The ability of the hiring entity to terminate or discharge the worker and/or the ability of the worker to leave before the task is completed without becoming liable for nonperformance under the contract or agreement also are factors examined in determining whether an employment relationship exists.

It is important to note, however, that none of the above factors, standing alone, will determine whether an employment relationship exists. The most important factor is the hiring entity's right to control the manner and means of completing the work. Doubtful situations generally are resolved by examining the facts of the specific case in light of all relevant factors.

If an employment relationship exists, the legal requirements placed on employers will apply regardless of what the parties call the worker, regardless of how payments are measured or made, and regardless of whether the person works part time or full time, unless a statutory exception applies to the situation.

In some cases, an employment relationship may exist between the employee and more than one employer, creating a situation of joint employment. A common example of this is when businesses obtain employees on contract from a temporary employment agency. It is important for employers to know that when they are in a situation of joint employment, both employers are jointly responsible to ensure that the employee is paid in accordance with the federal Fair Labor Standards Act (FLSA), as described in the Labor Standards section of this chapter. Note also that the Equal Employment Opportunity Commission (EEOC) has issued guidance on the application of Title VII of the Civil Rights Act of 1964, the Age Discrimination in Employment Act (ADEA), the Americans with Disabilities Act (ADA) and the Equal Pay Act (EPA) to individuals placed in job assignments by temporary employment agencies and other staffing firms (the EEOC refers to such individuals as "contingent workers"). In that Guidance, the EEOC states that either the staffing firm or the client (i.e. the business to which the contingent workers have been supplied), or both, may properly be considered an employer. If either or both has "control" over the contingent worker's work, that party will be an employer under Title VII, the ADA, the ADEA, and the EPA. Also, even if either lacks such "control", it will be considered an employer of that contingent worker, if it has enough other employees so as to be subject to those laws.

STATUTORY EMPLOYEES

Even if a worker is not an employee under common law rules, he or she may be considered an employee for certain statutory purposes, such as FICA (Social Security and Medicare) tax, federal and state unemployment insurance taxes, workers' compensation, Fair Labor Standards Act compliance, occupational safety and health requirements, and other statutory programs. Likewise, a federal or state statute may exempt certain employers or employees from its application.

Because both federal and state statutes define employees covered by their respective laws, both sources must be consulted before concluding a legal requirement is not applicable to a specific situation. Special rules apply to certain occupations, such as salespersons, and to special situations such as family owned businesses that employ family members.

The definition of "employee" often involves a legal determination. For this reason, particularly in unclear cases, it is important to consult an attorney before concluding an individual is not an employee.

INDEPENDENT CONTRACTORS

Many companies engage independent contractors, rather than employees, to fill temporary and sometimes permanent staffing needs. Such an arrangement is often beneficial for both companies and workers. Companies avoid paying certain taxes applicable to employees and are able to pay their workers by the project, without overtime pay. Workers gain flexibility that might not be available as an employee. In determining whether a worker is an employee or an independent contractor, companies often use the IRS "right to control" standard.

Different statutes apply varying tests to determine whether a worker is an employee or an independent contractor. While the IRS applies "right to control" test, many other statutes, such as FLSA, apply a more employee-favorable standard such as "economic dependence" or "economic realities" test. In other words, even if the worker is not controlled by the company a worker may still be an employee if they are in fact economically dependent on the work just like an employee. The U.S. Department of Labor (DOL) takes the position that "most workers are employees under the FSLA's broad definitions," and explains that under the FLSA's very broad definition of employment, to employ means "to suffer or permit to work." For wage and hour purposes, the DOL looks to six factors in determining the nature of a working relationship: (1) Is the work an integral part of the employer's business? (If yes, employee status is indicated), (2) Does the worker's managerial skill affect the worker's opportunity for profit or loss? (If no, employee status is indicated), (3) How does the worker's relative investment in his or her business compare to the employer's investment? (If the worker's investment is minimal compared to the employer's investment, employee status is indicated), (4) Does the work performed require special skill and initiative? (If no, employee status is indicated), (5) Is the relationship between the worker and the employer permanent or indefinite? (If yes, employee status is indicated), and (6) What is the nature and degree of the employer's control over the worker? (If control is asserted by the employer, employee status is indicated.)

There are other factors which are immaterial in determining the existence of an employment relationship. For example, the fact the worker has signed an agreement stating that he or she is an independent contractor is not controlling because the reality of the working relationship - and not the label given to the relationship agreement - is determinitive. Likewise, the fact that the worker has incorporated a business and/or is licensed by a State/local government agency has little bearing on determining the existence of an employment relationship. Additionally, the Supreme Court has held that employee status is not determined by the time or mode of pay.

The DOL has explained that the misclassification of workers as independent contractors has been increasing. To combat this problem, the DOL has entered into a cooperation agreement with the IRS and the State of Minnesota. The cooperation agreement allows both the DOL and the IRS to share information when they determine misclassification has occurred. For employers this means that it is easier to get caught, more difficult to prove contractor status and there are substantially more penalties for misclassification.

Editor's note: The Wage and Hour Division of the U.S. Department of Labor has issued a proposed rule that would clarify employee and independent contractor status under the Fair Labor Standards Act (FLSA).

The proposed rule:

- Adopts an "economic reality" test to determine a worker's status as an FLSA employee or an independent contractor. The test considers whether a worker is in business for himself or herself (independent contractor) or is economically dependent on a putative employer for work (employee);

- Identifies and explains two "core factors," specifically the nature and degree of the worker's control over the work, and the worker's opportunity for profit or loss based on initiative and/or investment. These factors help determine if a worker is economically dependent on someone else's businesses or is in a business for himself or herself;

- Identifies three other factors that may serve as additional guideposts in the analysis: the amount of skill required or the work; the degree of permanence of the working relationship between the worker ad the potential employer; and whether the work is part of an integrated unit of production; and

- Advises that the actual practice is more relevant than what may be contractually or theoretically possible in determining whether a worker is an employee or an independent contractor.

The notice of proposed rulemaking can be found in the Federal Register/Vol 85, No. 187/Friday, September 25, 2020/Proposed Rules.

INDEPENDENT CONTRACTORS IN THE CONSTRUCTION INDUSTRY

An individual who performs public or private sector commercial or residential building construction or improvement services in Minnesota is an independent contractor if he or she:

1. maintains a separate business with the individual's own office, equipment, materials, and other facilities;
2. holds or has applied for a federal employer identification number or has filed business self-employment income tax returns with the federal Internal Revenue Service if the individual has performed services in the previous year;
3. is operating under contract to perform specific services for the person for specific amounts of money and under which the individual controls the means of performing the services;
4. is incurring the main expenses related to the services that the individual is performing for the person under the contract;
5. is responsible for the satisfactory completion of the services that the individual has contracted to perform for the person and is liable for a failure to complete the services;
6. receives compensation from the person for the services performed under the contract on a commission or per-job or competitive bid basis and not on any other basis;
7. may realize a profit or suffer a loss under the contract to perform services for the person;
8. has continuing or recurring business liabilities or obligations; and
9. the success or failure of the individual's business depends on the relationship of business receipts to expenditures.

In addition to compliance with this nine-factor test, business entities and their owners and officers are required to conduct business appropriately including active filing with the Secretary of State, if required; invoices are submitted in the name of the business entity, not individuals and payments are made to the business entity, not individuals.

Penalties may be assessed for failure to register with the Minnesota Department of Labor and Industry, hiring unregistered contractors, misclassifying workers or coercing others to form a business entity. Additional information is available at Independent Contractor Registration, http://www.dli.mn.gov/business/independent-contractor-registration.

INDEPENDENT CONTRACTORS IN THE TRUCKING AND MESSENGER/COURIER INDUSTRIES

Minn. Stat. § 176.043, lays out the criteria for when an operator in the trucking and messenger/courier industry is considered an employee or an independent contractor. There are seven factors that must all be present for a worker to be considered an independent contractor. Some of the factors include when the individual:

- owns the equipment or holds it under a bona fide lease agreement;
- is responsible for the equipment's maintenance;
- is responsible for the operating costs;

- is responsible for supplying the necessary personal services to operate the equipment;
- substantially controls the means and manner of the service performance; and
- enters into a written contract specifying that the relationship is one of an independent contractor and not that of an employee.

FURTHER INFORMATION

In addition to consulting a professional advisor, more detailed information on "Who is an Employee" for various purposes may be obtained from the following sources and at the addresses and telephone numbers listed in the Resource Directory section of this Guide. See also the section of this Guide titled "Checklist for Hiring an Employee."

- **Federal income, withholding and FICA (Social Security and Medicare) tax:** *Publication 15 (Circular E) Employer's Tax Guide* (https://www.irs.gov/forms-pubs/about-publication-15); *Publication 15-A, Employer's Supplemental Tax Guide (Supplement to Circular E, Employer's Tax Guide, Publication 15-A)* (https://www.irs.gov/forms-pubs/about-publication-15-a); and *Publication 1779, Employee or Independent Contractor* (https://www.irs.gov/pub/irs-pdf/p1779.pdf). The IRS also offers "Small Business Taxes: The Virtual Workshop", an online resource for business owners who are not sure if they have employees or independent contractors. See https://www.irsvideos.gov/SmallBusinessTaxpayer/virtualworkshop. Also refer to *Independent Contractor (Self-Employed) or Employee*? (https://www.irs.gov/businesses/small-businesses-self-employed/independent-contractor-self-employed-or-employee).

- **Minnesota income tax:** *Minnesota Income Tax Withholding Instruction Booklet & Tax Tables* (https://www.revenue.state.mn.us/sites/default/files/2019-12/wh_inst_20_0.pdf)available at Find a Form (https://www.revenue.state.mn.us/form-search?search_text=&field_document_type=All&field_audience=436&field_tax_type=All&field_tax_year=All).

  Also refer to the Minnesota Department of Revenue *Independent Contractor or Employee - Withholding Fact Sheet 8* (https://www.revenue.state.mn.us/sites/default/files/2020-01/FactSheet08.pdf). This fact sheet explains Minnesota income tax withholding responsibilities as they relate to classification of independent contractors.

- **Workers' Compensation:** Information on the Minnesota Worker's Compensation System is available from the Minnesota Department of Labor and Industry at Workers' Compensation - Businesses, http://www.dli.mn.gov/business/workers-compensation-businesses. The Department has adopted rules addressing the conditions under which workers will be considered employees or independent contractors for workers' compensation purposes. These rules can be found at Minnesota Rules Chapter 5224. Minnesota Rules is available on the Office of the Revisor of Statutes website at https://www.revisor.mn.gov/rules/, at law libraries, and many public libraries. The Department has information regarding *Contractor Registration - Nine-Factor Test* at http://www.dli.mn.gov/business/independent-contractor/contractor-registration-nine-factor-test.

- **Federal Fair Labor Standards Act:** U.S. Department of Labor, Wage and Hour Division *Fact Sheet #13, Employment Relationship Under the Fair Labor Standards Act (FLSA)* at, https://www.dol.gov/whd/regs/compliance/whdfs13.htm.

- **Minnesota Fair Labor Standards Act:** Minnesota Department of Labor and Industry, Labor Standards Division.

- **Human Rights:** Minnesota Department of Human Rights.

EMPLOYMENT AGREEMENTS

EMPLOYMENT AT WILL

The doctrine of employment at will generally states that an employment relationship may be terminated at any time by either party. In the absence of a collective bargaining agreement or other contract, the employer may discharge an employee at any time for any legal reason, or for no reason, with or without notice. Likewise, the employee may resign at any time for any reason, with or without notice. Minnesota follows this general rule.

The employment at will relationship can be contrasted with a contractual relationship, in which the rights and duties of the parties are governed by specific contractual provisions. The courts in recent years have identified several situations in which an employment at will relationship is changed to a contractual relationship, or where for public policy reasons the employment at will rule will be disregarded. These situations are discussed in the section on Employment Contracts, ahead.

EMPLOYMENT CONTRACTS

Employment contracts may be written or oral. Employment contracts may be provided to employees who would not otherwise accept employment without the security of a contract, or in cases where the employer wishes to secure certain protections, such as the protection of confidential information or trade secrets. Employment contracts typically set forth the term or length of employment, compensation and benefits, job duties, and circumstances for termination. Some contracts also may include provisions relating to confidentiality, assignment of intellectual property rights like patents or copyrights, and non-compete agreements.

In recent years, Minnesota courts have used contract-based theories to carve out exceptions to the employment at will doctrine for public policy reasons. For example, the courts have found a contract to exist where the employee provides something of value, in addition to performing the job, in exchange for a promise of continued employment. A contract also has been found where the employee, in reliance on an offer of employment, gave up another job to accept employment. Most recently, Minnesota courts have determined that statements in a personnel handbook may create an enforceable contract if the terms are sufficiently definite, are communicated to the employee, and the employee accepts the terms and provides value by continuing to work. Implied contracts may be found to exist in other situations.

In cases where employees are represented by a union, the employer and the collective bargaining agent negotiate a contract which governs the relationship of the parties throughout its term.

PROTECTION OF CONFIDENTIAL INFORMATION

Minnesota law protects employers' confidential information and trade secrets in several ways. First, an employee has a generally recognized duty of loyalty to not disclose trade secrets or proprietary information of the employer. Second, the statutory Uniform Trade Secrets Act, adopted by Minnesota, prohibits misappropriation of trade secrets. And third, employers may require employees to execute nondisclosure agreements to prevent release of trade secrets or confidential information during or after their employment.

To be protected as a trade secret under the Uniform Trade Secrets Act, the information must not be generally known or readily ascertainable by the general public, it must provide economic value to the employer, and the employer must make reasonable efforts to maintain its secrecy.

Confidentiality agreements must be supported by "adequate consideration," i.e., the employee must be given something of value in exchange for the promise not to disclose the information. Examples of adequate consideration vary from case to case but might include the initial hiring of the employee in exchange for the agreement, promotions, salary increases or cash payments. Continued employment, without more, generally is not recognized as adequate consideration to support a confidentiality agreement.

ASSIGNMENT OF PATENTS AND INVENTIONS

An employer may require an employee, as a condition of employment, to assign the employee's rights in certain inventions to the employer. Under state law, such an assignment must exclude inventions for which no equipment, supplies, facilities or trade secret information of the employer were used, and which were developed entirely on the employee's own time, and which do not relate directly to the employer's business or its actual or demonstrably anticipated research or development, or which do not result from any work performed by the employee for the employer.

LABOR STANDARDS

GENERAL INFORMATION

Wages, overtime pay and recordkeeping requirements are regulated at the federal level by the Fair Labor Standards Act, 29 USC § 201 *et seq.*; 29 CFR parts 510 to 794 and at the state level by the Minnesota Fair Labor Standards Act, Minn. Stat. Chapter 177. Each act specifies the employers and employees to which it applies, but where the Minnesota act and the federal act are different, the law providing more protection for the employee or setting the higher standard applies. The Fair Labor Standards Act (FLSA) is administered by the Wage and Hour Division (WHD) of the U.S. Department of Labor. Website, https://www.dol.gov/whd. The Minnesota Fair Labor Standards Act is administered by the Labor Standards Division of the Minnesota Department of Labor and Industry (DLI). Go to http://www.dli.mn.gov/laborlaw.

This section discusses provisions of the federal act and the Minnesota act pertaining to persons covered, minimum wage and overtime requirements, prevailing wage requirements, and wage records.

Before the implementation of federal regulations affecting the definition and compensation of executive, administrative, professional, computer and highly compensated outside sales employees, federal statutes and regulations set the higher standard for overtime compensation. Under current federal regulations, however, Minnesota Statutes and regulations may set the higher standard. In that situation employers who formerly were required to pay overtime under federal law may no longer be required to do so but will be required to pay overtime under Minnesota law.

Employers should familiarize themselves with the federal and state requirements for labor standards in general, and the new overtime standards in particular, by visiting the websites of the U.S. Department of Labor, https://www.dol.gov (Compliance Assistance information and assistance), and the Minnesota Department of Labor and Industry. Review the Minnesota Department of Labor and Industry Overtime Laws information at http://www.dli.mn.gov/business/employment-practices/overtime-laws. Additional addresses and telephone numbers for direct contact with the U.S. Department of Labor and the Minnesota Department of Labor and Industry are provided in the Resource Directory section of this Guide.

Employers should still assume that they are covered by the federal act unless they are told otherwise by legal counsel.

PERSONS COVERED

Federal Act

The federal act covers all workers employed by: 1) hospitals and residential care facilities; 2) public or private preschools, elementary or secondary schools, and institutions of higher education; 3) enterprises with annual gross sales of $500,000, or more, whose workers are engaged in interstate commerce, produce goods for interstate commerce, or handle, sell, or otherwise work on goods or materials that have been moved in or produced for interstate commerce; and 4) public agencies.

Other employees will be covered by the federal act if they are individually engaged in interstate commerce, the production of goods for interstate commerce, or in any closely related process or occupation directly essential to such production. Such employees include those who: work in communication and transportation; handle, ship or receive goods moving in interstate commerce; regularly use the mails, telephone, fax, or email for interstate communication or who keep records on interstate transactions; regularly cross state lines in the course of their work; and perform clerical, custodial, maintenance or other work for firms engaged in interstate commerce or in the production of goods for interstate commerce. Due to the broad nature of this category, an employer that wishes to assert that its employees are not involved in interstate commerce should seek the advice of counsel.

Exceptions to the federal act are discussed in the section on "Federal Act Exemptions" that follows.

The federal Fair Labor Standards Act (and other federal employment laws, such as the Occupational Safety and Health Act, unemployment insurance, and anti-discrimination laws) apply to working welfare recipients in the same manner as it applies to other workers. The welfare law does not exempt welfare recipients from these laws. Welfare recipients would probably be considered covered employees in many, if not most, of the work activities under the welfare law, and in "workfare" arrangements. Exceptions are most likely to include individuals engaged in activities such as vocational education, job search assistance, and secondary school attendance, because these programs are not ordinarily considered employment under the federal act.

Further information on the federal act may be obtained by contacting the U.S. Department of Labor, Wage and Hour Division at the local address and telephone number provided in the Resource Directory section of this Guide. If you have a question about the federal act and welfare recipients, a Wage and Hour publication entitled "How Workplace Laws Apply to Welfare Recipients" is available through the Wage and Hour Division, and can be found in the compliance information section of the Wage and Hour Division website.

Minnesota Act

The Minnesota act generally applies to all employers and employees in Minnesota who are not covered by the federal act. Also, the Minnesota Act will apply to employers and employees subject to the federal act when the Minnesota Act would provide more protection to the employee or would set a higher standard. Exceptions to the Minnesota act are discussed in the section on "Minnesota Act Exemptions" below.

EXEMPTIONS

Minimum Wage for Federal Contractors

As required by Executive Order 13658, the U.S. DOL publishes wage rates for employees of federal contractors and subcontractors. At the time this Guide west to press, 2021 inflation adjusted rates were not available.

Effective January 1, 2020, the minimum wage required for employees of covered federal contractors and subcontractors is $10.80 per hour.

Beginning January 2020, the required minimum cash wage that generally must be paid to tipped employees performing work on or in connection to covered contracts is $7.55 per hour.

Federal Act Exemptions. The federal act exempts some employees from federal minimum wage or overtime requirements, or both. These exemptions are carefully defined and applied on a workweek by workweek basis. A business that wishes to pay a worker as an exempt employee should carefully check the exact requirements to make sure the exemption is applicable. The fact that an employee is paid a salary or commission rather than an hourly wage does not by itself determine that an employee is exempt from overtime or minimum wage requirements. A job title is also insufficient for determining exempt or non-exempt status. All of the specific requirements for the exemption must be met in order for the employee to be classified as exempt.

Exemptions from Federal Minimum Wage and Overtime Requirements. In general, the following are exempt from both the minimum wage and overtime requirements of the federal act: executive, administrative and professional employees and outside sales persons, employees in certain computer related occupations, employees of certain seasonal or recreational establishments, employees engaged in fishing operations, and farm workers employed by anyone who used no more than 500 work-days of farm labor in any calendar quarter of the preceding calendar year. Casual baby-sitters, and persons employed as companions to the elderly or infirm in a private residence may also be exempt from the minimum wage and overtime requirements.

Exemptions from Federal Overtime Pay Requirements Only. Most exempt employees fall into one of four classifications: executive, administrative, professional, or outside salesperson.

To qualify as an exempt executive, administrative or professional employee, an employee generally must meet certain tests regarding his or her job duties and be paid on a salary or fee basis at not less than $455 per week. Up to 10 percent of the salary threshold for non-highly compensated employees can be satisfied by non-discretionary bonuses, incentive pay or commissions-basis payments that must be made on at least a quarterly basis. The salary threshold will automatically update every three years.

Executive Exemption

To qualify for the executive employee exemption, all of the following tests must be met:

- The employee must be compensated on a salary basis (as defined in the regulations) at a rate not less than $970 per week;
- The employee's primary duty must be managing the enterprise, or managing a customarily recognized department or subdivision of the enterprise;
- The employee must customarily and regularly direct the work of at least two or more other full-time employees or their equivalent;
- The employee must have the authority to hire or fire other employees, or the employee's suggestions and recommendations as to the hiring, firing, advancement, promotion or any other change of status of other employees must be given particular weight; and
- Business owners (those with at least a 20 percent ownership) who are "actively engaged in its management" are also considered exempt employees without regard to the salary threshold.

Administrative Exemption

To qualify for the administrative employee exemption, all of the following tests must be met:

- The employee must be compensated on a salary or fee basis (as defined in the regulations) at a rate not less than $970 per week;
- The employee's primary duty must be the performance of office or non-manual work directly related to the management or general business operations of the employer or the employer's customers; and
- The employee's primary duty includes the exercise of discretion and independent judgment with respect to matters of significance.

Professional Exemption

To qualify for the learned professional exemption, all of the following tests must be met:

- The employee must be compensated on a salary or fee basis (as defined in the regulations) at a rate not less than $970 per week;
- The employee's primary duty must be the performance of work requiring advanced knowledge, defined as work which is predominantly intellectual in character and which includes work requiring the consistent exercise of discretion and judgment;

- The advanced knowledge must be in a field of science or learning; and
- The advanced knowledge must be customarily acquired by a prolonged course of specialized intellectual instruction.

Computer Employee Exemption

To qualify for the computer employee exemption, the following tests must be met:

- The employee must be compensated either on a salary or fee basis (as defined in the regulations) at a rate not less than $970 per week;
- The employee must be employed as a computer systems analyst, computer programmer, software engineer or other similarly skilled worker in the computer field performing the duties described below;
- The employee's primary duty must consist of:
    1) The application of systems analysis techniques and procedures, including consulting with users, to determine hardware, software or system functional specifications;
    2) The design, development, documentation, analysis, creation, testing or modification of computer systems or programs, including prototypes, based on and related to user or system design specifications;
    3) The design, documentation, testing, creation or modification of computer programs related to machine operating systems; or
    4) A combination of the aforementioned duties, the performance of which requires the same level of skill.

Outside Sales Exemption

To qualify for the outside sales employee exemption, all of the following tests must be met:

- The employee's primary duty must be making sales (as defined in the FLSA), or obtain orders or contracts for services or for the use of facilities for which a consideration will be paid by the client or customer; and
- The employee must be customarily and regularly engaged away from the employer's place or places of business.

Highly Compensated Employees

Highly compensated employees performing office or non-manual work and paid total annual compensation of $134,004 or more are exempt from the FLSA if they customarily and regularly perform at least one of the duties of an exempt executive, administrative or professional employee identified in the standard tests for exemption.

Blue Collar Workers

The exemptions provided by FLSA Section 13(a)(1) apply only to "white collar" employees who meet the salary and duties tests set forth in the Part 541 regulations. The exemptions do not apply to manual laborers or other "blue collar" workers who perform work involving repetitive operations with their hands, physical skill and energy. FLSA-covered, non-management employees in production, maintenance, construction and similar occupations such as carpenters, electricians, mechanics, plumbers, iron workers, craftsmen, operating engineers, longshoremen, construction workers and laborers are entitled to minimum wage and overtime premium pay under the FLSA, and are not exempt under the Part 541 regulations no matter how highly paid they might be.

Police, Fire Fighters, Paramedics & Other First Responders

The exemptions also do not apply to police officers, detectives, deputy sheriffs, state troopers, highway patrol officers, investigators, inspectors, correctional officers, parole or probation officers, park rangers, fire fighters, paramedics, emergency medical technicians, ambulance personnel, rescue workers, hazardous materials workers and similar employees, regardless of rank or pay level, who perform work such as preventing, controlling or extinguishing fires of any type; rescuing fire, crime or accident victims; preventing or detecting crimes; conducting investigations or inspections for violations of law; performing surveillance; pursuing, restraining and apprehending suspects; detaining or supervising suspected and convicted criminals, including those on probation or parole; interviewing witnesses; interrogating and fingerprinting suspects; preparing investigative reports; or other similar work.

Other Laws & Collective Bargaining Agreements

The FLSA provides minimum standards that may be exceeded, but cannot be waived or reduced. Employers must comply, for example, with any Federal, State or municipal laws, regulations or ordinances establishing a higher minimum wage or lower maximum workweek than those established under the FLSA. Similarly, employers may, on their own initiative or under a collective bargaining agreement, provide a higher wage, shorter workweek, or higher overtime premium than provided under the FLSA. While collective bargaining agreements cannot waive or reduce FLSA protections, nothing in the FLSA or the Part 541 regulation relieves employers from their contractual obligations under such bargaining agreements.

Minnesota Act Exemptions

Like the federal act, the Minnesota act exempts certain workers from its coverage. A business that wishes to rely on any of the exemptions should check the law carefully to be sure that the exemption is applicable to the firm's situation.

Exemptions from Minnesota Minimum Wage and Overtime Requirements. The Minnesota act covers all employees of an employer unless there is a specific statutory exemption. The following are some of the more common exemptions for for-profit employers.

- Individuals employed in a *bona fide* executive, administrative, or professional capacity, or a sales person who conducts no more than 20 percent of sales on the premises of the employer.

This exemption is discussed more fully under "Exemptions from Minnesota Overtime Pay Provisions" below.

- Taxicab drivers.
- Individual babysitters.
- Retail or service employees paid on a commission basis if the regular rate of pay exceeds one-and-one half times the minimum wage.
- Some salaried farm employees and farm employees under age 18 except corn detasselers and hand field workers when one or both of the minor's parents or physical custodians also are hand field workers. (Corn detasselers under age 18 are exempt from the state minimum wage provision, but must be paid for overtime.)

Other exemptions apply to certain employees of governmental units, nonprofit organizations and religious groups. Information on these exemptions may be obtained from the Labor Standards Division of the Department of Labor and Industry.

Exemptions from Minnesota Overtime Pay Requirements. The requirement for employers to pay employees premium pay for overtime is determined by whether the worker is an exempt or nonexempt employee. The fact that an employee is paid a salary or commission rather than an hourly wage does not by itself determine whether overtime pay is required. The specific requirements of the law must be met. Four types of workers are exempt from overtime pay requirements. They are: executive, administrative, professional, and outside sales workers.

- **Executive:** An employee who is paid no less than $250 a week in salary may qualify for exemption from overtime if: (1) the work consists mainly of the management of the business or management of a department or some other division of the company, and (2) if the employee regularly supervises and directs the work of at least two employees in the department or division (working foremen do not qualify.)
- **Administrative:** An employee who is paid no less than $250 a week in salary may qualify for exemption from overtime if: (1) the work performed is office or non-manual work directly involved in management policy or the general operations of the company or its customers, and (2) if the work calls for use of discretion and independent judgment. An employee must have enough authority to make policy decisions.
- **Professional:** An employee who is paid no less than $250 a week in salary may qualify as an exempt employee if: (1) the majority of the work is in performance of tasks which assume a knowledge in an advanced field of learning, teaching or science, with consistent use of discretion and judgment; or (2) if the work performed is in a field of artistic endeavor, such as invention or use of imagination or talent. Generally, an advanced degree is a requirement of the job.
- **Outside Sales Worker:** This person is hired for, and is usually away from the place of business for, the purpose of making service calls or obtaining orders and contracts for products or services provided by the employer. The working hours require spending at least 80 percent of the workweek outside the employer's premises. In addition the outside work may not be conducted at any one fixed place, even if not owned by the employer.

Employees earning less than the amounts specified in each category above may still qualify as exempt, but they must fulfill work requirements more detailed than indicated above.

Other employees subject to the Minnesota act but exempt from overtime requirements are:

- Seasonal employees of a carnival, circus, fair, or ski resort.
- Construction workers of on-farm silos or installers of appurtenant equipment who are paid on a unit or piece rate.
- Salesperson, parts person, or mechanic paid on a commission or incentive basis if employed by a non-manufacturing establishment primarily engaged in selling automobiles, trailers, trucks or farm implements to ultimate purchasers.
- Employees of a retail or service establishment if the regular rate of pay is in excess of one and one half times the minimum wage and more than half the compensation represents commissions on goods or services.

MINIMUM WAGE REQUIREMENTS

Federal Minimum Wage Requirements

The federal minimum wage to be paid by covered employers is $7.25 an hour. These employers include businesses that produce or handle goods for interstate commerce; businesses with annual dollar volume of business of $500,000 or more; and certain other businesses, including hospitals and nursing homes, private and public schools, and federal, state and local government agencies.

Minnesota Minimum Wage Requirements

Minimum wage applies only to "non-exempt" employees. "Non-exempt" employees are those employees who do not fall within one of the law's narrow "exempt" categories (e.g. executives, professionals, certain limited administrative employees, outside sales employees, etc. discussed at the end of this section). In practical terms, "non-exempt" is the default classification that applies to the majority of employees. All "non-exempt" employees must receive no less than the applicable minimum wage for each hour worked, keep a written record of all time worked, and receive overtime pay (time and one half) for all hours worked over the applicable number (40 hours under federal wage law; 48 hours under Minnesota wage law) in a workweek (the company's designated 7-day work period).

When both the federal and state wage laws apply and their minimum wages differ, an employer must pay its non-exempt employees the higher applicable minimum wage for each regular hour worked.

Minnesota's minimum wage rates will be adjusted for inflation on January 1, 2021, to $10.08 an hour for large employers and $8.21 an hour for other state minimum wages.

The current large employer minimum wage$ 10.00, will increase by eight cents to $10.08. Other state minimum wages, including the small employer, youth an training wages, as well as the summer work travel exchange visitor program wage, which are all currently $8.15, will increase by six cents to $8.21. These state minimum wage rates will not apply to work performed in the cities of Minneapolis and St. Paul, which have higher minimum wage rates.

Prohibition of Displacement: The new law prohibits employers from displacing other employees to take advantage of the lower minimum wage rates for employees under the age of 18, employees under the age of 20, or employees who qualify for the summer work travel exception. This prohibition includes total displacement of employees as well as partial displacement through a reduction in hours, wages, or employment benefits.

In cases where an employee is subject to both the state and federal minimum wage laws, the employee is entitled to the higher of the two minimum wages.

Minimum wage rates apply to all hours work, whether part time or full time. Employers are required to pay for all hours worked including waiting time, call time, training time and any other time the employee is restricted to the premises of the employer.

Cities may push their minimum wage base higher than state minimums. Minneapolis has approved a municipal ordinance that requires large employers to pay Minneapolis employees $15 an hour in five years and gives small employers seven years to reach that target wage. There is a tiered phase-in period (starting January 1, 2018) for small and large businesses. Large businesses are defined as having more than 100 employees and small businesses as 100 or fewer employees. The minimum wage will be targeted to inflation after the $15 an hour is reached. There is no exception for tipped employees - all employees are subject to the minimum wage. Contact the City of Minneapolis for additional information. The July 1, 2021 rate for businesses with 100 or fewer employees is $12.50 an hour and for businesses with more than 100 employees, the minimum wage is $14.25 per hour.

Updating Wage Postings

Employers are required to post a current notice of the applicable federal minimum wage rates and related obligations. Failure to post an updated notice may result in fines of up to $10,000. Updated posters may be downloaded free of charge from the U.S. Department of Labor. View these links: Workplace Posters - https://www.dol.gov/general/topics/posters/; elaws FirstStep Poster Advisor - https://webapps.dol.gov/elaws/posters.html; and Wage and Hour Division (WHD) - Workplace Posters - https://www.dol.gov/whd/resources/posters.htm.

Wages Using Payroll Card Accounts

Employers are allowed to pay employee wages via payroll card accounts. Employers are not required to use payroll card accounts, even if requested by employees.

Payroll debit cards allow an employee's net pay to be applied to a payroll account. The employee can then use the card to make purchases and withdraw cash at ATMs. Payroll accounts allow wages to be electronically transferred, eliminating the need for check cashing charges.

Before using payroll card accounts, employers first must file the required Minnesota Department of Labor and Industry's registration form found at http://www.dli.mn.gov/business/employment-practices/payroll-cards-minnesota. In addition before using payroll card accounts, an employer must provide employees written disclosure, in plain language, of all the employee's wage payment options. The disclosure must also include certain information, such as fees that would apply.

Use of a payroll card account cannot be a condition of hire or of continued employment, and employers may use the accounts only for those employees who voluntarily consent in writing on the disclosure form. The employer must retain the signed disclosure and provide a copy to the employee.

Employers must not charge employees any initiation, participation, loading or other fees to receive their wages via payroll card accounts, and payroll card issuers must not impose inactivity or dormancy fees. Also, any allowable fees imposed by the employer or the payroll card issuer that were not disclosed to the employee at the time of providing written consent may not be deducted or charged.

The law requires that an employee must be able to withdraw, by a free transaction, wages transferred to the account on the employee's regular payday. Employers are required to provide employees, upon request, one free transaction history each month.

The linking of payroll cards and accounts with credit, including loans against future pay and cash advances, is prohibited. Employers are also prohibited from using personal information generated by an employee's use or possession of the card or account for any purpose other than processing transactions and administering the account.

Employers may continue to pay employees via cash, paycheck and direct deposit. Employees may opt out of direct deposit by written objection to the employer. Employer's must give employees wishing to switch from payroll card accounts to another payment method a written form on which to indicate the change; the employer has 14 days to implement the new requested method.

OVERTIME PAY REQUIREMENTS

Federal Overtime Pay Requirements

The Federal act requires that covered non-exempt employees receive overtime pay at a rate of one and one-half times their regular rate of pay after 40 hours of work in a workweek. Exemptions from the federal overtime pay requirements are addressed above.

A workweek is a period of 168 hours during seven consecutive 24-hour periods. It may begin on any day of the week and any hour of the day established by the employer, but the established workweek must remain consistent. For purposes of computing overtime pay, each workweek stands alone; there can be no averaging of two or more workweeks (except for hospital or nursing home employees on an "8 and 80").

Overtime pay must be based on the regular rate. Generally, the regular rate includes all payments made by the employer to or on behalf of the employee (i.e., non-discretionary bonuses, incentive pay, shift differentials), although some statutory exceptions may apply. To calculate the regular rate, divide all pay received by all hours worked in the work week.

Overtime compensation must be paid in cash wages. There is an exception for public sector employees who can accrue hours worked over 40 as compensatory time to be paid out at a rate of time and one-half, in lieu of cash wages.

Minnesota Overtime Pay Requirements (Minn. Stat. § 177.25)

As a general rule, employers covered by the Minnesota act are required to pay nonexempt employees time and a half for all time worked in excess of 48 hours in one workweek. Each workweek stands by itself. The employer may not average the worker's hours over the two weeks. A special overtime law, Minn. Stat. § 177.25, subd. 2, applies to hospitals and the health care field.

Exemptions from the Minnesota overtime pay requirements are addressed earlier in this section. An exception to the 48 hour rule for payment of overtime appears at Minn. Stats. §§ 177.41 to 177.44. This statute, the Minnesota Prevailing Wage Law, requires that employees who work on state-funded construction projects be paid time-and-one-half for all time worked in excess of eight hours per day and 40 hours per week.

Premium pay need not be made for a period when no work is performed, such as sick days, holidays, and vacations. Overtime applies only after 48 hours of actual work, not hours paid.

PREVAILING WAGE LAWS

Both the federal government and the State of Minnesota by law require contractors who are awarded government funds for public works projects to pay their employees the prevailing wage for the locality in which the project is located. The Minnesota Legislature extended the provisions of its prevailing wage law to recipients of state funds for certain economic development projects.

The law applies to three forms of state financial assistance:

- Economic development grants where a single business receives $200,000 or more of the grant proceeds;
- Loans made by a state agency for economic development purposes where the loan recipient receives $500,000 or more of the loan proceeds, and
- Sales tax reductions or abatements made for economic development purposes in certain geographic areas.

Economic development is defined as financial assistance provided to a person directly or to a local unit of government or nonprofit organization on behalf of a person who is engaged in the manufacture or sale of goods and services, except for financial assistance provided for certain housing projects.

The law requires the person receiving or benefiting from the financial assistance, as a condition of receiving the assistance, to certify to the Commissioner of Labor and Industry that laborers and mechanics assigned to the project will be paid the prevailing wage rate for the area. The prevailing wage rate is determined periodically by the Department of Labor and Industry.

The federal government enforces the Davis-Bacon and related acts, which require the payment of prevailing wage rates and fringe benefits on federally-financed or assisted construction, and the Service Contract Act, which requires the payment of prevailing wage rates and fringe benefits on contracts to provide services to the federal government.

The prevailing wage rate is defined as the hourly basic rate of pay plus the employer's contribution for health and welfare, vacation, pension, and other economic benefits paid to the largest number of workers engaged in the same class of labor in the area. Area is defined as the county or other locality from which labor for any project normally is secured.

Current prevailing wage rates are available on the website of the Minnesota Department of Labor and Industry at http://www.dli.mn.gov/business/employment-practices/prevailing-wage-information.

RECORDKEEPING REQUIREMENTS

Federal Recordkeeping Requirements

Federal employer recordkeeping requirements are specified by regulation of the U.S. Department of Labor. Most of the information is of the kind generally maintained by employers in ordinary business practice and in compliance with other laws and regulations. The records do not have to be kept in any particular form and time clocks need not be used. The following records must be kept on all employees subject to the minimum wage and overtime provisions of the federal act.

The following is a listing of the basic records that an employer must maintain.

- Employee's full name and Social Security number.
- Address, including zip code.
- Birth date, if younger than 19.
- Sex and occupation.
- Time and day of week when employee's workweek begins.
- Hours worked each day.
- Total hours worked each workweek.
- Basis on which employee's wages are paid (e.g., "$6 an hour", "$220 a week", "piecework").
- Regular hourly pay rate.
- Total daily or weekly straight-time earnings.
- Total overtime earnings for the workweek.
- All additions to or deductions from the employee's wages.
- Total wages paid each pay period;
- Date of payment and the pay period covered by the payment.

Records required for exempt employees differ from those for nonexempt workers and special information is required on employees working under uncommon pay arrangements or to whom lodging or other facilities are furnished. Firms that employ industrial home workers must keep records in handbooks supplied by the U.S. Department of Labor.

In addition to the recordkeeping requirements imposed for records relating to employee compensation, a number of federal statutes impose record retention requirements on documents associated with employee recruitment and selection. These records include job postings and advertisements, test papers, interview records, lists of applicants, applicant resumes, ranking and valuative criteria and other records. Requirements range from six months to five-year retention. Each year a comprehensive update of federal record retention requirements is published in the *Federal Register.* A business or government reference librarian can direct employers to the latest compilation.

Minnesota Recordkeeping Requirements (Minn. Stat. § 177.30).

Employers must maintain records for three years. In 2019 Minnesota's record keeping requirements were amended (1Sp 2019 c7 art 3 s5), and the new law requires that the records be kept where the employees are working or in a place where records may be accessible and deliverable to the Minnesota Department of Labor and Industry within 72 hours of request.

The following records must be kept by an employer for the three year period:

- Each employee's name, address and occupation;
- Each employee's rate of pay and the gross and net amount paid in each pay period;
- Each employee's hours worked each day and each workweek, including, for all employees paid at a piece rate, the number of pieces completed at each piece rate;
- A list of personnel policies with brief descriptions of each policy that were provided to each employee, including the date the policies were given to the employee;
- A copy of the notice to and signed by each employee and a copy of any written changes to the notice that were provided to each employee;
- For each employer subject to the Minnesota Prevailing Wage Act, for public works projects funded in whole or in part with state funds, employers must furnish a certified payroll report every two week signed under oath by an owner or officer of the employer stating the wages and benefits paid each employee during the preceding weeks, and specifying for each employee:
    - Name
    - Identifying number
    - Prevailing wage master job classification
    - Hours worked each day
    - Rate of pay
    - Gross amount earned
    - Each deduction for taxes
    - Total deductions for taxes
    - Net pay for the week

- o Dollars contributed per hour for each benefit, including names and addresses of administrator
- o Benefit account number
- o Telephone number for health and welfare, vacation or holiday, apprenticeship training, pension or other benefit programs

- Any other information the commissioner finds necessary and appropriate to enforce the prevailing wage.

Timing for Making Wage Payments (Minn. Stat. § 181.101). The law specifies that employers must pay all wages (salary, earnings and gratuities) to employees at least once every 31 days. All commissions earned must be paid at least once every three months on a regular payday.

The new law allows the commissioner to require an employer to pay wages or commissions owed to an employee, pay owed wages or commissions as liquidated damages, pay compensatory damages incurred by an employee, and pay civil penalties for repeated or willful violations (Minn. Stat. § 177.27, subd 2).

The commissioner may impose penalties of up to $5,000 for each repeated failure to submit or deliver records required by law and for each repeated failure to keep and maintain the required records. For each day that wages are not paid to an employee in accordance with the commissioner's order, the commissioner may penalize the employer with the average amount of daily wages for that employee or an amount equal to 1/15th of the commissions earned by the employee.

Criminal Wage Theft. (Minn. Stat. § 609.52). The new law defines "wage theft" as not paying an employee the agreed upon wage, earning, or commissions, directly or indirectly causing an employee to give a receipt for an amount more than was paid, directly or indirectly demanding or receiving a rebate or refund for money that was not due, or where the employer attempts to show greater payment to an employee than was actually paid.

The punishment for criminal wage theft varies greatly. Penalties range from up to $100,000 in fines and no more than 20 years in prison, to no more than one year in prison and a $3,000 fine, depending on the amount at issue. When determining damages, the law allows the wages to be aggregated for up to six months.

Retaliation (Minn. Stat. § 181.03). The new law has non-retaliation protections. An employer who retaliates against employees for asserting rights or remedies under Minnesota's wage and hour laws may be fined $700 - $3,000 for each violation.

Retainage (Minn. Stats. §§ 15.72 and 337.10). Changes to Minnesota laws affecting construction in 2019, the legislature incorporated changes to retainage requirements for both public and private projects in Minnesota. Contact the Minnesota Department of Labor and Industry for specific information.

ADDITIONAL MINNESOTA REQUIREMENTS

As referenced above, the Minnesota Legislature this past year amended existing state labor laws and created significant new notice and recordkeeping requirements, recognized "wage theft", and imposed serious civil and criminal penalties for violations. This applies to all companies and organizations with Minnesota-based employees. The new legislation also allows the Commissioner of the Minnesota Department of Labor and Industry (DLI) to enter the places of business of employers, during working hours, to investigate potential violations. The investigation authority includes the ability to collect various evidence or potential violations and to interview witnesses.

The purpose of this new law is to create greater transparency and clarity of payment calculations for employees, especially those who are overtime-eligible. With this new law, employers must provide employees with information regarding components of their compensation, overtime eligibility status, timing of wage payments, potential deductions from pay, and company contact information.

The Minnesota Department of Labor and Industry provides an excellent series of guidance documents, a question and answer page and sample notice forms businesses can use to comply with these changes. Employers should familiarize themselves with the requirements in full to ensure compliance. Minnesota Department of Labor and Industry resources can be found at (1) Wage Theft Legislation 2019 and Summaries (https://www.dli.mn.gov/business/employment-practices/wage-theft-legislation-2019-and-summaries), (2) Guidance for employers on Minnesota's new Wage Theft Law (https://www.dli.mn.gov/sites/default/files/pdf/wage_theft_summary_employers.pdf), (3) Wage Theft Q & A (https://www.dli.mn.gov/business/employment-practices/wage-theft-qa) and (4) For Employers: Summary of Minnesota's new Wage Theft Law (https://www.dli.mn.gov/sites/default/files/pdf/wage_theft_law_summary.pdf), (5) Employee Wage Notice Examples (https://www.dli.mn.gov/sites/default/files/pdf/employee_notice_form.pdf and https://www.dli.mn.gov/sites/default/files/doc/employee_notice_form.docx).

Information to be disclosed to new employees by employers (Minn. Stat. § 181.032) The new law requires all employers to provide each employee with a written notice at the start of their employment.

First, employers must provide (more) detailed information to employees ((Minn. Stat. § 181.032 (d)-(f).)) At the start of employment, Minnesota employers must now provide a written notice that includes the following:

- The rate or rates of pay and basis thereof, including whether the employee is paid by the hour, shift, day, week, salary, piece, commission, or other method, and the specific application of any additional rates;
- Allowances, if any, claimed pursuant to permitted meals and lodging;
- Paid vacation, sick time, or other paid time-off accruals and terms of use;
- The employee's employment status and whether the employee is exempt from minimum wage, overtime, and other provisions of chapter 177, and on what basis;
- A list of deductions that may be made from the employee's pay;
- The number of days in a pay period, the regularly scheduled pay day, and the pay day on which the employee will receive the first payment of wages earned;

- The legal name of the employer and the operating name of the employer if different from the legal name; the physical address of the employer's main office or principal place of business, and a mailing address if different; and
- The telephone number of the employer.

Employers are required to keep a copy of the signed notice for each employee. All employers must provide the notice in English, with text that informs employees that they may request the notice be provided to them in another language. The Minnesota Department of Labor and Industry will provide, in multiple languages, the text that must be included in the notice. If an employee requests the notice in another language, the employer must provide it. Employers are also required to provide employees in writing any changes to the information in the notice before the date the changes take place.

Earnings Statement Requirements. In addition to the notice an employee must receive and sign at the start of employment, the new law adds the following requirements to the specific information that must be included in the earnings statement provided to employees each pay period ((Minn. Stat. § 181.032 (d)):

- The employee's rate of pay and basis thereof, including whether the employee is paid by the hour, shift, day, week, salary, piece, commission, or other method, and the specific application of any additional rates;
- Allowances, if any claimed pursuant to permitted meals and lodging;
- Paid vacation, sick time, or other paid time-off accruals and terms of use;
- The employee's employment status and whether the employee is exempt from minimum wage, overtime, and other provisions of Chapter 177, and on what basis;
- A list of deductions that may be made from the employee's pay;
- The number of days in the pay period, the regularly scheduled pay day, and the pay day on which the employee will receive the first payment of wages earned;
- The legal name of the employer and the operating name of the employer if different from the legal name;
- The physical address of the employer's main office or principal place of business, and a mailing address if different; and
- The telephone number of the employer.

Deductions from Wages

In General. By Minnesota statute, employers may only deduct certain items from an employee's wages. The employee must authorize the deduction in writing. Deductions authorized by law include deductions for union dues, life insurance premiums, hospitalization and surgical insurance, group accident and health insurance, group term life insurance, group annuities, contributions to credit unions or a community chest fund, contributions to a local arts council, local science council or Minnesota benefit association, contributions to a federally or state registered political action committee, and contributions to an employee stock purchase plan or savings plan. Minn. Stat. § 181.06, Subd. 2.

Uniforms and Equipment. Minnesota law limits the deductions directly or indirectly that may be made for uniforms, equipment and consumable supplies used on the job, and travel expenses. No deductions may be made for these items if the deduction would reduce the employee's wages below minimum wage. Deductions for uniforms or equipment may not exceed $50, and when employment is terminated, the employer must reimburse the full amount deducted. The employer may require the employee to surrender items for which reimbursement is made, but may not hold the employee's last check for failure to return the items. Minn. Stat. § 177.24, subd. 4 and 5; Minn. Stat. § 181.79.

Lost or Damaged Property. An employer may not deduct from wages any amount for lost, stolen or damaged property, or recover any claimed amount owed by the employee to the employer, unless the employee voluntarily authorizes the employer in writing to make the deduction after the loss has occurred, or unless the employee is found liable by a court for the loss or indebtedness. There are specific statutory limits on the amount which may be deducted in each pay period.

Child Support or Spousal Maintenance and Medical Support Obligations. The Minnesota Department of Human Services is directed to have employers participate in a centralized work reporting system for child support enforcement purposes. Employers are required to report certain information on newly-hired employees, and on independent contractors, within fifteen days of hiring or engaging that person.

Employers also must ask all new employees whether they have court-ordered medical support or dependent health or dental insurance obligations that must be withheld from income, and the terms of any court order. If medical support must be withheld, the employer must do the appropriate withholding. If the employee is required to obtain dependent insurance the employer must tell the employee about the application process and enroll the employee and dependents in the plan. An employer who willfully fails to comply is liable for the health or dental expenses incurred by dependents during the time they were eligible to be enrolled. The law also requires a court to order the parent with the better health care insurance plan to provide it for the children, if the plan is paid for by the employer or union.

Garnishment of Wages. An employer may be required to garnish and pay over money an employee owes to third persons. Certain statutory requirements must be met, and there is a limit on the amount of wages that may be garnished. These requirements and limitations are provided in the garnishment notice. An employer is prohibited by law from retaliating against an employee due to garnishment. An employer may charge the employee $3 for each written response the employer must provide for purposes of administering the garnishment of wages.

Access to Personnel Records (Other Than Employee Assistance Records)

Employers who employ one or more employees must allow those workers to review their personnel records and to obtain a copy under certain circumstances.

A worker must request the right to review his or her personnel file in writing, and can only do so once in a six-month period. An employee who separates from service may review the file once a year for as long as the personnel record is maintained. After the employee makes the request, the employer must comply within seven working days if the personnel record is in Minnesota, and within 14 days if the record is outside the state.

The file must be made available for review during the employer's normal hours of operation, but need not be made available during the employee's working hours. For separated employees, this requirement is met if the employee is given a copy of the file. The employer may require that the review be done in the presence of the employer or the employer's designee. After the review and upon the employee's written request, the employer must provide a copy of the record to the employee. The employer may not charge a fee for the copy. A request to review the record may be denied if the employer determines it is not made in good faith.

The law specifies a procedure for removal or revision of information that is disputed by the employee. If the employer and employee cannot agree on removal of disputed information, the employee may submit a written statement of up to five pages specifically identifying the disputed information and explaining the employee's position. The employee's statement must be included along with the disputed information for as long as the information is maintained in the employee's personnel record. A copy of the employee's statement must be provided to any person who receives a copy of the disputed information.

Communication of information obtained through a review of the employee's personnel record cannot be the basis of a defamation action, unless the employer refuses to follow the dispute resolution procedure. The law specifies conditions under which a defamation action may be maintained.

The law specifically prohibits retaliation against an employee for asserting his or her rights under the law. An employee may bring a civil action against an employer for violation of the law. Generally, the employee may recover actual damages and costs. If the employer is found to have unlawfully retaliated against the employee, the employee also may recover back pay, reinstatement or other equitable relief, and reasonable attorney's fees. The Minnesota Department of Labor and Industry may also assess a fine of up to $5,000 for violations of the law.

Employer References

Minn. Stat. § 181.967, provides that a private employer (defined as an employer "that is not a public entity as defined in Minn. Stat. § 13.02") is protected from liability for disclosure of the kinds of information noted below unless the current or former employee demonstrates "by clear and convincing evidence" that the information was false and defamatory and that the employer knew or should have known that the information was false and acted with malicious intent to injure the current or former employee.

The protection applies to disclosure of information "in response to a request for the information" about:

1) dates of employment;

2) compensation and wage history;

3) job description and duties;

4) training and education provided by the employer;

5) acts of violence, theft, harassment, or illegal conduct documented in the personnel record that resulted in disciplinary action or resignation and the employee's written response, if any, contained in the employee's personnel record.

Any disclosure of the information in number five above must be in writing with a copy sent contemporaneously by regular mail to the employee's last known address.

The protection also applies to liability for written disclosure of the information below when the current or past employee has provided the employer with written authorization for disclosure:

1) written employee evaluations conducted before the employee's separation from the employer, and the employee's written response, if any, contained in the employee's personnel record;
2) written disciplinary warnings and actions in the five years before the date of the authorization, and the employee's written response, if any, contained in the employee's personnel record;
3) written reasons for separation from employment.

For information disclosed under this section the employer must contemporaneously provide the employee or former employee with a copy of the information disclosed and to whom it was disclosed by mailing this information to the employee or former employee.

The prospective employer or employment agency shall not disclose written information received under this section without the written authorization of the employee.

The protections of the law do not apply to an employee's action involving an alleged violation of Minn. Stat. Chapter 363 (the Minnesota Human Rights Act) nor does the law diminish or impair the rights of a person under a collective bargaining agreement.

Access to Personnel Records Relating to Employee Assistance Programs

When employees avail themselves of an employer's employee assistance program, Minn. Stat. § 181.980 governs what must be done with the resulting records. An employee assistance provider must give, upon written request of a person who has received such services (or the parent or guardian of a minor person who has received such services), that person an opportunity to review and obtain copies of that person's employee assistance records. No fee may be charged for copies of records, and the employee assistance provider must comply with such a request no later than seven working days after receipt of such request, if the records are located in Minnesota, or fourteen working days if the records are elsewhere. Also, that statute mandates that such records "must be maintained separate from personnel records and must not become part of an employee's personnel file." The statute also prohibits disclosure of such records, or the fact of the participation in such a program, to a third person, including the employer or its representative, absent the prior written authorization of the person receiving the services, or his or her legal representative. There are some exceptions to that prohibition. The statute also provides that its rights and obligations "are in addition to rights or obligations created under a contract or other law governing access to records." Finally, the statute provides that "[i]n addition to other remedies provided by law, the recipient of employee assistance services may bring a civil action to compel compliance with this section and to recover damages, plus costs and reasonable attorney fees."

Indemnification of Employees

Minnesota employers are required by state statute to indemnify their employees for civil damages, fines and penalties arising out of their employment. To receive indemnification, employees must have acted within the scope of their duties and not have engaged in intentional misconduct, willful neglect of duty, or bad faith. Exceptions apply when another law or private agreement provides for indemnification.

REST BREAKS AND LEAVE TIME

Editor's Note: On March 20, 2020, Congress passed the Families First Coronavirus Response Act (FFCRA) the second emergency legislation adopted in response to COVID-19. The FFCRA was amended in part on March 27, 2020 by the Coronavirus Aid, Relief, and Economic Security (CARES) Act, the third emergency federal legislation adopted in response to COVID-19.

The FFCRA enacted (1) the Emergency Paid Sick Leave Act (Sick Leave Act) and (2) the Emergency Family and Medical Leave Expansion Act (Expansion Act) and, together with the Sick Leave Act, (the Acts). The Sick Leave Act at is the first ever federal paid sick leave mandate for private sector employers, and the Expansion Act temporarily amends the FMLA. The Acts apply to private employers with fewer than 500 U.S. employees and to public employers. The Acts became effective on April 1, 2020 and apply to eligible leave taken between April 1 and December 1, 2020. The Acts grant the U.S. Secretary of Labor the authority to issue regulations necessary to carry out the purposes of and to ensure consistency between the Acts.

The U.S. Department of Labor issued regulations implementing the Families First Coronavirus Response Act leave provisions, April 16, 2020, updated April 22, 2020, August 7, 2020, September 4, 2020, and September 17, 2020.

Unless a collective bargaining agreement provides otherwise, employers generally are free to establish their own policies regarding rest breaks and leave time. This section discusses several exceptions to the general rule.

REST BREAKS

Employers must permit each employee who works eight or more consecutive hours sufficient time to eat a meal. The employer is not required to pay the employee during the meal break as long as the employee is completely relieved of his or her duties for 20 minutes or longer (generally 30 minutes under Federal rules). An employer also must allow each employee adequate time within each four consecutive hours of work to utilize the nearest convenient restroom. A collective bargaining agreement may establish different rest and meal breaks.

Accommodation for Nursing Mothers

Minn. Stat. § 181.939 requires employers to provide "reasonable unpaid break time each day to an employee who needs to express breast milk for her infant child," unless to do so would "unduly disrupt the operations of the employer." The statute also provides that the break time must, if possible, run concurrently with any break time already provided to the employee. An employer must make reasonable efforts to provide a nursing mother with a room or other location to express milk that is shielded from view and free from intrusion from coworkers and the public and includes an electrical outlet. Employers are prohibited from retaliating against employees for asserting rights or remedies under this section. The Minnesota Department of Labor and Industry enforces this section. An amendment to Minn. Stat. § 617.23 makes clear that it is not a violation of the state "indecent exposure" law for a woman to breast feed.

LEAVE TIME

Vacation, Holiday, and Sick Leave

Minnesota employers are not required by law to provide vacation, holiday or sick time for their employees. Most employers do provide such leave, however. Employers should provide employees with notice of their vacation, holiday and sick leave policies in an employee handbook, or otherwise communicate these policies to employees in writing. These policies should address whether vacation or sick leave can be carried over from year to year, or whether it is forfeited if unused by the end of the year. The policies also should address whether the employee will be paid for unused leave. If the employer has a policy stating that employees will be paid any unused accrued vacation at termination, failure to make such payments, may result in an employer being found guilty of a gross misdemeanor.

Family Leave

Family and Medical Leave (Federal Law). The federal Family and Medical Leave Act (FMLA) requires employers engaged in interstate commerce or in an industry affecting interstate commerce, of 50 or more employees in 20 or more weeks in the current or prior calendar year to provide up to 12 weeks of unpaid leave or accrued paid leave to eligible employees for certain family and medical reasons. Employees are eligible if they have worked for a covered employer for at least 12 months, and for 1,250 hours over the previous 12 months immediately preceding the need for FMLA leave, and are employed at a worksite where the employer employs at least 50 people within 75 miles.[1]

In determining if the business meets the 50 or more criteria, the employer should include those people whose names appear on the employer's payroll, including part-time employees, those currently on approved leaves of absence or disciplinary suspensions and jointly owned (e.g., leased) employees. Employees on long term or indefinite layoff are not counted. Employees whose work sites are outside the United States, its territories or possessions are not covered for purposes of determining employer coverage nor are they protected by FMLA.

Employers must grant leave to employees in connection with the birth, placement or adoption of a child, to care for a spouse, minor or incompetent child or parent who has a serious health condition, or for their own serious health condition that makes them unable to perform their job. A serious health condition according to Regulations promulgated by the U.S. Department of Labor (DOL), includes an illness, injury, impairment, or physical or mental condition that involves either hospital care; absence plus continuing treatment; pregnancy; a chronic condition requiring treatment; permanent long-term supervision; or multiple treatments (non-chronic conditions).

Note that many courts, including the Eighth Circuit Court of Appeals, have been asked to interpret those Regulations; as those courts have reached varying conclusions, anyone with questions in this area is urged to seek the advice of counsel. Employees may be required to provide advance notice of the leave and medical certification as established by the FMLA and Regulations of the U.S. Department of Labor.

---

[1] The U.S. Department of Labor's Regulations on the FMLA are at 29 CFR Chapter 825.

Editor's note: In March 2015, DOL's final rule went into effect and states that of the term "spouse" will be defined using the "site of celebration or marriage" rather than the "site of domicile or residency" rule. What this means is that all lawfully married couples will be recognized for purposes of qualifying for FMLA leave to care for one another based on where they were married- or the "site of celebration or marriage" - rather than where they currently live. The "site of celebration" rule has been adopted by the IRS and the DOL, respectively for purposes of tax filing and ERISA-qualifying benefits. The primary effect of the rule is that employers in states where same-sex spouses to care for one another state or jurisdiction where same-sex marriage was legal at the time of the marriage. (29 CFR Part 825)

The FMLA requires all covered employers to comply with notification requirements, including posting information on the FMLA in a general location where all employees would have an opportunity to see it, providing general written information regarding employee rights under the FMLA to all employees, either in an employee handbook or as a handout, and providing all employees requesting or on FMLA leave with written notice detailing the specific obligations and expectations of the employee, and the consequences of failing to meet such obligations.

Although the law does not require the employer to provide paid leave, in some cases certain kinds of paid leave may run concurrently with FMLA leave. During the leave, employers must maintain group medical insurance coverage under conditions the employer would have provided coverage had the employee continued working. (Employers may in some cases recover premiums paid for maintaining health coverage from employees who do not return to work following the leave.) Upon return from FMLA leave, employees must be restored to their original or an equivalent position with equivalent pay, benefits and other employment terms. The FMLA allows employers to deny job restoration to "key employees" (employees who are paid on a salary basis and are the highest paid ten percent of the workforce) if reinstatement of the employee would cause "substantial and grievous economic harm" to the employer, and if the employer has provided the specific notification as required by the FMLA for "key employees". The law does not supersede any state or local law which provides greater family or medical leave rights, nor does it affect greater leave rights provided under a collective bargaining agreement.

Also, employers may adopt policies more generous than those required by the FMLA. Employers must post a notice, available from the U.S. Department of Labor, explaining employee rights and responsibilities under the law. This notice obligation also includes posting notices in languages necessary to accommodate the employer's workforce.

Editor's note. The US Department of Labor has issued an Administrative Interpretation clarifying its opinion that employees are entitled to take FMLA leave for birth, bonding or to care for the child of a domestic partner or same-sex domestic partner, as well as other children for whom an employee has responsibility for day-to-day care or financial responsibility, even though the employee has no biological or legal relationship to the child. (Administrator's Interpretation No. 2010-3). Military leave under the FMLA is governed by different definitions.

Parenting Leave (Minnesota Law). A Minnesota employer must grant an unpaid leave of absence to certain employees in conjunction with the birth or adoption of a child. This includes prenatal care and incapacity due to pregnancy. The law applies to employers who have more than 21 employees. The employee must have been employed by the employer for 12 months preceding the request, on at least a half-time basis.

The length of the leave may not exceed 12 weeks, unless otherwise agreed to by the employer, and must begin at a time requested by the employee. The employer may adopt reasonable policies governing the timing of requests for unpaid leave. The length of leave may be reduced by any period of paid parental or disability leave, but not accrued sick leave, provided by the employer so that the total leave does not exceed 12 weeks unless otherwise agreed by the employer. The employer may provide additional parental leave benefits. In the case of parenting leave taken in conjunction with the birth or adoption of a child, leave may begin anytime within 12 months after the birth or adoption of a child, or within 12 months after the child leaves the hospital, if the child remains in the hospital longer than the mother.

The employer must not retaliate against an employee for requesting or obtaining a leave of absence, and must continue to make group insurance or health care coverage available to the employee during the leave. The employer is not required to pay the cost of the insurance or health care coverage while the employee is on leave of absence.

If the leave is longer than one month, the employee must give the employer reasonable notice prior to returning to work.

An employee returning from a leave of absence is entitled to return to employment in the former position or in a position of comparable duties, number of hours, and pay. Certain exceptions apply to situations where the employer experiences a layoff that would have affected the employee and to collective bargaining situations.

Upon return to work, the employee is entitled to the rate of pay the employee was receiving at the time of the leave, plus any automatic adjustments in the employee's pay scale that occurred during the leave period. The employee retains all accrued preleave benefits of employment and seniority.

An employee who is injured by a violation of this law may sue for damages and to recover attorney's fees, and may seek an injunction or other equitable relief from the courts.

Employers or employees with questions about the interaction of federal and state parenting or family leave laws should seek professional advice.

Sick Leave Benefits; Care of Relatives. (Minn. Stat. § 181.940) Minnesota employers are not required to provide sick leave benefit for their employees. However, employers who are covered by the Care of Relatives Act (that is, employers with 21 or more employees at one site) must allow eligible employees (employees who have worked at least half time for a covered employer at least 12 months prior to their request) to use any sick leave that is provided to care for their children (including biological, adopted, foster, or step-child), a spouse, sibling, parent, grandparent, or stepparent, and also mother-in-law, father-in-law, or a grandchild (including a step-grandchild and a biological adopted or foster grandchild) on the same terms upon which the employee may use sick leave for him or herself. An employer may limit the use of sick leave for an employee's adult child, spouse, sibling, parent, grandparent, or stepparent to no less than 160 hours in a 12-month period. No limit may be placed on sick leave for a minor child. Employers who are covered by the federal Family and Medical Leave Act (FMLA) will have the added burden of coordinating FMLA leave and state Care of Relatives Leave when leaves of absence qualify under both laws.

Employers with more than 20 employees must allow employees to use personal sick leave benefits for absences due to illness or injury of their children, for reasonable periods of time, on the same terms as the employees are able to use sick leave benefits for their own illness. The child must be under age 18 or under age 20 if he or she is attending secondary school. To qualify for sick child leave, an employee must have worked for the employer for 12 consecutive months immediately preceding the request on at least a half-time basis. Salary continuation and disability payments are not included in determining benefits available for sick child leave. This section applies only to sick leave benefits paid from the employer's general assets, and (presumably) does not apply to sick leave benefits paid by a third-party insurer.

School Leave

Employers with one or more employees must grant leave of up to 16 hours during any twelvemonth period to enable a parent to attend a child's or foster child's school conferences or school-related activities and day care or kindergarten activities if those conferences or activities cannot be scheduled during nonwork hours. Employees are eligible for school leave if they work on at least a half-time basis. Employees need not be paid for school leave, but they may use accrued paid vacation leave or other appropriate leave for this purpose. Where the need for school leave is foreseeable, the employee must give the employer reasonable prior notice and must make a reasonable effort to schedule the leave so as not to unduly disrupt operations.

Bone Marrow Donations

Employers with 20 or more employees must grant paid leaves of absence of up to 40 work hours to an employee who seeks to undergo a medical procedure to donate bone marrow. The employer may not retaliate against the employee for requesting or obtaining the leave. The employer may require a doctor's statement verifying the purpose and length of the leave. If there is a medical determination that the employee does not qualify as a bone marrow donor, paid leave granted prior to the medical determination is not forfeited. There is no requirement that the employee be employed by the employer for a certain period of time before becoming eligible for the leave.

Military Leave

Employers must allow regular employees who are members of the Military Reserve or National Guard or Civil Air Patrol unpaid time off for military duty and training. The employee generally must be reinstated to a position of like seniority, status and pay following discharge or release from active duty.

The federal Uniformed Services Employment and Reemployment Rights Act (USERRA) (38 U.S.C. 43) provides reemployment protection to veterans and employees who perform military service in the active military, the National Guard or Reserves. That law applies to federal, state and local governments and all civilian employers regardless of size. If an employee leaves employment for voluntary or involuntary military service that employee upon his return from active duty is entitled to return to the employee's job, with accrued seniority, provided the employee meets the act's five eligibility criteria: (1) the employee must have held a civilian job with the employer; (2) the employee must have informed the employer that the employee was leaving for service in the uniformed services; (3) the period of service must not exceed five years; (4) the employee must have been released from the service under honorable conditions; (5) the employee must have reported to his civilian employer in a timely manner or submitted a timely application for reemployment.

The FMLA provide two forms of leave. (1) Exigency leave is available to service members of any branch of the Armed Services deployed to a foreign country. (2) Family caregiver leave applies to family members of veterans for up to five years after the veteran leaves service. Family leave to care for a covered service member is available up to five years after the veteran leaves the service if the veteran develops an injury or illness that was incurred or aggravated while on active duty. The five year window for veterans is intended to help veterans who suffer from post-traumatic stress disorder and other conditions that are not necessarily evident at the time the service member leaves active duty.

USERRA provides that employees serving in the uniformed services can elect to continue their group health coverage under an employer-sponsored group health plan for a period of up to 18 months. The Act increases that maximum period of group health plan coverage available for employees covered by USERRA from 18 months to 24 months, and applies to continuation coverage elections made on or after December 10, 2004. Employers dealing with service member employment and benefit protections can get more information from the U.S. Department of Labor website at https://www.dol.gov/vets. Information on USERRA is available at https://webapps.dol.gov/elaws/vets/userra/, and Notice Requirement is covered at Compliance Assistance, https://www.dol.gov/vets/programs/userra/compliance.

Employment Protection for Attendance at Military Events

Employers cannot fire or take adverse employment action against any employee, or keep them from attending certain events relating to military service of the employee's spouse, parent or child to which the employee is invited. This could include departure or return ceremonies, family training or reintegration programs.

The employee must provide reasonable notice to the employer when requesting time off, and the employer must provide a reasonable amount of nonpaid time off for the employee, not to exceed two consecutive days or six days in a calendar year. The employer must not compel the employee to use accumulated but unused vacation for these events.

Other Minnesota Military Leave Protections

In addition, three other Minnesota Statutes provide employees with job-protected time away from their jobs for military-related activities. They include Minn. Stats. §§ 181.947, 181.948, and 192.325. The protection of these three statutes overlap in some respects and, in summary, provide as follows:

1) Employers must allow employees up to two consecutive days and up to six total days per calendar year of unpaid leave to attend departure or return ceremonies upon deployment to or return from military service, family training or readiness events sponsored or conducted by the military, and other events held as part of the official reintegration programs for an employee's spouse, parent or child;

2) Employers must allow employees to take one day of unpaid leave per calendar year to attend the military send-off or homecoming ceremony for a grandparent, legal guardian, sibling, grandchild, fiancé; and

3) Employers must allow up to 10 working days of unpaid leave for employees, independent contractors, and those working for independent contractors for compensation when a parent, child, grandparent, sibling or spouse has been injured or killed while engaged in active service of the U.S. Armed Forces.

Finally, Minn. Stat. § 192.261 prohibits employers from asking an applicant for employment if he or she is a member of the National Guard or a reserve component of the U.S. Armed Forces and from requesting any type of oral or written statement concerning that status.

Note: Also refer to the publication *Employing Servicemembers: What You Should Know About USERRA*. The publication is available without charge from the Small Business Assistance Office.

Jury Service

Under Minnesota law an employer cannot deprive an employee of employment, or threaten or coerce an employee with respect to his or her employment, because the employee is called for, or responds to, a summons for jury service. An employer who violates the statute may be found guilty of criminal contempt and fined up to $700 or imprisoned up to six months or both.

If the employer discharges an employee because he or she is called for or responds to a summons for jury service, the employee may bring a civil action for recovery of lost wages and reinstatement. The civil action must be brought within 30 days of the discharge. Recoverable damages cannot exceed lost wages for six weeks. An employee who prevails in the civil action may be allowed reasonable attorney fees. Minnesota law does not require an employer to pay the employee during the period of jury service unless salaried.

Election Judge

An employee must be given paid time off to serve as an election judge. The employee must give 20 days' written notice. The employer may reduce the pay by the amount paid to the election judge by the appointing authority. The paid time off requirement applies to all state elections unless otherwise provided by law.

Time Off to Vote

Employers must allow their employees who are eligible to vote at a regularly scheduled state primary or general election; an election to fill a vacancy in the office of United States senator or United States representative; and a presidential primary election, to be absent from work for the purpose of voting at any time during his or her scheduled hours, without penalty or deduction from salary or wages because of the absence.

Political Convention Leave

An employee who is a member of the state central committee or executive committee of a major political party, or who is a delegate to a political convention, is entitled to an unpaid leave to attend a meeting of the committee or attend the convention. Employees must provide ten day's written notice to the employer.

EMPLOYEE TESTING AND BACKGROUND CHECKS

PRE-EMPLOYMENT TESTING

A Minnesota employer may require an applicant to take a pre-employment test (other than a physical exam or alcohol or drug test) so long as the test is not given for the purpose of discriminating against any member of any protected class. (Protected classes are discussed in the section of this Guide on Human Rights.)

The test must measure only essential job-related abilities and must be required of all applicants for the same position, regardless of disability (except for tests authorized under the workers' compensation law). The test must accurately measure the applicant's aptitude, achievement level or other relevant factors and it may not reflect the applicant's impaired sensory, manual or speaking skills except when those skills are what are being legitimately tested.

Employers who employ at least 15 employees during each of 20 or more calendar weeks in the current or preceding calendar year also must comply with the federal Equal Employment Opportunity Commission (EEOC) guidelines for pre-employment tests. Under those guidelines, an employer may be required to prove that its test has no adverse impact on any member of any protected group. Employers who must comply with the EEOC guidelines are advised to seek the advice of counsel.

An employer conducting a pre-employment test should be able to demonstrate that the test truly measures essential job-related abilities. If a facially neutral test or other business practice has a statistically significant, disparate impact within a protected class, such as sex or race, an employer may need to show the practice is job related and, if so, that no comparable, effective practice exists which has a significantly lesser adverse impact. Unless the test is obviously job-related, such as a typing test for an applicant for a typing job, the employer may want to consult an expert to be sure the requirements of the law are met.

PRE-EMPLOYMENT PHYSICAL EXAMINATIONS

A Minnesota employer at their own cost, may require an applicant, as a condition of hire, to submit to a pre-employment physical examination, which may include a medical history, if the applicant has first received an offer of employment contingent only upon passing the physical exam; the exam tests only for essential job-related abilities; and the exam is required of all persons conditionally offered employment for the same position, regardless of disability (except for exams authorized under the workers' compensation law). The physical may include a drug and alcohol test if the requirements of the Minnesota drug testing statute are followed.

An employer may not refuse to employ an applicant due to physical inability to perform the job unless the applicant is unable to perform the essential requirements of the job. If it appears, pursuant to competent medical advice, that the applicant may not be able to perform the essential duties of the job, certain employers have an obligation to "reasonably accommodate" the applicant, unless the employer can demonstrate that the accommodation would impose undue hardship on the company. Reasonable accommodation means taking steps to accommodate the known physical or mental limitations of a qualified disabled person. The reasonable accommodation requirement applies to those employers with 15 or more employees. See the section of this Guide entitled "Issues for Employers – Human Rights."

EMPLOYEE DRUG TESTING

By statute, an employer may not require an employee or job applicant to undergo drug testing unless testing is done pursuant to a written drug testing policy that meets statutory criteria, and testing is conducted by an approved laboratory. The statute applies to both alcohol and drug testing.

An employer may not discipline, discharge, discriminate against or require rehabilitation of an employee on the basis of a positive test unless the test is verified by a confirmatory test. An employee or job applicant who is damaged by violation of the statute may bring a civil action against the employer or laboratory. An action for an injunction or equitable relief such as reinstatement with back pay also may be brought, and attorney's fees may be awarded.

Employers with at least one employee required to hold a commercial driver's license are urged to seek the advice of counsel regarding the potential applicability of federal regulations requiring drug testing.

POLYGRAPH TESTING

State and federal laws prohibit employers from using the results of a polygraph or lie detector test to take adverse employment action against an employee or prospective employee. The federal law requires employers to inform employees of their rights under the law by posting a notice available from the U.S. Department of Labor. The Minnesota law is enforced by the Department of Labor and Industry, and the federal law is enforced by the U.S. Department of Labor. In addition to enforcement actions brought by the government agencies, an employee who is injured by a violation of the law may bring a private civil action against the employer.

GENETIC TESTING

State law prohibits an employer or employment agency from, as a condition of employment, directly or indirectly administering a genetic test or requesting or requiring protected genetic information; that law also prohibits an employer or employment agency from affecting the terms or conditions of employment, or terminating the employment of any person, based on protected genetic information. Likewise, the state law provides that no person shall provide or interpret for any employer or employment agency protected genetic information on a current or prospective employee. Any person aggrieved by a violation of this law may bring a civil action and the court may award up to three times the actual damage suffered due to the violation, plus punitive damages, reasonable costs, attorneys' fees and injunctive or other equitable relief.

Similarly, the new federal Genetic Information Nondiscrimination Act provides protection against the misuse of genetic information by employers. Employers may not use genetic information when making employment decisions such as hiring, firing and promotion or any other terms of employment.

USE OF CONSUMER REPORTS FOR EMPLOYMENT PURPOSES

Employers who wish to obtain a consumer report for employment purposes should be aware of notice and consent requirements on employers who seek to obtain credit reports for use in connection with the hiring or promotion process. (A consumer report is a report prepared by a consumer reporting agency bearing on a person's credit worthiness, credit standing, credit capacity, character, general reputation, personal character or mode of living that is used in connection with employment, or eligibility for credit or insurance). Prior to obtaining a report, an employer must fulfill notice and consent requirements. First, the employer must provide notices to the applicant, in "clear and conspicuous" language contained in a separate written disclosure form that discusses only the notice, that a report may be obtained for employment purposes. Second, the employer must obtain the applicant's written authorization to obtain the report. Third, the employer must certify to the reporting service that it has properly notified the applicant; that a copy of the report and summary of consumer rights will be provided to the applicant if any adverse action is taken based on the report; and that information from the report will not be used in violation of any applicable Federal or State equal employment opportunity law or regulation. Finally, before taking any adverse action based on information in the report, the employer must provide the applicant with a copy of the report and a summary of consumer rights.

Employers who obtain credit reports for job applicants, whether potential or current employees, should develop disclosure and consent documents. The Federal Trade Commission, which implements and enforces the Federal Fair Credit and Reporting Act for most industries, has issued sample notices.

Federal Trade Commission rules require all businesses that use consumer reports to properly dispose of sensitive information that they receive from the consumer reports. The affected businesses include lenders, insurers, employers, landlords, automobile dealers, and debt collectors. Proper disposal includes burning or shredding paper documents and destroying or erasing electronic media. The destruction can be outsourced if appropriate due diligence is conducted. For further information about the FTC's Disposal Rule, see https://www.ftc.gov/tips-advice/business-center/guidance/disposing-consumer-report-information-rule-tells-how.

TESTING RECORDKEEPING

The federal Age Discrimination in Employment Act requires retention for one year from date of personnel action of the results of employment and physical testing or examinations. Federal regulations on testing for the use of alcohol or controlled substances impose various recordkeeping requirements of from one to five years. Each year a comprehensive update of federal record retention requirements is published in the *Federal Register.* A business or government reference librarian can direct employers to the latest compilation.

BACKGROUND CHECKS

When hiring persons to perform certain jobs, employers are required by statute to perform a background check. For example, employers hiring security guards are required to check their backgrounds with the Minnesota Board of Criminal Apprehension; employers hiring certain counselors are required to check their references for evidence of sexual contact with patients or former patients. Also, other Minnesota laws require rental property owners to request background information from the Minnesota Bureau of Criminal Apprehension before hiring property managers. Likewise, employees, contractors and volunteers of a home health care provider or hospice are subject to background checks. New this year is the requirement of fingerprinting of all new employees who care for seniors, disabled and other potentially vulnerable groups.

Employers in other instances may be interested in performing background checks of potential employees. Those employers are strongly urged to seek the advice of counsel before performing those background checks. That is for many reasons, including but not limited to avoid any claims of discriminatory use of background checks and to ensure compliance with the Americans with Disabilities Act, the Minnesota Human Rights Act, the Fair Credit Reporting Act and the Minnesota Access to Consumer Reports law.

Private employers may not inquire into a job applicant's "criminal record or criminal history" before an interview or, if there is no interview, before a conditional offer of employment is made to the applicant.

Employers may not require an employee or prospective employee to pay for expenses incurred in criminal or background checks, credit checks or orientation, or to pay for the expense of training or testing that is required by federal or state law or is required by the employer for the employee to maintain the employee's current position, unless the training or testing is required to obtain or maintain a license, registration, or certification for the employee or prospective employee.

EMPLOYMENT OF MINORS

Minnesota employers generally are covered by the Minnesota Child Labor Standards Act. Federal child labor laws apply if the employer is under the jurisdiction of the federal Fair Labor Standards Act and the federal act would provide more protection or set a higher standard. Information on federal child labor laws may be obtained from the United States Department of Labor.[1] Information on state child labor laws may be obtained from the Minnesota Department of Labor and Industry. Addresses and telephone numbers for both are listed in the Resource Directory section of this Guide.

FEDERAL CHILD LABOR STANDARDS

The child labor provisions of the federal act are designed to protect the educational opportunities of minors and prohibit their employment in jobs and under conditions detrimental to their health or well-being. The provisions include lists of hazardous occupation orders for both farm and nonfarm jobs declared by the Secretary of Labor as being too dangerous for minors to perform:

- 18 years or older: any job, whether hazardous or not, for unlimited hours.
- 16 and 17 years old: any nonhazardous job, for unlimited hours. (However, the State requirements do not allow high school students to work after 11 p.m. on the night before a school day, or before 5 a.m. on a school day, subject to some exceptions.)
- 14 and 15 years old: outside of school hours in various nonmanufacturing, nonmining, nonhazardous jobs, under these conditions: no more than three hours on a school day, 18 hours in a school week, eight hours on a nonschool day or 40 hours in a nonschool week. Also, work may not begin before 7 a.m. nor end after 7 p.m., except from June 1 through Labor Day, when evening hours are extended to 9 p.m.

[1] The U.S. Department of Labor has issued various Regulations on the Federal Child Labor Laws. These can be found in various Chapters in 29 CFR (including Chapters 570, 575 and 579).

Regulations governing youth employment in nonfarm jobs differ somewhat from those pertaining to agricultural employment. In nonfarm work, the permissible kinds and hours of work, by age, are:

- 14 is the minimum age for most nonfarm work. However, at any age, youths may deliver newspapers, perform in radio, television, movie or theatrical productions, work for parents in their solely owned nonfarm business (except in manufacturing or on hazardous jobs), gather evergreens and make evergreen wreaths.

- Under a special provision 14- and 15-year-olds enrolled in an approved Work Experience and Career Exploration Program (WECEP) may be employed for up to 23 hours in school weeks and three hours on school days (including during school hours).

Hazardous occupations which are not permitted for any minor under age 18 are: working with explosives and radioactive materials; operating certain power-driven woodworking, metalworking, bakery, meat processing, and paper products machinery; operating various types of power-driven saws and guillotine shears; operating most power-driven hoisting apparatus such as non-automatic elevators, fork lifts, and cranes; most jobs in slaughtering and meat packing establishments; most jobs in excavation, logging and sawmilling; roofing, wrecking, demolition,and shipbreaking; operating motor vehicles or working as outside helpers on motor vehicles; and most jobs in the manufacturing of bricks, tiles, and similar products. Exemptions from some of the Department of Labor's hazardous occupation orders apply for apprentices and students in vocational education programs.

In addition to the hazardous prohibitions that apply to all minor workers, the Final Rule makes it clear that 14- and 15-year-olds may only work in those jobs that the Secretary of Labor allows, viz. "Employment that is not specifically permitted is prohibited." Accordingly, the Final Rule clarifies, details and expands both prohibited and permitted jobs for 14- and 15-year-olds:

- Safe, Allowable Tasks: The Final Rule expands the number and types of tasks that 14- and 15-year-olds are permitted to perform. This expansion builds on the former regulations that allowed them to work in food service, retail, and gasoline service establishments. Permitted activities now include: office work; work of an intellectually or artistically creative nature; most restaurant tasks; most retail tasks, including cashiering, stock work, and clean-up work; errand and delivery work by foot, bicycle, or public transportation; work in such fields as advertising, teaching, banking and information technology; most gasoline service station tasks; and, under certain conditions, work inside and outside of places that use power-driven machinery to process word products. Additionally, 15-year-olds (but not 14-year-olds) may work as lifeguards at traditional swimming pools and water parks, as defined in the Final Rule.

- Newly Prohibited Tasks: The Final Rule also adds or makes explicit prohibitions on 14- and 15-year-olds performing the following tasks: door-to-door sales, or peddling (with an exception for doing so on behalf of charitable organizations or public agencies); poultry catching and cooping; and promotional activity like sign waving, unless performed directly outside the employer's establishment.

- Clarifications: Some provisions relating to employment tasks are clarified including: When youth may ride inside or outside of passenger compartments of motor vehicles; the types of materials and situations in which youth may load and unload motor vehicles; and provisions regarding meat coolers and freezers.

The Final Rule also clarifies regulations relating to hours of work permitted for 14- and 15-year-olds. First, it clarifies that the 3 hour limit on employment on school days includes Fridays. Second, the prohibition on working during "school hours" is clarified as being "determined by the local public school district" where the minor resides, regardless of whether the student attends public school. Third, the Final Rule requires employers to use the same "week" (the 168 hour period that is used for computing whether employees are due overtime) to determine compliance with the child labor laws.

Additionally, the Final Rule creates a work-study program for 14- and 15-year-old students in college preparatory curricula, recognizing that various work-study programs are already in place throughout the country. The new work-study program must meet specific requirements set out in the Final Rule, but it allows 14- and 15-year-old students to work during school hours, whereas child labor regulations otherwise prohibit working during school hours.

The Child Labor provisions do not apply to children under 16 years of age employed by their parents in occupations other than manufacturing or mining or occupations declared hazardous by the Secretary of Labor. However, this exception only applies when the parent is the sole employer of the minor.

Although an employer is not required by federal law to obtain an age certificate or work permit in order to hire minors, Minnesota law does require an employer to have proof of age of any employee or applicant who is a minor. Employers may, however protect themselves from unintentional violations of the child labor laws by keeping on file an age certificate or work permit for each minor employed. Employers who are found to have violated the federal child labor laws may be fined up to $10,000 for each violation.

MINNESOTA CHILD LABOR STANDARDS

Under the Minnesota Child Labor Standards Act, a minor under 14 may not be employed, except:

- If at least 11 years old, as a newspaper carrier.
- If at least 12 years old, in agricultural operations with parent's or guardian's permission.
- As an actor or model with approval from the Minnesota Department of Labor and Industry.
- As an assistant soccer referee.

A minor under 16 may not work:

- Before 7 a.m. or after 9 p.m. except as a newspaper carrier.
- More than 40 hours a week or eight hours in a 24-hour period except in an agricultural operation.
- On school days during school hours, unless an Employment Certificate is issued by the appropriate school officials and kept on file by the employer.

High school students may not work:

- After 11 p.m. on evenings before school days (11:30 p.m. with written permission of a parent or guardian) or
- Before 5 a.m. on school days (4:30 a.m. with written permission of a parent or guardian).

  A high school student age 18 or older may make a written request to the employer to work during restricted hours.

A minor may not be employed in an occupation found by the Commissioner of Labor and Industry to be particularly hazardous or detrimental to the well-being of minors. The list of occupations is extensive. Some of the types of occupations that are prohibited for minors include those where the minor may be exposed to hazardous substances; those involving power-driven machinery and equipment; those which involve operation of amusement rides; jobs in processing plants, and jobs in establishments where intoxicating liquors are served. Questions concerning whether a particular occupation is prohibited for minors should be directed to the Labor Standards Unit of the Department of Labor and Industry at the address and telephone number provided in the Resource Directory section of this Guide.

The following are exceptions to the general rule prohibiting employment of minors in hazardous occupations:

- A minor may be employed at tasks away from or outside of the area of hazardous operation, equipment or materials.
- The law does not apply to a minor employed to do home chores or to babysit or to a minor employed by his or her parents. Home chore work is that which is usual to the home of the employer. Work performed in connection with or as part of the business, trade, or profession of the employer is not a home chore. Home chores are all those variable tasks normal to the running of a household and include but are not limited to mowing lawns, raking leaves, removing snow, light housekeeping, washing clothes or dishes, vacuuming, yard cleaning and food preparation.
- The prohibitions do not apply to a minor training in a state-approved apprenticeship program or a program approved by the Division of Vocational Technical Education, Minnesota Department of Education.
- The prohibitions do not apply to 17-year-old high school graduates.
- The prohibitions do not apply if the corporation the minor works for is totally owned by, and its daily business is supervised by, one or both parents. If the minor's parent is a member of the family farm corporation where the minor works, the prohibitions also do not apply.

Every employer in Minnesota is required to have proof of age of any employee or applicant who is a minor. (Minn. Stat. § 181A.06.) This must be secured from the minor in the form of an age certificate, a copy of the minor's birth certificate, a copy of the minor's driver's license, or a United States Department of Justice Immigration and Naturalization Service Employment Eligibility Verification Form I-9.

The Commissioner of the Department of Labor and Industry may impose a fine of up to $5,000 for each child labor law violation. Misdemeanor and gross misdemeanor charges also may be brought.

PROTECTION OF EMPLOYEES WHO REPORT VIOLATIONS OF LAW

"WHISTLEBLOWERS"

A Minnesota employer cannot discharge, discipline, threaten, otherwise discriminate against, or penalize an employee regarding the employee's compensation, terms, conditions, location, or privileges of employment because:

- The employee, or a person acting on behalf of an employee, in good faith, reports a violation or suspected violation, or planned violation of any federal or state law or common law or rule adopted pursuant to law to an employer or to any government body or law enforcement official;
- The employee is requested by a public body or office to participate in an investigation, hearing or inquiry; or
- The employee refuses an employer's order to perform an action that the employee has an objective basis in fact to believe violates any state or federal law or rule or regulation adopted pursuant to law, and the employee informs the employer that the order is being refused for that reason.
- The employee, in good faith, reports a situation in which the quality of health care services provided by a health care facility, organization, or health care provider violates a standard established by federal or state law or a professionally recognized national clinical or ethical standard and potentially places the public at risk of harm.

An employee whose employment is involuntarily terminated may, within five working days following termination, request in writing that the employer provide the reason for the termination. The employer must provide the truthful reason for the termination in writing within five working days following receipt of the request. If the employee was terminated for "whistleblowing" activities, and the employer fails to provide the written reason for termination within the time period specified by law, the employer may be subject to a civil penalty of $25 per day per injured employee, up to a maximum of $750 per injured employee. Communication of the statement furnished by the employer cannot be the subject of a defamation action by the employee against the employer.

The identity of an employee making a report or providing information must be kept confidential by the public official or law enforcement officer unless the employee consents to identification or the investigator determines that disclosure is necessary for prosecution. If disclosure is necessary for prosecution, the employee must be informed prior to the disclosure. The law does not permit an employee to make statements or disclosures knowing they are false or that they are in reckless disregard of the truth. The law also does not permit disclosures that would violate federal or state law or diminish or impair the rights of any person to the continued protection of confidentiality of communications provided by common law.

Employers must notify employees of their rights by posting a summary of the law. A summary is included on the minimum wage poster available from the Minnesota Department of Labor and Industry.

OTHER STATUTORY PROTECTIONS

In addition to the protections of the "whistleblower" law discussed above, other Minnesota laws prohibit employers from discriminating, retaliating, or taking adverse action against employees for exercising their legal rights. Some of these laws include the Minnesota Human Rights Act, the federal Age Discrimination in Employment Act, the Americans with Disabilities Act, the state and federal Fair Labor Standards Acts, the Occupational Safety and Health Act, Workers' Compensation laws, the Employee Retirement Income Security Act, and the Minnesota Parenting Leave law. Employers also may not take adverse employment action against employees whose wages are subject to garnishment, employees who are required to report child abuse and who do so, employees who participate in a strike, employees who are called to jury duty or who are summoned to court, and employees who request access to their personnel files as permitted by state law.

The Clean Air Act, the federal Water Pollution Control Act, the Energy Reorganization Act, the Age Discrimination in Employment Act, the Asbestos Hazard Emergency Response Act, Asbestos School Hazard Detection Act, the Civil Rights Act of 1991, the Civil Service Reform Act, the Employee Polygraph Protection Act, the Employee Retirement Income Security Act, the False Claims Act, the Federal Mine Safety and Health Act, the Financial Institution Reform, Recovery and Enforcement Act, the National Labor Relations Act, the Occupational Safety and Health Act, the Resource Conservation and Recovery Act, the Sarbanes-Oxley Act of 2002, the Surface Mine Reclamation And Control Act, the Toxic Substance Control Act and the Whistleblower Protection Program of the Wendell H. Ford Aviation Investment and Reform Act for the 21st Century all provide specific protections from termination for employees who report violations of these federal laws.

The Sarbanes-Oxley Act protects investors by improving the accuracy and reliability of corporate disclosures made pursuant to the securities laws. The law includes a whistleblower provision aimed at protecting employees of publicly traded companies who report fraud against shareholders. In addition, employees are protected against discrimination when they have filed, testified in, participated in, or otherwise assisted in a proceeding filed or about to be filed against publicly traded companies relating to any securities law or other federal law pertaining to fraud against shareholders or any alleged violation. While Sarbanes-Oxley and the related rulemaking by the SEC and the stock exchanges has profoundly impacted the corporate governance and financial reporting processes at public companies, private companies should also pay attention to the provisions of these regulations and may realize benefits from improving their processes in order to respond effectively to internal or external complaints.

HUMAN RIGHTS

FEDERAL LAWS PROHIBITING DISCRIMINATION

Under Title VII of the U.S. Civil Rights Act of 1964, it is unlawful for any employer of 15 or more employees to refuse to hire, to discharge, or to treat employees differently in any way because of their race, color, religion, sex or national origin. Employers may not limit, segregate, or classify employees in any manner so as to deprive them of employment opportunities or adversely affect a worker's employment status because of race, color, religion, sex or national origin. All aspects of the employment relationship are covered.

The Genetic Information Nondiscrimination Act (GINA) expands Title VII by prohibiting employers from discriminating against employees on the basis of "genetic information".

The Age Discrimination in Employment Act (ADEA) protects persons age 40 or older from discrimination by employers of 20 or more employees. Under that law, employers also must provide the same level of health care benefits to persons over the age of 65 as offered to younger employees. Note that the EEOC has issued guidance on, and many courts have decided cases involving, the type of waivers of claims under the ADEA that employers may lawfully obtain from their employees.

As a result of amendments, these laws are also applicable to state and local governments, government agencies, and other political subdivisions.

The Rehabilitation Act of 1973 prohibits discrimination because of physical or mental disability and applies to any employer who receives federal financial assistance or is a federal contractor. This law is enforced by the Office of Civil Rights, in the U.S. Department of Health and Human Services, Chicago, Illinois and the U.S. Department of Labor. Any employer with a federal contract of $2,500 or more must comply with an affirmative requirement to employ disabled persons. Alleged violations of this part of the Act are handled by the U.S. Office of Federal Contract Compliance.

The Americans with Disabilities Act prohibits discrimination on the basis of disability. The employment provisions of this Act are substantially similar to those in the Rehabilitation Act of 1973. The employment provisions of the Act apply to employers of 15 or more employees. To assist businesses in making structural modifications necessary to make their facilities accessible to disabled persons, both the Internal Revenue Code and Minnesota Statutes allow some or all of these expenses to be deducted in computing income tax.

The Uniformed Services Employment and Reemployment Rights Act of 1994 prohibits employers from discriminating with respect to the employment, promotion or employee benefits of persons who serve, or apply to serve, in the uniformed services. As that Act is written in broad terms, employers are urged to seek the advice of counsel in this area.

For the most part, the federal laws are administered by the Equal Employment Opportunity Commission (EEOC).

STATE LAW PROHIBITING DISCRIMINATION

The Minnesota law prohibiting illegal discrimination (including reprisals against persons who sought relief against discrimination) is the Minnesota Human Rights Act, Minn. Stat. Chapter 363. Generally, it has wider application than the federal anti-discrimination laws. It applies to all employers in the state who have one or more employees, as well as to employment agencies, labor organizations and temporary help agencies.

The state law makes it an unfair employment practice, except when based on a limited, statutory exception or a *bona fide* occupational qualification, for an employer to refuse to hire, to discharge, or otherwise to treat a person differently with respect to hire, tenure, compensation, terms, upgrading, conditions, facilities or privileges of employment, because of race, color, creed, religion, national origin, sex, marital status, status with regard to public assistance, disability, age, or sexual orientation; or in reprisal for objecting to, or participating in the investigation or litigation of, alleged discrimination or for associating with a disabled person or persons of a different race, color, creed, religion, sexual orientation or national origin. WESA amends the Human Rights Act to also prohibit discrimination against applicants and employees based on "familial status." The familial status protection applies to a person who is pregnant or who is in the process of securing legal custody of a minor. Familial status further is defined as "the condition of one or more minors being domiciled with (1) their parent (s) or the minors legal guardian or (2) the designee of the parent (s) or guardian" with written permission. Employers may not use these protected characteristics as a factor in making any employment decision. In rare instances, certain jobs may require persons to be chosen on the basis of one of these characteristics, but there is a strict burden of proof on the employer to show that the discrimination was demanded by the job in that all or virtually all persons excluded on the basis of the protected characteristic could not perform the job or that some other compelling business reason exists that justifies the action.

Before hiring, an employer may not require or request from applicants, or from any source, information which pertains to a protected characteristic, including on an application form or in an interview. An employer may, however, seek information to determine whether a person can safely and efficiently perform the duties of the position at issue. This may include requiring or requesting a physical examination, if the requirements of the law are met (see the section of this Guide on pre-employment testing). In general, employers also may, with the consent of the employee, after employment has commenced, obtain additional medical information to assess continuing ability to perform the job or to assess employee health insurance eligibility; for purposes mandated by law; for purposes of assessing the need to reasonably accommodate an employee; or pursuant to the state drug testing law; or other legitimate business reasons not otherwise prohibited by law. With limited exceptions, medical documentation must be collected and maintained on separate forms and kept confidential.

Under the state law, businesses with 15 or more full-time or part-time employees must provide reasonable accommodation for their employees' and job applicants' known disabilities, unless the business can demonstrate that the accommodation would impose an undue hardship on the business. This requirement is similar to that required by the federal Americans with Disabilities Act. "Reasonable accommodation" under the state law generally means making facilities readily accessible to the disabled person, or initiating practices like job restructuring, work schedule modifications, reassignment to a vacant position, acquisition or modification of equipment or devices, or providing aides on a temporary or periodic basis. "Undue hardship" is determined by evaluating a number of factors, including the size of the business, the type of operation, work force size and composition, the nature and cost of the needed accommodation, the employer's ability to finance the accommodation, and good faith efforts to explore less restrictive or less expensive alternatives with the employee and individuals or organizations knowledgeable about the needs of disabled persons.

The state law provides that whenever health care records or medical information adversely influence any hiring, firing or promotional decision about an applicant or employee, the employer must notify that person of that fact within 10 days of the final decision. There is no requirement in the state law that the employee must first request the information from the employer.

The Act also makes it a discriminatory practice for an employer not to treat women who are pregnant, or who have pregnancy-related disabilities, the same as other persons who are not so affected, but who are similar in their ability or inability to work. An employer's duty to make reasonable accommodation, as discussed above, also applies to women disabled by pregnancy, childbirth or related disabilities.

The Human Rights Act prohibits a business from refusing to do business with a woman based on her use of her current or former surname; and a business may not intentionally refuse to do business with or contract with, or discriminate in the basic terms of the contract because of a person's race, national origin, color, sex, sexual orientation or disability, unless it is for a legitimate business purpose.

Businesses are also prohibited from discriminating in the extension of personal or commercial credit, because of race, color, creed, religion, disability, national origin, sex, sexual orientation, marital status, or receipt of public assistance, including medical or rental assistance.

Another Minnesota law (Minn. Stat. § 181.938) prohibits an employer from retaliating against an employee or prospective employee who engages in the lawful use of food, alcoholic beverages, or tobacco during non-working hours. Exceptions apply for *bona fide* occupational requirements or to avoid a conflict of interest, and in certain other circumstances.

Valid, voluntary or required affirmative action programs are not prohibited by the Human Rights Act. Obtaining otherwise prohibited information from applicants is allowed for affirmative action purposes, but it must be kept separate and apart from other job application information and not be provided to or considered by any person involved in the selection of an employee, except when an effort is being made to make a hiring decision from among candidates in an underutilized protected group, pursuant to a *bona fide* affirmative action plan.

The Human Rights Act prohibits advertisements for employment that state a preference for applicants based on any of the protected characteristics, such as race, color, creed, religion, sex, age, sexual orientation, or marital status. Employers should avoid using terms which convey a preference for persons of a particular age or gender, e.g., "girl Friday," or "maintenance man."

As a place of public accommodation, a business is prohibited from discriminating against the public on the basis of race, color, creed, religion, disability, national origin, marital status, sexual orientation, or sex. Thus, a business must make reasonable accommodation, including removal of physical barriers and modification of policies, for a person with a disability, unless such access would pose a direct threat. A properly identified service animal, accompanying a person with a disability, must be allowed in a public place, provided the animal is properly leashed.

CHARGES OF DISCRIMINATION

An employee or applicant who feels discriminated against because of his or her age, race, sex, religion or other protected characteristic may file a charge with the Minnesota Department of Human Rights within one year of the occurrence of the discriminatory practice. The Department, after determining jurisdiction and accepting a charge for filing, will gather facts relevant to the charge and weigh the evidence provided by both sides. While parties to a charge may be represented by legal counsel, every effort is made to keep the procedure simple enough so that neither side will necessarily have to retain an attorney. Both sides are encouraged to settle the matter at any time in the process. In Minnesota, aggrieved parties may bypass the Human Rights Department and go directly to state district court to bring suit against the employer.

If the evidence does not support the charge, the Department will issue a "no probable cause" finding on the merits of the charge. Note also that whether or not the Department concludes that the evidence supports the charging party's allegations, the Department has the discretion to "dismiss" charges for a variety of reasons, such as not warranting the resources of that Department or a failure of the charging party to submit a rebuttal to the responding party's answer to the charge. Note that both a finding of "no probable cause" and a "dismissal" may be appealed (although there are different time periods for each appeal). Note again that a charging party, no matter what the Department concludes, may file a private lawsuit in district court. If the charge of discrimination is supported by the evidence, action is taken to stop the discriminatory act or practice and relief is sought for the person who was discriminated against. If relief is not obtained through this conciliation, the Department or the charging party may take the matter to court or to a public hearing.

Relief in employment discrimination cases may include the hiring, reinstatement, or upgrading of a person; up to three times back pay, including compensation for fringe benefits and interest accrued; and adoption of policies or participation in a training program. Relief could also include other compensatory damages, punitive damages, and damages for mental anguish. Violators of the law also may be assessed a civil penalty payable to the state. A person who violates the laws regarding public accommodations discrimination is guilty of a misdemeanor.

Minnesota Rules 5000.2250 requires that an employer charged with discrimination must retain all charge-related documents, under its control, until the Department informs the employer that the charge has been resolved. All job applicant and employment records must be retained by an employer for at least one year after they are made, whether or not a charge has been filed.

In addition, a number of federal statutes govern the retention of records regarding employees' charges of discrimination, including disability discrimination, improper termination, or violation of civil rights. These impose retention requirements of from one year to final disposition of charges, whichever is later. Each year a comprehensive update of federal recordkeeping requirements is published in the *Federal Register.* A business or government reference librarian can direct employers to the latest compilation.

GUIDELINES FOR PREVENTING DISCRIMINATION IN HIRING

When interviewing job applicants, the employer should only ask questions which reasonably relate to the job in question. The burden of proof is on the employer to demonstrate that questions are not used to discriminate. Asking an applicant to supply information that is not job-related or that might reveal an applicant's protected status could lead to charges of discrimination. Inquiries that may improperly request protected status information include those about age, date of birth, marital status (including identity or situation of spouse), sexual orientation, sex, race, creed, color, religion, national origin, and disabilities.

The employer may ask questions that help assess the applicant's ability to do the job, and which are asked of all applicants for the job. Inquiries that elicit information about the applicant's education, experience, abilities, licenses and certifications that are job related generally are permissible, as are inquiries about willingness to travel, salary expectations, references, and the applicant's interest in the job. It generally is permissible to talk about job duties and responsibilities, the business itself, career growth potential, and opportunities for advancement, so long as these topics are relevant to the job and are presented consistently to applicants, regardless of their individual status within a protected class.

An employer may not use prohibited information obtained from any source for the purpose of making a hiring or job decision. Employers should examine job requirements to ensure that they are not based on assumptions or stereotypes that are unrelated to job performance. Employers with questions in this area may contact the Minnesota Department of Human Rights at the address and telephone number provided in the Resource Directory section of this Guide.

AMERICANS WITH DISABILITIES ACT (ADA)

The ADA is a complex piece of federal legislation that prohibits discrimination against people with disabilities in everyday activities, such as buying an item at a store, going to the movies, enjoying a meal at a restaurant, exercising at the health club, or having the car serviced at a garage.

To meet the goals of the ADA, the law established requirements for businesses of all sizes. These requirements initially went into effect in 1992 and have been evolving since. Businesses that serve the public must modify policies and practices that discriminate against people with disabilities; comply with accessible design standards when constructing or altering facilities; remove barriers in existing facilities where achievable; and provide auxiliary aids and services when needed to ensure effective communication with people who have hearing, vision, or speech impairments. All businesses, even those that do not serve the public, must comply with accessible design standards when constructing or altering facilities.

Title I of the ADA requires employers of 15 or more employees, to provide qualified individuals with disabilities an equal opportunity to benefit from the full range of employment-related opportunities available to others. For example, it prohibits discrimination in recruitment, hiring, promotions, training, pay, social activities, and other privileges of employment. It restricts questions that can be asked about an applicant's disability before a job offer is made, and it requires that employers make reasonable accommodation to the known physical or mental limitations of otherwise qualified individuals with disabilities, unless it results in undue hardship.

Title I with respect to private employers is enforced by the Equal Employment Opportunity Commission (EEOC).

Title II of the ADA applies the laws on both hiring and access to local, state and federal government agencies and public transportation. Title II (other than transportation) is enforced by the U.S. Department of Justice.

Title III of the ADA prohibits discrimination against persons with disabilities in places of public accommodation and commercial facilities. Places of public accommodation include privately owned businesses, establishments of all sizes such as restaurants, hotels, theaters, convention centers, medical offices, retail stores, museums, libraries, private schools, health spas, and day care centers. Commercial facilities are businesses whose operations affect commerce, such as office buildings, factories, and warehouses. Public accommodations (that is, every business that opens its doors to the public) must: provide goods and services in an integrated setting, unless separate or different measures are necessary to ensure equal opportunity; eliminate unnecessary eligibility standards or rules that deny individuals with disabilities an equal opportunity to enjoy the goods and services of a place of public accommodation; and make reasonable modifications in policies, practices and procedures that deny equal access to individuals with disabilities, unless a fundamental alteration would result in the nature of goods and services provided. (Examples of policies and procedures would be if a store has a policy to exclude all animals, the policy should be changed to permit people who use service animals, such as "seeing-eye dogs" and "hearing-assist-dogs" to enter the store with their service animals. A store that has a special accessible entrance that remains locked during business hours will need to change the policy and keep the door unlocked when the store is open. If security is a problem, an accessible call box or buzzer, identified by a sign and mounted in an accessible location and height, should be installed to enable people with disabilities to call staff to unlock the door. A restaurant that restricts seating of people with disabilities to one area must revise the policy to permit the range of choices enjoyed by others.) They must also ensure effective communication through the use of auxiliary aids and services when necessary, unless an undue burden or fundamental alteration would result. (Examples of auxiliary aids and services include reading written information to a person who is blind or who has low vision or providing large print, audiotape or Braille; and using written notes, sign language interpreters or using captioning to communicate with a person who is deaf, hard of hearing or who has a speech disability.) They must remove architectural and structural communication barriers in existing facilities where readily achievable, and provide goods and services through alternative measures when removal of barriers is not readily achievable. ("Readily achievable" means easily accomplished without much difficulty or expense. The "readily achievable" requirement is based on the size and resources of the business. The Justice Department, as part of new ADA regulations, is adopting a "safe harbor" allowing businesses that comply with 1991 ADA standards to postpone compliance with 2010 standards until the building or building elements are altered. Larger businesses with more resources are expected to take a more active role in removing barriers than small businesses. The ADA also recognizes that economic conditions vary. When a business has the resources to remove barriers, it is expected to do so; but when profits are low, barrier removal may be reduced or delayed. Barrier removal is an ongoing obligation. Businesses are expected to remove barriers in the future as resources become available.) When public accommodations or commercial facilities design and construct new facilities, or alter existing facilities, they must do so in accordance with the Standards of Accessible Design. (In some cases, existing conditions, limited resources, or both will make it not "readily achievable" to follow the Standards fully. If this occurs, barrier removal measures may deviate from the Standards so long as the measures do not pose a significant risk to the health or safety of individuals with disabilities or others.) New proposals also address the ADA accessibility of websites, movie theaters, and equipment and furniture. Title III is enforced by the U.S. Department of Justice.

To be protected by the ADA, one must have a disability or have a relationship or association with an individual with a disability. An individual with a disability is defined by the ADA as a person who has a physical or mental impairment that substantially limits one or more major life activities, a person who has a history or record of such an impairment, or a person who is perceived by others as having such an impairment. The ADA does not specifically name all of the impairments that are covered, recent amendments mandate the definition of "disability" to be construed in favor of broad coverage of individuals. Employers can expect more employees to fall within the definition of "disabled" which will trigger the employer's duty to engage in the interactive process and provide reasonable accommodation more often.

There is a lot of guidance available regarding the ADA. For small businesses, compliance with the ADA is not difficult. To help businesses with their compliance efforts, Congress has established various technical assistance programs to answer questions about the ADA and has provided tax incentives. A listing of the various resources and tax code provisions is included in the Federal Government Listings and Additional Resources section of the Resource Directory of this Guide.

The ADA Amendments Act (ADAAA) significantly broadens the coverage of the ADA so that more employees with less severe impairments are protected by the definition of "disability". Employers are strongly encouraged to consult with legal counsel regarding disability assessments and reasonable accommodation issues, particularly in light of the ADAAA amendments.

AFFIRMATIVE ACTION REQUIREMENTS FOR GOVERNMENT CONTRACTORS

Businesses that contract with the government may be subject to affirmative action requirements. Federal, state and local laws each have different criteria to determine if a business must comply with their respective affirmative action or equal employment opportunity requirements.

Under Executive Order 11246 ("Non-Discrimination in Employment by Government Contractors and Subcontractors"), as amended, and its implementing Regulations issued on November 13, 2000, by the U.S. Department of Labor's Office of Federal Contract Compliance Programs (OFCCP), a business with 50 or more employees that has a non-construction contract (or subcontract) with the federal government of $50,000 or more, or a business receiving in excess of $10,000 for a federally assisted construction project, must develop an affirmative action plan. Note that those Regulations, according to the OFCCP, refocus compliance emphasis from the development of a written affirmative action plan to the implementation of such a plan into the overall management of the contracting or subcontracting business. Note also that those Regulations place greater emphasis on (and give OFCCP greater/monitoring powers over) whether such businesses are discriminating with respect to employee pay. Compliance with the Executive Order is monitored by the Office of Federal Contract Compliance Programs.

In summer 2014, the President signed several Executive Orders affecting the affirmative action obligations of federal contractors. Executive Order 13665 prohibits federal contractors from discharging or in any other manner discriminating against employees because they inquire about, discussed, or disclosed their own compensation or the compensation information of another employee. Executive Order 13672 prohibits federal contractors from discriminating against applicants or employees based on sexual orientation or gender identity. Executive Order 13673 requires employers seeking new federal contracts to disclose whether there have been any administrative or judicial judgements against it for labor and employment violations in the past three years.

In addition, in March 2014, the Office of Federal Contract Compliance issued final rules implementing amendments to the Rehabilitation Act and the Veterans Readjustment Assistance Act. The effect of these was to impose on federal contractors an obligation to establish annual hiring benchmarks for individuals with disabilities and veterans with a utilization goal of seven percent of the workforce.

Under Minn. Stat. § 363A.36, vendors who intend to bid on any purchases or contracts exceeding $100,000, and have had on any single working day in the past year more than 40 employees in Minnesota, must apply for a Certificate of Compliance from the Minnesota Department of Human Rights. State agencies cannot accept bids or proposals on purchases or contracts exceeding $100,000 from Minnesota vendors unless the Commissioner of the Minnesota Department of Human Rights has received the vendor's affirmative action plan for the employment of minority persons, women, and disabled individuals. State agencies cannot make awards exceeding $100,000 to Minnesota vendors unless the Commissioner of the Minnesota Department of Human Rights has approved the vendor's affirmative action plan and issued a certificate of compliance to the vendor. Vendors who have more than 40 employees in the state in which their principal place of business is located, will be required to certify that the business is in compliance with federal affirmative action requirements in order to receive awards exceeding $100,000. The Minnesota Department of Human Rights charges a $75 fee for each certificate of compliance issued. In addition, under the Women's Economic Security Act (WESA), an employer with 40 or more full time employees in Minnesota must obtain an equal pay certificate from the State if it does business with the State in excess of $500,000. This certificate is good for four years. The Minnesota Department of Human rights is responsible for enforcing compliance.

The cities of Minneapolis and St. Paul have city ordinances which require compliance with their specific affirmative action requirements. The Minneapolis Department of Civil Rights and the St. Paul Department of Human Rights are the agencies which enforce the respective city ordinances. Other cities or counties in Minnesota also may have affirmative action or equal employment opportunity requirements for businesses who contract with them. The entity awarding the contract should be able to inform the business of its affirmative action requirements.

IMMIGRATION LAW COMPLIANCE

The federal Immigration and Nationality Act (18 U.S.C. § 1324a) requires employers to verify that all persons they hire are legally authorized to work in the United States. The law also prohibits employers from knowingly hiring or continuing to employ persons not authorized to work in the United States as well as knowingly contracting for work by someone not authorized to work in the United States. The law applies to all employers, regardless of the number of employees they have, and to all individuals hired after November 6, 1986. Note that merely because a person holds a visa authorizing entrance into the United States, that person does not necessarily have authorization to be employed in the United States. It is the employer's responsibility to determine whether a person has that authorization to work in the United States. (Most functions of the former U.S. Immigration and Naturalization Service have been transferred to the U.S. Department of Homeland Security and divided into separate agencies. INS immigration services are now part of the Bureau of Citizen and Immigration Services (USCIS) and INS enforcement activities are part of the Bureau of Immigration and Customs Enforcement (ICE) within the Directorate of Border and Transportation Security.)

Employment verification is documented on Form I-9, available from the U.S. Citizenship and Immigration Services, I-9 Central at https://www.uscis.gov/i-9-central. The law requires the employer to ensure that every employee completes Section 1 of Form I-9 at the time the employee begins work. The law also requires the employer, within three days of hire, to review the documents establishing the employee's identity and eligibility to work and to properly complete Section 2 of Form I-9. The documents that satisfy the verification requirements are listed on Form I-9.

A self-employed person who is a sole proprietor need not complete a Form I-9 on himself or herself. If, however, the business owner is an employee of the business entity (i.e., an employee of a corporation), a Form I-9 is required.

Employers must keep the verification forms on file for three years from the date of hire or for one year following the employee's separation from service, whichever is later. The forms may be inspected by the Immigration and Customs Enforcement and the U.S. Department of Labor, and the Office of Special Counsel for Immigration Related Unfair Employment Practices.

The administrative tasks associated with the preparation and storage of Form I-9 have become more flexible as a result of a new electronic signature and storage law passed in 2005. Public Law 108-390 amended Minn. Stat. Chapter 274A of the Immigration and Nationality Act by authorizing the use of electronic signatures by employers and employees to attest verification of identity and eligibility documents when completing Form I-9; maintenance of I-9 forms in PDF format, rather than (or in addition to) the previously accepted paper, microfiche or microfilm formats; and conversion of existing paper I-9 forms into electronic formats.

Sanctions for failure to comply with the law include warnings, cease and desist orders, and civil penalties ranging from $275 to $2,200 per violation. Total fines may exceed these amounts. Criminal penalties may be imposed for a pattern and practice of violations.

The Immigration Reform and Control Act (IRCA) and Title VII of the Civil Rights Act of 1964 prohibit employment discrimination. Employers with four or more employees may not discriminate in the hiring, firing, or recruitment or referral for a fee of employees on the basis of the employee's national origin or citizenship status. In practice, this means that employers must treat all employees the same when completing Form I-9. Employers cannot set different employment eligibility verification standards or require that different documents be presented by different groups of employees. Employees can choose which documents they want to present from the lists of acceptable documents. An employer cannot request that an employee present more or different documents than are required or refuse to honor documents which on their face reasonably appear to be genuine and to relate to the person presenting them. An employer also cannot refuse to accept a document or refuse to hire an individual, because a document has a future expiration date. Penalties may be imposed upon violators. To minimize charges of discrimination, employers are encouraged to make hiring decisions irrespective of the national origin or citizenship status of applicants authorized to work in the United States. Questions like "What is your national origin?" and "Are you a United States citizen?" may be considered discriminatory. It is permissible, however, to ask whether an applicant is legally authorized to work in this country.

Employment verification is an area identified by the U.S. Immigration and Customs Enforcement (ICE) for audited review. Employers should make sure they are using current I-9 forms.

E-VERIFY

E-Verify (https://www.uscis.gov/e-verify) is an online system operated jointly by the Department of Homeland Security and the Social Security Administration (SSA). Participating employers can check the work status of new hires by comparing information from an employee's I-9 form against SSA and the Department of Homeland Security databases.

E-Verify is free and voluntary (with certain exceptions) and is the best means available for determining employment eligibility of new hires and the validity of their Social Security numbers. Federal departments and agencies require contractors to use an electronic system to verify worker's employment eligibility. The use of E-Verify in Minnesota is voluntary except for the Executive Branch of the State, recipients (vendors and subcontractors) of state contracts in excess of $50,000 and recipients of business subsidy agreements with the State.

Employees in Minnesota can verify their own employment eligibility status through Self-Check, part of the E-Verify system. Self-Check allows workers to check their own status.

Prior to applying for employment, a worker over the age of 16 may enter the same information into Self-Check that employers would enter from an employee's Form I-9 into E-Verify. The information comes from documents that establish a worker's identity and employment eligibility in the U.S. The worker then may compare his or her information with information in the same databases that E-Verify uses so that the worker may identify and address any existing mismatching information before applying with an employer who uses E-Verify.

E-Verify program information can be found at the address, telephone number and website address in the Resource Directory Section of this Guide.

OCCUPATIONAL SAFETY AND HEALTH

GENERAL INFORMATION

The Occupational Safety and Health Division of the Minnesota Department of Labor and Industry administers the Minnesota Occupational Safety and Health Act. The express legislative purpose of this Act is "to assure so far as possible every working man and woman in the State of Minnesota safe and healthful working conditions and to preserve our human resources."

The Minnesota Occupational Safety and Health Rules and Regulations adopt by reference the federal Occupational Safety and Health Standards. In addition, Minnesota has adopted some localized standards that apply to hazards not covered by the federal OSHA standards. Minnesota OSHA standards apply to all places of employment in the state with the exception of those under the exclusive jurisdiction of the federal government.

All places of employment are subject to inspection to ascertain compliance with published Minnesota Occupational Safety and Health Rules and Regulations. Inspections are scheduled following the guidelines of an administrative inspection scheduling plan approved by the federal Occupational Safety and Health Administration and in accordance with established priorities. Those priorities are: (1) imminent danger conditions; (2) catastrophes/fatalities/ serious injuries; (3) employee complaints; (4) target industry inspections; and (5) follow-up inspections. If violations are found, a citation will be issued specifying abatement dates for all violations. A monetary penalty may also be assessed. Criminal penalties including imprisonment and fines also may be assessed for knowing or willful violations.

EMPLOYER RIGHTS AND RESPONSIBILITIES

An employer's rights and responsibilities under the Act include, but are not limited to, the following:

- An employer must furnish to employees conditions of employment that are free from recognized hazards that are causing or are likely to cause death or serious injury.
- Employers are entitled to participate in the development, revision or revocation of OSHA standards by commenting on proposed standards, participating in hearings concerning standards, or by requesting the development of a new standard.

- An employer may request a variance from the requirements of a particular OSHA standard if the employer is unable to meet the mandates of that standard and wishes to use alternative means of compliance.
- Employers are entitled to protection of trade secrets or other legally privileged communications.
- Employers must post the *"Safety and Health Protection on the Job"* (https://www.dli.mn.gov/sites/default/files/pdf/mnosha_poster.pdf) poster in their places of employment. Posters may be obtained from the Minnesota Department of Labor and Industry. Contact information provided in the Resource Directory section of this Guide.
- Employers must provide to their employees all necessary protective equipment required by OSHA standards at no cost to the employee.
- An employer who receives a citation and/or proposed monetary penalty following an OSHA inspection may contest the citation or penalty by submitting a Notice of Contest to the Commissioner of the Department of Labor and Industry.
- Employers may obtain technical assistance from OSHA by writing or calling any of the area offices listed in the Resource Directory section of this Guide or by accessing the Minnesota Department of Labor and Industry or federal OSHA on the internet.

Employers can be fined up to $25,000 if a violation of state standards, rules, or orders results in the death of an employee.

A small employer exception helps protect small companies (fewer than 50 employees) from bankruptcy by allowing the $25,000 fine to be broken up into five annual $5,000 installments as long as the violation is not deemed to be willful or repeated. The state labor and industry commissioner can elect to waive the fine each year after the first if the employer is not cited for any more violations.

Businesses will be exempt from such fines if the owner or an employee with a controlling interest in the company is the one who dies.

Separate provisions of the law lengthen employee notice requirements by requiring employers to post notices of a citation at or near the place where a violation occurred for 20 days. Previous law required 15 days.

RECORDKEEPING

Under OSHA's recordkeeping regulation, certain covered employers are required to prepare and maintain records of occupational injuries and illness using OSHA 300 log. This information is important to employers, workers and OSHA in evaluating the safety of a workplace, understanding industry hazards, and implementing worker protections to reduce or eliminate hazards.

A revised rule updates the list of industries that are exempt from the requirement to routinely keep OSHA injury and illness records due to relatively low occupational injury and illness rates. These changes to OSHA's injury reporting rule became effective at the federal level January 1, 2015. Minnesota OSHSA adopted the new injury reporting requirements March 16, 2015, with an effective date of October 1, 2015.

Changes to OSHA's recordkeeping requirements (for low-hazard industries) were not adopted by Minnesota OSHA, which is consistent with past requirements in Minnesota.

Further information is available on the Minnesota OSHA website at https://www.dli.mn.gov/business/workplace-safety-and-health/mnosha-compliance-standards-and-regulations or at the federal OSHA Injury and Illness Recordkeeping and Reporting Requirements, https://www.osha.gov/recordkeeping.

REPORTING SEVERE INJURY AND WORK-RELATED FATALITIES

Employers must report work-related fatalities that result in the death of at least one employee, or incidents that result in the in-patient hospitalization of at least three employees, to Minnesota OSHA within eight hours after the death or hospitalization. Such a report must be made orally, in person or by telephone, to one of the area offices listed in the Resource Directory section of this Guide. After normal business hours, the report can be made by telephoning 800-321-6742.

Severe on-the-job injuries that do not result in death but require hospitalization must be reported within 24 hours. Such reports must be filed regardless of the size of the business.

WORKPLACE SAFETY PLAN

Employers in certain industries must develop and implement a written workplace accident and injury reduction program to promote safe and healthful working conditions. Industries where a plan is required are identified by the Commissioner of Labor and Industry by Standard Industrial Classification, based on the industry segment's Bureau of Labor Statistics' injury and illness record. The list is updated every two years and is published in Minnesota Rules 5208.1500.

An employer who is in a designated industry must develop its written plan within six months following the date the standard industrial classification (SIC) code for the industry is placed on the list. The program must have clearly stated goals and objectives, and must describe responsibility for implementing the program; management participation; methods used to identify, analyze, and control new or existing hazards, conditions and operations; communication of the plan to affected employees; investigation of workplace accidents and corrective action; and enforcement of safe work practices. The employer must conduct and document a review of the workplace accident and injury reduction program at least annually and document how procedures described in the program are met.

EMPLOYEE RIGHTS AND RESPONSIBILITIES

Although the primary responsibility for compliance with the law rests with the employer, employees are obliged to comply with OSHA standards and regulations which are applicable to their own actions and conduct. Employees cannot be cited or fined for noncompliance; employers must set up their own disciplinary procedures for employees who violate standards or regulations. Employee rights include, but are not limited to, the following:

- Employees have the right to request an OSHA inspection by filing a written complaint with the Minnesota Occupational Safety and Health Division describing the hazardous conditions that exist at the work facility. The complaint must be filed by a current employee or an authorized employee representative and must be signed. A complainant's name is not revealed nor is it part of any inspection record made available for review.

- Employees may participate in standards development activities.
- Employees must be notified of a variance request filed by their employer; employees may petition for a hearing on the variance request.
- Employee representatives may participate in the opening conference, walk-around inspection and closing conference conducted as part of an OSHA inspection; employees who exercise this right must be paid their usual wage.
- Employees may not be discriminated against because they exercised any right afforded them under the Minnesota OSHA Act. In addition, note that when an employee sues, alleging discrimination or discharge due to his or her assertion of rights under that Act, any communication between that employee and attorneys representing the Minnesota Department of Labor and Industry is, per Minn. Stat. § 182.669, subd. 1, "privileged as would be communications between an attorney and a client."

EMPLOYEE RIGHT-TO-KNOW ACT

The Minnesota Employee Right-to-Know Act is intended to ensure that employees are aware of the dangers associated with hazardous substances, harmful physical agents, or infectious agents that they may be exposed to in their workplaces. The Act requires employers to evaluate their workplaces for the presence of hazardous substances, harmful physical agents, and infectious agents and to provide training to employees concerning those substances or agents to which employees may be exposed. Written information on hazardous substances, harmful physical agents or infectious agents must be readily accessible to employees or their representatives. Labeling requirements for containers of hazardous substances and equipment or work areas that generate harmful physical agents are also included.

The Employee Right-to-Know Act applies to all Minnesota employers regardless of size (with the exception of federal agencies). Special provisions apply to certain technically qualified individuals as defined in the standard, farming operations, and waste service employers regulated by the federal Resource Conservation and Recovery Act.

Employers should conduct an inventory of their workplaces to determine what hazardous substances, harmful physical agents or infectious agents are present and which employees are at risk of exposure. Once the survey is completed, the employer must obtain, and have accessible to employees, written information on those substances or agents. This written information on hazardous substances is usually in the form of a material safety data sheet (MSDS) which can be obtained from the manufacturer of the substance. Material safety data sheets will provide the basic information that must be presented in the oral training program.

The Employee Right-to-Know Standard is being enforced as part of the Minnesota Occupational Safety and Health program. The standard provides guidelines concerning the type of information that must be included in the written training program, how often training must be provided, requirements for documentation and maintenance of training records, and labeling of hazardous substance containers and equipment that generates a harmful physical agent or infectious agents. The standard also includes lists of hazardous substances, harmful physical agents and infectious agents to assist employers in evaluating their workplaces. A copy of the Employee Right-to-Know

Standard may be obtained by contacting the Minnesota Bookstore at the address and telephone number provided in the Resource Directory section of this Guide or online at https://www.dli.mn.gov/business/workplace-safety-and-health/mnosha-compliance-standards-and-regulations. Questions concerning the Employee Right-to-Know Act may be directed to one of the Occupational Safety and Health Division offices, also listed in the Resource Directory section of this Guide.

WORKPLACE SAFETY CONSULTATION

The Minnesota Department of Labor and Industry Workplace Safety Consultation (WSC) offers a number of programs, including a grant program, to employers to identify potential hazards at their work sites and improve their safety management systems. For more information on these topics, see http://www.dli.mn.gov/about-department/our-areas-service/minnesota-osha-workplace-safety-consultation.

Safety Consultation

WSC offers free, confidential assistance, on request, to help employers improve their safety and health record, lower the cost of accidents and reduce OSHA-issue citations and penalties. This program targets small, high-hazard businesses. No citations or penalties are issued as a result of using these services, although any problems identified by a WSC consultant that are not corrected by the employer can be reported to MN OSHA Compliance staff for further investigation.

WSC consultants will help employers recognize hazards, make recommendations for solving problems and suggest other sources of help that may be available. In order to receive these services, the employer must commit to the timely correction of any serious safety or health hazard that may be found during the site visit by WSC consultants. Once an employer makes that commitment, the WCS consultant conducts a site visit and issues a report containing recommendations.

Minnesota Safety and Health Achievement Recognition Program (MNSHARP)

MNSHARP is a voluntary, consultation-based program that assists small, high-hazard employers in achieving safety and health improvements and recognizes them for doing so. Eligibility is limited to employers with up to 250 employees at the work site and not more than 500 at all sites corporation-wide; priority is given to employers with fewer than 100 employees. Participating employers receive a comprehensive safety and health consultation survey that results in a one-year action plan. During that year, participating employers must correct identified hazards and develop and implement an effective safety and health program; all employees must participate in these efforts. When the participating employer has met the requirements of the preceding sentence, and its lost-workday injury and illness rate falls below the national average for their industry, that employer is awarded with a MNSHARP Certificate of Recognition and for the next year that employer is exempted from programmed inspections from MNOSHA. Participating employers can enjoy renewed Certificates, as well as a continuance of their exemption from those programmed exemptions, if an on-site safety and health survey by WSC confirms that the employer is continuing to meet the requirements of MNSHARP.

MNSTAR Program

This program is a voluntary one, available to any employer in Minnesota, including small employers who previously successfully participated in MNSHARP. MNSTAR relies mainly on self-assessment by the employer, using the federal Voluntary Protection Program (see OSHA Instruction TED 8.1A, *Revised Voluntary Protection Programs (VPP) Policies and Procedures Manual*). Participating in MNSTAR requires the employer to commit to completing an extensive application, which will include providing WSC with copies of all the written policies and programs of the employer that WSC requests. In addition, the employer's lost workday injury and illness rate must be below state and national levels for its industry.

Labor-Management Safety and Health Committees

All employers with at least 25 employees are required to have a safety and health committee comprised of representatives from labor and management. Also, any other employer is likewise required to have such a committee if: that employer has a lost workday cases incidence rate in the top ten percent of all rates for employers in the same industry; or the workers' compensation premium classification assigned to the greatest portion of the payroll for that employer has a pure premium rate, as reported by the workers' compensation rating association, in the top 25 percent of premium rates for all classes. If both the labor and management representatives request it, WSC is available to help interpret OSHA standards, offer training in self-inspection techniques, and prepare and assist in the preparation and implementation of educational and training programs.

Safety and Health Education Outreach Program

WSC offers workshops to help educate employers and employees about workplace safety and health hazards and the OSHA standards that address them. The goal of these workshops is to lower injury and illness rates, and reduce workplace injury costs, by helping employers implement and maintain effective safety and health programs.

WSC, in partnership with 13 organizations throughout the state, offers a series of one-day safety and health seminars. Specific topics change each calendar quarter. In addition, upon request WSC will offer safety and health training to individual companies or organizations, by means of either an informal training session accompanied by an on-site consultation, or a formal training session.

Safety Grants Program

The Safety Grant program awards up to $10,000 to qualifying employers for the cost of projects designed to reduce the risk of injury and illness to their employees. To qualify, an employer must have workers' compensation insurance, be under MNOSHA's jurisdiction; a qualified safety professional must have conducted an on-site safety inspection and issued a written report with recommendations based on that inspection; the project must be consistent with the recommendations of that inspection, it must reduce the risk of injury or disease, and it must be feasible; the employer must be committed to the project's implementation, including an ability to provide funds to match the awarded grant amount, as well as be able to cover all estimated project costs by available funds, and; the project must comply with all federal, state and local laws and regulations. Priority for funds is given first to manufacturing businesses, then to workplaces that have had jobs lost due to safety issues, and then, finally, to all other projects.

WORKPLACE VIOLENCE PROTECTION

Due to the degree to which workplace violence occurs, employers must affirmatively ensure that their own employees are free from job related violence, not only to create a safe working environment for their employees but also to reduce the likelihood of costly litigation and/or compliance settlements arising out of workplace violence issues.

While there is currently no standard that regulates violence in the workplace, OSHA's "general duty clause" (a clause designed to cover hazards where no specific standard exists) is available to place an affirmative duty upon employers to investigate and evaluate workplace hazards, and to develop and implement preventive programs to curb violence and protect employees. The general duty clause could serve as the basis for a MNOSHA citation related to workplace violence. In addition, federal OSHA has developed guidelines concerning job-related violence in late-night retail establishments, health care and social service industries, and for taxi drivers.

WSC helps employers and employees reduce the incidence of violence in workplaces by providing on-site consultation, telephone assistance, education and training seminars, and a resource center. These efforts are targeted towards workplaces at high risk of violence, such as convenience stores, service stations, taxi and transit operations, restaurants and bars, motels, guard services, patient care facilities, schools, social service industries, residential care facilities and correctional institutions.

OSHA provides guidance on COVID-19 issues such as recording and reporting cases of COVID-19, determining whether a COVID-19 case is work related and creating preparedness plans for safe workplaces.

WORKERS' COMPENSATION INSURANCE

WHAT IS WORKERS' COMPENSATION INSURANCE?

Workers' compensation insurance provides compensation to employees who have a work-related injury or disease. Compensation includes partial wage replacement and full payment of medical and vocational rehabilitation costs. In case of death, workers' compensation benefits are paid to the employee's dependents. Workers' compensation insurance companies and self-insured employers pay these benefits and collect the premiums. The Minnesota workers' compensation law was designed to standardize benefits, reduce litigation, and encourage early rehabilitation intervention, good employee/employer relationships and return-to-work programs.

WHO IS REQUIRED TO HAVE WORKERS' COMPENSATION INSURANCE?

Generally all employers are required to have workers' compensation insurance and display the name of their insurer in a conspicuous place on a poster provided by the Minnesota Department of Labor and Industry. Under Minn. Stat. § 176.021, every employer is liable to pay compensation in every case of personal injury or death arising out of and in the course of employment. Minn. Stat. § 176.181, subd. 2. requires employers who have not been approved for self-insurance (through the Minnesota Department of Commerce) to provide workers' compensation insurance for their employees. Employees are generally defined as persons performing services for another for hire including minors and workers who are not citizens. A person who employs a child care provider (nanny) or other person (domestic) to work for them at the person's home may be required to provide worker's compensation insurance.

Some entities, if they have no employees are not employers so they have no one to insure:

- Sole Proprietorships: Individually or family run, non-incorporated businesses owned by one person, including true independent contractors, where any employees are immediate family members (a spouse, parent or child, regardless of age). Note: Once a non-immediate family member is hired, insurance is required.
- Partnerships: Partners in business or farm operations where every employee is a partner or a spouse, parent or child of a partner, regardless of age.

Other categories of employment are excluded from the workers' compensation requirement:

- Closely Held Corporations: Executive officers owning 25 percent or more of a closely held corporation or spouse, parent or child of the executive officer, regardless of age, may be automatically excluded unless the business elects to cover them. To qualify for this exemption, such corporation must have 10 or fewer shareholders and less than 22,800 hours of payroll in the preceding calendar year.

  Employees of such a corporation who are within the third degree of kindred according to the rules of civil law related by blood or marriage to an executive officer of the corporation may also be excluded by filing a written request to be excluded. This includes brothers, sisters, aunts, uncles, grandparents and grandchildren. Cousins may not be excluded from coverage.
- Limited Liability Companies: For the purpose of worker's compensation exclusions, managers of the LLC and their family members are treated the same as executive officers of closely held corporations.
- Family Farm Operations: Persons employed by a family farm which pays or is obligated to pay cash wages during the preceding calendar year of less than $8,000 in cash wages, or less than the statewide average annual wage when the farm operation has a total liability and medical payment coverage equal to $300,000 and $5,000, respectively, under a farm liability insurance policy, and the policy covers injuries to farm laborers. The farmer-employer's immediate family members, farmers or their family members exchanging work within the community and their employees are also exempted from coverage. Executive officers of a family farm corporation are excluded.
- Casual Employees: An employee who is not working in the usual course of the trade, business, profession or occupation of the employer and both the employee and the employer understand that the employment is meant to be for one time or infrequent rather than permanent or periodically regular.
- Household Workers: This includes a domestic worker, a repairer, groundskeeper or maintenance worker at a private household who earns less than $1,000 cash during a quarter of the year unless more than $1,000 was earned in any quarter of the previous year.

The Minnesota Department of Labor and Industry has information sheets which expand the definitions and criteria above. They can be accessed at the address, phone number or website listed in the Resource Directory section of this Guide.

The Minnesota Workers' Compensation Act provides that insurance coverage may be purchased for many of the above named classes of persons. When coverage is provided, the insured person becomes an "employee" as defined within the statute. When coverage is elected or terminated, written notice must be provided to the insurer and becomes effective the day following receipt of the notice or at a later date requested in the notice.

An employer contracting with an independent contractor may also provide insurance for that person. The employer may only charge the independent contractor a fee for the coverage if the independent contractor elects in writing to be covered and is issued an endorsement setting forth the terms of the coverage, the names of the persons covered, the fee charged and how the fee is calculated.

Employers who do not obtain the required insurance face serious consequences including penalties of up to $1,000 per employee per week and an order prohibiting the employer from employing any person. In addition, the employer of any nonresidential construction, repair, or remodeling project that fails to provide workers' compensation coverage for employees may be sued for damages by any losing bidder on the project. The losing bidder may be entitled to recover the amount of profit the winning contractor expected to make on the project, as well as costs and attorney fees.

WORKER IDENTIFICATION NUMBER

The Minnesota Department of Labor and Industry Workers' Compensation Division generates a worker identification number – or WID number into its system that may be used instead of a Social Security Number (SSN) to identify claims.

The WID number is person-specific: a unique two- to eight-character number is automatically generated within the Workers' Compensation Division computer system when a claim-generating document is received (such as a claim petition where a First Report of Injury form has not been filed). It may be used rather than the SSN, with the date of the injury, to identify a specific case file.

The WID number is optional for now and will be for some time. Contact the Minnesota Department of Labor and Industry Workers' Compensation Division for more information.

WHAT INJURIES AND DISEASES ARE COVERED?

Workers' compensation insurance covers injuries and diseases that arise out of and in the course and scope of the employment. A work-related injury or disease is generally a physical condition that is caused, aggravated, precipitated or accelerated by the work or the work environment. Covered injuries can occur at the work place or outside the work place if the employee is on an assignment or is in transit between different work sites. Employees who experience a tragic event at work that results in post-traumatic stress disorder may also apply for worker's compensation.

New legislation (2018 Minn. Session Laws, Chapter 185) specifies that PTSD (Post Traumatic Stress Disorder) is presumed to be an occupational disease for certain occupations effective January 1, 2019. See the above statute for additional information.

EMPLOYEES WHO ARE INJURED OUT OF STATE

Employees who are hired in Minnesota by a Minnesota employer or generally work here and also work out of state are covered by the Minnesota workers' compensation law. If a worker is employed in another state but is injured on the job in Minnesota, he or she can choose to be covered by the Minnesota workers' compensation law or by the law in his or her resident state.

A special provision for North Dakota employees limits the circumstances under which an employee hired in that state by a North Dakota employer could receive benefits under Minnesota law for injuries while temporarily working in Minnesota. Such an employee, who works in Minnesota fewer than 15 consecutive calendar days, or a maximum of 240 hours in a calendar year, will receive benefits under North Dakota law.

WHAT TO DO WHEN AN EMPLOYEE IS INJURED

When an employee is injured, it is the employer's responsibility – not the employee's – to complete a First Report of Injury form. The employer must give the employee the "Minnesota Workers' Compensation System Employee Information Sheet" at the time the employee is given a copy of the First Report of Injury Form. This form must be sent to the employer's workers' compensation insurance company so that it is received no later than 10 days after knowledge of the injury. The insurance company in turn must send the report to the Department of Labor and Industry so that it is received no later than 14 days after the injury if the injured worker is disabled more than three days. If the report is not filed within these deadlines, the employer or insurance company can be fined by the department. Self-insured employers have 14 days in which to file the report with the department.

It is important that the report is filed promptly so the insurance company will have adequate time to investigate the claim. If the work-related injury is serious or results in a fatality, the Minnesota Department of Labor and Industry must be notified by telephone within 48 hours. The First Report of Injury form also must be filed.

Completing a First Report of Injury form does not mean that the employer accepts liability for the injury. The insurance company will pay on the claim only after it has been investigated and determined that it is most likely compensable.

RETURNING AN EMPLOYEE TO WORK

Employers are strongly encouraged to bring their injured workers back to work as soon as they can. In cases of serious injuries, this might mean reasonably accommodating employees as they improve or modifying jobs they had before they were injured. Employers are encouraged to establish disability management programs to plan for these cases. The employer's workers' compensation insurer can assist in establishing such a program.

If the employee requests it or if the employee remains (or is expected to remain) off work more than 90 days and a valid request for waiver of rehabilitation services is not filed by the employer/insurer, the employee is entitled to receive a vocational rehabilitation consultation to determine whether the employee is qualified to receive vocational services. A rehabilitation consultation is provided at the request of the employer, the insurer, the employee, or the Minnesota Department of Labor and Industry and must be conducted by a qualified rehabilitation consultant registered with the Department.

It is important to coordinate these return-to-work programs with the employee's union, if there is one, to see that a return-to-work program does not conflict with seniority provisions in union contracts.

For employers of more than fifteen full-time employees, Minnesota law provides a civil penalty for an employer's refusal without reasonable cause to offer continued employment to an employee when continued employment is available within the employee's physical limitations. That penalty is one year's wages for the employee, up to $15,000.

MAKING A SUITABLE JOB OFFER

A suitable job offer is the offer of a job that is within the injured employee's medical restrictions and that returns the employee as close as possible to the economic status he or she enjoyed before the injury. Economic status includes not only wages, but also opportunities for promotion and advancement. Employee fringe benefits also may be considered in determining economic status. For example, if the employee had a minor injury, the only appropriate suitable job would be his or her old job or one similar to it. Any job, even a job with another employer, can qualify as a suitable job if it meets the tests of medical appropriateness and economic status, and takes into account the employee's former employment age, education, previous work history, interests and skills.

DISPUTE RESOLUTION

The majority of workers' compensation claims are administered without disputes arising. The Minnesota Department of Labor and Industry "must make efforts to settle problems of employees and employers by contacting third parties, including attorneys, insurers, and health care providers, on behalf of employers and employees and using the department's persuasion to settle issues quickly and cooperatively." (Minn. Stat. § 176.261).

For this purpose, the Minnesota Department of Labor and Industry has workers' compensation specialists and attorneys available to the public either by telephone or on a walk-in basis. Contact information can be found in the Resource Directory section of this Guide.

If informal methods are unable to resolve the problem, the Minnesota Department of Labor and Industry and the Office of Administrative Hearings offer administrative conferences and mediation sessions.

The Minnesota Department of Labor and Industry offers administrative conferences to try to resolve medical and rehabilitation benefit issues. The judges at the Office of Administrative Hearings conduct conferences to determine if the workers' compensation insurers are to be granted their request to discontinue disability benefits to an injured worker. The holder of an administrative conference will attempt to help the parties reach acceptable resolutions of the issues, but if this is not possible, the Minnesota Department of Labor and Industry will issue a decision and order, which is appealable.

Administrative conferences are designed to be fast, informal proceedings to resolve workers' compensation disputes. Attorneys may represent the parties but are not mandatory.

Mediation sessions are also used as a method to expedite the handling of disputed workers' compensation claims. The Minnesota Department of Labor and Industry will conduct a mediation session at the request of the parties. All parties must be agreeable to the mediation. Unlike other types of dispute resolution proceedings, the presiding official does not issue a decision. The mediator assists the parties in their efforts to work towards solutions and makes sure the agreements are in conformity with the workers' compensation laws. If the parties are successful in reaching resolutions, the mediator will prepare the mediation award and arrange for it to be properly signed, awarded, served and filed. As with administrative conferences, attorneys may represent the parties, but are not mandatory.

Other dispute resolution services offered at the Office of Administrative Hearings are settlement conferences, small claims court, special terms hearings, attorney fees and cost hearings, and formal hearings on workers' compensation issues. Some decisions are appealable to the Workers' Compensation Court of Appeals and the Minnesota Supreme Court.

REDUCING WORKERS' COMPENSATION COSTS

Workers' compensation insurance rates are set within broad limitations by the insurance company. Rates are adjusted by payroll risk classifications and by the employer's experience rating, which is the history of injuries in the business.

It is difficult to control the payroll risk classification because it is determined by the nature of the business and the type of work employees do. However, there are a number of ways to control the cost of workers' compensation premiums for the future. Employers who have accident prevention programs generally will have lower workers' compensation costs. The employer can take an active role in lowering workers' compensation costs by:

- Developing wellness programs that incorporate physical fitness and health education.
- Providing employee education on proper lifting techniques and appropriate body mechanics.
- Initiating return-to-work policies that include reasonable accommodation.
- Contacting Workplace Safety Consultation at the Minnesota Department of Labor and Industry, which provides a free, nonenforcement service to assist small private-sector employers in high hazard industries in their voluntary efforts to improve workplace safety and health. The Workplace Safety Consultation Division can be reached at the address and telephone number provided in the Resource Directory section of this Guide.

Under state law, all high hazard employers and those with more than 25 employees must establish a joint labor-management safety committee to address workers' compensation and workplace safety issues.

The employer's insurance company or agent can provide more information about accident prevention, safety and health programs and return-to-work programs.

BUYING WORKERS' COMPENSATION INSURANCE

There are several thousand licensed insurance agents who sell workers' compensation insurance in Minnesota. It is best to contact several agents to review the business and to quote prices for the insurance. In Minnesota, workers' compensation insurance is sold through open competition, which means insurance companies establish rates and compete for business. All workers' compensation policies provide coverage mandated by law; therefore, only the price and quality of service varies, and shopping for insurance can save money. Other factors to consider in choosing a carrier are claims servicing, safety counseling, and the carrier's reputation.

Options other than insurance may be available to cover an employer's workers' compensation liability. For example, some large employers or groups of employers are approved by the Department of Commerce to self-insure, which allows them to directly manage their workers' compensation claims and contain their costs. Many large employers who are approved to self-insure their risk hire a claims administration company.

Occasionally, an employer is unable to obtain workers' compensation insurance on the open market because the business is too small to justify the expense of selling and servicing the account or because of the nature of the risk involved in the business. In this case, the employer would buy the insurance through the Assigned Risk Pool. Additional information about this type of plan can be obtained from an insurance agent.

SEMINARS ON WORKERS' COMPENSATION

The Minnesota Department of Labor and Industry provides speakers and sponsors seminars and programs for employers on controlling workers' compensation costs. Refer to WC Training for Employers, http://www.dli.mn.gov/business/workers-compensation/wc-training-employers. Contact information about workers' compensation seminars may be obtained from the Minnesota Department of Labor and Industry at the address and telephone number provided in the Resource Directory section of this Guide.

FURTHER INFORMATION

Additional information on workers' compensation may be obtained by calling the Workers' Compensation Division at the address and telephone numbers provided in the Resource Directory section of this Guide. The Division also produces a primer about HIPPA (privacy of health information) and workers' compensation which will be helpful to employers.

EMPLOYEE BENEFITS

Employers commonly provide some form of health care, life insurance and retirement benefits for their employees. Although employers are not required to provide these plans, if the plans are provided they must comply with federal and state laws.

FEDERAL EMPLOYEE RETIREMENT INCOME SECURITY ACT

At the federal level, the Employee Retirement Income Security Act (ERISA), 29 United States Code §§ 1001-1461, governs pension plans and medical, surgical, sickness, disability and death benefit plans sponsored by employers who are engaged in interstate commerce or in other activities affecting interstate commerce. ERISA establishes standards governing information to be provided participants, eligibility for participation, benefit rights and benefit accrual, vesting, employer and employee contributions, payment of benefits, plan termination and mergers, and survivor benefits. Federal agencies charged with enforcing ERISA include the U.S. Department of Labor, the Treasury Department, the Internal Revenue Service, and the Pension Benefit Guaranty Fund.

Information on ERISA may be obtained from the U.S. Department of Labor's Employee Benefits Security Administration at the contact information provided in the Resource Directory section of this Guide.

ERISA is an extremely complex and technical law. Historically it has been amended frequently by Congress, and been the subject of a great deal of litigation. Failure to conform to its requirements can create civil liability for the employer, and can cause the employer to lose a tax deduction for amounts contributed to the benefit plan. For these reasons, employers who are contemplating benefit plans covered by ERISA should obtain the advice of experts in this field before setting up the plan.

MINNESOTA REQUIREMENTS FOR GROUP HEALTH AND LIFE INSURANCE

Minnesota employers who offer group health insurance, health maintenance (HMO) coverage, or group life insurance must comply with Minnesota Statutes and regulations of the Minnesota Department of Commerce concerning those products. In addition, HMO coverage is also regulated by Minnesota statutes and regulations of the Minnesota Department of Health. This is the case regardless of whether the employer is also covered by ERISA, although in some situations ERISA may preempt state law.

The state statutes and regulations establish minimum standards and requirements in areas like filing and obtaining approval of policy forms and certificates, minimum coverage requirements, content requirements for insurance certificates, limitations on cancellation and conversion procedures on termination of employment.

As with ERISA, the state requirements governing these plans are technical and complex. Expert advice should be sought before establishing any of these plans.

Insurance is regulated in Minnesota by the Minnesota Department of Commerce and, in the case of HMO coverage, by the Minnesota Department of Health. The departments may be contacted at the address and telephone number provided in the Resource Directory section of this Guide.

RECORDKEEPING

Both federal and state laws impose recordkeeping requirements on documents relating to employee benefit plans. These include plan descriptions, participants' elections, worksheets and other documents. Retention periods range from six years to duration of the plan plus one year. Each year a comprehensive update of federal record retention requirements is published in the *Federal Register.* A business or government reference librarian can direct employers to the latest compilation.

COBRA NOTIFICATION

Health Insurance

The federal Consolidated Omnibus Budget Reconciliation Act of 1985 (COBRA) requires employers who sponsor group health plans to offer covered individuals the right to elect continuation of the group coverage under certain circumstances. Minnesota law imposes additional requirements on employers whose health plans are funded through insurance contracts.

Employers who offer these types of benefits must provide employees (and, if covered, their spouses and dependents) with notice of their continuation rights when an event occurs that would otherwise cause a loss of coverage. The covered individual may elect to obtain for a limited period of time continuation of the coverage they had before the event. The individual may be required to pay up to 102 percent of the cost of the premium for their coverage.

COBRA requirements are complex. Firms that offer group health insurance to their employees should consult with legal counsel to assure that their notice procedures conform to federal and state law.

Life Insurance

There is no right under federal law to continue employer-provided life insurance coverage after employment terminates. Under Minnesota law, however, group term life insurance policies issued within the state must permit covered employees who are voluntarily or involuntarily terminated, incur a reduction in hours to the point where they are no longer eligible for coverage, or are laid off, to elect continuation of the coverage for themselves and their dependents. Coverage ends after 18 months or on the date on which coverage is obtained under another group policy, whichever occurs first. As with health insurance continuation coverage, the employee can be required to pay the cost of the life insurance continuation.

PLANT CLOSINGS

FEDERAL LAW

The federal Worker Adjustment and Retraining Notification Act (WARN) applies to employers of 100 or more full time employees. Employers with fewer employees are encouraged to comply with the spirit of the law, although they are not bound by it.

The federal law requires employers to provide 60 days' notice to several entities before ordering a plant closing or massive layoff. These entities include affected employees or their collective bargaining representative, the state dislocated worker unit (in Minnesota, the Department of Employment and Economic Development and its Rapid Response Team, listed in the Resource Directory section of this Guide), and the chief elected official of the unit of local government in which the business is located. If the firm is situated in more than one locality, notice must be given to the local governmental unit to which the employer pays the highest taxes.

Employers who violate the law may be liable to employees for back pay and benefits for which they would have been eligible under an employee benefit plan. An employer who fails to notify the local governmental unit of the plant closing may be liable for a civil penalty of up to $500 per day of violation.

MINNESOTA LAW

Minnesota law requires all employers who must provide notice under WARN to notify the Department of Employment and Economic Development (specifically, it's Rapid Response Team) of the names, addresses and occupations of the employees whose jobs will be terminated. The law encourages, but does not mandate, businesses that are considering a plant closing, substantial layoff or relocation of operations outside Minnesota to give early notice of that decision to the Department of Employment and Economic Development, the employees of the affected establishment, any collective bargaining agent representing the employees, and the local government unit in which the establishment is located. This notice is in addition to any notice required by WARN.

The law directs the Department of Employment and Economic Development to establish a program to help employers, employees and the community to respond quickly to the plant closing or layoff by providing information and technical assistance for dislocated workers. The law also provides information and technical assistance on accessing public and private services and programs for dislocated workers and establishes a grant program for examining the feasibility of alternatives to the plant closing. The Dislocated Worker Program is funded by a special payroll assessment that is paid with unemployment insurance taxes.

A new law provides employers facing economic hardship with an alternative to laying off their employees by participating in a shared work plan with the Minnesota Department of Employment and Economic Development.

BANKRUPTCY NOTIFICATION

Under Minnesota law, an employer must notify employees and job applicants that it has filed a petition for bankruptcy or has had an involuntary bankruptcy petition filed against it. Failure to provide the required notice is a misdemeanor.

POSTER REQUIREMENTS

A number of federal and state statutes require that employers post certain notices in places on the company's premises where employees are likely to see them. Examples of these locations include bulletin boards, entrances and time clocks and other conspicuous places. Where a company has more than one work site, posters must be placed at each site. Poster requirements are listed below. Posters are available **FREE** from the agencies listed, at the address and telephone number provided in the Resource Directory section of this Guide.

FEDERAL POSTER REQUIREMENTS

Please note that posting requirements vary by statute; that is, not all employers are covered by the US Department of Labor's statutes and thus may not be required to post a specific notice. For example, some small businesses may not be covered by the Family and Medical Leave Act and thus would not be subject to the Act's posting requirements. For information on coverage, visit the U.S. Department of Labor's elaws Poster and Recordkeeping at https://webapps.dol.gov/elaws/posters.html and elaws FirstStep Poster Advisor at https://webapps.dol.gov/elaws/posters.htm.

Fair Labor Standards

The U.S. Department of Labor requires employers to display posters on the federal minimum wage, overtime and child labor laws, and the Family and Medical Leave Act. Employees also must be notified of their rights under the Polygraph Protection Act of 1988. The Walsh-Healy Federal Contracts Act, the Davis Bacon and Related Acts, and the McNamara-O'Hara Service Contract Act require contractors to provide certain notices to employees working on government contracts. Posters and information are available from the U.S. Department of Labor, Wage and Hour Division.-Workplace Posters, https://www.dol.gov/whd/resources/posters.htm.

Equal Employment Opportunity

Information on federal requirements including equal employment opportunity, age discrimination, federal contract compliance, and compliance with the Rehabilitation Act of 1973 may be obtained from the federal Equal Employment Opportunity Commission.

Uniformed Services Employment and Reemployment Rights Act (USERRA)

Employers are required to provide to persons entitled to rights and benefits under USERRA, a notice of the rights, benefits and obligations of such persons and such employers under USERRA. Employers may provide the notice, "Your Rights Under USERRA" (https://www.dol.gov/vets/programs/userra/poster.htm), by posting it where employee notices are customarily placed. However, employers are free to provide the notice to employees in other ways that will minimize costs while ensuring that the full text of the notice is provided (e.g. by handling or mailing out the notice, or distributing the notice via electronic mail). Posters and information are available from the U.S. Department of Labor, Veterans' Employment and Training Services, USERRA, Compliance Assistance, https://www.dol.gov/agencies/vets/programs/userra/compliance.

Note: Also refer to the publication *Employing Servicemembers: What You Should Know About USERRA* publication available without charge from the Small Business Assistance Office.

STATE POSTER REQUIREMENTS

Fair Labor Standards, Occupational Safety and Health, and Workers' Compensation

The State of Minnesota requires employers to display posters on the state minimum wage law, including the provision for an employee's right to the reason for termination, and on the state mandatory retirement law. The state also requires employers to display posters on the Occupational Safety and Health law and on workers' compensation rights of employees. All required posters including the Unemployment Insurance poster described below are available from the Minnesota Department of Labor and Industry (DLI). The worker's compensation poster is available in many languages, including Spanish, Lao, Vietnamese, Cambodian, Hmong, and English and can be downloaded from DL, Workplace Posters page at http://www.dli.mn.gov/about-department/workplace-posters. Posters on parental leave, age discrimination, and whistleblower protection are also required.

Unemployment Insurance

Posters informing employees of their rights under state unemployment insurance law may be obtained from the Minnesota Department of Labor and Industry or can be printed from the Department's website at Workplace Posters, http://www.dli.mn.gov/about-department/workplace-posters.

Minnesota Clean Indoor Air Act

Employers should post no-smoking signs throughout the workplace in order to ensure employees understand the provisions of the Act and are not exposed to secondhand smoke while at work.

CHECKLIST FOR HIRING AN EMPLOYEE

The following information generally outlines federal and state tax and other requirements that apply to the employment relationship. Detailed descriptions of these requirements, including any exceptions and special requirements that may apply, can be found in information bulletins and instruction booklets published by the agency listed. Addresses and telephone numbers appear in the Resource Directory section of this Guide. For specific advice on individual situations consultation with a qualified professional advisor is strongly recommended.

Note: Corporations wholly-owned by the person who also performs services for that business are generally considered to be employers, and that owner is likewise generally considered to be an employee. As explained elsewhere in this Guide, persons working in the construction industry may be treated as employees for purposes of workers' compensation unless certain conditions are met.

1. **Determine whether the worker is an employee.**

   A worker generally is considered an "employee" if the person who obtains the worker's services has the legal right to control the manner and means of performing the work. A worker may be considered an employee for certain purposes, such as payment of FICA taxes – and not for other purposes, such as income tax withholding.

   If a worker is an employee, the requirements described in this checklist will apply whether the person is employed full-time or part-time. Before determining that a worker is not an employee it is advisable to consult with your attorney or with the appropriate agency – such as the Internal Revenue Service, Minnesota Department of Revenue, Minnesota Department of Employment and Economic Development, or Minnesota Department of Labor and Industry.

   Detailed discussion of whether a worker is an employee appears in the section of this Guide titled "Who is an Employee." The following forms and materials are available to help determine if a worker is an employee.

   Income tax withholding, FICA and Federal unemployment taxes:

   Form: SS-8, Determination of Worker Status for Purposes of Federal Employment Taxes and Income Tax Withholding, https://www.irs.gov/forms-pubs/about-form-ss-8.

   Publication 15-A, Employers' Supplemental Tax Guide, https://www.irs.gov/forms-pubs/about-publication-15-a, provides further information.

   Available from: Internal Revenue Service.

   Filed with: The IRS Service Center designated on the form.

   How often: In response to worker's request for determination of status for purposes of federal employment taxes and income tax withholding.

Minnesota Unemployment Insurance

Register with the Minnesota Unemployment Insurance (UI) Program of the Minnesota Department of Employment and Economic Development through its self-service unemployment insurance reporting system. The MN UI Program determinations whether a worker is an employee or independent contractor based on Minnesota Statute. Refer to the Unemployment Insurance (UI) Employer Handbook at https://www.uimn.org/employers/help-and-support/emp-hbook/index.jsp.

Register: Minnesota Unemployment Insurance (UI) Program website, https://www.uimn.org/employers.

When: As soon as possible after first wages are paid for covered employment.

Workers' compensation

The Minnesota Department of Labor and Industry has adopted rules addressing the conditions under which workers will be considered employees or independent contractors for workers' compensation purposes. These rules can be found at Minnesota Rules 5224. Copies of Minnesota Rules are available at law libraries and many public libraries, and may be purchased from the Minnesota Bookstore.

2. Obtain federal Employer Identification Number (EIN).

Form: SS-4, Application for Employer Identification Number, https://www.irs.gov/pub/irs-pdf/fss4.pdf

Available from: Forms and instructions are available online at https://www.irs.gov/forms-pubs/about-form-ss-4

Filed with: The IRS. It helps to have a completed Form SS-4 available before beginning the online application process.

Review How to Apply for an EIN, https://www.irs.gov/businesses/small-businesses-self-employed/how-to-apply-for-an-ein.

Apply online: https://www.irs.gov/businesses/small-businesses-self-employed/apply-for-an-employer-identification-number-ein-online

Apply by Fax: 855-641-6935 toll-free.

Apply by mail: Internal Revenue Service, Attn: EIN Operation, Cincinnati, OH 45999.

The IRS no longer issues EINs by telephone for domestic taxpayers. Only international applicants can receive an EIN by telephone.

How often: Once, unless business ownership or form of organization changes.

3. **Obtain Minnesota Taxpayer Identification Number.**

Form: ABR, Application for Business Registration, https://www.revenue.state.mn.us/sites/default/files/2020-01/FactSheet08.pdf.

Register with the Minnesota Dept. of Revenue:

- Online at https://www.mndor.state.mn.us/tp/webreg/_/.
- By phone at 651-282-5225 or 800-657-3605.

Available from: Minnesota Department of Revenue.

Filed with: Minnesota Department of Revenue.

How often: Once, unless business ownership or form of organization changes.

4. **Obtain Minnesota workers' compensation insurance.**

Form: None required.

Available from: Coverage is obtained through the employer's insurance company.

Filed with: Not applicable.

How often: Workers' compensation coverage is required for the entire time the employer has employees. Certain exemptions may exist. For information on these exemptions, contact your insurance company or the Minnesota Department of Labor and Industry, Workers' Compensation Division.

5. **Obtain Minnesota Unemployment Insurance (UI) Employer Account Number.**

Form: Unemployment Insurance (UI) Employer Account Number. Register:

- Online at Minnesota Unemployment Insurance (UI) Program, https://www.uimn.org/employers/index.jsp.
- By phone at 651-296-6141, option 4.

Available from: Minnesota Department of Employment and Economic Development, Unemployment Insurance (UI) Program.

Filed with: Minnesota Department of Employment and Economic Development, Unemployment Insurance (UI) Program.

How often: Under Minnesota Unemployment Insurance Law, every individual or organization that pays covered wages in Minnesota must register with the MN Unemployment Insurance (UI) Program. Registration should be done as soon as possible after the first wages are paid for covered employment in Minnesota. Registration must occur prior to the due date of the first quarterly wage detail report the employer is required to submit.

Do not register until covered wages have actually been paid.

Refer to the *Employer Handbook* at https://www.uimn.org/employers/help-and-support/emp-hbook/index.jsp, sections *Who Needs to Register* and *How to Register*.

6. Verify compliance with immigration law.

Form: Refer to Refer to Complete and Correct Form I-9, https://www.uscis.gov/i-9-central/complete-and-correct-form-i-9 and I-9, Employment Eligibility Verification, and Handbook for Employers M-274, https://www.uscis.gov/i-9-central/handbook-employers-m-274. See discussion of E-Verify earlier in this Guide.

Available from: Bureau of U.S. Citizenship and Immigration Services (USCIS).

Filed with: The Form I-9 is not filed with any government agency but is subject to audit and inspection by the U.S. Departments of Homeland Security and the U.S. Department of Labor.

Form I-9 must be retained by the employer for three years following the date of hire or one year after the individual's employment is terminated, whichever is later.

How often: Generally, a new Form I-9 must be completed each time an individual is hired within three business days of the employee's first day of work. An employer who rehires a person within three years of the date the I-9 was originally completed may be able to update and re-verify employment eligibility on the original Form I-9.

Details are available at USCIS's I-9 Central at https://www.uscis.gov/I-9Central.

7. Obtain employee withholding information (Forms W-4, W-4MN; child support and spousal maintenance obligations).

Form: Federal Form W-4, Employee's Withholding Allowance Certificate, https://www.irs.gov/forms-pubs/about-form-w-4, is used to determine the amount of federal income tax withholding.

Minnesota form, W-4MN, Minnesota Employee Withholding Allowance /Exemption Certificate, https://www.revenue.state.mn.us/sites/default/files/2020-01/w-4mn_0.pdf, should be completed in addition to federal Form W-4 in all cases.

Available from: Internal Revenue Service (Federal Form W-4) and the Minnesota Department of Revenue (Form W-4MN).

Filed with: Employers must keep copies of completed federal Forms, W-4 or state Forms W-4MN for their employees in their files. The forms verify that federal and state income taxes are being withheld according to the employee's instructions and needs to be available for inspection by the IRS or the state.

Employers may be directed, in written notice or in published guidance, to send certain W-4 forms to the IRS.

Employers must send copies of Form W-4MN to the Minnesota Department of Revenue if any of the following apply:

- The employee claims more than 10 Minnesota withholding allowances.
- The employee claims to be exempt from Minnesota withholding and you reasonably expect the employee's wages to exceed $200 per week. Exception: If the employee is a resident of reciprocity states, Michigan or North Dakota and has completed Form MWR, Reciprocity Exemption/Affidavit of Residency for Tax Year 2020, https://www.revenue.state.mn.us/sites/default/files/2019-12/mwr_20.pdf
- You believe the employee is not entitled to the number of allowances claimed.

Mail to: Minnesota Department of Revenue, Mail Station 6501, St. Paul, MN 55146-6501.

How often: Forms W-4 and W-4MN are generally valid until the employee provide new ones. But employees who claim to be exempt from withholding must renew the exemption annually by filing new Forms W-4 or W-4MN by February 15 each year.

When an employee replaces existing Forms W-4 or W-4MN with a new one, the employer must put the new information into effect no later than the start of the first payroll period ending on or after the 30th day after the day on which the replacement Form W-4 or W-4MN is received.

If there is no payroll period, the replacement Forms W-4 or W-4MN must be put into effect with the first payment of wages on or after the 30th day after the day on which the replacement Forms W-4 or W-4MN is received. The replacement Forms W-4 or W-4MN can be put into effect sooner, if the employer wishes.

8. New Hire Reporting.

The Claims Resolution Act of 2012 requires all employers to report all newly hired, re-hired and returning to work employees to a state directory within 20 days of the date they are hired, rehired, or return to work.

Form: The Minnesota New Hire Reporting Form or W-4 Form.

Available from: Minnesota Department of Human Services (DHS).

Filed with: Minnesota New Hire Reporting Center. You can file:

- Online at https://newhire-reporting.com/MN-Newhire/default.aspx.
- By mail at Minnesota New Hire Reporting Center, P.O. Box 64212, St. Paul, MN 55164-0212.

How often: Employers must report within 20 days of a new employee's hire date. Employers who submit reports electronically must do so in two monthly transmissions not more than 16 days apart.

In addition to reporting to the Minnesota Department of Human Services, employers must ask all new employees if they have court-ordered medical support or dependent insurance obligations that must be withheld from income, and the terms of any court order.

If amounts for medical support must be withheld, the employer must do the appropriate withholding. If the employee is required to obtain dependent insurance the employer must tell the employee about the application process and enroll the employee and the dependents in the plan. Employers are required to make such withholdings within a specific time period, and there are limits on the percentage of wages that can be withheld.

9. Withhold federal income tax and FICA tax (employee share) and withhold Minnesota income taxes.

Form: No specific form is required. These are accounting entries on the employer's books. The amounts also must be listed on the employee's pay statement.

Tables showing amounts to be withheld are provided by the Internal Revenue Service, see Publication 15 (Circular E) Employer's Tax Guide at https://www.irs.gov/forms-pubs/about-publication-15, and the Minnesota Department of Revenue, see Minnesota Income Tax Withholding Instruction Booklet and Tax Tables at https://www.revenue.state.mn.us/sites/default/files/2019-12/wh_inst_20_0.pdf.

Available from: Not applicable.

Filed with: Accounting records are retained by the employer and are subject to inspection by the Internal Revenue Service and Minnesota Department of Revenue.

How often: Withholding must be done each time wages are paid.

10. Account for employer's share of payroll taxes.

Payroll taxes include the employer's share of the FICA (Social Security and Medicare) tax, Federal Unemployment Tax Act (FUTA) and Minnesota unemployment tax.

Form: No specific form is required. These are accounting entries made on the employer's books each time wages are paid. The taxes are paid through deposits or with quarterly or annual tax returns.

Available from: Not applicable.

Filed with: These taxes must be deposited in a bank as specified by, or paid directly to, the Internal Revenue Service and the Minnesota Department of Employment and Economic Development.

Note: Electronic filing of these taxes may be required.

How often: The accounting entries are made each time wages are paid.

11. Deposit withheld federal income tax and employer's and employees' share of FICA tax and deposit federal unemployment (FUTA) tax.

Form: With few exceptions, electronic fund transfers are made using Electronic Federal Tax Payment System (EFTPS) for all federal tax deposits.

Filed with: Deposits are made to the U.S. Department of Treasury using EFTPS.

Information on EFTPS may found at https://www.eftps.com/eftps/ or by calling the U.S. Treasury Department customer service at 800-555-4477.

How often: For federal income tax and FICA tax, the accumulated liability usually must be deposited monthly or semiweekly (or by the next day if the liability is $100,000 or more). The "liability" is the sum of the withheld federal income tax, the employees' and the employer's share of Social Security and Medicare.

Generally, employers with a liability of $50,000 or less accrued during a designated four-quarter period will deposit monthly, and employers whose liability is more than $50,000 are required to deposit semi-weekly. The employer will follow the appropriate deposit schedule for the entire calendar year.

The specific rules may be found in IRS Publication 15, Circular E, Employer's Tax Guide which may be obtained from the Internal Revenue Service.

FUTA tax deposits are made quarterly (by the end of the month following the end of the quarter), unless the amount of FUTA tax owed but not deposited is $500 or less. If the tax is $500 or less at the end of the quarter, no deposit is required. The tax is added to the tax for the next quarter.

12. Deposit withheld Minnesota income tax.

Form: The employer can make Minnesota tax deposits in one of three ways:

1. Online with Minnesota Department of Revenue e-Services Payment Voucher System at https://www.mndor.state.mn.us/tp/paymentvoucher/_/.
2. By phone at 800-570-3329.
3. By mail with a payment voucher.

Some employers are required to pay electronically.

Filed with: Minnesota Department of Revenue.

How often: The employer must deposit Minnesota withholding tax following a semi-weekly or monthly schedule.

For deposit schedule information, see the Minnesota Income Tax Withholding Instruction Booklet and Tax Tables, https://www.revenue.state.mn.us/sites/default/files/2019-12/wh_inst_20_0.pdf.

13. File federal withholding return (quarterly) or employment taxes (annually)

Quarterly filers

Form: Form 941, Employer's QUARTERLY Federal Tax Return, https://www.irs.gov/forms-pubs/about-form-941

Different forms are required for employers of agricultural employees.

Available from: Internal Revenue Service.

Filed with: The IRS Service Center designated on the form.

How often: The employer must file a return quarterly.

Annually for employers of agricultural employees using Form 943, Employer's Annual Federal Tax Return for Agricultural Employees, https://www.irs.gov/pub/irs-pdf/f943.pdf.

Annual filers

Form: Form 944, Employer's Annual Federal Tax Return, https://www.irs.gov/forms-pubs/about-form-944 (optional).

Available from: Internal Revenue Service.

Small businesses may be affected by changes to Form 944, Employers Annual Federal Tax Return, https://www.irs.gov/forms-pubs/about-form-944. The changes include the ability for small employers to elect whether they want to file Form 944 or Form 941, Employer's Quarterly Federal Tax Return, https://www.irs.gov/pub/irs-pdf/f941.pdf.

Filed with: Employers who have estimated employment tax liability of $1,000 or less for the entire calendar year are eligible to file annual Form 944 rather than the quarterly Form 941. In the past, filing this form has been mandatory for employers who met the qualifications and were notified by the Internal Revenue Service to file Form 944.

How often: Employers who are Form 944 filers can opt out by telephone at 800-829-4933 no later than April 1 of the current year, or in writing no later than March 15 of the current year. Form 941 employers, who want to file Form 944 and are eligible, can opt in to filing a Form 944 during the same election period by the same methods. Whether opting in or opting out of Form 944 filing, after contacting the IRS, the taxpayer will be notified in writing about which return to file.

Information about filing employment taxes annually is available at Certain Taxpayers May Now File Their Employment Taxes Annually, https://www.irs.gov/businesses/small-businesses-self-employed/certain-taxpayers-may-now-file-their-employment-taxes-annually.

14. File Minnesota quarterly withholding return.

Form: Quarterly Withholding Tax Return

Available from: Minnesota Department of Revenue

Filed with: Returns must be filed electronically, either:

- Online with Minnesota Department of Revenue e-Services at https://www.mndor.state.mn.us/tp/eservices/_/.
- By phone at 800-570-3329.

How often: Quarterly. A return must be filed even if the employer paid no wages subject to withholding, had no employees during the quarter or had no tax withheld or deposited.

15. File Minnesota unemployment insurance wage detail.

Form: All wage detail reports must be submitted electronically. For more information see Wages & Taxes, https://www.uimn.org/employers/wages-taxes/index.jsp.

Available from: Minnesota Department of Employment and Economic Development, Unemployment Insurance (UI) Program.

Filed with: Minnesota Department of Employment and Economic Development, Unemployment Insurance (UI) Program.

How often: Quarterly. A wage detail report must be filed even if the employer paid no wages or had no employees during the quarter.

16. File federal unemployment tax (FUTA) return.

Form: Form 940, Employer's Annual Federal Unemployment (FUTA) Tax Return, https://www.irs.gov/forms-pubs/about-form-940.

Available from: Internal Revenue Service.

Filed with: The IRS Service Center designated on the form.

How often: Annually, by January 31 of each year.

17. Provide Form W-2 to employee and others.

Form: W-2, Wage and Tax Statement, https://www.irs.gov/forms-pubs/about-form-w-2

Available from: Internal Revenue Service

Filed with: Employee (three copies).

Social Security Administration (one copy).

Minnesota Department of Revenue (one copy).

One copy is retained by the employer.

How often: At the end of the year, the employer must complete Form W-2, Wage and Tax Statement (PDF) to report wages, tips and other compensation paid to an employee. A copy of this form must be given to the employee by January 31 for the previous year.

If the employee stops working for the employer and requests the W-2 before the January 31 deadline, it must be provided within 30 days following the request. The employer must also send a copy of the W-2 to the Social Security Administration (SSA) by January 31.

Employers can prepare and file up to 20 W-2s at a time at the Social Security Administration's website. Using SSA's online W-2 filing. Go to Employer W-2 Filing Instructions & Information, https://www.ssa.gov/employer/. Employers can also print out all the necessary copies of the W-2 for their employees, state taxing agencies, etc. Also refer to Minnesota Department of Revenue Submitting Form W-2, W-2c, and 1099, https://www.revenue.state.mn.us/submitting-forms-w-2-w-2c-and-1099.

Forms W-2 and W-3 may be obtained from the Internal Revenue Service by ordering online at Online Ordering for Information Returns and Employer Returns, https://www.irs.gov/businesses/online-ordering-for-information-returns-and-employer-returns.

18. File Minnesota annual withholding return (approved annual filers only).

Form: Annual Withholding Tax Return

Available from: Minnesota Department of Revenue

Filed with: Returns must be filed electronically, either:

- Online with Minnesota Department of Revenue e-Services at https://www.mndor.state.mn.us/tp/eservices/_/.
- By phone at 800-570-3329.

How often: Annually, by January 31 of each year.

To qualify for annual filing, you must have a filing history of $500 or less of withholding in the prior calendar year. If you believe you qualify and want to file your returns annually, contact the Minnesota Department of Revenue.

19. Information returns, pensions and other payments.

Form: Form 1099-MISC.

Employers who make payments to consultants, independent contractors, and others who are exempt from withholding may be required to provide a federal Form 1099-MISC to those individuals, and file the form with the Internal Revenue Service.

The IRS has brought back Form 1099-NEC, to be used beginning with 2020 information returns.

Refer to IRS information: Forms and Associated Taxes for Independent Contractors,https://www.irs.gov/businesses/small-businesses-self-employed/forms-and-associated-taxes-for-independent-contractors; About Form 1099-MISC, Miscellaneous Income, https://www.irs.gov/forms-pubs/about-form-1099-misc; and 2020 Instructions for Form 1099-MISC and Form 1099-NEC, https://www.irs.gov/pub/irs-pdf/i1099msc.pdf.

Available from: Internal Revenue Service.

Filed with: Internal Revenue Services.

How often: Annually.

Public Law 114-113, Division Q, section 201, requires Form 1099-MISC to be filed on or before January 31 when you are reporting nonemployee compensation payments in box 7.

Otherwise, file by February 28, if you file on paper, or by April 1, if you file electronically. The due dates for furnishing payee statements remain the same.

Refer to the IRS General Instructions for Certain Information Returns (Forms 1097, 1098, 1099, 3921, 3922, 5498, and W-2G), https://www.irs.gov/pub/irs-pdf/i1099gi.pdf.

Employers who pay pensions are required to issue Form 1099R to the recipients. The Internal Revenue Service and the Minnesota Department of Revenue have established special rules applicable to these situations.

BUSINESS TAXES

Common areas of small business tax liability include federal and state income taxes, state sales and use tax, FICA (Federal Insurance Contributions Act) (Social Security and Medicare) tax, FUTA (Federal Unemployment Tax Act), state unemployment tax, and tax withholding. In addition, businesses may be liable for less commonly applicable taxes such as taxes on the sale of fuel, alcohol products and cigarettes, and the hazardous waste generator tax. These taxes are discussed in more detail later in this section.

Note: Businesses operating in multiple jurisdictions, whether cities, states, or counties, need to be concerned about the taxes imposed by each of those jurisdictions, as well as the impact on the tax imposed by their home jurisdiction. This also applies equally to businesses using the Internet to sell goods or services.

SOURCES OF INFORMATION

Business owners, who wish to learn more about state taxation can attend free workshops and seminars offered throughout the state. These workshops are geared towards new businesses, new employers, and others interested in an introduction to business tax responsibilities.

Agency-Sponsored Business Education Workshops/Seminars

The **Minnesota Department of Revenue** offers classes, workshops and training events to help business owners understand their tax obligations and how to meet them.

Classroom Training: Basic Sales and Use Tax Classes; Lawful Gambling Education Seminars; MinnesotaCare Educational; Seminars; Partnership Tax and S Corporation Tax Basics Class; Withholding Tax Education Seminars.

More information and schedules are available on the Business Education and Outreach web page at https://www.revenue.state.mn.us/business-education-and-outreach or call 651-296-6181 or 800-657-3777.

Webinars / Videos: Using e-Services for Withholding Tax; Minnesota Withholding Tax Employer Responsibilities.

The **Minnesota Unemployment Insurance (UI) Program**, Minnesota Business Tax Education Partnership and the Minnesota Department of Revenue have partnered to present information on state employment taxes. Topics include:

Seminars: Seminar schedules are available at http://www.uimn.org/uimn/employers/help-and-support/educational-seminars/index.jsp or call 651-259-0779.

The **Minnesota Department of Labor & Industry** offers worker's compensation training opportunities for:

Employees

Employers: Seminars and customized training for employers.

Health care providers: Customized training for health care providers.

Insurers: Basic adjusters' training; Customized training for insurers; Downloadable insurer training materials.

Rehabilitation providers

Information and schedules are available at https://www.dli.mn.gov/business/workers-compensation/work-comp-training-opportunities.

Written Information

Both the Internal Revenue Service and the Minnesota Department of Revenue have written information on certain business topics.

Internal Revenue Service. The IRS online Small Business and Self-Employed Tax Center, at https://www.irs.gov/businesses/small-businesses-self-employed, provides extensive tax information and online tools and resources especially for business. The IRS offers many education products that can be viewed or ordered online at any time.

The IRS has a workshop, *Small Business Taxes: The Virtual Workshop*, https://www.irsvideos.gov/SmallBusinessTaxpayer/virtualworkshop, is composed of nine interactive lessons designed to help new small business owners learn their tax rights and responsibilities.

For additional IRS audio and video presentations, visit the IRS Video Portal at https://www.irsvideos.gov.

Minnesota Department of Revenue. Information on Minnesota business taxes is available at Businesses, https://www.revenue.state.mn.us/businesses.

The Minnesota Sales and Use Tax Business Guide, https://www.revenue.state.mn.us/guide/minnesota-sales-and-use-tax-business-guide, and Sales Tax Fact Sheets and Industry Guides, https://www.revenue.state.mn.us/sales-tax-fact-sheets-and-industry-guides, provide detailed information on a variety of sales tax topics.

Withholding Tax Fact Sheets, https://www.revenue.state.mn.us/withholding-tax-fact-sheets, provide detailed information on a variety of withholding tax topics.

TAX IDENTIFICATION NUMBERS

Many Minnesota businesses will need one or more tax identification numbers. These include the federal Employer Identification Number, the Minnesota Taxpayer Identification Number, and the Minnesota Unemployment Insurance Employer Account Number. New tax identification numbers must be obtained each time the ownership or form of business organization changes.

Federal Employer Identification Number

Sole proprietors may be eligible to use their Social Security number as their Federal Employer Identification Number (FEIN) if they do not have employees, are not required to file information returns, do not have a retirement plan for themselves, and are not required to pay federal excise taxes in connection with their business. Single-member limited liability companies that have elected to be taxed as a sole proprietorship may follow the rule set out in the previous sentence. All other business entities are required to obtain a federal employer identification number by filing Form SS-4 with the Internal Revenue Service.

Note: An independent contractor doing commercial or residential building construction or improvements in the public or private sector is considered to be, for workers' compensation purposes, an employee of any person or entity for whom or which that independent contractor performs services unless, among other things, that independent contractor has a federal employer identification number.

Form SS-4 may be obtained from the Internal Revenue Service website at https://www.irs.gov/forms-pubs/about-form-ss-4-application-for-employer-identification-number-ein. You may order forms by mail by going to https://www.irs.gov/forms-pubs/forms-and-publications-by-us-mail. Or you may call the IRS at 800-829-3676 to order the form by mail.

You can apply for a FEIN online, by fax or by mail. It helps to have a completed SS-4 form available.

To apply online, go to https://www.irs.gov/businesses/small-businesses-self-employed/apply-for-an-employer-identification-number-ein-online.

Minnesota businesses seeking to apply via fax can submit their application by dialing 855-641-6935 (toll-free).

Mail applications, which can take up to 4 to 5 weeks, should be submitted—for Minnesota businesses—to IRS, EIN Operation, Cincinnati, OH 45999.

Minnesota Taxpayer Identification Number (Minnesota Tax ID Number)

Most businesses need a Minnesota Tax ID Number (a seven digit number assigned by the Minnesota Department of Revenue) if the business is required to make any of the following filings:

- ST1, Sales and Use Tax Return
- M3, Partnership Return
- M4, Corporate Franchise Tax Return

- M8, S Corporation Return
- M4R Minnesota Business Activity Report
- Withholding of Employee Minnesota Income Tax

A Minnesota Tax ID may be obtained online, by phone, or by mailing Form ABR, Application for Business Registration (https://www.revenue.state.mn.us/sites/default/files/2020-09/abr.pdf)

If you are filing online, go to Business Tax Registration, https://www.mndor.state.mn.us/tp/webreg/_/.

You will need:

- Your Federal Employer Identification Number (FEIN), if applicable;
- The legal name or sole proprietor name and business address
- The business name (Certificate of Assumed Name) if applicable
- North American Industry Classification (NAICS) code available from the U.S. Census Bureau's website
- Names and Social Security numbers of the sole proprietor, officers, partners or representatives
- Address and name of a contact person

If you do not have Internet access, call 651-282-5225 or 800-657-3605 to speak to a business registration representative.

If you already have a Minnesota Tax ID Number, you may need to apply for a new one if the business changes its legal organization, or you are required to apply for a new federal ID number.

If a business has a Minnesota Tax ID Number and is registered to collect sales tax, the Minnesota Department of Revenue will send a confirmation letter that will serve as a sales tax permit. It is not required that this letter be displayed, but suppliers may require a copy for their records. A copy of the registration confirmation may be printed by using e-Services and select Update business information at https://www.mndor.state.mn.us/tp/eservices/_/.

The Minnesota Tax ID Number is called other things, such as "sales tax exempt number", "resale exemption number", or "seller's permit". This is merely a difference in terminology, often encountered in dealing with suppliers from other states. If a business has a Minnesota Tax ID Number and is registered for the tax types that it needs to collect and submit, then it does not need to apply for any additional numbers from the Minnesota Department of Revenue.

If a business is registered to collect income tax withholding, the Minnesota Tax ID Number also serves as its Minnesota Employer ID for Minnesota individual income tax withholding purposes. This number **does not** serve as the Unemployment Insurance (UI) Employer Account Number.

Minnesota Unemployment Insurance (UI) Employer Account Number

The Minnesota Department of Employment and Economic Development, Unemployment Insurance (UI) Program issues identification numbers that are different from those issued by the Department of Revenue and the Internal Revenue Service. All business entities, other than sole proprietorships, single member limited liability companies, partnerships without employees or corporations and limited liability companies with no employees other than owner/officers with 25 percent or more ownership share, must register with the Unemployment Insurance (UI) Program. Registration is done online at https://www.uimn.org/employers/ or by calling the Unemployment Insurance (UI) Program at 651-296-6141, option 4. The UI Program requests that businesses not register for a UI Employer account number until wages have actually been paid.

TAXPAYER BILL OF RIGHTS

Both the United States Congress and the Minnesota Legislature have enacted a Taxpayer Bill of Rights that governs many taxpayer relationships with the Internal Revenue Service and the Minnesota Department of Revenue. These laws formalize and standardize many audit, appeal, and collection procedures and clarify rights and protections available to taxpayers.

Information on the federal Taxpayer Bill of Rights is available on the IRS website at https://www.irs.gov/Taxpayer-Bill-of-Rights. It is also available in Publication 1, *Your Rights as a Taxpayer,* which may be obtained online at https://www.irs.gov/forms-pubs/about-publication-1.

Information on the Minnesota taxpayer rights is available on the Minnesota Department of Revenue at https://www.revenue.state.mn.us/guide/taxpayer-rights or by calling the Department of Revenue.

ELECTRONIC FILING OF TAXES

Electronic Payment Requirements - Minnesota

Minnesota law requires some businesses pay their state taxes and fees electronically. If you meet the requirement for any tax or fee listed below during the last 12 months ending June 30, you must pay all Minnesota business taxes electronically starting January 1 of the following year. If you are required to pay business taxes electronically for one year, you must continue to do so for all future years. Failure to remit electronically after notification from the Commissioner may result in a 5 percent penalty for each payment that should have been remitted electronically.

The following table shows when the electronic payment requirement first applies for various business taxes.

	Electronic payments required if business had at least:
Alcoholic beverage tax	$10,000 in tax
Cigarette and tobacco tax	$10,000 in tax
Corporation franchise tax	$10,000 in estimated tax payments
Corporation franchise for nonprofits	$10,000 in tax
Fiduciary income tax	100 trusts
Insurance premium taxes	$10,000 in tax
Lawful gambling tax	$10,000 in tax
Metropolitan landfill fee	$10,000 in tax
MinnesotaCare taxes	$10,000 in tax
Petroleum tax	All electronic
Sales and use taxes	$10,000 in tax
Withholding tax	$10,000 in tax

In other words, if a business collects more than $120,000 in sales taxes annually, but its only other tax is $10,000 in employee withholding taxes, both the sales tax and the withholding taxes must be paid electronically. For this purpose, the Minnesota Department of Revenue measures the tax collected or owed for the period from July 1 to June 30 of the following year, not the calendar year.

Any business exceeding one of the above thresholds is notified by a letter from the Minnesota Department of Revenue in the November following the end of the measuring period. The letter will indicate that as of the next January 1 all of that business's taxes must be filed electronically.

See e-Services (https://www.mndor.state.mn.us/tp/eservices/_/), Minnesota Department of Revenue's electronic file and pay system.

Electronic Payment Requirements - Federal

For federal tax purposes, many businesses will be required to file tax payments electronically, through the Electronic Federal Tax Payment System (EFTPS). See the section of this Guide titled "Business Taxes – Income Tax Withholding – Withholding Tax Deposit and Filing Requirements".

Certain mid-sized corporations, with assets between $10 million and $50 million, are required to e-file their Forms 1120 or 1120S for tax years ending on or after December 31, 2006. Large corporations with assets of $50 million or more were required to start e-filing with their 2005 Forms 1120 or 1120S.

Corporations required to e-file are those that meet the asset threshold and that file 250 or more federal returns a year, including excise tax, employment tax and information returns such as Forms W-2 and 1099.

Refer to the IRS information, e-file for Business and Self-Employed Taxpayers at https://www.irs.gov/e-file-providers/e-file-for-business-and-self-employed-taxpayers.

BUSINESS INCOME TAX RETURNS

This section describes the federal and state income tax returns that must be filed by various business entities. Businesses may also be liable for estimated tax payments, sales and use tax, and other taxes.

SOLE PROPRIETORSHIP

Federal Income Tax Returns

The sole proprietor reports income and expenses from the business on Schedule C (Form 1040) and any related forms and schedules. The net income or loss from the business is then reported on proprietor's individual Form 1040. The proprietor uses Schedule SE (Form 1040) to report net self-employment income to compute the Social Security and Medicare self-employment taxes.

Minnesota Income Tax Returns

The proprietor uses Form M1, Individual Income Tax Return. A copy of the Form 1040, Schedule C and other supporting schedules, must be attached to Form M1.

PARTNERSHIP

Federal Income Tax Returns

The partnership files Form 1065, which is an information return. Generally no tax is paid by the partnership with this return. Other forms and schedules may be required, including Schedules K and K-1.

Individual partners use Schedule E (Form 1040), which is prepared using information from their Schedule K-1 (Form 1065), to report their distributive share of partnership income, deductions, credits and losses on the individual Form 1040. Information from Schedule K-1 may be reported on other schedules in the 1040 series. Schedule SE (Form 1040) is used to compute Social Security and Medicare self-employment taxes.

A married couple who jointly operate an unincorporated business and file a joint federal income tax return can elect not to be treated as a partnership for federal tax purposes provided that the husband and wife are the only members of the joint venture and materially participate in the running of the business. For more information, see Married Couples in Business at https://www.irs.gov/businesses/small-businesses-self-employed/married-couples-in-business and Election for Married Couples Unincorporated Businesses at https://www.irs.gov/businesses/small-businesses-elf-employed/election-for-married-couples-unincorporated-businesses, from the IRS. This election carries over to the Minnesota tax return.

Minnesota Income Tax Returns

The partnership completes Form M3, Partnership Return, and files it with a copy of federal Form 1065 and Schedules K and K-1. The partnership may also have to pay a minimum fee based on property, payroll, and sales attributable to Minnesota. If the partnership has items of income, credits or modifications that are different from its federal return, the partnership must also issue Schedule KPI and/or Schedule KPC to its partners and include copies with Form M3.

If the partnership has nonresident individual partners, it may pay composite income tax on their behalf using Schedule KPI. Individual partners who are not included on the composite income tax may be required to complete Form M1, Individual Income Tax. If it has nonresident individual partners who will not be included in the composite income tax, generally the partnership is required to withhold income tax (called nonresident withholding) on behalf of such partners and remit it with Form M3, by using Schedule KPI.

C CORPORATION

Federal Income Tax Returns

The C corporation reports its income, deductions and credits, and computes its tax on Form 1120. Supporting forms and schedules may be required. If the corporation issues dividends, it must annually send Form 1099-DIV to its shareholders who receive more than $10 in dividends, stating the amount of ordinary income and qualified dividends paid. A copy of Form 1099-DIV is filed with the IRS.

Shareholders report dividends received from the corporation on their individual Form 1040. Shareholders may be required to file Schedule B (1040) to report their dividend and interest income.

Minnesota Income Tax Returns

The C corporation reports state tax on Form M4, Corporation Franchise Tax Return. The corporation also may have to pay a minimum fee based on property, payroll, and sales attributable to Minnesota.

S CORPORATION

Federal Income Tax Returns

The S corporation generally is not separately taxed. The S corporation files Form 1120-S and supporting forms and schedules, including Schedules K (Form 1120-S) and K-1 (Form 1120-S). Individual shareholders report their share of the S corporation's income, deductions, and credits on their individual Form 1040, using information on Schedule K-1.

Minnesota Income Tax Returns

S corporations file Form M8, S Corporation Return, with copies of federal Form 1120-S and supporting forms and schedules. The S corporation may have to pay a minimum fee based on property, payroll, and sales attributable to Minnesota. If the S corporation has items of income, credits or modifications that are different from the federal return it must also issue Schedule KS to its shareholders and include copies with Form M8.

If the S corporation has nonresident individual shareholders it may pay composite income tax on their behalf using Schedule KS. Individual shareholders who are not included on the composite income tax may be required to complete Form M1, Individual Income Tax Return.

If there are nonresident individual shareholders who will not be included in the composite income tax, generally the S corporation is required to withhold income tax (called nonresident withholding) on behalf of such shareholders and remit it with Form M8 by using Schedule KS.

LIMITED LIABILITY COMPANY

Under IRS Treasury Regulations the organizers of a limited liability company (LLC) can choose how the LLC will be taxed. Generally, a LLC with one member may be taxed either as a corporation or as a sole proprietorship. LLCs with two or more members may be taxed either as a partnership or as a corporation.

Note: For LLCs with one member, this decision will also impact whether the LLC needs a tax identification number.

A Minnesota LLC will receive the same tax treatment for state purposes that it receives for federal purposes. Persons considering forming a LLC are advised to consult with a tax professional regarding state and federal tax treatment.

See the section "Choosing the Form of Business Organization – Tax and Non-Tax Considerations" in this Guide.

TAX CREDITS AND INCENTIVES

Minnesota Tax Credits and Incentives

- **Credit For Increasing Research Activities:** Provides a credit of 10 percent of the first $2 million in incremental eligible research and development expenses above a base amount. For eligible expenses above $2 million, the credit is 4 percent. (Minn. Stat. § 290.068)

- **Alternative Minimum Tax Carryover Credit**: Provides a credit for prior year alternative minimum tax liability caused by timing items. The credit cannot be claimed in a year for which the taxpayer was subject to alternative minimum tax.

  For C corporations
  This allows a credit against corporate income tax for qualified alternative minimum tax previously paid. The entire amount of the credit must be carried into the earliest taxable year into which the credit may be carried, and any unused portion of the credit must be carried into the following taxable year. The credit may not be claimed in the same year the C corporation is paying Alternative Minimum Tax. (Minn. Stat. § 290.0921, subd. 8)

  For Individuals, Estates and Trusts
  This allows a credit against income tax equal to the adjusted net minimum tax reduced by the minimum tax credits allowable in a prior tax year. Special definitions apply to computation of tax involving part-time Minnesota residents, income from private activity bond revenue, and income from depletion. (Minn. Stat. § 290.091, subd. 6)

- **Greater Minnesota Job Expansion Program**: Provides tax benefits to businesses located outside the Twin Cities metro area that increase employment. Qualifying businesses that meet job-growth goals may receive sales tax refunds for purchases made during a seven-year period.

  Business must increase employment by a minimum of two FTE employees or 10 percent of the current number of employees at the facility, whichever is greater, within three years of being certified, and pay compensation to all the facility's employees of at least 120 percent of the federal poverty level for a family of four. The business must not be primarily engaged in retail sales or in several other specified industries. A maximum of $7 million per year may be refunded to all businesses participating in the program.

- **Border Cities Enterprize Zone Program:** Provides property and sales tax credits to businesses located or existing in the of Breckenridge, Dilworth, East Grand Forks, Moorhead, Ortonville, and Taylors Falls. The city provides the business with a tax credit certificate in a specific amount, and the business files a claim for a refund from the Minnesota Department of Revenue. (Minn. Stat. § 469.1732)
- **Data Center Sales Tax Incentives:** Available to companies that build data or network operations centers of at least 25,000 square feet and invest $30 million in the first four years.
- **Employers Transit Pass Credit:** For employers who purchased transit passes to give or resell to employees for use in Minnesota. The credit is 30 percent of the difference between what employers paid for the passes and charged for employees. (Minn. Stat. § 290.06, subd. 28).
- **Angel Tax Credit:** A refundable income tax credit to encourage investment in startup companies of certain industries located in Minnesota. (Minn. Stat. §§ 116J.8737 and 290.0692).
- **Beginning Farmer Tax Credit:** Provides tax credits for the rent or sale of farm land or a variety of farm assets to beginning farmers. Beginning farmers that participate in an approved financial management program. (Minn. Stat. §§ 41B.0391, subd. 3 and 290.06, subd. 38).
- **Owners of Agricultural Assets Credit**: Available to property owners who sell or rent qualified assets to beginning farmers. The credit is available in varying amounts based on the selling or rental agreement. (Minn. Stat. §§ 41B.0391, subd. 2 and 290.06, subd. 37).

Federal Tax Credits

- **Work Opportunity Federal Tax Credit:** Provides an incentive to hire individuals from targeted groups. The PATH Act expanded the targeted groups of individuals to include qualified long-term unemployment recipients.

  In Minnesota, the Department of Employment and Economic Development (DEED), (Work Opportunity Tax Credit (WOTC) Unit) certifies members of targeted groups. For more information, see Work Opportunity Tax Credit from DEED, https://mn.gov/deed/business/finding-workers/incentives/wotc.jsp, and IRS-Work Opportunity Tax Credit, https://www.irs.gov/businesses/small-businesses-self-employed/work-opportunity-tax-credit.

- **Small Business Health Care Tax Credit:** Receive a tax credit of up to 50 percent of annual premiums paid toward health insurance for employees, (35 percent for tax years (2010-2013).

  Offers a tax credit benefit to employers that:

  - Have fewer than 25 full-time equivalent employees
  - Pay average wages of less than $50,000 a year per full-time equivalent
  - Offer a qualified health plan to its employees through a Small Business Health Options Program Marketplace (or qualify for a limited exception to this requirement)
  - Pay at least 50 percent of the cost of employee-only – not family or dependent – health care coverage for each employee

The maximum credit is up to 50 percent of premiums paid for small business employers and up to 35 percent of premiums paid for small tax-exempt employers. The credit is available to eligible employers for two consecutive taxable years.

For more detailed information regarding the credit, visit the IRS at Small Business Health Care Tax Credit and the SHOP Marketplace, https://www.irs.gov/affordable-care-act/employers/small-business-health-care-tax-credit-and-the-shop-marketplace.

For information about qualified health plans offered through the SHOP Marketplace, visit Healthcare.gov, https://www.healthcare.gov/small-businesses/.

TAXATION OF NON-MINNESOTA BUSINESSES DOING BUSINESS IN MINNESOTA

Non-Minnesota businesses that do business or own property in Minnesota may be subject to state taxes if they have sufficient nexus. Generally, businesses that meet all of these activities that have nexus:

- Having a place of business in Minnesota
- Having employees or independent contractors conducting business in Minnesota
- Owning or leasing real property or tangible personal property in Minnesota
    - Obtaining or soliciting business within Minnesota such as
    - Selling products or services to customers in Minnesota who receive the product or service in Minnesota
    - Engaging in transactions with customers in Minnesota that involve intangible property and results in income
- Direct mail, phone solicitation, or various forms of advertising in Minnesota

Nexus can be complicated to determine. Contact the Minnesota Department of Revenue for assistance.

TAXATION OF BUSINESSES OPERATING WITHIN AND OUTSIDE MINNESOTA

Businesses that operate within and outside Minnesota are required to calculate the amount of income subject to Minnesota tax. They must allocate the business income to Minnesota based on the percentage of sales to Minnesota customers compared to total sales.

"Throwback Rule"

Minnesota does not use the "Throwback Rule" for sales received in another state. The rule is including sales received in another state as in-state sales when the seller lacks taxable nexus in the other state.

Instead, Minnesota uses the location of sales received (destination) to determine what is an in-state sale for the apportionment formula. For example, if the destination of a sale is in Minnesota, the sale is included in the sales factor as an in-state sale. If the destination of the sale is in another state, the sale is not an in-state sale.

BUSINESS ACTIVITY REPORT

Every business that has property or personnel in Minnesota or receives income from Minnesota sources is required to file the Form M4R Minnesota Business Activity Report, with the Minnesota Department of Revenue unless the business files a timely state corporation income tax return (Form M4, Corporation Franchise Tax Return or Form M8, S Corporation Return), has a certificate of authority to do business in Minnesota, or is otherwise exempt from this requirement.

A business that is required to file a Business Activities Report that fails to do so does not have any cause of action to bring suit under Minnesota law. It cannot use Minnesota courts for all contracts executed and all causes of action that arose before the accounting period for which the business failed to file the report. The Commissioner of Revenue may disclose to litigants whether a Business Activity Report has been filed by a party to a lawsuit.

Contact the Minnesota Department of Revenue for questions and copies of Form M4R.

ESTIMATED TAX

Individuals who are sole proprietors, partners, S corporation shareholders, and members of limited liability companies generally will be required to make federal and Minnesota estimated tax payments if their income tax and - for federal purposes, self-employment tax - will exceed taxes paid through withholding and credits by $500 or more ($1,000 for federal individual income tax purposes). The tax is determined on income from all sources, not just on income from the business.

Individuals may use federal Form 1040-ES, Estimated Taxes for Individuals, to determine and pay estimated taxes. To make federal tax payments, individuals may or may use the Electronic Federal Tax Payments System (EFTPS). The IRS also offers a secure service called Direct Pay with Bank Account to pay estimated taxes. For more information, see https://www.irs.gov/payments/direct-pay.

Minnesota estimated payments may be made through the Minnesota Department of Revenue website using direct debit or by credit/debit card (additional fees apply). Minnesota estimated tax payments made by check must include a voucher. Payment vouchers can be created using the Payment Voucher System. For more information see payment options for Estimated Tax, https://www.revenue.state.mn.us/estimated-tax.

C corporations use federal Form 1120-W and Minnesota Form M4, Corporate Franchise Tax Return, to calculate estimated tax payments. C corporations are not required to pay estimated taxes for the first year they are subject to tax in Minnesota. Federal estimated tax payments are deposited with an authorized financial institution. Minnesota payments are made with the Department of Revenue.

Partnerships and S corporations must make Minnesota estimated tax payments if their minimum fee and S corporation taxes are expected to be $500 or more, or if they have any nonresident individuals whose tax is expected to be $500 or more and who are included on the entity's composite income tax. Withholding of tax for nonresident partners or shareholders is subject to estimated tax requirements.

INCOME TAX PENALTIES AND INTEREST

Both the IRS and the Minnesota Department of Revenue may assess monetary penalties and interest for various reasons, including but not limited to:

- Failure to pay a required tax
- A substantial underpayment of tax
- Failure to file a return
- Failure to file and pay
- Filing a fraudulent, false, or frivolous return

The IRS also may impose a penalty for underpayment of tax due to negligence or disregard of the tax rules, or for a substantial understatement of income. In addition, the federal government and the state may impose criminal penalties for deliberately failing to file a return or deliberately filing a false return.

The interest rate on unpaid taxes is adjusted periodically by the IRS and the state to reflect current market rates.

SALES AND USE TAX

SALES AND USE TAX REGISTRATION

Every person who makes taxable retail sales or provides taxable services in Minnesota must obtain a Minnesota tax identification number and register to collect and remit Minnesota sales and use tax. This must be done before making any taxable sales in Minnesota.

You must register and collect sales tax in Minnesota if you have a taxable presence (nexus) in Minnesota, even if you are an out-of-state retailer or marketplace provider.

You have presence in Minnesota if your business does any of the following:

o Maintains a physical location in Minnesota (office, warehouse, or distribution, sales, or sample room)

o Sells products to customers into Minnesota, using the Internet, mail order, or telephone, without having a physical presence in that state and does not meet the small seller exemption

o Makes 200 or more retail sales shipped to Minnesota over a period of 12 consecutive months

o Makes retail sales shipped to Minnesota that total more than $100,000 over a period of 12 consecutive months

o Has an employee, representative, agent, or independent contractor that does work on behalf of the retailer in Minnesota

o Facilitates the sale of taxable goods or services on behalf of a Minnesota business

o Delivers items into Minnesota in your own vehicles

o Provides taxable services in Minnesota

o Owns property in Minnesota

o Keeps inventory in a Marketplace Provider's fulfillment center in Minnesota

o Is an affiliate of a Minnesota retailer that promotes or provides other services to you and your business and the retailer are related parties

o Enters into an agreement with a Minnesota resident for a commission or similar consideration and directly or indirectly refers potential customers to the seller through website links or otherwise

If you do not make taxable sales, but make purchases subject to use tax, you must register to remit use tax.

For more information on who needs to register, see Who Needs to Register? at https://www.revenue.state.mn.us/guide/who-needs-register and Registering Your Business at https://www.revenue.state.mn.us/guide/registering-your-business, or call 651-296-6181 or 800-657-3777.

To obtain a Minnesota Tax ID Number, go to Business Tax Registration at https://www.mndor.state.mn.us/tp/webreg/_/ or call 651-282-5225 or 800-657-3605.

MINNESOTA SALES TAX

Minnesota has a 6.875 percent general sales tax rate. The sales tax applies to retail sales of taxable services, tangible personal property or specific digital products made in Minnesota. Businesses collect and remit the sales tax due on items and services sold at retail on behalf of the state.

Most retail sales are taxable in Minnesota. A "retail sale" means any sale, lease or rental of tangible personal property for any purpose other than resale, sublease or subrent. A retail sale also includes services for any purposes other than for resale. However, some sales are specifically exempted by law from the sales and use tax. These exemptions are discussed later in this section.

The Minnesota Department of Revenue has the Minnesota Sales and Use Tax Business Guide, https://www.revenue.state.mn.us/guide/minnesota-sales-and-use-tax-business-guide, and Sales Tax Fact Sheets and Industry Guides, https://www.revenue.state.mn.us/sales-tax-fact-sheets-and-industry-guides.

The Minnesota Department of Revenue does not issue a physical sales tax permit. Upon registration, the taxpayer is given a letter confirming they have registered for sales and use tax. There is no requirement for the taxpayer to post the confirmation letter in their retail store or anywhere else.

MINNESOTA USE TAX

The use tax complements and is similar to the sales tax. It applies when you buy, lease or rent taxable items on services used in your business without paying sales tax to the seller. The use tax rate is the same as the sales tax rate. The rate is applied to the cost of the taxable purchases on which the sales tax is not paid. The buyer pays use tax directly to the state.

Both businesses and individuals are subject to use tax. For more information review Sales and Use Tax, https://www.revenue.state.mn.us/sales-and-use-tax; Fact Sheet 146, Use Tax for Businesses, https://www.revenue.state.mn.us/sites/default/files/2020-02/FS146.pdf: or Fact Sheet 156, Use Tax for Individuals, https://www.revenue.state.mn.us/sites/default/files/2019-11/FS156.pdf.

See also Fact Sheet 164, Local Sales and Use Taxes, https://www.revenue.state.mn.us/sites/default/files/2020-08/FS164.pdf.

Common examples of when use tax is due:

- Items purchased outside Minnesota from retailers who do not collect Minnesota sales tax, if the items are for use, storage or consumption in Minnesota.
- Items originally purchased for resale, if the items are taken out of inventory for business or personal use. When items are taken out of inventory, use tax is calculated on the purchase prices of the items.
- Items originally purchased for use in agricultural or industrial production, if the items are put to a taxable use. The use tax must be paid when the item is put to taxable use.
- Items and taxable services purchased from a Minnesota seller who does not collect the sales tax, if the items are put to a taxable use.
- Items given away or donated to individuals or businesses, including nonprofit organizations.

Businesses that have registered for sales and use tax should report their cost of the use tax items when they electronically file their sales and use tax return. Individuals must file a Form UT1, Individual Use Tax Return, which is due April 15 following the end of the calendar year. Local use tax is also due if the items are used in an area that imposes a local sales and use tax. Local use taxes are reported on the taxpayer's state return.

LOCAL SALES AND USE TAXES

The Minnesota Department of Revenue currently administers several local sales and use taxes. General local taxes apply the same as general Minnesota sales and use tax laws. If you make retail sales in any city or county with a local sales tax, you must also register to collect the local tax.

Local taxes are reported when you file your Minnesota sales and use tax. Each local tax has a separate line to report the sales separately. You must be registered for each local tax you report.

Local tax applies to sales when a sale is made in the local area, a service performed in the local area, or taxable items are shipped into the local area. To figure the total tax, combine the state tax rate and the local tax rates; apply the combined rate to the taxable sales price.

Local use tax applies when items or services are bought for business or personal use in the local area without paying local sales tax to the seller. Use tax is similar to sales tax and the rates are identical. It is based on the cost of taxable purchases. Common examples of when local use tax is due:

- Items are bought outside the local area and the seller did not collect local sales tax, and then the item is used for business or personal use in the local area.
- A taxable item is bought for your business from an out-of-state seller who did not collect local sales tax.

Refer to Local Sales Tax Information at https://www.revenue.state.mn.us/local-sales-tax-information.

EXEMPTION CERTIFICATES

Generally, all sales of items and services are presumed to be subject to the sales tax, unless an exemption applies. To purchase qualifying items exempt from sales tax give your supplier a completed Form ST3, Certificate of Exemption, https://www.revenue.state.mn.us/sites/default/files/2019-07/st3.pdf. Form available at Sales and Use Tax, https://www.revenue.state.mn.us/sales-and-use-tax.

Unless the customer gives the seller a completed exemption certificate, the seller is required to collect and remit the sales tax. It is not sufficient for the customer to provide only its sales and use tax number.

An exemption certificate may be for either a single purchase or a blanket exemption. Customers who frequently make exempt purchases from one seller should give that seller a blanket exemption certificate to cover future purchases. That way, the seller will not need to collect a new certificate each time the customer makes a purchase.

A completed exemption certificate should be retained in the seller's files to substantiate the exemption. Certificates are subject to inspection by the Minnesota Department of Revenue, but they should not be mailed to the department.

EXEMPTIONS AND EXEMPT ORGANIZATIONS

Certain sales are exempt from sales and use tax. Exemptions commonly encountered by Minnesota businesses are listed below. Detailed information on the exemptions may be obtained at Sales Tax Exemptions, https://www.revenue.state.mn.us/guide/sales-tax-exemptions.

Food, Clothing and Prescription Drugs

Generally, the sale of clothing, prescription drugs and most food is exempt from the sales and use tax. However, the exemption for sales of food does not apply to prepared food purchased from restaurants, bars, delicatessens or caterers, and does not include candy, soft drinks or dietary supplements.

Capital Equipment Purchases

Capital equipment means machinery and equipment purchased or leased, and used in Minnesota by the purchaser or lessee primarily for manufacturing, fabricating, mining, or refining tangible personal property to be sold ultimately at retail if the machinery and equipment are essential to the integrated production process of manufacturing, fabricating, mining, or refining. Capital equipment also includes machinery and equipment used primarily to electronically transmit results retrieved by a customer of an on-line computerized data retrieval system. Capital equipment includes all machinery and equipment that is essential to the integrated production process; also included are repair and replacement parts, materials used for foundations that support machinery or equipment, and materials used to construct and install special purpose buildings used in the production process.

Purchases of qualifying capital equipment are exempt upfront with a completed Form ST3, Certificate of Exemption.

See Sales Tax Fact Sheets and Industry Guides, https://www.revenue.state.mn.us/sales-tax-fact-sheets-and-industry-guides, for more information.

Resource Recovery

An exemption from sales and use tax is allowed for purchases of equipment used for processing solid or hazardous waste at a resource recovery facility. The exemption requires prior approval by the Minnesota Department of Revenue. For more information, contact the department, Sales and Use Tax Division.

Sales to Nonprofit Organizations

Nonprofit organizations may, in certain instances, be exempt from paying sales tax. The exemption only applies to groups organized exclusively for charitable purposes, senior citizen groups, religious, and educational organizations. This exemption applies to purchases made by the nonprofit organization; it does not allow them to sell items without collecting and remitting sales tax. To apply, use Form ST16, Application for Nonprofit Exempt Status - Sales Tax.

The exemption does not apply to the purchases of meals, lodging, or motor vehicles, and also does not apply to the additional 9.2 percent tax or 5 percent fee on short term rental of vehicles. Qualifying exempt organizations must provide a completed Form ST3, Certificate of Exemption.

Sales to Government Agencies

Sales to the federal government and its agencies are not taxable. The federal agency must give the seller a purchase order, payment voucher, work order, or completed Form ST3, Certificate of Exemption, to purchase exempt from tax. Sales to employees of the federal government are taxable.

Minnesota State agencies use a direct pay authorization. This means that state agencies do not pay the sales tax to the seller, but instead pay the tax directly to the Department of Revenue. Purchase orders used by Minnesota State agencies contain information about the direct pay authorization, so it is not necessary for vendors to obtain a copy of it. There are exceptions to the use of direct pay authorization. Sellers of prepared food or beverages, lodging and related services, admissions to amusement or athletic events, motor vehicles or certain services to the State of Minnesota must collect and remit sales tax on those sales from the purchasing Minnesota State agency.

Cities and counties are exempt from sales and use tax on purchases used in providing certain government services. Townships have had this exemption since October 1, 2011. In 2017 this exemption was expanded to special districts; instrumentality of a statutory or home rule charter city, county, or township; and joint powers board or organization. To claim the exemption, these purchasers must provide a Form ST3, Certificate of Exemption to their sellers. However, sales of prepared food, candy, soft drinks, alcoholic beverages or lodging to those entities are not exempt.

FILING THE SALES AND USE TAX RETURN

A sales and use tax account is set up on either a monthly, quarterly or annual filing basis depending on how much tax is owed each month.

Annual Filing. Tax must average less than $100 per month.

Quarterly Filing. Tax must average less than $500 per month.

Monthly Filing. Tax average is $500 or more per month.

Seasonal Filing. If the business is not open year-round, request seasonal filing. With seasonal filing you only need to file returns for those periods when the business is open.

One-time Filing. If you will be making taxable sales in Minnesota at only one event or during one month, ask for one-time filing. Do not apply for one-time filing if you plan to make taxable sales in the future.

If the amount of tax you report is consistently higher or lower than the limits, you can change your filing cycles when you log into e-Services Minnesota to file or pay taxes. If Internet service is not available, contact the Minnesota Department of Revenue.

The following are the due dates:

Monthly Filers. 20th day of the following month.

Quarterly Filers. April 20, July 20, October 20 and January 20.

Annual Filers**.** February 5 of the following year. Annual filers must file on a calendar-year basis, not a fiscal year basis.

Unregistered Individuals Filing Annual Return. April 15 of the following year.

Payments must be electronically received or postmarked by the due date. If the due date falls on a legal holiday or weekend, the return is due the next business day.

Mandatory electronic payment. Taxpayers who have a sales and use tax liability of $10,000 or more in the state's fiscal year (July 1 - June 30) must **pay** all taxes electronically starting with the next calendar year.

Associated payers. If you are required to electronically pay any business tax type to the Minnesota Department of Revenue, you must pay all business taxes electronically.

June accelerated payment. The June accelerated payment is due two business days before June 30, and the remaining payment and return for June is due August 20. For more information on the June accelerated payment, go to June Accelerated Filer, https://www.revenue.state.mn.us/june-accelerated-filer.

FICA TAX

The Social Security and Medicare benefit programs are financed by taxes paid by employers and employees under the Federal Insurance Contributions Act (FICA), and by self-employed individuals through the self-employment tax.

FICA taxes are levied on both the employer and the employee. The employer is responsible for the employer's share of FICA taxes, and also is required to collect and pay the employee's part of the tax, which is withheld from the employee's pay in much the same way as income tax is withheld. Self-employed individuals compute their self-employment tax on Internal Revenue Service Schedule SE of Form 1040.

Special rules apply to tipped employees, and to persons who receive both wages and self -employment income. Special rules also apply to payments in kind made by employers, such as the furnishing of meals, lodging, clothing or services to employees.

It should be noted that the FICA rates and wage base limitations are subject to change by congressional action. Typically wage base limitations change each year. The wage base for 2021 is $142,800.

The following IRS publications can provide additional information on FICA contributions, withholding and self-employment taxes: *Publication 15, Employer's Tax Guide (Circular E)*, https://www.irs.gov/forms-pubs/about-publication-15; and *Publication 15-A, Employer's Supplemental Tax Guide (Supplement to Circular E, Employer's Tax Guide, Publication 15)*, https://www.irs.gov/forms-pubs/about-publication-15-a. To obtain these publications contact the Internal Revenue Service at the address and telephone number provided in the Resource Directory section of this Guide or visit https://www.irs.gov/publications.

INCOME TAX WITHHOLDING

INTRODUCTION

Employers must withhold federal and Minnesota income tax and the employee's share of the FICA tax from their employee's wages and pay those taxes to the federal and state government. The amount of withholding is based on the wages or salary paid to the employee, and the number of withholding allowances claimed by the employee on Form W-4MN, Minnesota Employee Withholding Allowance/Exemption Certificate, https://www.revenue.state.mn.us/sites/default/files/2020-01/w-4mn_0.pdf or the amount determined on Form W-4, Employee's Withholding Allowance Certificate, https://www.irs.gov/forms-pubs/about-form-w-4, which the employee completes at the time of hiring. (Withholding Allowance Certificates are discussed later in this section.) Employers are required to withhold both federal and state income taxes and FICA tax from their employees' wages as soon as they are paid. Note that special rules may apply to the withholding of taxes on "supplemental" wages (e.g., on a bonus paid to an employee).

The Internal Revenue Service and the Minnesota Department of Revenue provide withholding tables to enable the employer to determine the appropriate withholding amount. These tables are available on the agencies websites. These agencies also send periodic newsletters and/or notices to employers about changes in the law or procedures. Employers must comply with these changes.

TAX IDENTIFICATION NUMBER

All business entities that have employees must obtain a federal employer identification number. If the employer employs anyone who works in Minnesota, or any Minnesota resident, that employer must also obtain a Minnesota tax identification number. Employers should apply for their tax identification numbers before they expect to hire their first employee, to allow for adequate processing time. A penalty may be assessed for failure to apply on time.

A federal identification number is obtained from the Internal Revenue Service online. Information is available at How to Apply for an EIN at https://www.irs.gov/businesses/small-businesses-self-employed/how-to-apply-for-an-ein.

To register for a Minnesota Tax ID Number go to Registering Your Business at https://www.revenue.state.mn.us/guide/registering-your-business. If you do not have Internet access, call the Business Registration office at 651-282-5225 or 800-657-3605.

Further information on the procedure for obtaining these numbers is provided in the section of this Guide on Business Taxes or may be obtained from the Internal Revenue Service or Minnesota Department of Revenue at the address and telephone numbers provided in the Resource Directory section of this Guide.

Following receipt and processing of the applications for tax identification numbers, the Internal Revenue Service and the Minnesota Department of Revenue provides the employer with respective identification numbers. Employers must file Minnesota withholding tax returns electronically over the Internet using e-services, or by touchtone telephone. If the employer is not required to pay electronically and chooses to pay by check, they can create a payment voucher found on the Minnesota Department of Revenue website for federal payments, the employer will automatically be enrolled in the Electronic Federal Tax Payment System—EFTPS—so they can make all deposits online or by phone. Within a few days they will receive by mail an EFTPS enrollment confirmation, as well as a Personal Identification Number (PIN) and complete instructions for using EFTPS. The employer will need to wait until they receive the EFTPS information in the mail before making a payment electronically. Once they receive the EFTPS Confirmation Package, they can begin making EFTPS payments.

WITHHOLDING ALLOWANCE CERTIFICATES

Federal Form W-4, Employee's Withholding Certificate, https://www.irs.gov/forms-pubs/about-form-w-4, is completed by the employee at the time of hiring, and is used by the employer to determine how much federal tax to withhold from the employee's paycheck. Employers may refer employees to the IRS Withholding Estimator at https://www.irs.gov/individuals/tax-withholding-estimator, to determine how to fill out Form W-4. Form W-4 can also be downloaded from the IRS at https://www.irs.gov/forms-pubs/about-form-w-4.

The Minnesota Department of Revenue provides Form W-4MN, Minnesota Employee Withholding Allowance/Exemption Certificate, https://www.revenue.state.mn.us/sites/default/files/2020-01/w-4mn_0.pdf, for state tax withholding. An employee must complete Form W-4MN and provide it to the employer any time they start employment or change their federal Form W-4, or claims to be exempt from Minnesota income tax withholding.

You must send copies of Form W-4MN to the Minnesota Department of Revenue if any of the following apply:

- The employee claims more than 10 Minnesota withholding allowances: or
- The employee claims to be exempt from Minnesota withholding and you reasonably expect the employee's wages to exceed $200 per week (Exception: if the employee is a resident of Michigan or North Dakota and has completed Form MWR)
- You believe the employee is not entitled to the number of allowances claimed

The employer should honor the employee's W-4 or W-4MN unless notified by the Internal Revenue Service or the Minnesota Department of Revenue that the form is not valid. Penalties apply to employees knowingly filing incorrect W-4 or W-4MN forms and employers who fail to provide federal or state tax authorities with, Forms W-4 or W-4MN when required.

FURNISHING WAGE AND TAX STATEMENT TO EMPLOYEES

The employer must issue a wage and tax statement, federal Form W-2, https://www.irs.gov/forms-pubs/about-form-w-2, to each employee on or before January 31 of the following year, or within 30 days of a written request from the employee if his or her employment was terminated.

Employers may furnish Form W-2 to employees electronically provided certain criteria are met. Employees must affirmatively consent to receive the Form W-2 in an electronic format and prior to, or at the time of the consent, the employer must provide a disclosure statement containing certain disclosures. Additionally, the electronic version of Form W-2 must contain all required information and comply with applicable revenue procedures relating to substitute statements to recipients. If the statement is furnished on a website, the employer must notify the employee, via mail, electronic mail, or in person, that the statement is posted on a website and provide instructions on accessing and printing the statement.*

*Most employers are required to submit W-2 and 1099 information electronically. For more information go to the Minnesota Department of Revenue, Withholding Tax Fact Sheets at https://www.revenue.state.mn.us/withholding-tax-fact-sheets, and select Fact Sheet #2 or #2a.

The federal copy of Form W-2, https://www.irs.gov/forms-pubs/about-form-w-2, together with Form W-3, Transmittal of Wage and Tax Statements, https://www.irs.gov/forms-pubs/about-form-w-3, must be filed annually with the Social Security Administration no later than January 31. No other forms should be sent with the W-2s. The state copy of Form W-2 must be filed with the Minnesota Department of Revenue by January 31. Information Returns (1099s) that show Minnesota tax withheld should be sent with the W-2 Forms.

Forms W-2 and W-3 may be obtained from the Internal Revenue Service, Online Ordering for Information Returns and Employer Returns at https://www.irs.gov/businesses/online-ordering-for-information-returns-and-employer-returns.

DEFINITION OF EMPLOYER AND EMPLOYEE

Generally, an employer is a person or organization for whom a worker performs a service as an employee. The employer usually provides the tools and place to work and has the right to hire and discharge an employee. A person may be an employer for purposes of one kind of tax but not for another.

Generally, employees can be defined either under common law or under special statutes for special purposes. Generally speaking, a common law employee is anyone who performs services that can be controlled by an employer (what will be done and how it will be done). This is true even when the employer gives the employee freedom of action. What matters is that the employer has the legal right to control the method and result of the services.

Further information on determining whether an individual is an employee is provided in the sections of this Guide titled "Issues for Employers" and "Checklist for Hiring an Employee" or refer to Federal Publication 15A, Employer's Supplemental Tax Guide.

ISSUES FOR NONRESIDENT EMPLOYERS AND EMPLOYEES

North Dakota and Michigan Residents Working in Minnesota

Minnesota has tax reciprocity agreements with these states. Under these agreements, residents of North Dakota or Michigan who work in Minnesota are not required to have Minnesota income tax withheld from their Minnesota compensation if they complete Form MWR, Reciprocity Exemption/Affidavit of Residency, https://www.revenue.state.mn.us/sites/default/files/2019-12/mwr_20.pdf. Instead, they pay state tax to the state in which they live.

A North Dakota or Michigan resident who works in Minnesota and does not want Minnesota income tax withheld from his or her wages must complete and give to the employer Form MWR, Reciprocity Exemption/Affidavit of Residency. The employer must retain one copy for his or her records and forward one copy to the Minnesota Department of Revenue. Form MWR should be completed by the employee each year by February 28 or within 30 days after they begin working or they change their residence.

The employer must send a copy of Form MWR to the Minnesota Department of Revenue no later than March 31 each year, or within thirty days after a hire of a new employee, an employee changes his or her residence, when the employee submits the form to the employer.

Employees of Interstate Carrier Companies

Interstate carrier companies that have employees such as truck drivers, bus drivers or railroad workers who regularly perform assigned duties in more than one state should withhold income tax for the employee's state of residence only.

Interstate air carrier companies who have employees who perform regularly assigned duties on aircraft in more than one state are required to withhold for their state of residence as well as any state in which more than 50 percent of their compensation is earned. An employee is considered to have earned more than 50 percent of their compensation in any state in which scheduled flight time in that state is more than 50 percent of total scheduled flight time for the calendar year.

Tax on Nonresident Entertainment Entities

Nonresident entertainers such as musicians, actors, dancers, athletes and public speakers may be subject to a two percent tax on the gross compensation they receive for entertainment performed in Minnesota. The tax is imposed on the entertainment entity. The person who has legal control of the payment of the compensation is responsible for withholding and depositing the tax. This tax does not apply to residents of North Dakota or Michigan if the individual provided a properly completed Form MWR, reciprocity exemption/affidavit of residency.

More information on Nonresident Entertainer Tax is available at https://www.revenue.state.mn.us/nonresident-entertainer-tax.

Minnesota Residents Employed Outside Minnesota

In Other States. An employer of a Minnesota resident who does not work in Minnesota but works in another state and who withholds federal income tax from the wages of that employee may also be required to withhold Minnesota income tax. The employer may be required to withhold taxes in the state in which the work is being performed and Minnesota if the company in the other state has Minnesota nexus. The term nexus is used in tax law to describe a situation in which a business has a presence in a state and is subject to the state's jurisdiction to tax. In general, a business has nexus if it derives income from sources within the state, owns or leases property in the state, employs personnel in the state in activities that exceed "mere solicitation", or has capital or property in the state. Reciprocity agreements apply for the states of North Dakota and Michigan. An employer who is required to withhold both Minnesota income tax and income tax for another state should first determine the amount of income tax to be withheld for each state. If the amount of Minnesota income tax is greater than the amount to be withheld from the state in which the employee is working, the employer should send the difference to the Minnesota Department of Revenue.

If the amount to be withheld for the other state is greater than the amount to be withheld for Minnesota, do not withhold Minnesota income tax.

Outside the United States. A Minnesota resident who is transferred to a location outside the United States remains a Minnesota resident unless:

(1) the employee is a "qualified individual" for the foreign earned income exclusion of Section 911(d)(1) of the Internal Revenue Code, and

(2) the employee does not have an interest in any homesteaded property in Minnesota. If the employee does not meet these criteria, the employer must continue to withhold Minnesota income tax from the employee's wages.

If you are required to withhold Minnesota State tax, follow the same rules as tax withheld from employees working in Minnesota. (See the section titled "Withholding Tax Deposit and Filing Requirements" below.)

If the employee changes his or her domicile and requests that you stop withholding Minnesota income tax, send the Department of Revenue a copy of the employee's W-4 and a letter explaining in detail why the employee thinks his or her domicile has changed.

WITHHOLDING TAX DEPOSIT AND FILING REQUIREMENTS

Overview

Both the Internal Revenue Service and the Minnesota Department of Revenue require employers to deposit withheld tax on a periodic basis, and to file periodic returns. Deposit and filing requirements are discussed below. Employers should note that for purposes of determining the frequency of payment, federal and state withholdings are totaled separately.

Deposit Requirements

Annual Requirement (Federal only). Agricultural employers who accumulate less than $2,500 federal tax liability during the year may pay the tax and file the return annually.

Annual Requirement (Minnesota only). Minnesota employers with $500 or less in Minnesota withholding tax in a year may be approved by the Department of Revenue to file on an annual basis. If during the year the Minnesota withholding tax exceeds $500, the employer is required to make a deposit at the end of the month following the month in which withholding tax exceeded $500. To make a deposit, the employer should use Minnesota Department of Revenue e-Services at https://www.mndor.state.mn.us/tp/eservices/_/, telephone 800-570-3329, or use a payment voucher.

Quarterly Requirement. Employers with federal deposit liability of less than $2,500 in the current quarter or state withholdings of $1,500 or less in the prior quarter must pay the entire amount to the Internal Revenue Service or Minnesota Department of Revenue quarterly. The payment is due the last day of the month following the end of the quarter.

General Rule for Making Deposits (Minnesota). If an employer withholds more than $1,500 in Minnesota tax during the previous quarter, the employer is required to make Minnesota deposits in the next quarter as often as it is required to make federal deposits, either monthly or semiweekly.

Monthly Requirement. New employers and employers whose total federal tax liability for the four quarters in the lookback period is $50,000 or less are required to deposit employment taxes each month by the fifteenth day of the following month. The lookback period is the four quarters beginning July 1 of the second preceding year and ending June 30 of the prior year. Employers should consult IRS Publication 15, Circular E, and the Minnesota Department of Revenue Income Tax Withholding Instruction Booklet and Tax Tables for specific rules and exceptions.

Semi-weekly Requirement. Employers whose total tax liability for the lookback period is more than $50,000 are required to deposit employment taxes on Wednesday and/or Friday, according to their payroll day. Employers should consult IRS Publication 15, Circular E, Employer's Tax Guide, and the Minnesota Department of Revenue Income Tax Withholding Instructions for specific rules.

One-Day Requirement (Federal only). Employers who accumulate taxes of $100,000 or more on any day during a deposit period are required to make the deposit by the close of the next banking day, whether they are a monthly or semi-weekly depositor.

Personal Liability for Payment of Employment Taxes. To encourage prompt payment of withheld income and employment taxes, including Social Security taxes, railroad retirement taxes, or collected excise taxes, Congress passed a law that provides for the TFRP (Trust Fund Recovery Penalty). These taxes are called trust fund taxes because you actually hold the employee's money in trust until you make a federal tax deposit in that amount. In the event that an employer fails to pay its employment taxes, its individual officers, members, directors, owners or others, who are responsible for collecting or paying withheld income and employment taxes and willfully fail to collect or pay them may be held personally liable for unpaid taxes. See the IRS Employment Taxes and the Trust Fund Recovery Penalty (TFRP) information at https://www.irs.gov/businesses/small-businesses-self-employed/employment-taxes-and-the-trust-fund-recovery-penalty-tfrp.

Electronic Federal Tax Payment System (EFTPS). The EFTPS is the system sponsored by the U.S. Department of Treasury that taxpayers use to initiate Federal tax payments electronically. As of January 1, 2011, all required Federal Tax Deposits must be made electronically using EFTPS. For more information or to enroll in EFTPS visit https://www.eftps.com/eftps/ or call the EFTPS Customer Service Center at 800-555-4477, or 800-733-4829 (TDD hearing-impaired), or 800-244-4829 (Español).

Electronic State Deposits. State tax deposits must be made electronically if state tax withholdings total more than $10,000 in Minnesota income tax during the last 12-month period ending June 30, if they use a payroll service company, or they are required to electronically pay any other Minnesota business tax to the Minnesota Department of Revenue. If you are required to pay business taxes electronically for one year, you must continue to do so for all future years. For more information see the Minnesota Income Tax Withholding Instruction Booklet and Tax Tables.

Filing Requirements

Quarterly Withholding Tax Return. Each quarter, all employers (except annual filers) must file federal Form 941, Employer's Quarterly Federal Tax Return with the Internal Revenue Service. In addition, all employers (except Minnesota annual filers) must file a Minnesota Quarterly Tax Withholding Return for each quarter. These returns must be filed electronically via Minnesota Department of Revenue e-Services at https://www.mndor.state.mn.us/tp/eservices/_/ or by phone 800-570-3329.

W-2 filing. Federal Form W-3, Transmittal of Income and Tax Statements, must be filed annually with the federal copies of each employee's Form W-2 to the Social Security Administration. The federal Form W-3 of the W-2 must be filed no later than January 31 in the year following the taxable year, or within 30 days of going out of business. The state copies of each employee's Form W-2 and 1099s that show Minnesota withholding must be filed with the Minnesota Department of Revenue. For requirements regarding the filing of Forms W-2 and 1099 see Withholding Tax Fact Sheets #2 and #2a at Withholding Tax Fact Sheets, https://www.revenue.state.mn.us/withholding-tax-fact-sheets. The federal Form W-3 and the state copies of the W-2 must be filed no later than January 31 in the year following the taxable year, or within 30 days of going out of business.

Annual Filing. If you have been approved by the Minnesota Department of Revenue to be an annual filer, you do not file quarterly returns. Your annual withholding tax return is due by January 31 of the year following the end of the taxable year. The return must be filed electronically using Minnesota Department of Revenue e-Services or by calling 800-570-3329.

Forms

Deposits through EFTPS require no coupon. Deposits of Minnesota taxes are made using the Minnesota e-Services system, by touchtone phone, or by mail using a payment voucher. Quarterly returns are filed using federal Form 941, Employer's Quarterly Federal Tax Return. State returns must be filed electronically using the Minnesota Department of Revenue e-Services or touchtone telephone. Note: both federal and state returns must be filed, even if all deposits have been made or there is zero tax due. You must file a zero withholding tax return.

Due Dates

All federal quarterly 941 returns are due April 30, July 31, October 31 and January 31. Minnesota quarterly withholding returns are due April 30, July 31, October 31, and January 31. The return for annual filers is due January 31. Federal returns and deposits and state deposits and returns will be considered on time if received or postmarked on or before the due date. The postmark must be a United States postmark and must not be from a postage meter. If deposits are made electronically, refer to the specific instructions for the type of deposit.

WITHHOLDING TAX PENALTIES AND INTEREST

Both the Internal Revenue Service and the Minnesota Department of Revenue assess penalties and interest for the failure to make deposits on time, the failure to file required returns on time, and the failure to file Form W-2 and 1099 forms. The amount of penalty for late deposits or late filing is based on the length of time the payment or return is late. The Internal Revenue Service imposes a penalty on failure to provide correct information on W-2 forms, and failure to provide a correct Taxpayer Identification Number. In addition, the Minnesota Department of Revenue imposes a penalty on failure to provide Form W-2 information to the department and for refusing to provide all information required on the forms.

Any person responsible for paying withholding tax may be held personally liable for failure to do so. A penalty equal to 100 percent of the amount of income tax, Social Security and Medicare tax, withheld from an employee's paycheck, may also be imposed. The IRS calls this the Trust Fund Recovery penalty.

Interest is assessed on unpaid withholding tax (plus penalties). Interest accrues from the date the payment should have been made to the date the payment actually is made. The interest rate is adjusted to reflect market rates.

CONTRACTOR AND SUBCONTRACTOR CLEARANCE

A prime contractor, contractor or subcontractor who performs work on a project for the State of Minnesota or any of Minnesota's political or governmental subdivisions (e.g., counties, cities, school districts) must file a Contractor Affidavit with the Minnesota Department of Revenue certifying that the contractor has complied with Minnesota's withholding tax laws in order to receive final payment for the work.

A **contractor** is a person who is awarded a contract to perform work and who performed the work personally or through his or her employees. A **prime contractor** is a contractor who is awarded a contract to perform work but who subcontracts all or part of the work to other contractors. A **subcontractor** is hired by a prime contractor to perform all or part of the work on a contract. A **subcontractor** files a contractor affidavit when the subcontractor completes its part of the project. A **prime contractor** or **contractor** files a contractor affidavit when the entire project is completed.

Go to the Minnesota Department of Revenue's website to submit a withholding Contractor Affidavit (see Contractor Affidavit Requirements at https://www.revenue.state.mn.us/sites/default/files/2019-12/mwr_20.pdf) for approval.

SUCCESSOR LIABILITY FOR CERTAIN TAXES WHEN A BUSINESS OR ITS ASSETS ARE TRANSFERRED

Whenever a business or its assets are transferred outside the ordinary course of business, and a lien for unpaid sales or withholding taxes has been filed, in certain situations the new owner can be liable for the amount of the lien and any related interest and penalties, and any other unpaid sales or withholding taxes. In order to avoid liability for these taxes, the potential new owner must send a notice to the Commissioner of the Department of Revenue at least twenty days before taking possession of the assets or paying the purchase price. That notice must contain information regarding the transfer of the business or its assets, the terms and conditions of that transfer, and the tax identification number of the business being transferred.

The Commissioner then has twenty days to notify the potential new owner of any additional sales or withholding taxes (including interest and penalties); the Commissioner may also notify the potential new owner of the amount needed to satisfy the lien, or that there are no taxes due in addition to the amount shown on the lien, or that additional tax returns are due. If the Commissioner fails to give the required notice within the twenty-day period, the potential new owner is not liable for any taxes other than those shown on the lien.

These rules apply to transfers of businesses or business assets, whether by sales or gift. In the case of sales transfers, the amount of the tax liability cannot exceed the purchase price. In the case of gift transfers, the tax liability is presumed to be the value of the transferred assets or business. Also, for transfers by gift, the tax liability can be avoided by returning the gifted property. These rules also apply to changes in the type of business entity or changes to the name of the business, so long as one business is being discontinued and another one started.

If an IRS Notice of Federal Tax Lien has been filed, contact the IRS to apply for a Certificate of Discharge. See IRS Publication 783 for more information.

REVOCATION OR PREVENTION OF LICENSE ISSUANCE OR RENEWAL

Existing licenses can be revoked if the Minnesota Department of Revenue notifies the licensing authority that the license holder owes the state for back taxes, penalties or interest. The Commissioner of Revenue is authorized to stop, by issuing a Notice of Requirement for Tax Clearance, the issuance or renewal of any business, trade, occupational or professional license issued by the state, a county or a municipality to businesses that have a state tax liability of more than $500 (Minn. Stat. § 270C.72).

If a licensing agency receives a Notice of Requirement for Tax Clearance for a business, a license may not be issued, renewed or transferred until the agency receives a tax clearance certificate from the Commissioner of Revenue. A tax clearance certificate is issued only upon resolution of the tax delinquency.

The Commissioner of Revenue is responsible for all negotiations, disputes and appeals resulting from a license denial under this statute. Further information regarding the requirements or application of this law may be obtained from the Minnesota Department of Revenue's Collection Enforcement group, at the address and telephone number provided in the Resource Directory section of this Guide.

UNEMPLOYMENT INSURANCE TAXES

Unemployment insurance taxes, paid by the employers, are funds used to pay unemployment benefits. The amount of tax paid by Minnesota employers is based on their unemployment history.

Unemployment benefits provide a temporary partial wage replacement to those Minnesota workers who become unemployed through no fault of their own. These payments are an economic stabilizer/stimulator in times of economic downturn, and help to maintain an available skilled workforce for Minnesota employers.

Federal unemployment tax (generally referred to as FUTA tax) is a separate tax used to fund the administration of the program at both the federal and state levels. FUTA taxes are collected by the Internal Revenue Service on behalf of the U.S. Department of Labor, Employment Standards Administration. State unemployment insurance taxes and the Minnesota Unemployment Insurance Law are administered by the Minnesota Unemployment Insurance Program, a division of the Department of Employment and Economic Development. Information on the federal and state programs may be obtained from the U.S. Department of Labor (federal program) and the Minnesota Unemployment Insurance (UI) Program (state program) at the addresses and telephone numbers provided in the Resource Directory section of this Guide. Both the federal and the state unemployment insurance taxes are employer-funded. Therefore, no deductions for it may be made from employees' wages.

FEDERAL UNEMPLOYMENT TAXES

Filing Requirements

The FUTA tax return is prepared once per year and is generally due one month after the year ends.

A FUTA tax return must be filed by any employer who meets any one of the following tests:

- The employer pays $1,500 or more in wages in any one calendar quarter for the reporting year, or;
- The employer had one or more employees for some part of a day in any of 20 different weeks during the reporting year. For this test, all regular, temporary, and part-time employees are counted. Note: Partners of a partnership, and sole proprietors and their spouses, parents, and minor children are not counted for this purpose. (This test is known as the "general" test), or;
- The employer paid cash wages of $20,000 or more to farm workers during any calendar quarter for the reporting year, or;
- The employer had 10 or more farm workers for some part of a day in each of 20 different weeks in the reporting year. Aliens admitted to the United States on a temporary basis to perform farm labor are counted for this purpose. (This test is known as the "farm workers" test), or;
- The employer paid cash wages of $1,000 in any calendar quarter in the reporting year for household work done in a private home, local college club, or local chapter of a fraternity or sorority. (This test is known as the "household employees" test).

Figuring the Tax

The federal unemployment tax is figured on the first $7,000 in wages paid ("wage base") to each employee during the year. The federal unemployment tax rate is 6.0 percent of the wage base (Note: The wage base and tax rate are subject to change annually); however, the employer is given a credit of up to 5.4 percent if the state unemployment insurance tax payments were timely. Therefore, the tax rate can be as low as 0.6 percent (6.0 percent minus the 5.4 percentage point credit). An employer may not take FUTA credit for any state taxes the employer did not actually pay.

In computing the employee wage base for FUTA, an employer who takes over the business of another employer who was subject to the federal unemployment tax may count wages paid by the first employer to those employees who continue to work for the second employer.

Additionally, wages paid to an owner/officer who owns 25 percent or more of a corporation or limited liability company (LLC), and has not opted to be covered under the Minnesota Unemployment Insurance (UI) Program (i.e. wages on which no Minnesota unemployment insurance tax has been paid), are not eligible for the 5.4 percentage point FUTA credit. For more information on this topic, see the section entitled "Coverage" under STATE UNEMPLOYMENT INSURANCE TAXES below.

Reporting and Paying the Tax

FUTA tax is reported on Form 940. The form covers one calendar year, and is due January 31st of the following year. An employer may, however, be required to make deposits of the tax before filing the return. If at the end of any calendar quarter the employer owes but has not yet deposited more than $500 in FUTA tax for the year, the employer must make a deposit by the end of the following month. If the tax is $500 or less at the end of a quarter, no deposit is required. Instead, it is added to the tax for the next quarter. If the total undeposited tax is more than $500 in the next quarter, a deposit is required. These payments must be made electronically via the Electronic Federal Tax Payment System (EFTPS). To enroll, visit https://www.eftps.com/eftps/.

Penalties

An employer can avoid penalties and interest by making tax deposits when they are due, correct returns, and paying the proper amount of tax when due. Penalties may be imposed for filing late deposits and late filing, unless the employer can show reasonable cause for the delay. Information on penalties can be obtained from the Internal Revenue Service at the address and telephone number provided in the Resource Directory section of this Guide.

STATE UNEMPLOYMENT INSURANCE TAXES

Coverage

All firms or organizations having services performed for them in Minnesota are subject to the provisions of the Minnesota Unemployment Insurance Law, and most of these firms or organizations are required to pay unemployment insurance taxes. In lieu of taxes, governmental entities and some nonprofits reimburse unemployment benefits paid to their former employees on a dollar-for-dollar basis. Whether or not a business is required to report wages and pay unemployment insurance taxes depends on the amount and type of employment, the amount of wages paid and other factors present in special situations. As discussed in "FEDERAL UNEMPLOYMENT TAXES" above, the wages paid to an owner/officer who owns 25 percent or more of a corporation or limited liability company (LLC), and has not chosen to be covered under the Minnesota Unemployment Insurance (UI) Program, are not subject to Minnesota unemployment insurance tax, nor do they need to be reported on the Wage Detail Report (discussed below in "Wage Detail Reports").

Registering for a Minnesota Unemployment Insurance (UI) Employer Account

All entities that pay wages to employees performing covered services in Minnesota are required to register with the Minnesota Unemployment Insurance (UI) Program. Registration is done either online or by automated phone system, and should be completed as soon as possible after wages are paid to employees performing covered services in Minnesota, but not later than the due date of the first Wage Detail Report (discussed below in "Wage Detail Reports"). Based on the information provided, the Minnesota Unemployment Insurance (UI) Program will determine if the entity is required to report the wages paid to its employees and pay Minnesota unemployment insurance taxes on those wages, or (if eligible) reimburse any unemployment benefits that are paid to the entity's former employees. If the entity meets the reporting requirements, it will be assigned an unemployment insurance employer account number.

The following entities do not need to register for a Minnesota Unemployment Insurance (UI) Employer Account:

- sole proprietorships whose only employees are the spouse, parents, and/or minor children of the sole proprietor, or;
- corporations and LLCs whose only employees are owner/officers who directly or indirectly own 25 percent or more of the business and have not chosen to be covered under the Minnesota Unemployment Insurance Program, or;
- partnerships whose only workers are the partners of the partnership.

Acquisitions

When an employer acquires all or part of a business that was required to pay unemployment insurance taxes in Minnesota, that transaction can affect the acquiring employer's UI tax rate. Depending on the circumstances, taxable wages and benefits paid charges associated with the predecessor employer's UI account may be transferred to the successor employer's UI account. This transfer is effective the date of the acquisition or merger; the Minnesota Unemployment Insurance (UI) Program will then recalculate the successor's tax rate effective the first day of the calendar quarter following the effective date of the transfer. Visit https://www.uimn.org for details.

Tax Rates

Visit Minnesota Unemployment Insurance (UI) Program, Wages & Taxes, https://www.uimn.org/employers/wages-taxes/index.jsp, for details on UI tax rate calculations.

New employers

The tax rate for new employers is based on the average tax rate for the employer's industry. This ensures that each new employer has a rate that aligns with other businesses in their industry. Industries are defined by the North American Industry Classification System (NAICS).

Experience rating

The Minnesota Unemployment Insurance (UI) Program assigns an experience rating to each employer that has paid taxable wages for a minimum period of time. An experience rating is a ratio of the employer's total taxable wages and total UI benefit charges. The more unemployment that an employer causes during its experience rating period, the higher the employer's experience rating will be.

To calculate an experience rate, the UI Program looks to an employer's history of taxable wages and benefits paid charges over the prior 48-month period. The experience rating period ends on June 30 of the year prior to the year for which the experience rate is being computed. For example, experience rates assigned to employers for 2020 were based on the time period beginning July 1, 2014, and ending June 30, 2019.

Employers are not required to have had employees during the entire 48 month period to receive an experience rating. If an employer paid wages on or before July 1 of their first year of coverage, they will be eligible for an experience rating in the third year. For example, an employer that first paid wages on or before June 30, 2018, will receive an experience rating in 2020. In other words, to receive an experience rating, an employer must have paid wages for a minimum of 18 months.

By relating employer UI tax rates to taxable wages and benefits paid charges, experience ratings help ensure that each employer pays UI taxes commensurate to the unemployment for which the employer is responsible.

Additional and Special Assessments

If the balance in the Minnesota UI Fund on March 31 falls below certain levels, an additional assessment takes effect for the following year. There is also a provision in the law for a special assessment to pay interest on federal loans which help to keep the Trust Fund solvent during periods of high unemployment.

Special Assessment for Workforce Development

A Special Workforce Development Assessment is paid with the quarterly unemployment insurance tax. The assessment collected is deposited in the Minnesota Workforce Development Fund, and is used to fund programs that help unemployed workers with retraining and re-employment, helping to keep them a valuable part of their local economy in Minnesota. Visit Minnesota Unemployment Insurance (UI) Program, https://www.uimn.org, for details.

Wage Detail Reports

Minnesota requires employers to file wage reports and pay Unemployment Insurance tax on a quarterly basis. When employers pay covered wages to employees for services provided, they are required to submit quarterly wage reports detailing the wages they paid to each employee, and pay tax on the wages reported. All covered wages paid to both full and part-time employees during the calendar quarter must be reported (this includes commissions, bonuses, tips as well as the cash value of any remuneration paid by a means other than cash), except those wages excluded by law. Examples of covered/noncovered employment are listed in the Unemployment Insurance (UI) Employer Handbook at Covered vs. noncovered employment, https://www.uimn.org/employers/help-and-support/emp-hbook/covered-employment.jsp#non-covered.

Not all covered wages are taxable. Unemployment insurance tax is only paid on wages up to an annual taxable maximum per employee. Visit https://www.uimn.org for details.

The wage information that is required quarterly for each employee is:

- full name;
- Social Security number;
- total wages paid in the quarter;
- number of hours worked in the quarter, and;
- work location(s).

Employers are also required to report the total number of covered workers who worked or received pay during the payroll period which included the 12th of the month for each month in the reporting period. The wage detail report and the related taxes and other assessments are due within one month after the end of each calendar quarter. The due dates are April 30, July 31, October 31 and January 31. If any of these dates falls on a weekend or state government holiday, the due date is the next state government business day. Wage Detail Reports are required from all covered employers, even though they may have had no employees during the quarter, and therefore owe no tax. Even though no tax is due, a late fee will still apply if the report is filed late. Reports must be electronically filed and accepted by the due date. The electronic receipt date of the accepted report will determine timeliness. Instructions on how to file a Zero Wage Report are listed in the Minnesota Unemployment Insurance (UI) Program Employer Self-Service System User Guide, https://www.uimn.org/employers/help-and-support/employer-user-guide/index.jsp.

Wage Detail Reports are filed online or with an automated phone option using the Employer Self-Service System. Features of the System include:

- All tax and wage reporting is done on a secure website or using automated telephone reporting (for employers with few employees and no access to the Internet).
- Wage and tax reports are combined - the System calculates taxable wages and the amount of tax and other assessments due.
- Several standard electronic file formats and submission types are accepted.
- Electronic Payments—Electronic payment options using either ACH debit or ACH credit are available for all employers, and required for employers reporting 50 or more employees and all third-party processors paying on behalf of their clients. The posting date of the payment (not the postmark date for paper check payments) will determine its timeliness.
- Features allow the user to view and update account information, view payment history and wage detail information, make changes to account information, view benefits paid charges and receive and respond to Determinations of Benefit Account and Eligibility—all online.

Interest Charged on Late Tax Payments

If the taxes due are not received by the due date, the employer is assessed interest at the rate of 1.0 percent per month or any part thereof, from the due date until payment is received by the Minnesota Unemployment Insurance (UI) Program. Interest assessments may be removed if a late payment is attributable to certain extenuating circumstances. All requests for interest removal must be in writing, and the reasons for late payment must be substantiated.

Late Fees for Failure to File Timely Reports

An employer who knowingly fails to submit a Wage Detail Report by the due date is required to pay a late fee in addition to the interest. An employer who submits the Wage Detail Report, but knowingly fails to include any part of the required information or knowingly enters erroneous information is also subject to an administrative fee. Additional information on interest and administrative fees is available on the Minnesota Unemployment Insurance (UI) Program's website at https://www.uimn.org/employers/.

Adjustments and Refunds

An employer that overpays the tax due may apply for an adjustment within four years from the date the tax was paid. To obtain an adjustment the employer should complete an adjustment transaction using the Unemployment Insurance Employer Self-Service System. Upon approval of the submission, the employer will receive a credit that can be applied to future taxes. When specifically requested, a refund check will be issued for the full amount of the credit. An employer who fails to include all wages in a previous report should complete an adjustment transaction via the Minnesota Unemployment Insurance (UI) Employer Self-Service System. Upon review and approval of the completed submission, the necessary adjustments will be made. Adjustments for a prior quarter should not be made on a subsequent quarter's Wage Detail Report. All adjustments should be made to the quarter and year to which they relate. Overpayments or underpayments may also result from an unemployment insurance audit of an employer's payroll records. In such cases, all adjustments will automatically be made, and the employer will be notified of any overpayment or underpayment.

Audits

Unemployment Insurance Auditors perform regular examinations of employer payroll records. An audit to verify wage items and employment is generally confined to a single year, but may be expanded if errors or exclusions are found. All of the employer's records, including subsidiary records, must be made available to the auditor. Auditors may also inspect records for the purpose of establishing an employer's liability under the law, to obtain information regarding an application for unemployment benefits and in connection with unemployment insurance fraud investigations. The Minnesota Unemployment Insurance Law provides that the records of any employing unit must be open to inspection, audit and verification at any reasonable time, and as often as may be deemed necessary.

Records

True and accurate employment records must be kept by all Minnesota employers, whether or not they are covered under the Minnesota Unemployment Insurance Law.

Since an employer's reporting requirements cannot be properly determined without such records, the records must be open to inspection as requested by the Audits & Special Accounts Section of the Minnesota Unemployment Insurance (UI) Program. The law provides penalties and administrative fees to ensure compliance. Records should contain the following information for each employee:

- full name;
- complete home address;
- Social Security number;
- the beginning and ending dates of the pay period and the date of payment;
- the days and number of hours in which the individual performed services;
- the location where the services were performed;
- the amount of gross wages paid and wages due but not paid for services performed;
- the rate and base unit of pay;
- any amounts paid as allowances or reimbursement for expenses; and
- the date of, and reason for, an employee's separation from employment.

For services performed both in Minnesota and outside Minnesota the records must also include:

- the state in which the employer maintains a base of operations used by the individual;
- the state from which the services are directed and controlled; and
- a list of the states in which the individual performs services, other than temporary or incidental services, and the dates services were performed in each state.

Wages paid and wages due but not paid must be broken down to show the character of each payment. For example, meals, lodging, bonuses and gifts must be shown separately. Employment records must be kept for a period of not less than four years in addition to the current calendar year.

Personal Liability for Payment of Unemployment Insurance Tax

In the event that an employer fails to pay its unemployment insurance tax, its individual officers, directors, governors, members, partners, or owners may be held personally liable for any unpaid taxes, interest and fees.

FEDERAL TAX REQUIREMENTS

YOU MAY BE LIABLE FOR	IF YOU ARE TAXED AS*	USE FORM	DUE ON OR BEFORE
Tax Identification Number	Sole proprietor with employees; Partnership; Corporation If you are a sole proprietor with no employees use your Social Security Number as your tax identification number	SS-4, Application for Employer Identification Number (EIN)	See Instructions on Form SS-4
Individual – Income Tax Return	Sole proprietor	Schedule C (Form 1040), Profit or Loss from Business (Sole Proprietorship)	April 15th or the 15th day of the 4th month after the end of the tax year
	Partner or S corporation shareholder	Schedule E (Form 1040), Supplemental Income or Loss	Same as above
Business – Income Tax Return	Partnership	Form 1065, U.S. Return of Partnership Income	15th day of the 3rd month following the close of the tax year
	S corporation	Form 1120-S, U.S. Income Tax Return for an S corporation	15th day of the 3rd month after the end of the tax year
	Corporation	Form 1120, U.S. Corporation Income Tax Return	15th day of the 4th month after the end of the tax year
Estimated Taxes – Individual	Sole Proprietor or individual who is a partner or S corporation shareholder	Form 1040-ES, Estimated Tax For Individuals	15th day of the 4th, 6th, and 9th months of tax year, 15th day of 1st month after end of tax year
Estimated Taxes – Corporation	Corporation	Form 1120-W, Estimated Tax for Corporations	15th day of the 4th, 6th, 9th and 12th months of tax year
Withholding of Income Tax and FICA Deposits	Business with Employees	EFTPS	See withholding and deposit instructions issued by IRS
Return for Reporting Withholding of Employee's Income Tax and FICA	Business with Employees	Form 941, Employer's Quarterly Federal Tax Return	End of month following end of quarter
Reporting Information on Wage and Tax Statements (Form W-2)	Business with Employees	W-3, Transmittal of Wage and Tax Statements	See Reporting Information on Wage and Tax Statements (Form W-2)
Unemployment Tax (FUTA)	Business with Employees	Form 940, Employer's Annual Federal Unemployment (FUTA) Tax Return	January 31
Unemployment Tax Deposits	Business with Employees	EFTPS	See FUTA Deposit Instructions issued by IRS
Information Returns	Business Required to File Form 1099, U.S. Information Returns	Form 1096, Annual Summary and Transmittal of U.S. Information Returns	Filed on or before January 31, 2020, when you are reporting nonemployee compensation payments in box 7. Otherwise, file by February 28, 2020, if you file on paper, or by March 31, 2020, if you file electronically.
Other Federal Taxes call the IRS			

Note that generally speaking, single-member LLCs may choose to be taxed as a sole proprietorship or a corporation. LLCs with at least two members may choose to be taxed either as a corporation or as a partnership.

STATE OF MINNESOTA TAX REQUIREMENTS

YOU MAY BE LIABLE FOR	IF YOU ARE TAXED AS*	USE FORM	DUE ON OR BEFORE
Tax Identification Number	Making taxable sales or withholding taxes; Partnership, Corporation	Register online at Minnesota Depatment of Revenueor file form Application for Business Registration (ABR)	See information at Minnesota Department of Revenue, Businesses at https://www.revenue.state.mn.us/businesses or call 651-282-5225
Income Tax	Sole Proprietor	M1, Individual Income Tax Return	April 15, or the 15th day of 4th month after the end of the tax year
	Individual who is a partner or S corporation shareholder	M1, Individual Income Tax Return	Same as above
	Partnership	M3, Partnership Return	Same as federal
	C Corporation	M4, Corporation Franchise Tax Return	Same as federal
		M11, Insurance Premium Tax Return for Property and Casualty Companies	March 1
	S corporation	M8 Corporation Return	Same as federal
Sales and Use Tax (sales tax returns must be filed using the e-Services Minnesota electronic filing system or by phone)	Organization that makes retail sales or provides taxable services	Filing of Sales and Use Tax return must be done online through e-Services system or by phone: Online – e-Services By phone – Call 800-570-3329 (toll-free)	Due date is based on filing cycle assigned by Department of Revenue – see instructions.
	Business that purchases taxable property for use in Minnesota without paying sales tax	Same as above	Included on Sales and Use Tax Return
	Consumer who purchases taxable property without paying sales tax	UT1, Individual Use Tax Return,	April 15th of following year
Estimated Tax	Sole proprietor or individual who is a partner or S corporation shareholder	-Pay through e-Services -See Make a Payment for other types of payment methods	15th day of 4th, 6th, and 9th months of tax year; and 15th day of 1st month after end of tax year
	Corporation	Payment Vouchers System	15th day of 3rd, 6th, 9th, and 12th months of tax year

* Note that generally speaking, single-member LLCs may choose to be taxed as a sole proprietorship or a corporation. LLCs with at least two members may choose to be taxed either as a corporation or as a partnership. For Minnesota unemployment insurance purposes, all LLCs are treated as corporations.

STATE OF MINNESOTA TAX REQUIREMENTS

YOU MAY BE LIABLE FOR	IF YOU ARE TAXED AS*	USE FORM	DUE ON OR BEFORE
Withholding of Income Tax	Sole proprietor, corporation, S corporation or partnership -Minnesota Withholding Tax Returns -Minnesota Withholding Tax Deposits	e-Services, touchtone phone or Income Tax Withholding payment voucher. See Payment Voucher System	See withholding instructions issued by the Minnesota Department of Revenue
Nonresident Partner or Shareholder Withholding	Partnership S corporation	M3 (Schedule KPI) M8 (Schedule KS)	Due date of tax return
Unemployment Tax	Sole proprietor, corporation, S corporation, partnership, limited liability partnership or limited liability company	Minnesota Unemployment Insurance (UI) Self-Service User System. Registration and login links available at http://www.uimn.org/employers/	Prior to the submission of the first quarterly wage detail report
		Unemployment Quarterly Wage Detail Report and Tax Payment using Minnesota Unemployment Insurance (UI) Self-Service User System. Registration and login links available at http://www.uimn.org/employers/	Within one month after end of each calendar quarter
Minimum Fee	Corporation	M4	Due date of tax return
	S Corporation	M8	
	Partnership	M3	
Other Taxes	Call Department of Revenue		

* Note that generally speaking, single-member LLCs may choose to be taxed as a sole proprietorship or a corporation. LLCs with at least two members may choose to be taxed either as a corporation or as a partnership. For Minnesota unemployment insurance purposes, all LLCs are treated as corporations.

SOURCES OF INFORMATION AND ASSISTANCE

STATE PROGRAMS

SMALL BUSINESS ASSISTANCE OFFICE

The Small Business Assistance Office, specifically created by Minn. Stat. § 116J.66, provides accurate, timely and comprehensive information and assistance to businesses in all areas of start-up, operation and expansion. Functionally, the office has two bureaus for service delivery: the Bureau of Business Licenses and the Bureau of Small Business. The specific services of the Bureau of Business Licenses and the Bureau of Small Business are described below. For further information on these programs or to order any of the publications, contact the Small Business Assistance Office at the address, telephone number and go to the website address listed in the Resource Directory section of this Guide.

Bureau of Business Licenses

The Bureau of Business Licenses provides a number of services at no charge. It publishes the ***State of Minnesota Directory of Licenses and Permits*** reproduced in this Guide. That Directory, along with additional license and permit information, is available online at Minnesota ELicensing, https://mn.gov/elicense/. The Bureau provides comprehensive information on the number and kind of licenses required for a business venture, the agencies which issue them and the affirmative burdens imposed on applicants. The Bureau will also provide opinions from licensing agencies on their use of discretion in issuing licenses, and the potential issues and difficulties in obtaining licenses based on a review of a potential applicant's business concept. Master application procedures for obtaining related and similar licenses from different licensing agencies of the state are available, as well as consolidation of hearings involved in obtaining multiple licenses and information on related licensing requirements of federal and local governments.

Bureau of Small Business

The Bureau of Small Business serves as a focal point within state government for small business related information. It publishes ***Checklist for Hiring an Employee*** (reprinted in this Guide), an outline of the federal and state requirements governing the hiring of an employee; ***A Guide to Intellectual Property Protection***, a primer for the inventor and the entrepreneur on the protection of new ideas and the products which result from them; ***An Employer's Guide to Employment Law Issues in Minnesota***, designed to alert Minnesota employers to issues which commonly arise in the employment relationship; ***Employing Servicemembers: What You Should Know About USERRA***, a manual concerning employers dealing with servicemember employees and the protections offered to those employees under the Uniformed Services

Employment and Reemployment Rights Act (USERRA); ***First Considerations In Starting a Family Child Care Business***, this publication is directed at persons considering the formation and operation of a family child care business; ***Raising Capital: Securities Law and Business Considerations***, providing a general overview of the various federal and state securities law considerations involved in raising capital and including such areas as "taking a company public," "due diligence," the investment agreement and tax consequences of capital financing; ***Minnesota's Angel Tax Credit June 2019***, describes eligibility requirements for credits, how the credit works, and other information; ***A Legal Guide to Technology Transactions A COVID-19 Update 2020***, is intended to better enable businesses considering information technology acquisition to frame up their questions and issues for their own staff, for technology suppliers, and for consultants and attorneys who will be involved in the contracting, acquisition, and use of the technology; ***A Legal Guide to the Use Of Social Media In The Workplace***, is designed to alert businesses to legal issues which commonly arise when social media is used in the workplace or as a business tool; ***A Legal Guide to Data and Privacy Security 2020***, represents the first ever attempt to compile Minnesota state data privacy and security laws as well as federal and global privacy laws in one publication; and ***Small Business Notes***, an electronic format serial publication presenting a brief overview of recent trends, developments and issues affecting small businesses. Some of these publications are available in print form and all of these publications are available on CD or USB Flash Drive. Publications are available online on the Minnesota Department of Employment and Economic Development (DEED) website at https://mn.gov/deed/business/help/sbao/. The Bureau continually produces new publications throughout the year. Contact the Bureau for a current publications list. All publications are available free of charge.

SMALL BUSINESS DEVELOPMENT CENTERS (SBDCs)

The Minnesota Small Business Development Centers (MnSBDCs) offer confidential one-on-one business counseling and group training to those that are interested in expanding or starting a small business in Minnesota. Most SBDCs are located within an hour drive of a business client's residence. The SBDCs operate through a network of nine statewide regional centers, and their satellite centers and outreach locations. The SBDC network is made up of committed professionals, each with distinctive credentials that qualify them to assist with both general and special business needs. Drawing on both formal education and years of practical business experience, each counselor understands well what it is like to operate a business.

The SBDC counseling service primarily focuses on assisting existing and growing businesses in the areas of business planning, marketing, E-commerce technology, financial analysis and loan packaging. Directly and through collaboration with other resource organizations, the SBDC program also offers assistance and referrals in areas like regulatory compliance assistance, information technology, exporting, government procurement, and federal research and development opportunities. Counseling is customized to meet the needs of the client, and may be provided by staff counselors or private consultants. The SBDCs also offer assistance to those who are considering starting a business by providing information and resources on pre-business planning and by working with resource partners to help the entrepreneur with exploring possibilities in determining whether to pursue the business venture. A request for counseling services can be accessed on the MnSBDC section of the Minnesota Department of Employment and Economic Development (DEED) website at https://mn.gov/deed/business/help/sbdc/.

Training seminars offered by the SBDCs are designed to help small business owners and managers strengthen their management skills. Training programs are specifically designed and delivered based on the needs of the local business community. Recent training seminar topics offered have included pre-business planning, access to capital, understanding and using financial statements, employment management issues, workplace communication, E-commerce technology, and market research and analysis. A listing of current training programs offered by the SBDC network can be found by visiting the MnSBDC website.

While the SBDCs do not administer loan or grant programs, its network of counselors does help small business to access funding options, evaluate eligibility, and help prepare documentation that lenders require. The SBDCs helps business owners to better understand the loan process and helps them to prepare a detailed and complete loan application.

Resource libraries at the SBDCs offer access to business development reference books, periodicals and computerized databases. Many SBDCs have computers and business software that may be used by clients to develop business plans. Most regional centers offer online counseling.

The MnSBDC program is a partnership of the U.S. Small Business Administration, the Minnesota Department of Employment and Economic Development, and the host institutions of the regional and satellite centers. Businesses served by the SBDC program must meet size standards and other requirements for assistance established by the U.S. Small Business Administration. Financial support of its funding partners allows the SBDC to offer counseling services at no cost to the business client. Training programs and special projects are provided either at no cost or for a nominal fee.

Contact information and locations of members of the MnSBDC network are listed in the Resource Directory section of this Guide.

MINNESOTA TRADE OFFICE

The Minnesota Trade Office (MTO), an office within the Minnesota Department of Employment and Economic Development (DEED), is the state agency that provides export assistance to Minnesota companies and works to attract foreign direct investment. The MTO delivers programs and services particularly focused on helping small and medium sized companies enter and compete in the international market. Most services are offered free of charge or at a nominal cost. MTO services include:

Export Counseling and Technical Assistance

The MTO is staffed with a team of international trade representatives with broad international business experience who can help guide companies through the challenges of conducting international business. Through confidential and personalized meetings, MTO trade representatives are available to evaluate your export readiness, advise on how to conduct market research and develop an export plan, assist with market entry strategies, identify market opportunities and provide market intelligence, provide shipping and tariff information, identify potential distributors, partners, agents, and buyers, and more.

Export Promotion Services

To help companies explore market opportunities firsthand and meet potential distributors, partners, agents, and buyers, the MTO arranges numerous export promotional events annually. The MTO organizes trade missions, including the governor's trade missions; provides exhibition opportunities at domestic and international trade shows; and arranges face-to-face meetings with potential foreign buyers. In addition to promotional events organized directly by the MTO, the trade office also can advise Minnesota companies of promotional events organized by other trade associations.

Export Education and Training Services

The MTO provides training seminars and workshops designed to provide companies the knowledge and tools necessary to be successful exporters. A complete listing of educational programs is posted on the MTO website at https://mn.gov/deed/business/exporting/ (click on Calendar of Events).

Market Intelligence and Research Resources

To ensure Minnesota companies have the very latest market intelligence at their disposal, the MTO works with the DEED library to maintain an extensive collection of information on foreign markets. Open to the public by appointment Monday through Friday (9:00 a.m. - 4:00 p.m.) and staffed with professional researchers, the DEED library is replete with economic data, export statistics, international trade periodicals, company directories, a wide variety of electronic and internet-based market research tools, as well as materials to help companies learn the mechanics of exporting and the art of conducting business in other cultures. Companies also can access valuable research resources on the MTO website.

To take advantage of the full range of MTO export assistance services, contact the MTO at the address and telephone number in the Resource Directory section of this Guide and visit the MTO website at https://mn.gov/deed/business/exporting/.

STEP (State Trade and Export Promotion Program) Export Assistance for Small Business

The STEP program provides financial and technical assistance to qualifying Minnesota small businesses with an active interest in exporting products or services to foreign markets. Participants may be first-time exporters or companies that are currently exporting but are interested in expanding into new international markets.

Invest in Minnesota

With staff in Minnesota and key international markets the Office of Foreign Direct Investment is available to help foreign companies explore the advantages of expanding in Minnesota.

MINNESOTA BUSINESS FIRST STOP

Minnesota Business First Stop streamlines the development process for complex business startups, expansions or relocations that involve financing, licensing, permitting, and regulatory issues that overlap multiple state agencies.

For more information about assistance and services provided see https://mn.gov/deed/business/help/first-stop/.

LAUNCH MINNESOTA

Launch Minnesota provides entrepreneurs and emerging technology companies with financial assistance in the form of grants as a spur to business growth. Launch Minnesota works with private industry to create financial incentives and programming to demonstrate that Minnesota is committed to fostering an innovation ecosystem that draws global attention. It is a joint initiative with private businesses and nonprofit organizations statewide. The program has an annual budget of $2.5 million.

A key goal of Launch Minnesota is to make the risks related to leaving a steady job to start a high technology company a little more manageable for entrepreneurs through:

- Grants to assist in attracting federal research and development funding
- Business liquidity grants to help entrepreneurs with capital constraints
- Child care and housing assistance
- Training in areas such as understanding equity capital, building toward scalability, and pitching venture capitalists

Launch Minnesota is set up to provide special consideration and social capital connectivity for startups and small businesses in Greater Minnesota as well as businesses started by women, veterans and people of color. Interested parties should visit http://www.launchminnesota.org/ and contact launchminnesota@state.mn.us.

VOCATIONAL REHABILITATION SERVICE

Small Business Assistance for People with Disabilities

People with disabilities who wish to start or continue operating a small business may be eligible to receive financial assistance and support through Vocational Rehabilitation Services.

Vocational Rehabilitation services funding is available for start-up costs when a qualifying individual with a disability wishes to start a new business. Funding is also available to cover business stabilization costs when an owner's disability forces changes to a product, service or method of operation, or when a disability causes suspensions or lengthy interruptions to business operations.

Eligible costs must be identified on a business plan that is developed and approved in collaboration with a vocational rehabilitation counselor. These costs could include such things as occupational licenses, tools, marketing materials, insurance, equipment, stocks and supplies.

For more information about assistance and services provided by Vocational Rehabilitation Services, and to find office locations, see https://mn.gov/deed/job-seekers/disabilities/.

EMPLOYMENT AND TRAINING PROGRAMS

Minnesota CareerForce Centers

The Minnesota Department of Employment and Economic Development has joined with other providers of employment and training services to create the Minnesota CareerForce Center System. The 49 CareerForce Centers have services provided by Job Service/Unemployment Insurance, local job training programs, State Services for the Blind, Veteran's Services, and Rehabilitation Services.

In addition, other organizations may be partners at each CareerForce Center, including Community Action Programs, Department of Human Services programs, local community or economic development groups, schools and colleges, and local government offices. The CareerForce Centers are nationally recognized for their accessibility and wide range of services offered.

Services of interest to businesses include:

- Self-service job postings and resume searches on MinnesotaWorks.net
- Job screening and computerized skills matching
- CareerOneStop
- Fee-based job analysis of position duties and tasks
- Employer advisory committees
- Labor market information
- Special programs, such as Shared Work and bonding programs
- Federal tax credits
- Conferences and seminars
- Veterans placement and representatives
- Plant closings and mass layoffs
- Job and career fairs

More information about CareerForce Centers and services to business is available at https://www.careerforcemn.com.

Shared Work Program

The Shared Work Program offers an alternative to layoffs for employers facing a temporary downturn in business. Administered by the Unemployment Insurance (UI) Program, it allows an employer to divide available hours of work among a group of employees as an alternative to full layoffs.

Affected employees may receive partial unemployment insurance benefits while working reduced hours. An employer can maintain morale, productivity and flexibility in the workplace by participating in the Shared Work Program. For more information about the program, contact the Coordinator or go to https://www.uimn.org/employers/alternative-layoff/index.jsp.

Apprenticeship Programs

Apprenticeship programs are located in the Minnesota Department of Labor and Industry. Apprenticeship Minnesota helps employers develop and register apprenticeship programs and promote workforce diversity through outreach and education. Minnesota's apprenticeship program allows employers to design their own apprenticeship program that provides apprentices with specific skills, training and job-related instruction tailored to the company's needs.

Apprenticeship is a successful and innovative employee training model that can be designed to meet employers' needs to recruit, train and retain 21st century talent. An apprentice earns, learns and works for their employers as they receive structured on-the-job training and related classroom instruction. Apprenticeships help businesses develop highly-skilled and motivated employees, reduce turnover rates, increase worker productivity and lower the cost of recruitment.

For more information about apprenticeship and dual training, contact the Minnesota Department of Labor and Industry or go to https://www.dli.mn.gov/about-department/our-areas-service/apprenticeship-minnesota.

MINNESOTA JOB SKILLS PARTNERSHIP

The Minnesota Jobs Skills Partnership (MJSP) works with businesses, educational institutions and nonprofit organizations to train or retrain workers, expand work opportunities and keep high-quality jobs in the state. The goal is to target short-term training for full-time employment in the growth sectors of the state's economy.

Grants are offered through a variety of programs to offset training-related expenses incurred by business, industry, nonprofit organizations and educational institutions to meet current and future workforce needs.

Grant programs available through the Minnesota Job Skills Partnership include:

- Partnership - Provides grants to educational institutions that are partnering with a business or a consortium of businesses to develop and deliver training to new or existing workers that is specific to the business needs.

- Pathways - Provides grants to educational institutions, or public, private, or nonprofit entities that are partnering with a business or a consortium of businesses to provide training for individuals who have incomes at or below 200 percent of the federal poverty guidelines or those who are making a transition from public assistance to work.

- Low Income Worker Training Program—Provides grants to public, private, or nonprofit entities to help low-income people gain new skills necessary move up the career ladder to higher paying jobs and greater economic self-sufficiency.
- Job Training Incentive Program— Provides training grants to new or expanding businesses located in Greater Minnesota.

The Minnesota Job Skills Partnership is located within the Business and Community Development Division of the Minnesota Department of Employment and Economic Development. For more information and applications, go to https://mn.gov/deed/business/financing-business/training-grant/.

DISLOCATED WORKER PROGRAM

The Dislocated Worker Program, located within the CareerForce Division of the Minnesota Department of Employment and Economic Development (DEED), provides employment and training services to workers laid off from their jobs due to no fault of their own and due to changes in technology, investment strategies, and consumption and competition. The program also serves veterans leaving active duty with the Armed Forces and certain individuals leaving active duty of the National Guard or Armed Forces Reserves.

DEED delivers dislocated worker services in two ways: For individual dislocated workers, resources are allocated to service providers in the CareerForce Centers, or in the event of a plant closing or mass layoff (usually 50 or more workers affected) DEED has developed a process which customizes services to the needs of the affected workers and businesses. The process begins in confidence with members of the Dislocated Worker Program Rapid Response Team. The most effective programs begin with at least 60 days' notice, in compliance with the Worker Adjustment and Retraining Notification Act (WARN).

For more information about the Dislocated Worker Program and Rapid Response Team, go to https://mn.gov/deed/programs-services/dislocated-worker/.

MINNESOTA FEDERAL BONDING SERVICE

The Minnesota Federal Bonding Service provides individual fidelity bonds (employee dishonesty insurance) to employers for job applicants who may be denied coverage by an employer's surety company due to risk factors. The Fidelity Bond insurance is issued as a policy of Travelers Property Casualty. The Minnesota Department of Employment and Economic Development (DEED) is an authorized agency for the issuance of these bonds.

This fidelity bond is issued at the request of the employer at the time of a job offer, or, if the employer chooses to bond someone already in his/her employment. Bond coverage becomes effective when the employer of the person to be bonded contacts the Bonding Coordinator for DEED. The person to be bonded must be working, full or part-time, in W2-paid employment in Minnesota. Self-employment is not eligible. The bond is provided at no cost to the employer or the job applicant. The duration of the bond is six months and the bond is ordinarily for $5,000. An employee is ineligible for this service if he/she has been in a bonded position before and a claim was made against that bond. This bond protects the employer only against employee theft of money or property. If there is not a claim against the bond, after six months, the employer will be offered the opportunity to continue the bond at standard rates, and the employee is considered "Bondable for Life."

For more information about the Federal Bonding Program go to https://mn.gov/deed/business/finding-workers/incentives/federal-bonding.jsp.

UNIVERSITY OF MINNESOTA EXTENSION

University of Minnesota Extension delivers educational programs and information to Minnesota citizens and communities. Extension's statewide network of researchers, educators, and volunteers focuses on community development and vitality; land, food, and environment; and youth development and family living. For more information, go to https://www.extension.umn.edu/.

GOVERNMENT PROCUREMENT ASSISTANCE

Governmental agencies at the federal, state and local level are major consumers of a variety of goods and services. Many such agencies have special set-aside or preference programs for small businesses in general and/or businesses which are owned, controlled and operated by minorities, women, service disabled veterans or businesses located in distressed areas.

To qualify for many of these programs, businesses must complete an application and be certified by the third party that the business meets the program qualifications. Information on the various federal, state, local and private certification programs can be found at the Federal Executive Board of Minnesota website, Small and Disadvantaged Business Opportunities Council (SADBOC) section at https://www.minnesota.feb.gov/programs/sadboc.

In addition, many units of government are increasingly using the Internet in their procurement processes. Businesses will need to prepare to participate in Internet procurement and electronic payment systems if they intend to be able to compete for government business.

FEDERAL PROCUREMENT

The Small Business Act authorizes federal agencies to conduct procurements that are exclusively reserved for small businesses called "small business set asides." There are different programs under which these set-asides are authorized.

The Small Business Reserve is a statutory provision that requires all agency purchases valued between $3,500 and $150,000 to be reserved for small businesses. It applies when there are two or more responsible businesses that can satisfy the agency's requirement at a fair market price. Contracts in this dollar range are made using simple procedures that make it easier for businesses to participate. Procurement opportunities valued above $150,000 are subject to more complicated procedures, and may be set aside for small businesses if there is an expectation that offers will be obtained from two or more small business concerns.

Federal agencies have goals for spending certain percentages of their contracting dollars for various subcategories of small businesses. For some of these categories, a small business may self-certify its status in the System for Award Management (SAM) at https://beta.sam.gov/. Small businesses, small disadvantaged small business, small women owned businesses, veteran owned small businesses, and service disabled veteran owned small businesses may self-certify their status. However, veteran owned small businesses and service disabled veteran owned small businesses wishing to do business with the U.S. Dept. of Veterans Affairs (VA) must have their eligibility verified. Visit the VA Office of Small and Disadvantaged Business Utilization (OSDBU) at https://www.va.gov/osdbu/.

Small business concerns that are located in and hire from historically underutilized business zones or HUBZones may qualify for procurement preferences. Qualified small business concerns trying to claim HUBZone status must first apply and be certified by the Small Business Administration (SBA). HUBZone information can be found at https://www.sba.gov/federal-contracting/contracting-assistance-programs/hubzone-program.

The federal government can also limit the competition on certain contracts to women-owned small business (WOSB) or economically disadvantaged women-owned small business (EDWOSB). Additional information is available at https://www.sba.gov/content/women-owned-small-business-program.

Several other federal procurement programs exist for small businesses. These programs address the areas of contractor responsibility, innovation research, technology, and business development.

Federal contracting officers must purchase goods and services from responsible contractors, meaning that the contractor has the capability, capacity, integrity, and financial resources to perform the contract. If a contracting officer proposes to reject the offer of a small business firm which is a low offeror because of questions related to the firm's ability to perform the contract on any of the above grounds, the case is referred to the SBA for a possible Certificate of Competency (COC). If the business demonstrates the ability to perform, the SBA issues a COC to the contracting officer requiring the award of that specific contract to the small business.

Under the Small Business Innovation Research (SBIR) Program, federal agencies having research and development budgets in excess of $100 million set aside a percent for awards to small high-technology firms. The SBIR program is discussed in the Procurement / Purchasing / Certification / Other Assistance section of the Resource Directory of this Guide.

Under the Small Business Technology Transfer Program (STTR) federal agencies having annual research and development budgets of more than $1 billion will set aside a percentage for awards to small high-technology firms that collaborate with nonprofit research institutions.

The 8(a) Business Development Program is designed to provide business assistance and training to help socially and economically disadvantaged citizens gain access to the economic mainstream. This nine year program, consisting of a four year developmental stage and a five year transition stage, provides specialized business training, counseling and the ability to obtain contracts through sole-source and restricted competition procedures. To learn more about the 8(a) BD program including eligibility requirements, application procedures and to access the online 8(a) BD application go to https://www.sba.gov/contracting/government-contracting-programs/8a-business-development-program.

Micro-purchases (government purchases at or below $3,000) are made using the simplest and most direct buying technique. Micro-purchases may be made by telephone, over the counter, by Internet transactions, or other means of electronic communication. These purchases are made by credit card. The credit card holders are generally outside of the purchasing department.

Simplified acquisition procedures apply to procurement with an estimated value of $150,000 and below. As mentioned above, procurement valued between $3,500 and $150,000 are reserved exclusively for small businesses. Simplified acquisitions are made using oral or written solicitations along with commercial cards or electronic purchasing techniques.

The largest volume of dollars expended by the federal government is made through the use of formal procedures for acquisitions above the $150,000 simplified acquisition threshold. Formal procedures include sealed bidding where an Invitation for Bids is used and negotiations where a Request for Proposals is used. Under sealed bidding procedures, contractors submit bids that are opened publicly at a time and place designated by the purchasing agency. Award is made to the lowest responsible bidder. Contract negotiation is used when the government wishes to consider factors in addition to price when selecting the successful offeror.

There is also a growing trend among federal agencies to negotiate long-term Multiple-Award Task Order contracts. These contracts frequently combine a wide range and large volume of work that had previously been the subject of individual contracts.

Resources

The Minnesota Procurement Technical Assistance Center (MN PTAC) helps businesses secure federal government contracts. See the information in the Procurement/Purchasing/Certification /Other Assistance section of the Resource Directory of this Guide.

Many federal agencies publish their requirements on their own home pages. The Small Business Act requires that agencies annually publish a list of their requirements for upcoming fiscal years. These requirements can be accessed through individual agency websites or the SBA website.

Beta.sam.gov is the single government point-of-entry for Federal Government Procurement opportunities over $25,000. Government buyers are able to publicize their business opportunities by posting information directly to beta.sam.gov at https://beta.sam.gov/. Vendors seeking federal markets for their products and services can search, monitor and retrieve opportunities solicited by the entire federal contracting community. A help line is available for assistance.

The SBA offers more contracting information on their website at https://www.sba.gov/contracting.

STATE PROCUREMENT

The state of Minnesota has a program for enabling small businesses and small businesses owned by targeted groups to participate in the state procurement process. Under this program, the state may set aside certain contracts for award to small businesses, may grant preferences for bids by small targeted group businesses, and may require state contractors to subcontract with small firms.

The small business procurement program and the targeted group procurement program are administered by the Minnesota Department of Administration through their Office of Equity in Procurement (OEP). Information about the office is available on their website at https://mn.gov/admin/business/vendor-info/oep/. Information on becoming a vendor to the State may be obtained at Vendor Information, https://mn.gov/admin/business/vendor-info/. The Department maintains a Solicitations Announcements site, http://www.mmd.admin.state.mn.us/solicitations.htm, with information on state contracts. Contact information for the Department of Administration is provided in the Resource Directory section of this Guide.

Purchases from Small Business in General

Each fiscal year the Department of Administration must ensure that small businesses receive at least 25 percent of the total value of anticipated total state procurement of goods and services, including printing and construction. In addition, every state agency must for each fiscal year designate for awarding to small businesses at least 25 percent of the anticipated procurements of that agency for professional and technical services.

To be eligible for the small business procurement program, a business must have its principal place of business in Minnesota; be a manufacturer, manufacturer's representative, dealer, jobber, distributor, contractor, or business engaged in a joint venture; not be a broker, third party lessor, or franchise; and comply with revenue or sales limitations for the industry established by the Department of Administration.

Purchases from Small Targeted Group Businesses

The purpose of the targeted group procurement program is to remedy the effects of past discrimination against members of targeted groups. Periodically, the Department of Administration studies whether effects of past discrimination continue to dampen the participation of members of targeted groups. To be considered under the program, a business must be so designated by the Commissioner of the Department of Administration; businesses can be designated under one of two possible avenues. First, for businesses majority owned and operated by women, persons with a substantial physical disability, or specific minorities, the designation is made on the basis of "purchasing categories". A business is eligible under the program if the Commissioner "determines there is a statistical disparity between the percentage of purchasing from businesses owned by group members and the representation of businesses owned by group members among all businesses in the state in the purchasing category." Second, the Commissioner may designate a business if the Commissioner "determines that inclusion is necessary to remedy discrimination against the owner based on race, gender, or disability in attempting to operate a business that would provide goods or services to public agencies." (Note that the statute specifically provides that such designations of purchasing categories and businesses are not rules for purposes of Minn. Stat. Chapter 14, and are not subject to the rulemaking provisions of that Chapter.)

To be eligible for the small targeted group procurement program, a business must be majority owned and operated by women, or by persons with a disability, or by specific minorities; and have its principal place of business in Minnesota. Also, to qualify a business must: not be a manufacturer, manufacturer's representative, dealer, jobber, distributor, contractor, or business engaged in a joint venture; not be a broker, third party lessor, or franchise; comply with revenue or sales limitations for the industry established by the Department of Administration; and be certified as eligible according to procedures and criteria established by the Department of Administration.

To qualify for the targeted group and economically disadvantaged procurement programs, the business must file an application for certification and supporting documentation with the Materials Management Division of the Department of Administration. The application and supporting documentation are reviewed by the staff of the Materials Management Division for conformity with applicable laws. A business that is certified by the Department of Administration is eligible to participate in small business procurement programs of the Department of Administration, and could be eligible to participate in similar programs of the state Department of Transportation and some metropolitan agencies, without further certification. Certified businesses must submit an annual report to the Materials Management Division verifying information on file with the Division.

The incentive for targeted group vendors is the pricing preference received on state contracts. Specifically, the Commissioner of Administration may award up to a six percent preference for specified goods or services (i.e., a bid for $106 is treated the same as a bid for $100 by a non-targeted business), when the bidder is a small targeted group business. The Commissioner may award a contract for goods, services, or construction directly to a small business or small targeted group business without going through a competitive solicitation process up to a total contract award of $25,000. Likewise, a pricing preference of up to six percent (four percent for construction projects) may be awarded for bids submitted by a small business located in an "economically disadvantaged area". For this purpose, a business can qualify by meeting one of three tests: the owner resides in or the business is located in a county in which the median income for married couples is less than 70 percent of the state median income for married couples; the owner resides in or the business is located in an area designated a "labor surplus" area by the U.S. Department of Labor; or, the business is a rehabilitation facility or work activity program. Also, the Department of Administration may designate a "targeted neighborhood" (so designated pursuant to Minn. Stat. § 469.202) or an "enterprise zone" (so designated pursuant to Minn. Stat. § 469.167) as "economically disadvantaged" for purposes of that 6 percent preference.

The Minnesota legislature made changes to state procurement contracts to certified veteran-owned small businesses (businesses that are majority-owned and operated by veterans). The commissioner may award contract for goods, services, or construction directly to a veteran-owned small business without going through a competitive solicitation process up to a total contract award value, including extension options, of $25,000. Equity select also extends to direct award to certified targeted group and economically disadvantaged small businesses.

All laws and rules pertaining to solicitations, bid evaluations, contract awards, and other procurement matters apply equally to procurements from small businesses. Before making an award under the small targeted group business program, the Department of Administration is directed by statute to evaluate whether the small business scheduled to receive the award is able to perform the contract. The determination includes consideration of production and financial capacity and technical competence.

Note, however, that Minnesota Statutes provide that the state may use a "reverse auction" procedure in which vendors compete in an open and interactive environment to deliver the lowest price for goods or services. When the Commissioner of the Minnesota Department of Administration determines that a reverse auction is the appropriate process the provisions of Minn. Stat. § 16C.06 on solicitations do not apply.

Registration as a vendor can be made via the state's online vendor registration system. You will need a Federal Tax Identification Number and Minnesota Tax Identification number (if applicable) when you register. Being registered is not a guarantee that you will be sent invitations to bid or requests for proposals – only that your name will appear on a list as a potential vendor of the products you sell or the services you provide.

Minnesota Procurement Technical Assistance Center (PTAC)

MN PTAC assists businesses by providing individualized technical assistance in navigating local, state, and federal contracting requirements as well as performance assistance. PTAC business counselors can help with market identification, registration assistance, contracting regulations/ compliance assistance, and ongoing technical support throughout the procurement process. The PTAC website is https://mn.gov/admin/business/vendor-info/ptac/about/. Contact information for the various federal, state, county, city and other procurement /purchasing certification offices are listed in the Procurement/Purchasing/Certification/Other Assistance section of the Resource Directory of this Guide.

LOCAL PROCUREMENT

Businesses interested in selling their goods or services to local units of government should contact each locality. Outside the immediate Twin Cities area the local city clerk or county auditor is the best first step in determining the potential for sales to local governments. Contact information for the various federal, state, county, city and other procurement /purchasing certification offices are listed in the Procurement/Purchasing/Certification/Other Assistance section of the Resource Directory of this Guide.

ACCOUNTING AND TAX ASSISTANCE

PUBLIC ACCOUNTANTS

A Certified Public Accountant (CPA) is a person licensed and certified by the state for professional competence and experience in the field of accounting whose education and experience background includes: completion of a college accounting program; passing a rigorous exam in accounting, auditing, income taxes and business law; qualifying for certification by the State Board of Accountancy; practicing according to a strict code of ethics; meeting continuing education requirements; and passing a peer review of their policies and procedures every three years. A Licensed Public Accountant (LPA) is also licensed by the state without having passed an examination. An LPA provides many of the same functions as a CPA and is also required to meet ongoing continuing professional education and peer review.

CPAs are qualified to provide a variety of services, but their services are particularly beneficial to start-up situations in three general areas: financial statement services; tax-related services; and financial planning and consulting services.

Financial Statement Services

Accounting is the language of business. It ties together the marketing and management operations of a business. CPAs use this language to communicate needed information to their clients. The financial statements are the medium through which pertinent information is transmitted to businesses. They usually include the accountant's report; balance sheet; income statement; cash flow statement; and notes to the financial statements.

Each statement gives a different aspect of the condition or result of operations for a period of time. The more one understands and respects the language, the more benefit one derives from the financial statements. The present and prospective activities of the business will often dictate that a CPA give independent, objective opinions on financial statements prepared by management. The reports rendered by the CPA on the financial statements are generally at one of three levels:

- **An Audit.** A positive assertion on financial statements that the financial statements do or do not present fairly the financial position, results of operations, and cash flows in accordance with generally accepted accounting principles or another comprehensive basis of accounting consistently applied.
- **A Review.** Limited assurance that nothing came to the accountant's attention to indicate the statements were not in accordance with generally accepted accounting principles or another comprehensive basis of accounting.
- **A Compilation.** An indication that the financial statements were compiled from information represented by management and that no assurance is given on them.

The level of reporting plays a significant role because it indicates the degree of assurance that the CPA is rendering on the financial statements. Where a business has borrowed from a financial institution, the size of the debt will usually dictate what level of assurance the bank would like to see.

Tax-Related Services

The entrepreneur often doesn't realize that tax planning is a source of business capital. Careful planning and the use of a CPA can enhance this source of funds. Income taxes must be paid on business profits; hence, they are expenses of a business. These income taxes, if properly planned, can be kept to a minimum, thus leaving cash available for financing your business. In addition, if a business should fail, you will want the most advantageous treatment of these losses. The CPA must always be aware of current changes in the tax law and can provide the proper vehicle for making the most of this source of funds. For example, the CPA can: assist in structuring the initial organization of proprietorships, partnerships (whether general, limited or limited liability) or corporations; assist in structuring a possible tax-free incorporation; assist in structuring business purchase, sale or liquidation transactions; prepare various compliance tax reports, such as individual, partnership and corporate income tax, payroll, sales tax, property taxes; handle tax examinations and tax planning strategies; assist in estate planning and personal tax planning; and assist in the implementation of executive compensation, retirement plans and employee benefit programs.

Financial Planning and Consulting Services

A CPA can assist a business:

- in choosing the form of business organization
- setting up an accounting system and procedures
- defining and obtaining reporting, operational and cost control needs
- developing and evaluating the business plan, forecasts and budgets
- strategic planning; preparing special purpose reports including statements prepared on comprehensive bases of accounting other than generally accepted accounting principles
- preparing reports with opinion on specific financial statement elements such as accounts receivable and inventory reports
- discussing results of applying agreed-upon procedures to specific financial statement elements; implementing cash flow and management reports
- structuring and implementing financing plans for the start-up, operation, and expansion stages
- preparing reports to management on the strengths and weaknesses of internal accounting controls along with recommendations to correct the weaknesses
- preparing bank loan applications for initial or expansion capital needs
- computer selection, implementation and training;
- providing advice on business valuations and mergers and acquisitions.

The Minnesota Society of Certified Public Accountants maintains a free referral service to put businesses in contact with qualified CPAs. Contact the MNCPA at https://www.mncpa.org/ and at the telephone number listed in the Resource Directory section of this Guide.

ENROLLED AGENTS

Enrolled Agents are trained and experienced tax professionals who have either passed a comprehensive examination given by the Department of the Treasury or have had five continuous years of experience with the Internal Revenue Service at the audit level. Enrolled Agents must maintain their credentials through continuing tax education which is reported directly to the Internal Revenue Service. Enrolled Agents are trained to handle complex tax returns for individuals, partnerships, corporations and other tax entities, and are authorized to represent taxpayers at all administrative levels before the Internal Revenue Service. Information and referrals may be obtained from the Minnesota Society of Enrolled Agents at https://mnsea.org/ and at the telephone number provided in the Resource Directory Section of this Guide.

PREPARE + PROSPER

Prepare + Prosper is a nonprofit organization that assists low- to moderate-income people to build financial well-being through free tax preparation and financial services, products, and coaching. Volunteers are trained—those in the tax clinics are IRS-certified.

Contact Prepare + Prosper at the contact information provided in the Resource Directory section of this guide or visit their website http://prepareandprosper.org/free-tax-preparation/.

TAXPAYER EDUCATION WORKSHOPS

The Minnesota Unemployment Insurance (UI) Program, Minnesota Business Tax Education Partnership offers free education seminars around the state to assist businesses. Visit https://www.uimn.org/uimn/employers/help-and-support/educational-seminars/index.jsp or call 651-259-0779.

The Minnesota Department of Revenue offers classes, workshops and training events to help business owners understand their tax obligations and how to meet them. More information and schedules are available from the Minnesota Department of Revenue, Sales Tax Education and at https://www.revenue.state.mn.us/business-education-and-outreach or call 651-296-6181 or 800-657-3777.

The Minnesota Department of Labor & Industry offers worker's compensation training opportunities for: employees, employers, health care providers, insurers, and rehabilitation providers. Information and schedules are available at https://www.dli.mn.gov/business/workers-compensation/work-comp-training-opportunities.

LIBRARIES

LIBRARY SERVICES

Libraries and librarians are an invaluable source of assistance to the business community, providing access to resources and information. While library resources can be directly used by patrons, entrepreneurs should not be shy about seeking the expertise of librarians who are familiar with search techniques and sources and can save patrons time, money and hassle. Today, public libraries serve the business community by featuring small business collections, offering workshops on such topics as creating business plans and researching patents and trademarks, and providing networking opportunities.

Entrepreneurs and small business owners can use library resources to prepare business plans, research competitors, track trends and perform market analysis. Researchers can use library databases to access business news and research, company information, trade and professional associations, annual reports, demographics and more. The business community can use libraries to research a range of topics, including product protection, employee rights and responsibilities, accounting, taxation, marketing, quality management, business plan development, economic trends and emerging technologies.

Many library resources can be searched from work or home via the Internet. While most users appropriately think first of public libraries, local public libraries can connect to other larger and specialized library collections. Business people should also consider nearby college and university libraries, which frequently serve their broader communities. In addition, libraries in government agencies offer unique publications and resources that may be useful. Finally, special libraries that serve corporations, law firms, medical institutions and other organizations may also be helpful.

At eLibraryMN, https://elibrarymn.org/, researchers are helped in locating public libraries and databases available to Minnesota residents.

Libraries subscribe to many online resources useful to business people. These resources are widely available at Minnesota libraries.

Databases for Business Information

The following databases provide access to business news, research, trends and reports:

- **ABI/INFORM Complete** - Features business information from trade journals, industry surveys and company reports - https://www.proquest.com/products-services/abi_inform_complete.html
- **Business Plans Handbook** - Offers model business plans on hundreds of businesses - https://www.referenceforbusiness.com/business-plans/
- **Business Source Premier** - Features full-text articles from business journals, industry -surveys, market research and country reports - https://www.ebscohost.com/academic/business-source-premier
- **IBISWorld** - comprehensive collection of U.S. Industry Market Research and Industry Risk Ratings - https://www.ibisworld.com/
- **NewsBank** - Provides full-text articles from business journals and domestic and international newspapers - https://www.newsbank.com/
- **Proquest Global Newsstream** - Provides full-text articles and abstracts from over 2,500 news sources - https://about.proquest.com/products-services/globalnewsstream.html
- **Regional Business News** - Features full-text coverage from regional business publications across the U.S. - https://www.ebscohost.com/academic/regional-business-news

Tools to Research Companies

These online and print sources offer company profiles, contact information, product descriptions and sales and employment figures. The following company directories are available at many Minnesota libraries:

- **GALE -Business Insights: Essentials** - Provides access to in-depth information on U.S. and international businesses, industries and products - https://www.gale.com/c/business-insights-essentials
- **Dun & Bradstreet** - Global commercial database contains more than 205 million business records - https://www.dnb.com
- **EDGAR** - Provides U.S. Securities and Exchange Commission filings on public companies - https://www.sec.gov/edgar.shtml#.VAoWBdd929I

- **D&B Hoovers** - Provides information on about 40,000 companies - http://www.hoovers.com/
- **Kompass** - Features a directory of 2.3 million companies in 66 countries - https://us.kompass.com/
- **Medical Alley Association** - Features a directory of Minnesota life sciences companies - https://www.medicalalley.org/
- **Mergent Online** - Provides information on public companies around the world - http://www.mergentonline.com/
- **Manufacturers' News Inc.** - Nation's largest compiler and publisher of industrial directories and databases - https://mni.net
- **ReferenceUSA** - Offers information on 14 million U.S. businesses - http://resource.referenceusa.com/
- **ThomasNet** - Includes manufacturers, distributors and service providers - https://www.thomasnet.com/

Minnesota Business Journals

These Minnesota resources cover business in Minnesota.

Finance & Commerce - https://finance-commerce.com/

Minneapolis / St. Paul Business Journal - https://www.bizjournals.com/twincities

Minneapolis / St. Paul Business Journal Book of Lists - https://www.bizjournals.com/twincities/digital-edition?issue_id=8909

REJournals.com - https://www.rejournals.com

Minnesota Precision Manufacturing Association - https://mpma.site-ym.com/default.aspx

Twin Cities Business - http://tcbmag.com/

Upsize Minnesota - http://www.upsizemag.com/

Minnesota Newspapers

Local newspapers are also a great source for business and company news. Use the Minnesota Newspaper Directory at http://www.mnnews.com/ to learn about the state's newspapers.

Business Reference Websites/Books

Here is a sample of popular titles:

Minnesota Business: Associations & Nonprofits

Encyclopedia of American Industries

Encyclopedia of Associations

Encyclopedia of Business Information Sources

Local Market Analyst

Manufacturing & Distribution USA

RMA (Risk Management Association) Annual Statement Studies

Small Business Sourcebook

Business Websites

Here are websites small business owners and entrepreneurs can use for free:

Business Plans

- **Bplans** - Access tips for creating business plan - https://www.bplans.com/sample_business_plans.php
- **Business Plans** - Lists types of small businesses and provides corresponding sample business plans, profiles and books - https://www.carnegielibrary.org/services/for-businesses/entrepreneurs-and-small-businesses/business-plans-index/
- **U.S. Small Business Administration (SBA)** - **Create your Business Plan** - https://www.sba.gov/starting-business/write-your-business-plan

Forms, Contracts

- **Entrepreneur.com** - Provides how-to guides on starting a business, including business forms and templates - https://www.entrepreneur.com/
- **FindLaw-Small Business Contracts & Forms and Corporate Counsel**
  - https://smallbusiness.findlaw.com/business-lawyer-resources/small-business-forms-contracts.html
  - https://contracts.corporate.findlaw.com/

Financing

- **GovLoans.gov** - Access information on federal government loans - https://www.govloans.gov/
- **SBA Loans & Grants** - Features a primer on financing options for your business - https://www.sba.gov/loans-grants#

General

- **Biz Info Library** - Offers information on starting and growing a business - http://www.bizinfolibrary.org/
- **Kauffman Entrepreneurs** - Links to information of interest to entrepreneurs - https://www.entrepreneurship.org/
- **Trade Show News Network (TSNN)** - Features a worldwide directory of trade shows, exhibitions and conferences - https://www.tsnn.com/
- **WSJ's Small Business** - Offers articles, forums and a toolkit for small business owners - https://www.wsj.com/news/types/small-business

Government Assistance

- **Business.USA.gov** - Links businesses to forms, assistance, laws and regulations - https://business.usa.gov/
- **Bureau of Labor Statistics** - Provides economic data and analysis on employment - https://www.bls.gov/
- **IRS Small Business and Self -Employed Tax Center** - https://www.irs.gov/businesses/small-businesses-self-employed
- **Small Business Administration** - Features guides to starting, financing and expanding a business - https://www.sba.gov/
- **U.S. Census Bureau** - Provides social, demographic and economic information - https://www.census.gov/

ADDITIONAL SOURCES OF ASSISTANCE

SPECIALIZED LEGAL RESEARCH AND ASSISTANCE

LegalCORPS, part of the Minnesota Bar Association, provides referrals to Minnesota attorneys and provides *pro bono* services to small businesses, private nonprofit organizations, and low-income innovators. For more information contact Legal Corps at 612-206-0780. Website, http://legalcorps.org/.

The Mitchell Hamline School of Law offers their Legal Practice Center, Business Law Clinic and Intellectual Property Law Clinic in which students assist with drafting contracts for nonprofit groups; filing patent applications; and forming business entities for new small enterprises. Website, https://mitchellhamline.edu/legal-practice-center/.

The University of Minnesota Business Law Concentration has experienced business law attorneys from several law firms supervise two-person teams of law students working with clinic clients. The clinic provides free legal assistance in non-litigation matters to small businesses, nonprofits and entrepreneurs with a viable business plan. For more information contact Business Law Clinic at 612-625-4641 and https://www.law.umn.edu/academics/concentrations/business-law-concentration.

LawMoose is a Minnesota legal search engine that, while not offering legal advice, offers an online legal reference library for researching Minnesota law, an online search engine focused on law related sites in Minnesota, and a Minnesota legal periodical index. The site, http://lawmoose.com/ assists users in framing legal questions and issues to address to their own legal counsel.

The Minnesota Judicial Branch offers legal help topics and forms through their website at http://www.mncourts.gov/Help-Topics.aspx.

MANAGEMENT ASSISTANCE FOR MINORITY BUSINESSES

There are a number of organizations which offer business planning and business management assistance specifically targeted to businesses owned and operated by racial minorities, women, disabled individuals, and other socially or economically disadvantaged persons. A listing of these organizations can be found in the Resource Directory section of this Guide.

INCUBATORS

Sometimes called enterprise centers, innovation centers or business and technology centers, incubators offer new, small firms a way to minimize both fixed and variable costs by providing low cost office and production space, shared office services, management assistance and – in some cases – financial assistance. A listing of these organizations can be found in the Resource Directory section of this Guide.

INVENTORS RESOURCES

Resources include The Inventors' Network, LegalCORPS Inventor Assistance Program (IAP) (free legal representation to low-income inventors seeking to patent their innovations with the U.S. Patent & Trademark Office (USPTO)), and the U.S. Patent and Trademark Depository Office, Inventors Assistance Center (IAC). A listing of these organizations can be found in the Resource Directory section of this Guide.

MINNESOTA STATE

All colleges and universities within the Minnesota State system provide programs for small business owners. These programs range from the certificate level to the master's degree. Some programs are focused on comprehensive business management such as the business marketing and management (A.A.S. degree) and the business administration master's degree. Other programs contain a number of courses which small business owners or those intending to become small business owners would find useful.

In addition to the above programs which result in an academic credential, Minnesota State's community and technical colleges also offer a large variety of non-credit workshops and seminars worthwhile to small business owners. These educational opportunities are available either through open enrollment to the public or through customized contracts with individual business.

REGIONAL DEVELOPMENT COMMISSIONS

Regional development commissions are established by statute to coordinate and conduct regional planning activities for the counties, cities and towns which comprise the region.

The commissions are responsible for preparing and adopting a regional development plan which prescribes the policies, goals, standards, and programs for the orderly development of the region. By statute, the plan must address the physical, economic and social needs of the region, including land use, parks and open space, access to sunlight for solar energy systems, airports, highways, transit facilities, hospitals, libraries, schools, housing and public buildings.

The commissions review applications for federal and state loans and grants, conduct urban and rural research, coordinate civil defense, community shelter planning and flood plain management within the region and may contract to provide services and technical assistance to local units of government in the conduct of local planning and development activities.

A list of the regional development commissions, the counties they include, and the office addresses can be found in the Resource Directory section of this Guide.

EXPORT / IMPORT ASSISTANCE

The U.S. Commerce Department, U.S. Commercial Service; Small Business Administration (SBA), Export Assistance Centers; U.S. Customs & Border Protection (CBP) and the Export-Import Bank of the United States are resources for information on federal export finance programs, exporting training and publications.

Additional resources include the Minnesota District Export Council (DEC) and the Minnesota Trade Office. Contact information for these resources is located in the Resource Directory section of this Guide.

SCORE

SCORE has volunteers who provide free and confidential one-on-one business counseling and mentoring. In Minnesota there are six SCORE chapters located in principal metropolitan areas of the state. These chapters operate branches in smaller communities. SCORE is a resource partner with the U.S. Small Business Administration (SBA).

SCORE programs include:

- Take a Workshop - live and recorded webinars, interactive courses on demand and in-person, local workshops from industry leaders and mentors on a variety of business topics.
- Browse the Library - free business templates, eguides, checklists, blogs, videos or other helpful resources.

SCORE sponsors seminars for small businesses. The “Going into Business” seminar is designed to help people minimize risks in the start-up and operation of a business. The “Business Loan” seminar offers an overview of SBA loan guarantee programs and funding options. The “Marketing” workshop provides details on how to develop a low cost marketing program for a small business. The “Business Planning” workshop assists in developing business plans. The Minneapolis, St. Paul, and South Metro chapters of SCORE hold workshops and seminars periodically throughout the year at a number of locations in the Twin Cities metro area. There is a nominal charge for these seminars.

A list of SCORE offices and branches can be found in the Management Assistance, General section of the Resource Directory of this Guide.

WOMEN'S BUSINESS CENTERS

There are three Women's Business Centers (WBCs) located throughout Minnesota offering business information, group training, and individual counseling primarily to women-owned small businesses. For more information or assistance, contact the Women's Business Center at the address and phone numbers in the Management Assistance for Minority Businesses section of the Resource Directory of this Guide. As a resource partner of the U. S. Small Business Administration (SBA) their services can be utilized by any small business owner.

RESOURCE DIRECTORY

RESOURCE DIRECTORY

CONTENTS

COOPERATIVES

Cooperative Development Services
145 University Ave. W., Suite 450
St. Paul, MN 55103
651-265-3678
http://www.cdsus.coop/

Cooperative Network
145 University Ave. W., Suite 450
St. Paul, MN 55103
651-228-0213
https://cooperativenetwork.coop/

USDA Rural Development
State Office
375 Jackson Street, Suite 410
St. Paul, MN 55101
651-602-7800
https://www.rd.usda.gov/mn

ENVIRONMENTAL

See Government, State
Minnesota Department of Administration,
Minnesota Environmental Quality Board
Minnesota Pollution Control Agency

EXPORT / IMPORT ASSISTANCE

U.S. Commercial Service
Minneapolis Field Office
330 2nd Ave. South, Suite 410
Minneapolis, MN 55401
612-348-1638 | office.minneapolis@trade.gov
https://2016.export.gov/minnesota/

A Basic Guide to Exporting
https://www.export.gov/article?id=Why-Companies-should-export

How to Export -video series
https://www.export.gov/How-to-Export

Ecommerce Export Resource Center -video series
https://www.export.gov/eCommerce

U.S. Customs & Border Protection (CBP) -
U.S. Dept. of Homeland Security (DHS)
Service Port—Minneapolis #3501
5600 W. American Blvd., Ste. 760
Bloomington, MN 55437
952-857-3100
https://www.cbp.gov/

Basic Importing and Exporting
https://www.cbp.gov/trade/basic-import-export

Locate a Port of Entry in Minnesota
https://www.cbp.gov/contact/ports/mn

Export Assistance Center - U.S. Small Business Administration (SBA)
330 2nd Ave. South, Suite 402A
Minneapolis, MN 55401
612-348-1642
https://www.sba.gov/content/export-assistance

Export Products
https://www.sba.gov/business-guide/grow-your-business/export-products

Minnesota Department of Agriculture (MDA)
Minnesota Research and Promotion Councils
MDA works with Minnesota's 13 research and promotion councils to promote the state's diverse agricultural sector. Also administer the process of check-off refunds, conduct elections, and provide other administrative oversight to commodity councils.
651-201-6494
http://www.mda.state.mn.us/minnesota-research-and-promotion-councils

Minnesota Trade Office
1st National Bank Building
332 Minnesota Street, Suite E200
St. Paul, MN 55101
651-259-7499 800-657-3858
https://mn.gov/deed/business/exporting/

STEP Grant (State Trade and Export Promotion Program)
Provides financial and technical assistance to qualifying Minnesota small businesses with an active interest in exporting products or services to foreign markets.
651-259-7481
https://mn.gov/deed/business/exporting/export-financing/

Trade Assistance Helpline
651-259-7498 | Mto.TradeAssistance@state.mn.us

Minnesota District Export Council (DEC)
A private, non-profit organization that brings together international business people who provide guidance and assistance in international markets.
330 2nd Ave. South, Suite 410
Minneapolis, MN 55401
612-348-1638
http://www.exportassistance.com

Export Basics & Training
http://www.exportassistance.com/export-basics

FINANCING, FEDERAL SOURCES

Federal Assistance Listings
https://sam.gov/

GovLoans.gov
800-333-4636
https://www.govloans.gov

Grants.gov
800-518-4726| support@grants.gov
https://www.grants.gov/

USA.gov -Small Business
844-872-4681
https://www.usa.gov/business?source=busa

U.S. Small Business Administration (SBA)
Minnesota District Office
330 2nd Ave. South, Suite 430
Minneapolis, MN 55401-2224
612-370-2324
https://www.sba.gov/offices/district/mn/minneapolis

Lender Match
A free online referral tool that connects small businesses with participating SBA-approved lenders for 7(a) Loans Program and the Microloan Program.
https://www.sba.gov/lendermatch

Microloan Program

Microloan Intermediaries
https://www.sba.gov/partners/lenders/microloan-program/list-lenders

African Development Center (ADC)
1931 South 5th Street
Minneapolis, MN 55454
612-333-4772 877-232-4775
http://www.adcminnesota.org

Rochester Office:
507-282-7333

Willmar Office:
518 Litchfield Ave. S.W.
Willmar, MN 56201
320-262-8545

Service Area: Anoka, Beltrami, Blue Earth, Carver, Chisago, Dakota, Faribault, Hennepin, Isanti, Kandiyohi, Lyon, Olmsted, Ramsey, Scott, Sherburne, Stearns, and Washington counties.

Hmong American Partnership
394 University Ave W. 2nd Floor
Saint Paul, MN 55103
651-495-9160
https://www.hmong.org/

Service Area: Anoka, Dakota, Hennepin, Ramsey, Scott, Washington counties.

Neighborhood Development Center (NDC)
663 University Ave., Suite 200
St. Paul, MN 55104
651-291-2480
http://www.ndc-mn.org/

Service area: Hennepin and Ramsey counties.

Entrepreneur Fund, Inc.
800-422-0374
https://www.entrepreneurfund.org/

Iron Range Office:
551 Hat Trick Ave.
Eveleth, MN 55734
218-749-4191

Duluth Office:
202 W. Superior Street, Suite 311
Duluth, MN 55802
218-623-5747

Grand Rapids Office:
(Co-located with Itasca Economic Dev. Corp.)
12 N.W. 3rd Street
Grand Rapids, MN 55744
218-322-6151

Hibbing Office:
301 Howard Street, Suite 22
Hibbing, MN 55746
218-421-6151

Little Falls Office:
309 1st Street N.E.
Little Falls, MN 56345
218-735-6033

Service Area: Aitkin, Carlton, Cass, Cook, Douglas, Itasca, Koochiching, Lake, Pine, St. Louis counties

Northwest Minnesota Foundation
201 3rd St. N.W.
Bemidji, MN 56601
218-759-2057 800-659-7859
https://www.nwmf.org

Service area: Beltrami, Clearwater, Hubbard, Kittson, Lake of the Woods, Mahnomen, Marshall, Norman, Pennington, Polk, Red Lake, and Roseau counties.

Southern Minnesota Initiative Foundation
525 Florence Ave.
Owatonna, MN 55060
507-455-3215 | inquiry@smifoundation.org
http://www.smifoundation.org

Service area: Faribault, Fillmore, Freeborn, Goodhue, Houston, Le Sueur, Martin, Mower, Nicollet, Olmsted, Rice, Sibley, Steele, Wabasha, Waseca, Watonwan, and Winona counties.

Southwest Initiative Foundation
15 3rd Ave. N.W.
Hutchinson, MN 55350
320-587-4848 800-594-9480
info@swifoundation.org
https://www.swifoundation.org

Service area: Big Stone, Carver, Chippewa, Cottonwood, Jackson, Kandiyohi, Lac qui Parle, Lincoln, Lyon, McLeod, Meeker, Murray, Nobles, Pipestone, Redwood, Renville, Rock, Swift, Wright, and Yellow Medicine counties.

WomenVenture
2021 E. Hennepin Ave., Suite 200
Minneapolis, MN 55413
612-224-9540
https://www.womenventure.org

Service area: Ten-county Twin Cities Metro area, which includes the counties of Anoka, Carver, Chisago, Dakota, Hennepin, Isanti, Ramsey, Scott, Steele, Washington and Wright.

7(a) Loan Program
https://www.sba.gov/partners/lenders/7a-loan-program/types-7a-loans

8(a) Business Development Program
https://www.sba.gov/contracting/government-contracting-programs/8a-business-development-program

CDC/504 Program
https://www.sba.gov/offices/headquarters/ofa/resources/4049

Certified Development Companies (CDCs)

Central Minnesota Development Company (CMDC)
1885 Station Parkway N.W.
Andover, MN 55304
763-784-3337
https://www.cmdcbusinessloans.com

Minnesota Business Finance Corporation
320-258-5000 800-593-0123
https://www.mbfc.org

Minneapolis Office:

601 Carlson Parkway, Suite 1062
Minnetonka, MN 55402
612-746-6905

Detroit Lakes:

119 Graystone Plaza, Suite 200
Detroit Lakes, MN 56501
218-844-4510

St. Cloud Office:

616 Roosevelt Road, Suite 200
St. Cloud, MN 56301
320-258-5000

Prairieland Economic Development Corp.
1 Prairie Drive
Slayton, MN 56172
507-836-6656 800-507-9003
info@prairielandedc.com
https://www.prairielandedc.com/

SPEDCO (St. Paul Metro East Dev. Corporation)
3900 Northwoods Drive, Suite 225
Arden Hills, MN 55112
651-631-4900 866-977-3326
http://www.spedco.com

504 Corporation
http://www.504corporation.com

Rochester Office:

220 South Broadway, Suite 100
Rochester, MN 55904
507-288-6442 877-504-5400

Mankato Office:

P.O. Box 4241
Mankato, MN 56002
507-625-6056

Twin Cities Metro Certified Development Co.
3495 Vadnais Center Drive
Vadnais Heights, MN 55110
651-481-8081 888-481-4504
https://www.504lending.com

Small Business Investment Companies (SBIC)
https://www.sba.gov/sbic

Bayview Capital Partners II, III, L.P.
301 Carlson Parkway, Suite 325
Minnetonka, MN 55305
952-345-2035
http://www.bayviewcap.com

Convergent Capital Partners II, III, L.P.
505 N. Highway 169, Suite 175
Minneapolis, MN 55441
763-432-4081
http://www.cvcap.com

GMB Mezzanine Capital, II, III, L.P.
50 South Sixth Street, Suite 1460
Minneapolis, MN 55402
612-243-4405
http://gmbmezz.com/

Marquette Capital Fund II, L.P.
60 South Sixth Street, Suite 3510
Minneapolis, MN 55402
612-661-3990
http://www.marquettecapital.com/

Medallion Capital, Inc.
3000 W. County Road 42, Suite 301
Burnsville, MN 55337
952-831-2025
http://www.medallioncapital.com/

Spell Capital Partners, LLC
222 South Ninth Street, Suite 2880
Minneapolis, MN 55402
612-371-9650
https://spellcapital.com/

USDA (U.S. Department of Agriculture)
Rural Development
State Office
375 Jackson Street, Suite 410
St. Paul, MN 55101
651-602-7800
https://www.rd.usda.gov/mn

FINANCING / TAX CREDITS, STATE SOURCES

Office of Grants Management
https://mn.gov/grants/

Agriculture (MDA), MN Department of
Orville L. Freeman Building
625 Robert Street N.
St. Paul, MN 55155
651-201-6000 800 967-2474
800-627-3529 (TDD) | mda.info@state.mn.us
https://www.mda.state.mn.us

Loan and Grant Programs
https://www.mda.state.mn.us/funding

Beginning Farmer Credits
Credit provides tax credits for the rent or sale of farm land or a variety of farm assets to beginning farmers. This includes incentives for the sale of farm land.
651-201-6004 | mda.bftc@state.mn.us
https://www.mda.state.mn.us/bftc

Employment and Economic Development (DEED), MN Department of
1st National Bank Building
332 Minnesota Street, Suite E200
St. Paul, MN 55101-1351
651-259-7114 | DEED.CustomerService@state.mn.us
https://mn.gov/deed/

Financing Programs:
https://mn.gov/deed/business/financing-business/deed-programs/

Minnesota Investment Fund (MIF)
Provides financing to help expand, add new workers, and retain high-quality jobs.
651-259-7430 800-657-3858
https://mn.gov/deed/business/financing-business/deed-programs/mif/

Minnesota Job Creation Fund
Provides financial incentives to new and expanding businesses that meet certain job creation and capital investment targets.
jobcreationfund@state.mn.us
https://mn.gov/deed/business/financing-business/deed-programs/mn-jcf/

Emerging Entrepreneur Loan Program (ELP)
Supports the growth of businesses owned and operated by minorities, low-income persons, women, veterans and/or persons with disabilities. DEED provides grant funds to a network of nonprofit lenders which use these funds for loans to start-up and expanding businesses throughout the state.
651-259-7450
https://mn.gov/deed/business/financing-business/deed-programs/elp/

Indian Business Loan Program
Program supports the development of Indian-owned and operated businesses and promotes economic opportunities for Indian people throughout Minnesota.
651-259-7483
https://mn.gov/deed/business/financing-business/deed-programs/indian/

Minnesota Reservist and Veteran Business Loan Program
Provides business loans to companies that are affected when certain employees are called to active military duty and to individual veterans who have returned from active duty and want to start their own business.
651-259-7427
https://mn.gov/deed/business/financing-business/deed-programs/reservists/

Tourism Business Septic Tank Replacement
651-259-7428 800-657-3858

Export Financing Programs:
https://mn.gov/deed/business/exporting/export-financing/

STEP (State Trade & Export Promotion Program) Grant Program
651-259-7487
https://mn.gov/deed/business/exporting/export-financing/

Tax Credits
https://mn.gov/deed/business/financing-business/tax-credits/

Border-Cities Enterprise Zone Program
Program provides business tax credits (property tax credits, debt financing credit on new construction, sales tax credit on construction equipment and materials, and new or existing employee credits) to qualifying businesses that are the source of investment, development, and job creation or retention in the Border-Cities Enterprise Zone cities of Breckenridge, Dilworth, East Grand Forks, Moorhead, and Ortonville.
651-259-7415 800-657-3858
https://mn.gov/deed/business/financing-business/tax-credits/border-cities/

Seed Capital Investment Credit Program
Program provides tax incentives for investing in innovative business located in the Minnesota border cities of Breckenridge, Dilworth, East Grand Forks, Moorhead, and Ortonville.
651-259-7415
https://mn.gov/deed/business/financing-business/tax-credits/seed-capital/

Data Center Sales Tax Incentives
Companies that build data or network operation centers of at least 25,000 square feet and invest $30 million in the first four years qualify for valuable tax breaks.
651-259-7415
https://mn.gov/deed/business/financing-business/tax-credits/data-center-credit/

Launch Minnesota
Provides financial incentives, training, and grants to people starting companies in technology sectors such as aerospace, agricultural processing, nanotechnology and medical devices.
launchminnesota@state.mn.us
http://www.launchminnesota.org

Iron Range Resources & Rehabilitation Board (IRRRB)
4261 Hwy 53 S.
Eveleth, MN 55734
218-735-3000 877-829-3936
https://mn.gov/irrrb/

Pollution Control Agency (MPCA), MN
520 Lafayette Road
St. Paul, MN 55155-4194
651-296-6300 800-657-3864
https://www.pca.state.mn.us

Environmental Assistance Grants & Loans
https://www.pca.state.mn.us/about-mpca/environmental-assistance-grants-and-loans

Environmental Assistance Grants
651-757-2459 800-657-3864
https://www.pca.state.mn.us/about-mpca/environmental-assistance-grants

Environmental Assistance Loans
651-757-2459 800-657-3864
https://www.pca.state.mn.us/about-mpca/environmental-assistance-loans

Financial Assistance: Grants and Loans
https://www.pca.state.mn.us/about-mpca/financial-assistance-grants-and-loans

Small Business Environmental Assistance
https://www.pca.state.mn.us/smallbizhelp

Small Business Environmental Improvement Loans
651-757-2218 800-657-3938
https://www.pca.state.mn.us/regulations/low-interest-environmental-loans

FINANCING, LOCAL SOURCES

Regional / County / City Economic Development Programs

Arrowhead Regional Development Commission (ARDC)
221 W. First Street
Duluth MN 55802
218-772-5545 800-232-0707
https://www.ardc.org

East Central Regional Development Commission
100 Park Street S.
Mora, MN 55051
320-679-4065 | ecrdc@ecrdc.org
http://www.ecrdc.org/

Greater Mankato Growth, Inc.
3 Civic Center Plaza, Suite 100
Mankato, MN 56001
507-385-6640 800-697-0652
https://www.greatermankato.com/financing-incentives

Region Five Development Commission
200 1st Street N.E., Suite 2
Staples, MN 56479
218-894-3233
https://www.regionfive.org

Aitkin County Economic Development
217 2nd Street N.W., Room 131
Aitkin, MN 56431
218-927-7305
https://www.co.aitkin.mn.us/departments/economic-dev/economic-develop.html

Alexandria Area Economic Development Commission (AAEDC)
324 Broadway, Suite 101
Alexandria, MN 56308
320-763-4545
https://livingalexarea.org/

Development Corporation of Austin (DCA)
329 N. Main Street, Suite 106 L
Austin, MN 55912
507-433-9495 | austindca@austindca.org
http://www.austindca.org/

Benton Economic Partnership, Inc.
c/o Falcon National Bank
183 Cedar Drive
Foley, MN 56329
320-968-6197
http://bentonpartnership.org/

Brainerd Lakes Area Development Corp. (BLADC)
224 W. Washington Street
Brainerd, MN 56401
218-828-0096 888-322-5232
info@growbrainerdlakes.org
http://www.growbrainerdlakes.org

Carlton County Economic Development Authority
Carlton County Courthouse
301 Walnut Ave., Room 106
Carlton, MN 55718
218-384-9597
http://co.carlton.mn.us/156/Economic-Development

Carver County Community Development Agency
705 Walnut Street N.
Chaska, MN 55318
952-448-7715
https://www.carvercda.org/

Cass County Economic Development Corporation
P.O. Box 1606
303 Minnesota Ave. W.
Walker, MN 56484
218-547-7262 | cass.edc@co.cass.mn.us
https://www.casscountyedc.com

Chisago County HRA-EDA
38871 7th Ave., P.O. Box 815
North Branch, Minnesota 55056
651-674-5664
http://www.chisagocounty.org

Cook County / Grand Marais EDA
15 North Broadway, P.O. Box 597
Grand Marais, MN 55604
218-387-3112
http://www.prosperitynorth.com

Dakota County Community Development Agency
1228 Town Centre Drive
Eagan, MN 55123
651-675-4400
https://www.dakotacda.org

Headwaters Regional Development Commission (HRDC) / Headwaters Regional Finance Corporation (HRFC)
403 Fourth Street N.W., Suite 310
P.O. Box 906
Bemidji, MN 56619
218-444-4732 | hrdc@hrdc.org
https://hrdc.org/business-finance/

Kandiyohi County and City of Willmar Economic Development Commission
222 20th Street S.E., P.O. Box 1783
Willmar, MN 56201
320-235-7370 866-665-4556
http://kandiyohi.com

Koochiching County Economic Development Authority (KEDA)
405 3rd Street, P.O. Box 138
International Falls, MN 56649
218-283-8585 800-452-3569
keda@businessupnorth.com
https://businessupnorth.com

Meeker County Economic Development Authority
114 N. Holcombe Ave., Suite 260
Litchfield, MN 55355
320-693-5272 | meekerdc@gmail.com
https://www.meekercodevcorp.com

Murray County Economic Development Authority
2500 28th Street
Slayton, MN 56172
507-836-6148
https://murraycountymn.com/murray-county-eda/

Red Lake County Economic Development Corp
P.O. Box 279
Red Lake Falls, MN 56570
218-253-2897 218-465-4246
https://www.co.red-lake.mn.us/

Redwood Area Development Corporation
200 S. Mill Street, P.O. Box 481
Redwood Falls, MN 56283
507-637-4004 | radc@redwoodfalls.org
https://www.radc.org/radc

Renville County HRA/EDA
105 South 5th Street, Suite 318
Olivia, MN 56277
320-523-3656 | hraeda@renvillecountymn.com
http://www.renville.com/

Rice County Economic Development
320 3rd Street N.W.
Faribault, MN 55021
507-332-6121 | RCED@co.rice.mn.us
http://www.co.rice.mn.us/315/Economic-Development

St. Cloud Economic Development Authority
400 2nd Street S.
St. Cloud, MN 56301
320-255-7218
http://www.ci.stcloud.mn.us/252/Economic-Development-Authority

St. Louis County Planning and Community Development
St. Louis County Government Services Center
320 West 2nd Street, Suite 301
Duluth, MN 55802
218-725-5008
https://www.stlouiscountymn.gov/departments-a-z/planning-development

Sherburne County Economic Development
Sherburne County Government Center
13880 Business Center Dr. N.W.
Elk River, MN 55330
763-765-3007 800-433-5229
https://www.co.sherburne.mn.us/193/Economic-Development

Sibley County Economic Development
Sibley County Courthouse
400 Court Ave., 2nd Floor
Gaylord, MN 55334
507-237-4117
https://www.co.sibley.mn.us/economic_development/index.php

Stevens County Economic Improvement Commission, Inc.
215 Atlantic Ave.
Morris, MN 52627
320-585-2609 | sceic@hometownsolutions.net
https://www.sceic.org

Swift County Rural Development Finance Auth. (RDA)
301 14th Street N., P.O. Box 288
Benson, MN 56215
218-330-7500
http://www.swiftcountyrda.com/swift

Todd County Development Corporation
347 Central Ave. Suite 1
Long Prairie, MN 56347
320-732-2128
http://www.toddcountydevelopment.org/

Worthington Regional Economic Development Corporation
1121 Third Ave.
Worthington, MN 56187
507-372-5515 | grow@worthington-minnesota.com
http://www.worthington-minnesota.com/

Wright County Economic Development Partnership
6800 Electric Drive, P.O. Box 525
Rockford, MN 55373
763-477-3086 | info@wrightpartnership.org
https://www.wrightpartnership.org

Barnesville Economic Development Authority
P.O. Box 550
Barnesville, MN 5651-4
218-354-2145 218-354-7570
https://www.barnesvillemn.com/government/boards-commissions/economic-development/

Brooklyn Park Businesses
5200 85th Ave. N.
Brooklyn Park, MN 55443
763-493-8145
https://www.brooklynpark.org/businesses/

East Side Neighborhood Development Company, Inc.
965 Payne Ave., Suite 200
St. Paul, MN 55130
651-288-8744
https://www.esndc.org/

Fergus Falls Economic Improvement Commission
112 Washington Ave. W.
Fergus Falls, MN 56537
218-332-5428 | eic@ci.fergus-falls.mn.us
https://www.ci.fergus-falls.mn.us/eic

Hibbing Economic Development Authority (HEDA)
401 E. 21st Street
Hibbing, MN 55746
218-362-5930
http://www.hibbing.mn.us/business/hibbing-economic-development-authority-heda

Minneapolis Community Planning and Economic Development Department (CPED)
Crown Roller Mill
105 Fifth Ave. South #200
Minneapolis, MN 55401
612-673-5095

Minneapolis Business Assistance
http://www.minneapolismn.gov/cped/ba/index.htm

Business Potal
https://business.minneapolismn.gov/

Homegrown Minneapolis
http://www.minneapolismn.gov/sustainability/homegrown/index.htm

Starting a Local Food Business
http://www2.minneapolismn.gov/sustainability/homegrown/WCMS1P-129851

Greater Fargo Moorhead Economic Development Corporation (GFMEDC)
51 Broadway, Suite 500
Fargo, ND 58102
701-364-1900 877-243-0821
https://gfmedc.com/

Moorhead Economic Development Authority
500 Center Ave. P.O. Box 779
Moorhead, MN 56561
218-299-5166
http://www.cityofmoorhead.com/government/boards-commissions/economic-development-authority

New Ulm Economic Development Corporation
1 North Minnesota Street, P.O. Box 384
New Ulm, MN 56073
507-233-4305 | nuedc@newulmtel.net
https://www.newulm.com/grow-new-ulm/economic-development/

Northside Economic Opportunity Network (NEON)
1007 W. Broadway Ave. N.
Minneapolis, MN 55411
612-302-1505 | info@neon-mn.org
https://www.neon-mn.org/

Pipestone Economic Development Authority (PEDA)
119 2nd Ave. S.W.
Pipestone, MN 56164
507-825-3324
http://www.progressivepipestone.com/154/Economic-Development

Rochester Area Economic Development, Inc. (RAEDI) - Southeast Minnesota Capital Fund
220 South Broadway, Suite 100
Rochester, MN 55904
507-288-0208
http://raedi.com/

St. Paul Department of Planning and Economic Development (PED), Economic Development
City Hall Annex
25 W. 4th Street, Suite 1300
St. Paul, MN 55102
651-266-6604
https://www.stpaul.gov/departments/planning-economic-development/economic-development

Business Assistance Tools

Technical Assistance
https://www.stpaul.gov/departments/planning-economic-development/economic-development/business-assistance-tools/business-0

Business Financial Programs
https://www.stpaul.gov/departments/planning-economic-development/economic-development/business-assistance-tools/business

Open for Business
651-266-6600 | businessresources@ci.stpaul.mn.us
https://www.stpaul.gov/businesses/OpenForBusiness

Pocket Guide to Opening a Business
https://saintpaulstg.prod.acquia-sites.com/businesses/open-business/opening-business

St. Paul Port Authority
380 St. Peter Street, Suite 850
St. Paul, MN 55102
651-224-5686 800-328-8417
https://www.sppa.com/energy-financing/overview

Two Harbors Development Commission
522 First Ave.
Two Harbors, MN 55616
218-830-0831
http://www.twoharborsmn.gov/city_departments/two_harbors_development_commission/index.php

Zumbrota Economic Development Authority
175 West Ave.
Zumbrota, MN 55992
507-732-7318
https://www.ci.zumbrota.mn.us

FINANCING, PRIVATE SOURCES

Rural Initiative Organizations

Initiative Foundation
405 First Street S.E.
Little Falls, MN 56345
877-632-9255 | info@ifound.org
https://www.ifound.org

Service area: Benton, Cass, Chisago, Crow Wing Isanti, Kanabec, Mille Lacs, Morrison, Pine, Sherburne, Stearns, Todd, Wadena, and Wright counties.

Northland Foundation
202 W. Superior Street, Suite 610
Duluth, MN 55802
218-723-4040 800-433-4045
info@northlandfdn.org
https://www.northlandfdn.org

Service area: Aitkin, Carlton, Cook, Itasca, Koochiching, Lake, and St. Louis counties.

Northwest Minnesota Foundation
201 3rd Street N.W.
Bemidji, MN 56601
218-759-2057 800-659-7859 | info@nwmf.org
https://www.nwmf.org

Service area: Beltrami, Clearwater, Hubbard, Kittson, Lake of the Woods, Mahnomen, Marshall, Norman, Pennington, Polk, Red Lake, and Roseau counties.

Southern Minnesota Initiative Foundation
525 Florence Ave.
Owatonna, MN 55060
507-455-3215 | inquiry@smifoundation.org
https://smifoundation.org/3

Service area: Blue Earth, Brown, Dodge, Faribault, Fillmore, Freeborn, Goodhue, Houston, Le Sueur, Martin, Mower, Nicollet, Olmsted, Rice, Sibley, Steele, Wabasha, Waseca, Watonwan, and Winona counties.

Southwest Initiative Foundation
15 3rd Ave. N.W.
Hutchinson, MN 55350
320-587-4848 800-594-9480
info@swifoundation.org
https://www.swifoundation.org

Service area: Big Stone, Chippewa, Cottonwood, Jackson, Kandiyohi, Lac qui Parle, Lincoln, Lyon, McLeod, Meeker, Murray, Nobles, Pipestone, Redwood, Renville, Rock, Swift, and Yellow Medicine counties.

West Central Initiative
P.O. Box 318
Fergus Falls, MN 56538
218-739-2239 800-735-2239 | wci@wcif.org
https://www.wcif.org

Service area: Becker, Clay, Douglas, Grant, Otter Tail, Pope, Stevens, Traverse, & Wilkin counties.

Seed Capital / Other

Beta.MN

Beta Group is a 501(c)(3) whose mission is to accelerate the success of Minnesota-based startups.
225 South 6th Street
Minneapolis, MN 55402
http://www.beta.mn

Norris Institute

University of St. Thomas
Opus College of Business
1000 LaSalle Ave.
Minneapolis, MN 55403
651-962-4092
https://business.stthomas.edu/centers-institutes/schulze-school/about-schulze/norris-institute/

MN Vest

MNvest is an exemption from registration under federal and Minnesota state securities laws. By meeting the requirements of MNvest, companies may raise capital within Minnesota state borders.
info@mnvest.org
http://mnvest.org/the-law/

GOVERNMENT, FEDERAL

USA.gov

The U.S. government's official web portal.
844-872-4681
https://www.usa.gov/ https://gobierno.usa.gov

USA.gov -Small Business

The official business link to the U.S. Government.
https://www.usa.gov/business?source=busa

Benefits.gov

The official benefits website of the U.S. government.
https://www.benefits.gov

beta.sam.gov

Federal business opportunities.
https://beta.sam.gov/

Agriculture (USDA), U.S. Department of

Minnesota Rural Development
375 Jackson Street, Suite 410
St. Paul, MN 55101
651-602-7800
https://www.rd.usda.gov/mn

Census Bureau, U.S.

Chicago Region Office
1111 W. 22nd Street, Suite 400
Oak Brook, IL 60523-1918
630-288-9200 800-865-6384
https://www.census.gov

NAICS

North American Industry Classification System (NAICS) is the standard used by Federal statistical agencies in classifying business establishments for the purpose of collecting, analyzing, and publishing statistical data related to the U.S. business economy.
https://www.census.gov/eos/www/naics/

Commerce, U.S. Department of

Minneapolis Office of the U.S. Commercial Service
330 2nd Ave. S., Suite 410
Minneapolis, MN 55401
612-348-1638 | office.minneapolis@trade.gov
https://2016.export.gov/minnesota/

Minority Business Development Agency
MDBA Business Center
250 Second Ave. S., Suite 106
612-259-6590
https://www.mbda.gov/business-center/minneapolis-mbda-business-center

Consumer Product and Safety Commission (CPSC), U.S.

4330 East West Highway
Bethesda, MD 20814
800-638-2772
https://www.cpsc.gov

Business & Manufacturing
https://www.cpsc.gov/Business--Manufacturing/

Small Business Resources
888-531-9070
https://www.cpsc.gov/Business--Manufacturing/Small-Business-Resources

Copyright Office, U.S.

Library of Congress
101 Independence Ave. S.E.
Washington, D.C. 20559-6000
202-707-5959 877-476-0778
https://www.copyright.gov

Environmental Protection Agency (EPA), U.S.

Region 5 -Minnesota
https://www.epa.gov/mn

Laws & Regulations
https://www.epa.gov/laws-regulations

Equal Employment Opportunity Commission (EEOC), U.S.

Minneapolis Area Office
Towle Building
330 Second Ave. South, Suite 720
Minneapolis, MN 55401
800-669-4000
https://www.eeoc.gov/field/minneapolis/index.cfm

Workplace Poster Order Form
800-669-3362 (voice)
https://www1.eeoc.gov/employers/poster.cfm

Federal Communications Commission (FCC)
445 12th Street S.W.
Washington, D.C. 20554
888-225-5322   888-835-5322 (TTY)
https://www.fcc.gov

Forms
888-CALL-FCC
https://www.fcc.gov/licensing-databases/forms

Licensing
https://www.fcc.gov/licensing

Media Bureau
MediaRelations@fcc.gov
https://www.fcc.gov/media

Audio Division
https://www.fcc.gov/media/radio/audio-division

Video Division
https://www.fcc.gov/media/television/video-division

Wireless Telecommunications Bureau
https://www.fcc.gov/wireless-telecommunications

Federal Trade Commission (FTC)
Bureau of Consumer Protection
600 Pennsylvania Ave. N.W.
Washington, D.C. 20580
https://www.ftc.gov

Business Center
https://www.ftc.gov/tips-advice/business-center

Consumer Information
https://www.consumer.ftc.gov

General Services Administration (GSA), U.S.
Great Lakes Office of Small Business Utilization
844-GSA-4111
https://www.gsa.gov/about-us/regions/welcome-to-the-great-lakes-region-5/great-lakes-office-of-small-business-utilization

Health and Human Services, U.S. Department of
Food and Drug Administration (FDA), U.S.
Minneapolis District Office
250 Marquette Ave., Suite 710
Minneapolis, MN 55401
612-334-4100
https://www.fda.gov/

Homeland Security, U.S. Department of
202-282-8000
https://www.dhs.gov

U.S. Citizenship and Immigration Services (USCIS)
https://www.uscis.gov

National Customer Service Center
800-375-5283   800-877-1833 (TTY)

Minnesota - St. Paul Field Office
250 Marquette Ave, Suite 710
Minneapolis, MN 55401
https://www.uscis.gov/about-us/find-a-uscis-office/field-offices

Application Support Center
1105 University Ave. W., Suite 102
St. Paul, MN 55104-4086

I-9 Central

Federal law requires every employer and agricultural recruiter/referrers for a fee hiring an individual for employment in the U.S. must complete Form I-9, Employment Eligibility Verification. Form I-9 will help to verify an employee's identity and employment authorization.

https://www.uscis.gov/i-9-central

Handbook for Employers
https://www.uscis.gov/i-9-central/handbook-employers-m-274

E-Verify
https://www.e-verify.gov/

Web-based system that allows enrolled employers to confirm the eligibility of their employees to work in the United States. E-Verify employers verify the identity and employment eligibility of newly hired employees by electronically matching information provided by employees on Form I-9, Employment Eligibility Verification, against records available to the Social Security Administration (SSA) and the Department of Homeland Security (DHS).

This is a voluntary program. However, employers with federal contracts or subcontracts that contain the Federal Acquisition Regulation (FAR) E-Verify clause are required to enroll in E-Verify as a condition of federal contracting. Employers may also be required to participate in E-Verify if their states have legislation mandating the use of E-Verify, such as a condition of business licensing. Some instances employers may be required to participate in E-Verify as a result of a legal ruling.

For employers/employer agents
https://www.e-verify.gov/employers

For employees
https://www.e-verify.gov/employees

Customs & Border Protection (CBP), U.S.
Service Port—Minneapolis
5600 W. American Blvd., Suite 760
Bloomington, MN 55437
952-857-3100
https://www.cbp.gov/contact/ports/minneapolis

Immigration & Customs Enforcement (ICE), U.S.
866-347-2423
https://www.ice.gov

Minneapolis/St. Paul Special Agent in Charge (SAC)
1 Federal Drive, Suite 1340
Fort Snelling, MN 55111
612-843-8800

Internal Revenue Service (IRS)
https://www.irs.gov https://www.irs.gov/es/spanish

Telephone Assistance for Individuals
800-829-1040

Telephone Assistance for Businesses
800-829-4933

Employer Identification Numbers (EINs)
https://www.irs.gov/businesses/small-businesses-self-employed/employer-id-numbers

To apply for an EIN online
https://www.irs.gov/businesses/small-businesses-self-employed/how-to-apply-for-an-ein

To apply for an EIN by fax
Complete and fax Form SS-4 and fax it to
855-641-6935 (toll free)

To apply for an EIN by mail
Forms are mailed to the designated Regional Service Center. For businesses with their principal place of business in Minnesota, mail to:

Internal Revenue Service
Attn: EIN Operation
Cincinnati, OH 45999

The IRS no longer issues EINs by telephone for domestic taxpayers. Only international applicants can receive an EIN by telephone.

Forms, Instructions and Publications
https://www.irs.gov/forms-instructions

Online Ordering for Information Returns and Employer Returns
https://www.irs.gov/businesses/online-ordering-for-information-returns-and-employer-returns

Small Business and Self-Employed Tax Center
https://www.irs.gov/businesses/small-businesses-self-employed

Taxpayer Advocate Service
Wells Fargo Place
30 E. 7th Street, Suite 817, Stop 1005 STP
St. Paul, MN 55101
651-312-7999 877-777-4778
800-829-4059 TTY/TTD
https://www.irs.gov/advocate/local-taxpayer-advocate#Minnesota

Tax Exempt and Government Entities Customer Account Services
877-829-5500

Video Portal
https://www.irsvideos.gov

Small Business Taxes: The Virtual Workshop
https://www.irsvideos.gov/SmallBusinessTaxpayer/virtualworkshop

Justice, U.S. Department of

ADA.gov
Americans with Disabilities Act (ADA) information and technical assistance.
https://www.ada.gov

ADA Information Line
800-514-0301 800-514-0383 (TTY)

ADA Primer for Small Businesses
https://www.ada.gov/regs2010/smallbusiness/smallbusprimer2010.htm

ADA Tax Incentives
https://www.ada.gov/taxincent.htm

Bureau of Alcohol, Tobacco, Firearms and Explosives (ATF)
St. Paul Field Division
30 E. Seventh Street, Suite 1900
St. Paul, Minnesota 55101
651-726-0220
https://www.atf.gov/

ATF Firearms Industry
https://www.atf.gov/firearms/tools-services-firearms-industry

Federal Firearms Licensing Center (FFLC)
Licensing firearms and explosives manufacturers, importers, collectors, users, and dealers.
866-662-2750 | FFLC@atf.gov

How to Become a Federal Firearms Licensee (FFL)
https://www.atf.gov/firearms/apply-license

Labor (DOL), U.S. Department of
https://www.dol.gov

National Contact Center
866-487-2365

Wage & Hour Division (WHD) - Mpls. Dist. Office
Tri-Tech Center, Suite 920
331 Second Ave. S.
Minneapolis, MN 55401-1321
612-370-3341 866-487-9243
https://www.dol.gov/agencies/whd/contact/local-offices#mn

Bureau of Labor Statistics
Standard Occupational Classification (SOC)
https://www.bls.gov/soc/

Disability Resources
https://www.dol.gov/odep/topics/disability.htm

elaws (Employment Laws Assistance for Workers and Small Businesses)
Employment laws assistance for workers and small businesses.
https://webapps.dol.gov/elaws/

elaws FirstStep Poster Advisor
https://webapps.dol.gov/elaws/posters.htm

Employee Benefits Security Administration
866-444-3272
https://www.dol.gov/agencies/ebsa

Office of Small & Disadvantaged Business Utilization (OSDBU)
OSDBU administers DOL's responsibility to ensure procurement opportunities for small businesses, small disadvantaged businesses, women-owned small businesses, HUBZone businesses, and businesses owned by service-disabled veterans
866-487-2365
https://www.dol.gov/agencies/oasam/business-operations-center/osdbu/programs

Workplace Poster Requirements
https://www.dol.gov/general/topics/posters/

Occupational Safety & Health Administration (OSHA)
Minnesota Dept. of Labor & Industry
Minnesota OSHA (MNOSHA)
443 Lafayette Road N.
St. Paul, MN 55155
651-284-5050 877-470-6742
http://www.dli.mn.gov/business/safety-and-health-work

Small Business
https://www.osha.gov/dcsp/smallbusiness/index.html

National Archives and Records Administration
Federal Register, Office of the (OFR)
8601 Adelphi Road
College Park, MD 20740-6001
866-272-6272
https://www.archives.gov/federal-register

National Labor Relations Board
Minneapolis Federal Office Building
212 Third Ave. S., Suite 200
Minneapolis, MN 55401
612-348-1757
https://www.nlrb.gov/region/minneapolis

Employee Rights Poster
https://www.nlrb.gov/news-publications/publications/employee-rights-poster

Patent and Trademark Office (USPTO), U.S.
Mailstop USPTO Contact Center
P.O. Box 1450
Alexandria, VA 22313-1450
571-272-1000 800-786-9199
https://www.uspto.gov/

Securities and Exchange Commission (SEC), U.S.
Office of Small Business
U.S. Securities and Exchange Commission
100 F Street N.E.
Washington, D.C. 20549-3628
202-551-3460 888-SEC-6585
https://www.sec.gov

Information for Small Businesses
https://www.sec.gov/smallbusiness

Forms List
202-551-4040
https://www.sec.gov/forms

Small Business Administration (SBA), U.S.
Minnesota District Office
330 2nd Ave. South, Suite 430
Minneapolis, MN 55401-2224
612-370-2324
https://www.sba.gov/offices/district/mn/minneapolis

Lender Match
Lender Match is a free online referral tool that connects small businesses with participating SBA-approved lenders.
https://www.sba.gov/lendermatch

7(a) Loan Program
https://www.sba.gov/partners/lenders/7a-loan-program/types-7a-loans

8(a) Business Development Program
https://www.sba.gov/contracting/government-contracting-programs/8a-business-development-program

Boots to Business
Is an entrepreneurial education and training program offered by the U.S. Small Business Administration (SBA) as part of the Department of Defense's Transition Assistance Program (TAP). B2B provides participants with an overview of business ownership and is open to transitioning service members (including National Guard and Reserve) and their spouses.
202-205-6773
https://www.sba.gov/offices/headquarters/ovbd/resources/160511

Business Guide
https://www.sba.gov/business-guide

Contracting
https://www.sba.gov/federal-contracting

Export Products
https://www.sba.gov/business-guide/grow-your-business/export-products

Funding Programs
https://www.sba.gov/funding-programs

HUBZone Certification
https://www.sba.gov/contracting/government-contracting-programs/hubzone-program

Learning Center
https://www.sba.gov/learning-center

Size Standards
https://www.sba.gov/federal-contracting/contracting-guide/size-standards

Veteran-Owned businesses
https://www.sba.gov/business-guide/grow/veteran-owned-businesses-programs

National Ombudsman
Primary mission is to assist small businesses when they experience excessive or unfair federal regulatory enforcement actions by a federal agency.
888-734-3247
https://www.sba.gov/ombudsman/

Social Security Administration (SSA), U.S.
332 Minnesota Street, Suite N650
St. Paul, MN 55101
800-772-1213 800-325-0778 (TTY)
https://www.ssa.gov/

Business Services Online
https://www.socialsecurity.gov/bso/bsowelcome.htm

Greater Twin Cities Metropolitan Area Social Security - Card Center
1811 Chicago Ave., Suite 2
Minneapolis, MN 55404-1998
800-772-1213 800-325-0778 (TTY)

Doing Business with Social Security
https://www.ssa.gov/thirdparty/business.html

Social Security Number Verification Service (SSNVS)
https://www.ssa.gov/employer/ssnv.htm

Publications & Forms
https://www.ssa.gov/employer/pub.htm

Treasury, U.S. Department of the

Alcohol and Tobacco Tax and Trade Bureau (TTB)
Collects Federal excise taxes on alcohol, tobacco, firearms, and ammunition.
Public Information Officer
1310 G Street, N.W., Suite 300
Washington, D.C. 20220
202-453-2000
https://www.ttb.gov

Beverage Alcohol
https://www.ttb.gov/what-we-do/program-areas/beverage-alcohol

Firearms and Ammunition Excise Tax
https://www.ttb.gov/firearms

Getting Started in a TTB-Related Industry
https://www.ttb.gov/resources/business-central/industry-startup-tutorial

Electronic Federal Tax Payment System (EFTPS)
800-555-3453
https://www.eftps.gov

EFTPS Customer Support -Business
800-555-4477 (English) 800-244-4829 (Espanol)

Veterans Affairs, U.S. Department of
202-303-3260
https://www.va.gov

Office of Small & Disadvanted Business (OSBDU)
Verification Assistance Program
https://www.va.gov/osdbu/verification/assistance

GOVERNMENT, STATE

Minnesota.gov
https://mn.gov
The official website for the State of Minnesota.

Minnesota Elicening
Web portal with access to information regarding licenses, permits and registrations administered by state agencies.
license.minnesota@state.mn.us
https://mn.gov/elicense/

Accountancy, MN Board of
85 E. 7th Place, Suite 125
St. Paul, MN 55101
651-296-7938 651-297-5353 (TTY)
800-627-3529 (TTY)
http://www.boa.state.mn.us

Administration, MN Department of

Office of State Procurement (OSP)
State of Minnesota's central procurement office.
MN Department of Administration
Room 112, State Administration Building
50 Sherburne Avenue
St. Paul, MN 55155
651-296-2600
http://www.mmd.admin.state.mn.us/

SWIFT (Statewide Integrated Financial Tools) Vendor Resources
https://mn.gov/mmb/accounting/swift/vendor-resources/

Vendor Information
https://mn.gov/admin/business/vendor-info/

Vendor Registration
http://www.mmd.admin.state.mn.us/mn02000.htm

Office of Equity in Procurement (OEP)
The office helps ensure greater equity in state contracting and construction. It promotes opportunities to do business with the state, and provide assistance to small businesses owned by women, minorities, people with substantial physical disabilities, and veterans as they seek state contracts.
651-201-2402 | procurement.equity@state.mn.us
https://mn.gov/admin/business/vendor-info/oep/

Small Business Procurement Program
Program for targeted group, economically disadvantaged and veteran-owned small businesses.
http://mn.gov/admin/business/vendor-info/oep/sbcp/

Archaeologists, MN Office of the State
328 W. Kellogg Blvd.
St. Paul, MN 55102
651-201-2263 | mn.osa@state.mn.us
https://mn.gov/admin/archaeologist/

Minnesota's Bookstore
The bookstore operates as a centralized publishing house for state agency products sold to the public and publishes the State Register, the official State of Minnesota publication.
660 Olive Street
St. Paul, MN 55155
651-297-3000 800-657-3757
711 (MN Relay Service)
https://mn.gov/admin/bookstore/

State Register
https://mn.gov/admin/bookstore/register.jsp

Agriculture (MDA), MN Department of
Orville L. Freeman Building
625 Robert Street N.
St. Paul, MN 55155
651-201-6000 800-967-2474
800-627-3529 (TDD) | mda.info@state.mn.us
https://www.mda.state.mn.us

Food Licenses
https://mda.state.mn.us/food-feed/food-licenses

Starting a Food Business
651-201-6081
MDA.FoodLicensingLiaison@state.mn.us

Licensing
651-201-6062 | mda.licensing@state.mn.us

Food Business Licensing and Food Safety Wizard
http://www2.mda.state.mn.us/webapp/foodlicensingwizard/

Pesticide & Fertilizer Management Division
651-201-6671

Loan, Grant and Other Funding Opportunities Program
https://www.mda.state.mn.us/funding

Minnesota FarmLink
Searchable tool to connect prospective farmers with retiring and experienced farmers.
320-842-6910
https://mda.state.mn.us/farmlink

Minnesota Grown
https://minnesotagrown.com

Animal Health (BAH), MN Board of
625 N. Robert Street
St. Paul, MN 55155
651-296-2942 800-627-3529 (TTY)
https://mn.gov/bah/

Architecture, Engineering, Land Surveying, Landscape Architecture, Geoscience and Interior Design (AELSLAGID), MN Board of
85 E. 7th Place, Suite 160
St. Paul, MN 55101
651-296-2388 800-627-3529 TTY
https://mn.gov/aelslagid/

Attorney General Office, MN
1400 Bremer Tower
445 Minnesota Street
St. Paul, MN 55101
651-296-3353 800-657-3787
651-297-7206 (TTY) 800-366-4812 (TTY)
https://www.ag.state.mn.us

Barber Examiners, MN Board of
2829 University Ave. S.E., Suite 425
Minneapolis, MN 55414
651-201-2820
https://mn.gov/boards/barber-examiners/

Behavioral Health & Therapy (BBHT), MN Board of
2829 University Ave. S.E., Suite 210
Minneapolis, MN 55414
651-201-2756| bbht.board@state.mn.us
https://mn.gov/boards/behavioral-health/

Bureau of Business Licenses
See Small Business Assistance Office, Employment and Economic Development (DEED), MN Dept. of

Campaign Finance and Disclosure Board, MN
190 Centennial Building
658 Cedar Street
St. Paul, MN 55155
651-539-1190 800-657-3889
https://cfb.mn.gov/

Chiropractic Examiners, MN Board of
2829 University Ave. S.E., Suite 300
Minneapolis, MN 55414-3220
651-201-2850
https://mn.gov/boards/chiropractic-examiners/

Commerce, MN Department of
85 7th Place E. Suite 500
St. Paul, MN 55101
https://mn.gov/commerce/

General Information
651-539-1500 | general.commerce@state.mn.us

Consumers
651-539-1600 800-657-3602 (MN only)
consumer.protection@state.mn.us
https://mn.gov/commerce/consumers/

Financial Institutions
651-539-1600 | financial.commerce@state.mn.us
https://mn.gov/commerce/industries/financial-institutions/

Insurance Information
651-539-1779 | insurance.commerce@state.mn.us
https://mn.gov/commerce/industries/insurance/

Small Business Health Plans
https://mn.gov/commerce/industries/insurance/businesses/

Licensing
651-539-1599 800-657-3978 (MN only)
licensing.commerce@state.mn.us

Securities Registration
651-539-1638 | securities.commerce@state.mn.us
https://mn.gov/commerce/industries/securities/

Telecommunications
651-539-1883 | telecom.commerce@state.mn.us

Scales & Meters
https://mn.gov/commerce/industries/scales-meters/

Cosmetology, MN Board of
1000 University Ave. W., Suite 100
St. Paul, MN 55104
651-201-2742 | cosmetology@state.mn.us
https://mn.gov/boards/cosmetology

Dentistry, MN Board of
2829 University Ave. S.E., Suite 450
Minneapolis, MN 55414
612-617-2250 888-240-4762
dental.board@state.mn.us
https://mn.gov/boards/dentistry/

Dietetics and Nutrition Practice, MN Board of
2829 University Ave. S.E., Suite 402
Minneapolis, MN 55414
651-201-2764
board.dietetics-nutrition@state.mn.us
https://mn.gov/boards/dietetics-and-nutrition/

Education, MN Department of
1500 MN Hwy. 36 West
Roseville, MN 55113
651-582-8200
https://education.state.mn.us/mde/index.html

Emergency Medical Services Regulatory Board (EMSRB), MN
2829 University Ave. S.E., Suite 310
Minneapolis, MN 55414
651-201-2800 800-747-2011
https://mn.gov/boards/emsrb/

Employment and Economic Development (DEED), MN Department of
1st National Bank Building
332 Minnesota Street, Suite E200
St. Paul, MN 55101-1351
651-259-7114 800-657-3858
651-296-3900 (TTY)
https://mn.gov/deed/

Border-Cities Enterprise Zone Program
Program provides business tax credits (property tax credits, debt financing credit on new construction, sales tax credit on construction equipment and materials, and new or existing employee credits) to qualifying businesses that are the source of investment, development, and job creation or retention in the Border-Cities Enterprise Zone cities of Breckenridge, Dilworth, East Grand Forks, Moorhead, and Ortonville.
651-259-7415 800-657-3858
https://mn.gov/deed/business/financing-business/tax-credits/border-cities/

Business Enterprises Program (BEP)
BEP provides profitable vending machine business opportunities for qualified legally blind individuals to operate to become self-supporting.
651-539-2284
https://mn.gov/deed/ssb/jobseekers/bep.jsp

Business Guidebooks
651-556-8425
https://mn.gov/deed/newscenter/publications/allpubs2.jsp#/list/appId/1/filterType/Category/filterValue/Guidebooks/page/1/sort//order/

Data Center - Labor Market Information
Collects, analyzes, & disseminates key labor market indicators, information, and analysis on the economy, workforce, industry base, and job market in Minnesota.
651-259-7384 888-234-1114 | deed.lmi@state.mn.us
https://mn.gov/deed/data/

Data Center Sales Tax Incentives
Companies that build data or network operation centers of at least 25,000 square feet and invest $30 million in the first four years qualify for valuable tax breaks.
651-259-7415
https://mn.gov/deed/business/financing-business/tax-credits/data-center-credit/

Dislocated Worker Program
Program assists to minimize the economic impact of layoffs and plant closings to employers and workers.
651-259-7537 866-213-1422 | deed.dw@state.mn.us
https://mn.gov/deed/programs-services/dislocated-worker

Rapid Response Team
651-259-7531 / 7548 / 7519 / 7535 / 7145 / 7552
866-213-1422

Emerging Entrepreneur Loan Program
Program provides loan capital for businesses that are owned and operated by minorities, low-income persons, women, veterans and/or persons with disabilities.
651-259-7450
https://mn.gov/deed/business/financing-business/deed-programs/elp/

Federal Bonding Service
651-259-7521 888-234-5521
https://mn.gov/deed/business/finding-workers/incentives/federal-bonding.jsp

Find Land, Sites, and Buildings
https://mn.gov/deed/ed/sites-buildings/

Shovel-Ready Site Certified Sites
Key legal, technical and regulatory tasks of developing these sites are already complete.
https://mn.gov/deed/government/shovel-ready/

Statewide Site Selection Tool
https://mn.gov/deed/business/locating-minnesota/land-bldg/statewide/

Greater Minnesota Job Expansion Program
Provides tax benefits to businesses located in Greater Minnesota that increase employment. Qualifying businesses that meet job-growth goals may receive sales tax refunds for purchases made during a seven-year period.
651-259-7434
https://mn.gov/deed/business/financing-business/tax-credits/greater-mn-job-expansion/

Hiring Foreign Workers
Learn about foreign labor certification and the responsibilities of Minnesota employers when hiring foreign workers as temporary or permanent employees.
651-259-7513 | deed.foreignlabor@state.mn.us
https://mn.gov/deed/business/finding-workers/hiring-foreign/

Hiring People with Disabilities
https://mn.gov/deed/business/finding-workers/hiring-disabilities/

Homemakers Returning to Work
Program provides pre-employment services for participants to enter or re-enter the labor market after having been homemakers.
651-259-7540

Indian Business Loan Program
Supports the development of Indian-owned and operated businesses for Native American people throughout Minnesota.
651-259-7483
https://mn.gov/deed/business/financing-business/deed-programs/indian/

Launch Minnesota
Provides financial incentives, training, and grants to people starting companies in technology sectors such as aerospace, agricultural processing, nanotechnology and medical devices.
launchminnesota@state.mn.us
http://www.launchminnesota.org/

Location and Expansion Assistance

Business Development Managers
Work closely with companies of all types to help them locate and expand in communities throughout Minnesota.
651-259-7432 | economic.development@state.mn.us
https://mn.gov/deed/business/help/location-assist/

Northwest Region:
Counties: Beltrami, Cass, Clearwater, Hubbard, Kittson, Lake of the Woods, Mahnomen, Marshall, Norman, Pennington, Polk, Red Lake, Roseau
651-259-7437 218-766-5282 (cell)

Northeast Region:
Counties: Aitkin, Carlton, Chisago, Cook, Isanti, Itasca, Kanabec, Koochiching, Lake, Mille Lacs, Pine, St. Louis
218-310-7757 (cell)

West Central Region:
Counties: Becker, Benton, Clay, Crow Wing, Douglas, Grant, Morrison, Otter Tail, Pope, Sherburne, Stevens, Todd, Traverse, Wadena, Wilkin, Wright
651-259-7468 612-849-1676 (cell)

Southwest Region:
Counties: Big Stone, Blue Earth, Brown, Chippewa, Cottonwood, Faribault, Jackson, Kandiyohi, Lac qui Parle, Le Sueur, Lincoln, Lyon, Martin, McLeod, Meeker, Murray, Rock, Nicollet, Nobles, Pipestone, Redwood, Renville, Sibley, Swift, Waseca, Watonwan, Yellow Medicine
507-344-2601 507-380-3220 (cell)

Southeast Region:
Counties: Dodge, Fillmore, Freeborn, Goodhue, Houston, Mower, Olmsted, Rice, Steele, Wabasha, Winona
507-205-6069 651-245-8674 (cell)

Twin Cities Metro:
Counties: Anoka, Carver, Dakota, Hennepin, Ramsey, Scott, Washington
651-259-7436 651-274-3584 (cell)
651-259-7445 651-276-0857 (cell)
800-657-3858

Industry Specialists

Biosciences and Medical Devices
651-259-7442 800-657-3858

Data Centers
651-259-7436 800-657-3858

Wind Industry
507-344-2601

Migrant and Seasonal Farm Workers
Migrant Labor Representatives
507-333-2086 507-344-2608
507-923-2827 320-441-6575
https://mn.gov/deed/job-seekers/find-a-job/targeted-services/migrants/

Minnesota Business First Stop
Streamlines the development process for complex business startups, expansions or relocations that involve financing, licensing, permitting, and regulatory issues that overlap multiple state agencies.
651-259-7463 855-893-2099
Deed.FirstStop@state.mn.us
https://mn.gov/deed/business/help/first-stop/

Minnesota Investment Fund (MIF)
Provides grants to help add new workers and retain high-quality jobs on a statewide basis.
651-259-7430 800-657-3858
https://mn.gov/deed/business/financing-business/deed-programs/mif/

Minnesota Job Creation Fund
Fund provides financial incentives to new and expanding businesses that meet certain job creation and capital investment targets.
651-259-7483 800-657-3858
https://mn.gov/deed/business/financing-business/deed-programs/mn-jcf/

Minnesota Job Skills Partnership (MJSP)
651-259-7514 | deed.mjsp@state.mn.us
https://mn.gov/deed/business/financing-business/training-grant/

MN Reservist and Veteran Business Loan Program
Provides business loans to companies that are affected when certain employees are called to active military duty and to individual veterans who have returned from active duty and want to start their own business.
651-259-7427
https://mn.gov/deed/business/financing-business/deed-programs/reservists/

MN SBIR/STTR (Small Business Innovation Research (SBIR) and Small Business Technology Transfer (STTR) Program)
State's focal point to assist seed, early stage, emerging and existing firms (1-500 employees) to successfully access non-dilutive federal funding through the programs.
Minnesota High Tech Association
400 South 4th St., Suite 416
Minneapolis, MN 55415
952-230-4540
https://www.mhta.org/mnsbir/

Minnesota Small Business Development Centers (Mn SBDCs)
Operating through a network of nine statewide regional centers, offering confidential consulting to help clients identify, and understand running a successful business.
651-259-7423 877-653-8333
https://mn.gov/deed/business/help/sbdc/

See **MANAGEMENT ASSISTANCE, GENERAL** for Mn SBDC locations throughout Minnesota.

Minnesota Trade Office (MTO)
Provides export assistance to Minnesota's manufacturers and service providers. Programs and services focus primarily on assisting small and medium-sized companies.
651-259-7499 800-657-3858
651-282-6142 800-366-2906 (TYY)
Mto.TradeAssistance@state.mn.us
https://mn.gov/deed/business/exporting/

Export Financing Programs:
https://mn.gov/deed/business/exporting/export-financing/

EB-5 Immigrant Investor Program
651-259-7398
https://mn.gov/deed/business/locating-minnesota/invest-mn/eb5.jsp

Export Counseling and Assistance:

International Trade Representatives:

651-259-7484 Greater China, Southeast Asia & Pacific Oceana
651-259-7486 Middle East & Africa
651-259-7492 Latin America & Caribbean
651-259-7490 Canada & Mexico (NAFTA)
651-259-7494 European Union & Western Europe
651-259-7495 Eastern Europe, Russia, & Central America
651-259-7482 Japan and Korea

Industry Experts:

651-259-7482 Medical & Health Care Industries
651-259-7494 Environmental and Energy Industries

International Business Services Directory
Mto.TradeAssistance@state.mn.us
https://apps.deed.state.mn.us/ExportMN/IBRsf/

STEP (State Trade and Export Promotion Program) Grant Program
651-259-7481
https://mn.gov/deed/business/exporting/export-financing/

Trade Assistance Helpline
651-259-7498

CareerForce
Centers help job seekers find employment, help businesses find workers, and help anyone at any stage explore and plan careers.
CareerForce@state.mn.us
https://www.careerforcemn.com/

CareerForce Locations
https://www.careerforcemn.com/locations

See also **JOB SERVICE AND JOB TRAINING**
MN DEPARTMENT of EMPLOYMENT and ECONOMIC DEVELOPMENT

MinnesotaWorks.net
An Internet-based self-service system where registered employers and job seekers can connect.
https://www.minnesotaworks.net

Office of Youth Development
This youth employment, training and education programs provide vital experience and guidance to help prepare Minnesota's neediest young people to succeed.
https://mn.gov/deed/programs-services/office-youth-development/

People with Disabilities
Programs that assists persons with significant disabilities to seek, gain, and retain employment.
651-259-7366 800-328-9095
651-296-3900 (TTY) 800-657-3973 (TTY)
877-672-3848 (Speech-to-Speech Telephone Re-Voice)
https://mn.gov/deed/job-seekers/disabilities/

SEED Capital Investment Credit Program
Provides tax incentives for investing in innovative business located in the Minnesota border cities of Breckenridge, Dilworth, East Grand Forks, Moorhead, and Ortonville.
651-259-7415
https://mn.gov/deed/business/financing-business/tax-credits/seed-capital/

Small Business Assistance Office (SBAO)
Office serves as a point of first and continuing contact for individuals and firms with questions about business start-up, business operation and business licensing.
651-556-8425 (Voicemail Publication Order Line)
651-259-7476 (Information and Assistance)
800-310-8323 | deed.mnsbao@state.mn.us
https://mn.gov/deed/business/help/sbao/

Business Guidebooks
https://mn.gov/deed/business/help/sbao/

State Services for the Blind (SSB)
2200 University Ave. W.
St. Paul, MN 55114
651-539-2300
https://mn.gov/deed/ssb/

For Job Seekers
651-539-2284 800-652-9000
https://mn.gov/deed/ssb/jobseekers/overview.jsp

SSB Office Locations
https://mn.gov/deed/ssb/about/contact/locations/

Tourism Business Septic Tank Replacement
Program makes low-interest financing available to existing tourism-related businesses that provide overnight lodging and need to replace a failed septic system.
800-657-3858
https://mn.gov/deed/business/financing-business/deed-programs/septic-tourism/

Trade Adjustment Assistance (TAA)
Program is available to workers who lose their jobs, hours or income as a result of increased foreign trade activity.
651-259-7543 888-234-1330 | DEED.TAA@state.mn.us
https://mn.gov/deed/job-seekers/recently-unemployed/layoff/trade-adjustment-assistance.jsp

Unemployment Insurance (UI) Program
Program provides temporary benefits to qualified persons out of work.
ui.mn@state.mn.us
http://www.uimn.org/employers/

Employer Account information
651-296-6141 select option 4 to speak with a customer service representative

Employer Handbook
http://www.uimn.org/employers/help-and-support/emp-hbook/index.jsp

Applicant contacts -general information
651-296-3644 Twin Cities Metro Area
877-898-9090 Greater MN 866-814-1252 (TTY)

Minnesota Business Tax Education Partnership Educational Seminars
The Minnesota Unemployment Insurance (UI) Program offers several types of free educational seminars around the state to assist businesses.
651-259-0779 | ui.mn@state.mn.us
http://www.uimn.org/employers/help-and-support/educational-seminars/index.jsp

Shared Work Program
An alternative to layoffs for employers facing a temporary downturn in business. It allows employers to divide available hours of work among a group of employees instead of implementing a full layoff.
shared.work@state.mn.us
http://www.uimn.org/employers/help-and-support/shared-work/

Veterans Employment Services Programs
Programs ensure that specialized employment and training services are provided to veterans.
https://mn.gov/deed/job-seekers/veteran-services/

Veterans Employment Representatives
https://www.careerforcemn.com/dedicated-veterans-employment-team

Transition Assistance Program (TAP)
Workshops for vets to take stock of their current situation, explore career options, develop job research and job-seeking skills.
651-259-7511
https://www.careerforcemn.com/more-veterans-resources

Work Opportunity Tax Credit (WOTC)
Federal tax credit available to all private sector businesses as an incentive to employers to hire workers in certain groups who experience high rates of unemployment.
651-259-7521 888-234-5521
https://mn.gov/deed/business/finding-workers/incentives/wotc.jsp

Environmental Quality Board (EQB), MN
520 Lafayette Road N.
St. Paul, MN 55155
651-757-2873
https://www.eqb.state.mn.us

Environmental Review Program
651-757-2873 | Env.Review@state.mn.us

Executives for Long Term Services and Supports (BELTSS), Board of
2829 University Ave. S.E., Suite 404
Minneapolis, MN 55414
651-201-2730 | benha@state.mn.us
https://mn.gov/boards/nursing-home/

Firefighter Training and Education, Minnesota Board of
445 Minnesota Street, Suite 146
St. Paul, MN 55101
651-201-7257| fire-training.board@state.mn.us
http://mn.gov/mbfte/

Gambling Control Board, MN
1711 W. County Road B, Suite 300 South
Roseville, MN 55113
651-639-1900
http://mn.gov/gcb/

Health (MDH), MN Department of
625 N. Robert Street
P.O. Box 64975
St. Paul, MN 55164-0975
651-201-5000 888-345-0823
https://www.health.state.mn.us/index.html

Asbestos Program
651-201-4620 | health.asbestos-lead@state.mn.us
https://www.health.state.mn.us/communities/environment/asbestos/index.html

Environmental Health Division -Program Contacts
651-201-4571
https://www.health.state.mn.us/about/org/eh/contacts.html

Environmental Health Specialist/Sanitarian
651-201-4500 | health.sanitarians@state.mn.us
https://www.health.state.mn.us/communities/environment/sanitarian/index.html

Food, Pools, and Lodging Services Section
Food, Beverage, and Lodging (FBL)
651-201-4500 | health.foodlodging@state.mn.us
https://www.health.state.mn.us/communities/environment/food/license/index.html

Human Rights (DHS), MN Department of
Freeman Building
625 Robert Street N.
St. Paul, MN 55155
651-539-1100 MN Relay 711
800-657-3704 | Info.MDHR@state.mn.us
https://mn.gov/mdhr/

Human Services (DHS), MN Department of
444 Lafayette Road N.
St. Paul, MN 55155
651-431-2000 800- 627-3529 (TTY/TDD)
dhs.healthcare-providers@state.mn.us
https://mn.gov/dhs/

Licensing Division
651-431-6500

Minnesota New Hire Reporting Center
Federal and State law requires employers to report newly hired and re-hired employees in Minnesota to the New Hire Reporting Center.
P.O. Box 64212
St. Paul, MN 55164-0212
800-672-4473 800-692-4473 (toll-free fax)
https://newhire-reporting.com/MN-Newhire/default.aspx

Judicial Branch, MN
Lawyer Registration Office, Minnesota
180 E. 5th Street, Suite 950
St. Paul, MN 55101
651-296-2254
lawyerregistration@mbcle.state.mn.us
https://www.lro.mn.gov/

Labor and Industry (DLI), MN Department of
443 Lafayette Road N.
St. Paul, MN 55155-4307
http://www.dli.mn.gov

General Information
651-284-5005 800-342-5354
dli.communications@state.mn.us

Apprenticeship
651-284-5005 800-342-5354
DLI.Apprenticeship@state.mn.us
http://www.dli.mn.gov/business/workforce/apprenticeship

Construction Codes & Licensing Division (CCLD)
651-284-5012 800-657-3944
http://www.dli.mn.gov/about-department/our-areas-service/construction-codes-and-licensing

For Business
651-284-5034 800-284-5034
DLI.License@state.mn.us
http://www.dli.mn.gov/business

For Workers
651-284-5031
http://www.dli.mn.gov/workers

Independent Contractor Registration
651-284-5074 | dli.register@state.mn.us
http://www.dli.mn.gov/business/independent-contractor-registration

Labor Standards
651-284-5070 | dli.laborstandards@state.mn.us
http://www.dli.mn.gov/laborlaw

Minnesota Occupational Safety and Health Administration (MNOSHA) Compliance
651-284-5050 877-470-6742
osha.compliance@state.mn.us
https://www.dli.mn.gov/business/workplace-safety-and-health/mnosha-compliance-standards-and-regulations

Compliance -Duluth Area Office
525 Lake Ave. S., Suite 330
Duluth, MN 55802
218-725-7722

Compliance -Mankato Area Office
12 Civic Center Plaza, Suite 1650
Mankato, MN 56001
507-304-6262 877-348-0508

Workplace Safety Consultation
651-284-5060 800-657-3776
osha.consultation@state.mn.us
http://www.dli.mn.gov/about-department/our-areas-service/minnesota-osha-workplace-safety-consultation

Workers' Compensation -Business
800-342-5354, press 3
http://www.dli.mn.gov/business/workers-compensation-businesses

Benefits / Claims Questions
651-284-5032 800-342-5354

Workers' Compensation Training for Employers
651-284-5431 | dli.wctraining@state.mn.us
http://www.dli.mn.gov/business/workers-compensation/wc-training-employers

Vocational Rehabilitation Unit (VRU)
St. Paul Metro Office
651-284-5038 888-772-5500
http://www.dli.mn.gov/business/workers-compensation/work-comp-dlis-vocational-rehabilitation-unit-vru

Workplace Posters
651-284-5042 800-342-5354
dli.post@state.mn.us
http://www.dli.mn.gov/about-department/workplace-posters

Office of Combative Sports, Minnesota
443 Lafayette Road N.
St. Paul, MN 55155
651-284-5366
http://www.dli.mn.gov/ocs

Management & Budget, MN
MNsure
Minnesota's health insurance marketplace where individuals, families and small businesses can shop, compare and choose health insurance coverage.
651-539-2099 855-366-7873
gethelp@mnsure.org
https://www.mnsure.org

Marriage and Family Therapy, MN Board of
2829 University Ave. S.E., Suite 400
Minneapolis, MN 55414
612-617-2220 800-627-3529 (MN Relay)
mft.board@state.mn.us
https://mn.gov/boards/marriage-and-family/

Medical Practice, MN Board of
2829 University Ave. S.E., Suite 500
Minneapolis, MN 55414-3246
612-617-2130 800-627-3529 (MN Relay)
medical.board@state.mn.us
https://mn.gov/boards/medical-practice/

Minnesota State Colleges and Universities
Wells Fargo Place
30 7th Street E.
St. Paul, MN 55101
651-556-0596 800-456-8519
https://www.minnstate.edu/

Natural Resources (DNR), Minnesota Dept. of
500 Lafayette Road
St. Paul, MN 55155-4040
https://www.dnr.state.mn.us

DNR Information / License Center
651-296-6157 888-646-6367
info.dnr@state.mn.us
https://www.dnr.state.mn.us/contact/index.html

Fish Minnesota
https://www.dnr.state.mn.us/fishing/index.html

Hunting & trapping
https://www.dnr.state.mn.us/hunting/index.html

Watercraft / Recreational Motor Vehicle / Snowmobile Registrations
651-296-6157 888-646-6367

Nursing, MN Board of
1210 Northland Drive #120
Mendota Heights, MN 55120
612-317-3000 800-627-3529 (MN Relay Service)
nursing.board@state.mn.us
https://mn.gov/boards/nursing/

Occupational Therapy Practice, MN Board of
2829 University Ave. S.E., Suite 415
Minneapolis, MN 55414
651-548-2179 | Occupational.therapy@state.mn.us
https://mn.gov/boards/occupational-therapy/

Office of Higher Education, MN
1450 Energy Park Drive, Suite 350
St. Paul, MN 55108
651-642-0567 800-657-3866
https://www.ohe.state.mn.us/

Optometry, MN Board of
2829 University Ave. S.E., Suite 403
Minneapolis, MN 55414
651-201-2762
optometry.board@state.mn.us
https://mn.gov/boards/optometry

Peace Officer Standards and Training (POST), MN Board of
1600 University Ave., Suite 200
St. Paul, MN 55104-3825
651-643-3060
https://dps.mn.gov/entity/post/Pages/default.aspx

Pharmacy, MN Board of
2829 University Ave. S.E., Suite 530
Minneapolis, MN 55414
651-201-2825
https://mn.gov/boards/pharmacy/

Physical Therapy, MN Board of
2829 University Ave. S.E., Suite 420
Minneapolis, MN 55414-3246
612-627-5406 | physical.therapy@state.mn.us
https://mn.gov/boards/physical-therapy/

Podiatric Medicine, MN Board of
2829 University Ave. S.E., Suite 430
Minneapolis, MN 55414
612-548-2175 | podiatric.medicine@state.mn.us
https://mn.gov/boards/podiatric-medicine/

Pollution Control Agency (MPCA), MN
520 Lafayette Road
St. Paul, MN 55155-4194
651-296-6300 800-657-3864
https://www.pca.state.mn.us

Environmental Assistance Grants & Loans
https://www.pca.state.mn.us/about-mpca/environmental-assistance-grants-and-loans

Environmental Assistance Grants
651-757-2459 800-657-3864
https://www.pca.state.mn.us/about-mpca/environmental-assistance-grants

Environmental Assistance Loans
651-757-2459 800-657-3864
https://www.pca.state.mn.us/about-mpca/environmental-assistance-loans

Financial Assistance: Grants and Loans
https://www.pca.state.mn.us/about-mpca/financial-assistance-grants-and-loans

Small Business Environmental Assistance
https://www.pca.state.mn.us/smallbizhelp

Low-interest Environmental Loans
651-757-2218 800-657-3938
https://www.pca.state.mn.us/regulations/low-interest-environmental-loans

Small Business Ombudsman Program
An independent entity responsible for reviewing environmental regulatory activities to ensure that they are fair, reasonable and appropriate for Minnesota's "small businesses" that have to comply with environmental regulations—independently owned and operated businesses with less than 100 employees.
651-757-2121 800-985-4247
https://www.pca.state.mn.us/regulations/small-business-ombudsman

Professional Educator Licensing and Standards Board (PELSB), MN
1500 Highway 36 West, Suite 300
Roseville, MN 55113-4055
651-539-4200 | pelsb@state.mn.us
https://mn.gov/pelsb/

Psychology, MN Board of
2829 University Ave. S.E., Suite 320
Minneapolis, MN 55414
612-617-2230 800-627-3529 (MN Relay Service)
psychology.board@state.mn.us
https://mn.gov/boards/psychology/

Public Safety (DPS), MN Department of
Central Office, Town Square Building
445 Minnesota Street
St. Paul, MN 55101
651-201-7000
https://dps.mn.gov

Alcohol & Gambling Enforcement Division
651-201-7507
https://dps.mn.gov/divisions/age/Pages/default.aspx

Driver and Vehicle Services (DVS)
445 Minnesota Street, Suite 190
St. Paul, MN 55101-5190
https://dps.mn.gov/divisions/DVS/contact/Pages/default.aspx

Driver Services
651-297-3298 |dvs.driverslicense@state.mn.us

Driver Evaluation, Work permits, violations, limited/revoked/suspended/canceled privileges, fines on driving records
651-296-2025

Office Locations
https://dps.mn.gov/divisions/dvs/locations/Pages/find-office-locations.aspx
651-297-2005

Schedule or Reschedule an Exam
https://driverservices.dps.mn.gov/EServices/_/#1

Vehicle Services
651-297-2126 | dvs.motor.vehicles@state.mn.us

Commercial Driver's License
651-297-5029

Motor Vehicle Dealer License
651-201-7800 | DVS.Dealerquestion@state.mn.us

Bureau of Criminal Apprehension (BCA)
1430 Maryland Ave. E.
St. Paul, MN 55106
651-793-7000
https://dps.mn.gov/divisions/bca/Pages/default.aspx

Private Detective and Protective Agent Services, State of MN Board of
1430 Maryland Ave. E.
St. Paul, MN 55106
651-793-2666 651-282-6555 (TTYL)
mn.pdb@state.mn.us
https://dps.mn.gov/entity/pdb/Pages/default.aspx

State Fire Marshal, MN
445 Minnesota Street, Suite 145
St. Paul, MN 55101-5145
651-201-7200 651-282-6555 (TTYL)
https://dps.mn.gov/divisions/sfm/Pages/default.aspx

Public Utilities Commission (PUC), MN
121 Seventh Place E., Suite 350
St. Paul, MN 55101
651-296-0406 800-657-3782
consumer.puc@state.mn.us
https://mn.gov/puc/

Racing Commission (MRC), MN
https://www.mrc.state.mn.us

Licensing Questions
mrclicensing@state.mn.us

Canterbury Park MRC Office
P.O. Box 630
Shakopee, MN 55379
952-496-7950
cbypark@canterburypark.com
https://www.canterburypark.com

Running Aces
15201 Zurich Street N.E., Suite 212
Columbus, MN 55025
651-925-3951 | info@runaces.com
https://runaces.com/

Revenue (DOR), MN Department of
600 N. Robert Street
St. Paul, MN 55146
https://www.revenue.state.mn.us

Registering Your Business
https://www.revenue.state.mn.us/guide/registering-your-business

Business Tax Registration / MN Sales Tax ID Number
651-282-5225 800-657-3605
https://www.mndor.state.mn.us/tp/webreg/_/

Collections Division
651-556-3003 800-657-3909
https://www.revenue.state.mn.us/collection-information

Corporations Franchise Tax / Business Income Tax
651-556-3075

e-Services
https://www.mndor.state.mn.us/tp/eservices/_/

Individual Income Tax
651-296-3781 800-652-9094
https://www.revenue.state.mn.us/individuals

File an Income Tax Return
https://www.revenue.state.mn.us/file-income-tax-return

Make a Payment
https://www.revenue.state.mn.us/make-payment

Finda a Form
https://www.revenue.state.mn.us/find-form

Where's My Refund?
https://www.revenue.state.mn.us/wheres-my-refund

Education and Outreach
Training opportunities for businesses to help meet their tax obligations.
651-282-5225
https://www.revenue.state.mn.us/business-education-and-outreach

Sales and Use Tax
651-296-6181 800-657-3777
https://www.revenue.state.mn.us/sales-and-use-tax

Sales Tax Fact Sheets and Industry Guides
https://www.revenue.state.mn.us/sales-tax-fact-sheets-and-industry-guides

Minnesota Sales and Use Tax Business Guide
https://www.revenue.state.mn.us/guide/minnesota-sales-and-use-tax-business-guide

Taxpayer Rights
https://www.revenue.state.mn.us/guide/taxpayer-rights

Withholding Tax
651-282-9999 800-657-3594
https://www.revenue.state.mn.us/withholding-tax

Assessors, MN State Board of
Minnesota Department of Revenue
Mail Station 3340
St. Paul, MN 55146-3340
651-556-6086
https://www.revenue.state.mn.us/minnesota-state-board-assessors

Secretary of State (SOS), Office of the Minnesota
https://www.sos.state.mn.us

Business and Nonprofit Services address:
Office of the Minnesota Secretary of State
Retirement Systems of Minnesota Building
60 Empire Dr., Suite 100
St. Paul, MN 55103
651-296-2803 877-551-6767 (Greater MN)
business.services@state.mn.us

Business Forms & Fees
https://www.sos.state.mn.us/business-liens/business-forms-fees/

Business Name Search / Availability
https://mblsportal.sos.state.mn.us/Business/Search

Create an Online Account
https://mblsportal.sos.state.mn.us/Account/Register

Notary & Apostille
https://www.sos.state.mn.us/notary-apostille/

How to Register a Business
https://www.sos.state.mn.us/business-liens/start-a-business/how-to-register-your-business/

Small Business Assistance Office (SBAO)
MN DEED
1st National Bank Building
332 Minnesota Street, Suite E200
St. Paul, MN 55101-1351
651-556-8425 (Voicemail Publication Order Line)

651-259-7476 (Information and Assistance)

800-310-8323 | deed.mnsbao@state.mn.us

https://mn.gov/deed/business/help/sbao/

State Legislature, MN
Office of the Revisor of Statutes
700 State Office Building
100 Rev. Dr. Martin Luther King Jr. Blvd.
St. Paul, MN 55155
651-296-2868
https://www.revisor.mn.gov

Statutes, Laws and Rules
https://www.revisor.mn.gov/pubs/

Transportation (MnDOT), MN Department of
395 John Ireland Blvd.
St. Paul, MN 55155-1899
651-296-3000
800-657-3774 800-627-3529 (MN Relay Service)
http://www.dot.state.mn.us

Commercial Vehicle Operations (CVO)
651-215-6330
http://www.dot.state.mn.us/cvo/index.html

Veterans Affairs, MN Department of
State Veterans Service Building
20 W. 12th Street, Room 206
St. Paul, MN 55155
651-296-2562 888-546-5838 LinkVet
https://mn.gov/mdva/
Equality and Diversity at MnDOT
https://www.dot.state.mn.us/equity-diversity/index.html

Veterinary Medicine, MN Board of
2829 University Ave. S.E., Suite 401
Minneapolis, MN 55414
651-201-2844 800-627-3529 (MN Relay Service)
https://mn.gov/boards/veterinary-medicine/

GOVERNMENT, REGIONAL

Regional Development Commissions

Northwest Regional Development Commission
109 South Minnesota Street
Warren, MN 56762
218-745-6733
https://www.nwrdc.org

Region 1. Serves Kittson, Marshall, Norman, Pennington, Polk, Red Lake, and Roseau counties

Headwaters Regional Development Commission
403 Fourth Street N.W., Suite 310, P.O. Box 906
Bemidji, MN 56619
218-444-4732 | hrdc@hrdc.org
http://www.hrdc.org

Region 2. Serves Beltrami, Clearwater, Hubbard, Lake of the Woods, and Mahnomen counties.

Arrowhead Regional Development Commission
221 W. 1st Street
Duluth, MN 55802
218-722-5545 800- 232-0707 | info@ardc.org
https://www.ardc.org

Region 3. Serves Aitkin, Carlton, Cook, Itasca, Koochiching, Lake, and St. Louis counties.

West Central Initiative
P.O. Box 318
Fergus Falls, MN 56537
218-739-2239 800- 735- 2239 | wci@wcif.org
https://www.wcif.org

Region 4. Becker, Clay, Douglas, Grant, Otter Tail, Pope, Stevens, Traverse, and Wilkin counties.

Region Five Development Commission / North Central Economic Development Association (NCEDA)
200 1st Street N.E., Suite 2
Staples, MN 56479
218-894-3233
https://www.regionfive.org

Region 5. Serves Cass, Crow Wing, Morrison, Todd, and Wadena counties.

Mid-Minnesota Development Commission
333 6th Street S.W., Suite 2
Willmar, MN 56201
320-235-8504 800-450-8608
mmrdc@mmrdc.org
http://www.mmrdc.org

Region 6E. Serves Kandiyohi, McLeod, Meeker, and Renville counties.

Upper Minnesota Valley Regional Development Commission (UMVRDC)
323 W. Schlieman Ave.
Appleton, MN 56208
320-289-1981 | info@umvrdc.org
https://umvrdc.org/

Region 6W. Serves Big Stone, Chippewa, Lac qui Parle, Swift, and Yellow Medicine counties.

East Central Regional Development Commission
100 Park Street S.
Mora, MN 55051
320-679-4065 | ecrdc@ecrdc.org
http://www.ecrdc.org/

Region 7E. Serves Chisago, Isanti, Kanabec, Mille Lacs, and Pine counties.

Southwest Regional Development Commission
2401 Broadway Ave., Suite 1
Slayton, MN 56172
507-836-8547 | srdc@swrdc.org
http://www.swrdc.org

Region 8. Serves Cottonwood, Jackson, Rock, Lincoln, Lyon, Murray, Nobles, Pipestone, and Redwood counties.

Region Nine Development Commission
10 Civic Center Plaza Suite 3
Mankato, MN 56002
507-387-5643
https://www.rndc.org

Region 9. Serves Blue Earth, Brown, Faribault, Le Sueur, Martin, Nicollet, Sibley, Waseca, and Watonwan counties.

Metropolitan Council
390 Robert Street N.
St. Paul, MN 55101
651-602-1000 | public.info@metc.state.mn.us
https://metrocouncil.org

Region 11. Serves Anoka, Carver, Dakota, Hennepin, Ramsey, Scott, and Washington counties.

INSURANCE

MNsure
A central marketplace for individuals, families and small employers can get affordable health insurance and access tax credits or assistance to help pay for health insurance coverage.
Golden Rule Building
85 7th Place East, Suite 120
St. Paul, MN 55101-2198
855-366-7873 651-539-2099
https://www.mnsure.org

Minnesota Joint Underwriting Association (MJUA)
The statutory purpose of the MJUA is to provide liability insurance coverage to those individuals or entities that are unable to obtain coverage through traditional methods if the insurance is required by law, or if the insurance is necessary to earn a livelihood serving a public purpose.
12400 Portland Ave. S., Suite 190
Burnsville, MN 55337
952-641-0260 | info@mjua.org
https://www.mjua.org

Minnesota Fair Plan
(Limited property insurance)
1128 Harmon Place, Suite 311
Minneapolis, MN 55403
612-338-7584 800-524-1640
http://www.mnfairplan.org

Minnesota Department of Commerce
Insurance Division
Small business insurance information
651-296-2488 800-657-3602 (MN only)
https://mn.gov/commerce/industries/insurance/businesses/

INVENTORS

Mitchell Hamline School of Law
Legal Practice Center / Intellectual Property Law Clinic
Assists with filing patent or trademark applications.
875 Summit Ave.
St. Paul, MN 55105
651-227-9171 888-962-5529
https://mitchellhamline.edu/legal-practice-center/

Inventors' Network
Monthly meeting location:
Eisenhower Community Center
1001 MN Hwy. 7
Hopkins, MN 55305
https://www.inventorsnetwork.org

LegalCORPS Inventor Assistance Program (IAP)
First program in the United States to provide free legal representation to low income inventors seeking to patent their innovations with the U.S. Patent & Trademark Office.
612-206-0780 | info@legalcorps.org
http://legalcorps.org/inventors

U.S. Patent and Trademark Office
Mailstop USPTO Contact Center
P.O. Box 1450
Alexandria, VA 22313-1450
https://www.uspto.gov

Inventors Assistance Center (IAC)
517-272-1000 800-786-9199
https://www.uspto.gov/learning-and-resources/support-centers/inventors-assistance-center-iac

Patents Ombudsman Program
https://www.uspto.gov/patent/ombudsman-program

U.S. Patent and Trademark Depository Library
Hennepin County Public Library -Central Business/Science/Government Documents Div.
300 Nicollet Ave.
Minneapolis, MN 55401
952-847-8095
https://www.hclib.org/browse/online-resources

JOB SERVICE and JOB TRAINING

Employment and Economic Development (DEED), Minnesota Department of

Minnesota Job Service

The focus of all services is to help job seekers find work and help employers find and retain qualified employees.

Most of the services are delivered through Minnesota's statewide network of CareerForce Centers.

https://mn.gov/deed/programs-services/mn-job-service/

Minnesota Job Skills Partnership (MJSP)

Program helps business and educational institutions develop cooperative training projects.

651-259-7514   800-657-3858
https://mn.gov/deed/business/financing-business/training-grant/

CareerForce

Job skills analysis, assessment and customized training.

6581-259-7501 | CareerForce@state.mn.us
https://www.careerforcemn.com/

CareerForce Locations:
https://www.careerforcemn.com/locations

CareerForce Albert Lea
2200 Riverland Drive
Albert Lea, MN 56007
507-369-1488

CareerForce Alexandria
303 22nd Ave. West, Suite 107
Alexandria, MN 56308
320-762-7800

CareerForce Austin
1600 8th Ave. N.W.
Austin, MN 55912
507-433-0555

CareerForce Bemidji
Downtown
616 America Ave. N.W., Suite 210
Bemidji, MN 56601
218-333-8200

Westbridge
2300 24th Street N.W.
Bemidji, MN 56601

CareerForce Blaine
1201 89th Ave. N.E., Suite 235
Blaine, MN 55434
763-324-2300

CareerForce Bloomington
4220 W. Old Shakopee Road, Suite 100
Bloomington, MN 55437
952-703-7730

CareerForce Brainerd
204 Laurel Street, Suite 21
Brainerd, MN 56401
218-828-2450

CareerForce Brooklyn Park
7225 Northland Dr., Suite 100
Brooklyn Park, MN 55428
763-279-4400

CareerForce Burnsville
2800 County Road 42 W.
Burnsville, MN 55337
952-703-3100

CareerForce Cambridge
140 Buchanan Street N., Suite 152
Cambridge, MN 55008
763-279-4492

CareerForce Chaska
602 East 4th Street
Chaska, MN 55318
952-361-1711

CareerForce Cloquet
14 N. 11th Street
Cloquet, MN 55720
218-878-5000

CareerForce Cottage Grove
13000 Ravine Parkway S.
Cottage Grove, MN 55016
651-430-4162

CareerForce Crookston
2015 Sahlstrom Dr
Crookston, MN 56716
218-277-7330

CareerForce Detroit Lakes
803 Roosevelt Ave.
Detroit Lakes, MN 56501
218-846-7377

CareerForce Duluth
402 W. 1st Street
Duluth, MN 55802
218-302-8400

CareerForce Fairmont
400 S. State Street, Suite 180
Fairmont, MN 56031
507-235-5518

CareerForce Faribault
201 Lyndale Ave. S., Suite 1
Faribault, MN 55021
507-333-2088

CareerForce Fergus Falls
125 West Lincoln Ave., Suite 1
Fergus Falls, MN 56537
218-739-7560

CareerForce Forest Lake
19955 Forest Road N.
Forest Lake, MN 55025
651-275-7265

CareerForce Grand Rapids
1215 Southeast 2nd Ave.
Grand Rapids, MN 55744
218-327-4480

CareerForce Hibbing
3920 13th Ave. E.
Hibbing, MN 55746
218-231-8590

CareerForce Hutchinson
2 Century Ave. S.E.
Hutchinson, MN 55350
320-587-4740

CareerForce International Falls
1501 Hwy. 71, SC 128
International Falls, MN 56649
218-283-9427

CareerForce Litchfield
114 Holcombe Ave. N., Suite 170
Litchfield, MN 55355
320-593-1056

CareerForce Little Falls
609 13th Ave. N.E., Suite G
Little Falls, MN 56345
320-232-2000

CareerForce Mankato
12 Civic Center Plaza, Suite 1600A
Mankato, MN 56001-7796
507-344-2622

CareerForce Marshall
607 W. Main Street
Marshall, MN 56258
507-476-4040

CareerForce Minneapolis North
800 West Broadway Ave.
Minneapolis, MN 55411
612-299-7200

CareerForce Minneapolis South
777 E. Lake Street
Minneapolis, MN 55407
612-821-4000

CareerForce Montevideo
202 North 1st Street
Montevideo, MN 56265
320-269-8819

CareerForce Monticello
406 E. 7th Street
Monticello MN 55362
763-271-3700

CareerForce Moorhead
715 11th Street N., Suite 302
Moorhead, MN 56560
218-287-5060

CareerForce Mora
903 Forest Ave E.
Mora, MN 55051
320-679-6484

CareerForce New Ulm
1618 South Broadway Street
New Ulm, MN 56073
507-354-3138

CareerForce North St. Paul
2266 2nd Street N.
North St. Paul, MN 55109
651-266-9890

CareerForce Red Wing
1606 West 3rd Street
Red Wing, MN 55066
651-385-6480

CareerForce Rochester
2070 College View Rd. E.
Rochester, MN 55904
507-923-2828

CareerForce Roseau
121 Center Street E, Suite 202
Roseau, MN 56751
218-463-2233

CareerForce Shakopee
752 Canterbury Road S.
Shakopee, MN 55379
952-496-8686

CareerForce St. Cloud
1542 Northway Drive, Door 2
St. Cloud, MN 56303
320-308-5320

CareerForce St. Paul
540 Fairview Ave N.
St. Paul, MN 55104
651-642-0363

CareerForce Thief River Falls
1301 Highway 1 East
Thief River Falls, MN 56701
218-683-8060

CareerForce Virginia
820 North 9th St., Suite 250
Virginia, MN 55792
218-735-3740

CareerForce Wadena
124 1st Street S.E., Suite 2
Wadena, MN 56482
218-631-7660

CareerForce West St. Paul
1 Mendota Road W., Suite 170
West St. Paul, MN 55118
651-554-5955

CareerForce Willmar
2200 23rd Street, N.E., Suite 2040
Willmar, MN 56201
320-441-6590

CareerForce Winona
1250 Homer Road, Suite 200
Winona, MN 55987
507-205-6060

CareerForce Woodbury
2150 Radio Dr.
Woodbury, MN 55125
651-275-8650

CareerForce Worthington
318 9th Street
Worthington, MN 56187
507-295-2020

MinnesotaWorks.net
An Internet-based self-service system where registered employers and job seekers can connect
https://www.minnesotaworks.net

Workforce Investment Act (WIA) Youth Program
Provides economically disadvantaged teenagers and young adults between the ages of 14 - 21 with year-round employment and training services.
651-259-7555
https://mn.gov/deed/job-seekers/find-a-job/targeted-services/youth-employment/wia-youth-program.jsp

LEGAL ASSISTANCE

Minnesota Judicial Branch
Self-Help Center
Website is intended for people who are representing themselves in a Minnesota District Court without a lawyer.
http://www.mncourts.gov/selfhelp

Minnesota State Bar Association
600 Nicollet Mall, Suite 380
Minneapolis, MN 55402
612-333-1183 800- 882-6722
https://www.mnbar.org

MN Find a Lawyer Directory
https://www.mnbar.org/member-directory/find-a-lawyer

LegalCORPS
Free legal assistance for small businesses and nonprofits.
100 LaSalle Ave., SCH 317
Minneapolis, MN 55403
612-206-0780 | info@legalcorps.org
http://legalcorps.org/

County Bar Associations / Other Assistance

Anoka County Bar Association
https://anokabar.com

Legal Assistance for Dakota County
https://mn.gov/law-library/assets/Dakota%20County_tcm1041-78737.pdf

Hennepin County Bar Association
Lawyer Referral and Information Service
612-752-6666
https://mnlawyerreferral.org/

Ramsey County Bar Association
Attorney Referral Service
651-224-1775 | ars@ramseybar.org
https://mnlawyerreferral.org/

Minnesota Hispanic Bar Association
https://minnhba.org/

Minnesota American Indian Bar Association
http://www.maiba.org

Minnesota Association of Black Lawyers
Lawyer Referrals
https://mabl.org/membership-directory/

Minnesota Lavender Bar Association
info@mnlavbar.org
https://www.mnlavbar.org

Foodblazer
Information and legal advice for food entrepreneurs.
http://www.foodblazer.com/

Lawmoose
Online legal reference library, online search engine focused on law related sites in Minnesota, and a Minnesota legal periodical index.
http://www.lawmoose.com

Law Schools

Mitchell Hamline School of Law
Legal Practice Center
Assists with forming business entities for new small businesses.
875 Summit Ave.
St. Paul, MN 55105
651-227-9171 888-962-5529
https://mitchellhamline.edu/legal-practice-center/

University of Minnesota Law School
Center for Business Law

Business Law Clinic
Clinic offers students the opportunity to represent business clients in a non-litigation context.
229 19th Ave. S.
Minneapolis, MN 55455
612-625-5515
https://www.law.umn.edu/course/7860/business-law-clinic

LIBRARIES

Primary Metropolitan Area Libraries

Anoka County Library
707 County Road 10 N.E.
Blaine, MN 55434
763-717-3267 763-717-3271 (TDD/TTY)
https://www.anokacounty.us/1758/Libraries

Carver County Library
Chaska Library
4 City Hall Plaza
Chaska, MN 55318
952-448-9395
https://www.carverlib.org

Dakota County Library
1340 Wescott Road
Eagan, MN 55123
651-450-2900
https://www.co.dakota.mn.us/libraries

Hennepin County Library
Minneapolis Central Library
300 Nicollet Ave.
Minneapolis, MN 55401
612-543-8000
https://www.hclib.org

Ramsey County Library
2180 Hamline Ave.
Roseville, MN 55113
651-724-6001, option #3
https://www.rclreads.org/

Scott County Library System
Savage Library
13090 Alabama Ave. S.
Savage, MN 55378
952-707-1770
https://www.scottlib.org/

St. Paul Public Library
Central Library
90 W. 4th Street
St. Paul, MN 55102
651-266-7000
https://www.sppl.org

workPLACE
https://sppl.org/workplace/

Washington County Library
8595 Central Park Place
Woodbury, MN 55125
651-731-1320
https://www.washcolib.org/

Minnesota Library Systems

Capitol Area Library Consortium (CALCO)
Provides access to state government library services and resources.
http://mn.gov/library/

Arrowhead Library System
5528 Emerald Ave.
Mountain Iron, MN 55768
218-741-3840
https://www.alslib.info/

Central Minnesota Libraries Exchange (CMLE)
St. Cloud State University - Miller Center 130-D
570 1st Street S.E.
St. Cloud, MN 56304
320-257-1933 | admin@cmle.org
https://cmle.org

Duluth Public Library
520 W. Superior Street
Duluth, MN 55802
218-730-4200
http://www.duluthlibrary.org

East Central Regional Library
244 S. Birch Street
Cambridge, MN 55008
763-689-7390 888-234-1293
https://ecrlib.org/

Great River Regional Library
1300 W. St. Germain Street
St. Cloud, MN 56301
320-650-2500
https://griver.org

Kitchigami Regional Library System
310 2nd Street N., P.O. Box 84
Pine River, MN 56474
218-587-2171
http://krls.org

Lake Agassiz Regional Library
118 5th Street S.
Moorhead, MN 56560
218-233-3757
https://larl.org

Metropolitan Library Service Agency (MELSA) / Metronet
1619 Dayton Ave., Suite 314
St. Paul, MN 55104
651-645-5731
http://www.melsa.org/
651-646-0475
http://metrolibraries.net/

Northern Lights Library Network (NLLN)
1104 7th Ave. S.
Moorhead, MN 56563
218-477-2934
https://nlln.org

Northwest Regional Library
210 LaBree Ave. N., P.O. Box 593
Thief River Falls, MN 56701
218-681-1066
http://nwrlib.org

Pioneerland Library System
410 5th Street S.W.
Willmar, MN 56201
320-235-6106
https://www.pioneerland.lib.mn.us

Plum Creek Library System Headquarters
290 S. Lake Street
Worthington, MN 56187
507-376-5803 800-439-3492
http://www.plumcreeklibrary.org

Prairielands Library Exchange
109 South 5th Street
Marshall, MN 56258
507-532-9013 800-788-6479
https://www.prairielands.org/

Southeastern Libraries Cooperating/Southeast Library Systems (SELCO/SELS)
2600 19th Street N.W.
Rochester, MN 55901
507-288-5513 800-992-5061
https://www.selco.info

Traverse des Sioux Library System
1400 Madison Ave., Suite 622
Mankato, MN 56001
507-625-6169
https://tdslib.org/

Viking Library System
1915 Fir Ave. W.
Fergus Falls, MN 56537
218-739-5286
https://www.viking.lib.mn.us

Law Libraries

Anoka County Law Library
325 E. Main Street
Anoka, MN 55303
763-422-7487
https://www.anokacounty.us/346/Law-Library

Carver County Law Library
Carver County Government Center
604 E. Fourth Street
Chaska, MN 55318
952-361-1564
https://www.carverlib.org/locations/law-library

Clay County Law Library
Clay County Courthouse -Lower level
807 11th Street N., P.O. Box 280
Moorhead, MN 56561
218-299-7522
https://claycountymn.gov/629/Law-Library

Dakota County Law Library - Hastings Judicial Center
1560 W. Highway 55
Hastings, MN 55033
651-438-8080
https://www.co.dakota.mn.us/LawJustice/LawLibrary/Pages/default.aspx

Mitchell Hamline School of Law
Warren E. Burger Law Library
875 Summit Ave.
St. Paul, MN 55105
651-290-6424
https://mitchellhamline.edu/library/

Hennepin County Law Library
C-2451 Government Center
300 S. 6th Street
Minneapolis, MN 55487
612-348-3022
https://www.hclawlib.org/

Minnesota State Law Library
Room G25, Minnesota Judicial Center
25 Rev. Dr. Martin Luther King, Jr. Blvd.
St. Paul, MN 55155
651-296-2775 800-627-3529 (TTY)
https://mn.gov/law-library/

Olmsted County Law Library
151 4th Street S.E., 1st Floor
Rochester, MN 55904
507-328-7605
https://www.olmstedlawlibrary.com/

Ramsey County Law Library
1815 Courthouse
15 Kellogg Blvd. W.
St. Paul, MN 55102
651-266-8391
https://www.ramseycounty.us/residents/libraries/law-library

St. Louis County Law Library
St. Louis County Government Center
100 North 5th Ave. W.
Duluth, MN 55802
218-726-2611 800-450-9777
https://www.stlouiscountymn.gov/departments-a-z/law-library

Scott County Law Library
Scott County Government Center
200 4th Ave. W.
Shakopee, MN 55379
952-496-8713
https://www.scottcountymn.gov/778/Law-Library

Sherburne County Law Library
Sherburne County Government Center
13880 Highway 10
Elk River, MN 55330-4608
763-229-3056
https://www.co.sherburne.mn.us/598/Law-Library

Stearns County Law Help Center
725 Courthouse Square, Room 105
St. Cloud, MN 56303
320-656-3678
https://www.stearnscountymn.gov/428/Law-Help-Center

U.S. Eighth Circuit Court Libraries
http://www.lb8.uscourts.gov

Minneapolis Branch:
1102 U.S. Courthouse
300 South Fourth Street
Minneapolis, Minnesota 55415
612-664-5830

St. Paul Branch:
316 N. Robert Street
100 Federal Building St. Paul, MN 55101
651-848-1300

University of Minnesota Law Library
120 Mondale Hall, U of M
229 19th Ave. S.
Minneapolis, MN 55455
612-625-1000
https://library.law.umn.edu

University of St. Thomas
Shoenecker Law Library
1000 LaSalle Ave.
Minneapolis, MN 55403
651-962-4902 | libweb@stthomas.edu
https://www.stthomas.edu/libraries/about/

Washington County Law Library
Government Center
14949 62nd St. N.
P.O. Box 6
Stillwater, MN 55082
651-430-6330
https://www.washcolib.org/lawlibrary

Note: There are county law libraries in each county. Information about the County Law Library Program is available from the Minnesota State Law Library. https://mn.gov/law-library/research-links/county-law-libraries.jsp

Government Document Depository Libraries

Anoka County Library
Northtown Library
711 Highway 10 N.E.
Blaine, MN 55434-2398
763-717-3267
https://www.anokacounty.us/1758/Libraries

Bemidji State University
A.C. Clark Library
1500 Birchmont Drive N.E.
Bemidji, MN 56601-2699
218-755-3342
https://www.bemidjistate.edu/library/

Carleton College
Lawrence McKinley Gould Library
One North College Street
Northfield, MN 55057
507-646-4264
https://apps.carleton.edu/campus/library/about/collections/government/

Dakota County Library System
Wescott Library
1340 Wescott Road
Eagan, MN 55123-1099
651-688-1500
https://www.co.dakota.mn.us/library

Duluth Public Library
520 West Superior Street
Duluth, MN 55802-1578
218-723-4243
http://www.duluthlibrary.org/

Gustavus Adolphus College
Folke Bernadotte Memorial Library
800 W. College Ave.
St. Peter, MN 56082
507-933-7567
https://gustavus.edu/library/govdocs/index.php

Hennepin County Library System
Minneapolis Central Library
Business/Science/Government Documents Division
300 Nicollet Ave.
Minneapolis, MN 55401
612-543-8095
https://www.hclib.org/browse/online-resources?category=Government-and-politics

Minnesota State Law Library
Room G25, Minnesota Judicial Center
25 Rev. Martin Luther King, Jr. Blvd.
St. Paul, MN 55155
651-296-2775
https://mn.gov/law-library/

Minnesota State University–Mankato
Memorial Library
601 Maywood Ave.
Mankato, MN 56002-8419
507-389-5952
http://lib.mnsu.edu/govdoc/index.html

Minnesota State University Moorhead
Livingston Lord Library
1104 7th Ave. S.
Moorhead, MN 56563
218-236-2349
https://www2.mnstate.edu/library/

Mitchell Hamline School of Law
Warren E. Burger Law Library
875 Summit Ave.
St. Paul, MN 55105
651-290-6424
https://mitchellhamline.edu/library/

St. Cloud State University
Learning Resources and Technical Services
James W. Miller Learning Resource Center, MC130-B
720 4th Ave. S.
St. Cloud, MN 56301-4998
320-308-4755
https://www.stcloudstate.edu/library/research/default.aspx

St. Olaf College
Rolvaag Memorial Library
1510 St. Olaf Ave.
Northfield, MN 55057-1093
507-646-3452
https://www.stolaf.edu/library/index.cfm

St. Paul Public Library
Central Library
Government Publications
90 W. 4th Street
St. Paul, MN 55102
651-226-7000
https://sppl.org/government-documents/

Southwest Minnesota State University Library
McFarland Library - Government Documents
1501 State Street
Marshall, MN 56258
507-537-6176
http://www.smsu.edu/library/collections.html

University of Minnesota
Government Publications Library
499 Wilson Library
309 19th Ave. S.
Minneapolis, MN 55455
612-624-0241 | govref@umn.edu
https://www.lib.umn.edu/govpubs

University of Minnesota
Magrath Library
Government Documents
1984 Buford Ave.
St. Paul, MN 55108
612-624-1212
https://www.lib.umn.edu/magrath

University of Minnesota Morris
Rodney A. Briggs Library
600 E. 4th Street
Morris, MN 56267
320-589-6175
https://library.morris.umn.edu/about-library/government-publications

University of Minnesota -Duluth
Kathryn A. Martin Library L274
416 Library Drive
Duluth, MN 55812
218-726-8100
https://lib.d.umn.edu/research-collections/government-information

Winona State University
Main Library
176 West Mark Street
Winona, MN 55987
507-457-5148
https://www.winona.edu/library/collections/govresources.asp

LOCAL ASSISTANCE FOR SMALL BUSINESSES

Business Accelerators / Incubators / Other

City Food Studio
3722 Chicago Ave. S.
Minneapolis, MN 55407
612-315-3399 | kitchen@cityfoodstudio.com
https://cityfoodstudio.com/

Cleantech Open Midwest
University of St. Thomas
1000 LaSalle Ave.
Minneapolis, MN 55403
midwest@cleantechopen.org
https://midwest.cleantechopen.org/

East Side Neighborhood Development Company, Inc.
965 Payne Ave., Suite 200
St. Paul, Minnesota 55130
651-288-8746
https://esndc.org/?home

Foodblazer
Information and legal advice for food entrepreneurs.
http://www.foodblazer.com/

Frogtown Entrepreneur Center / Frogtown Square
Neighborhood Development Center (NDC)
663 University Ave., Suite 200
St. Paul, MN 55104
651-291-2480
http://www.ndc-mn.org/what-we-do/business-incubators/

Garden Fresh Fresh Farms CSA & Commercial Kitchen
1065 MN Highway 36 E.
Maplewood, MN 55109
612-886-6631
http://www.gardenfreshfarms.com/

GIA Kitchen
955 N. Mackubin Street
St. Paul, MN 55117
https://sites.google.com/site/giakitchen/

Glen Nelson Center
500 Osborn370
370 Wabasha Street
St. Paul, MN 55102
651-333-3123
https://www.glennelson.org/

Kindred Kitchen
1206 W. Broadway Ave., Suite 180
Minneapolis, MN 55411
612-584-0728
https://www.kindredkitchen.org

Maker to Market Accelerator
Lakewinds Food Co-op and The Good Acre collaborated to create Maker to Market, a homegrown food accelerator
https://makertomarketmn.com/

Mayo Clinic Business Accelerator
221 First Ave. S.W., Suite 202
Rochester, MN 55902
507-288-0208
http://www.mcbusaccel.com

Mercado Central
Neighborhood Development Center (NDC)
1515 E. Lake Street
Minneapolis, MN 55407
612-728-5485 | info@mimercadocentral.com
http://mimercadocentral.com/

Midtown Global Market
Neighborhood Development Center (NDC)
920 E. Lake Street
Minneapolis, MN 55407
612-876-4451
https://www.midtownglobalmarket.org

Midwest Pantry
3147 California Street, Suite 100
Minneapolis, MN 55418
651-387-3218
http://www.midwestpantry.com/

MN Foodcrafters
865 Pierce Butler Route
St. Paul, MN 55104
651-336-7880

North Made
Bolin Headquarters
2523 Wayzata Blvd., Suite 300
Minneapolis, MN 55405
612-374-1200 800-876-6264
info@north-made.com
http://www.north-made.com/

Northfield Enterprise Center
510 Washington Street
Northfield, MN 55057
507-786-9065
director@northfieldenterprisecenter.com
http://www.northfieldenterprisecenter.com

Northside Economic Opportunity Network (NEON)
1007 W. Broadway Ave. N.
Minneapolis, MN 55411
612-302-1505 | info@neon-mn.org
https://www.neon-mn.org/

North Shore Business Enterprise Center
P.O. Box 248
Two Harbors, MN 55616
218-834-3384 | nsbec@lakenet.com
https://www.nsbec.com

Owatonna Area Business Development Center
1065 S.W. 24th Street
Owatonna, MN 55060
507-451-0517
https://www.owatonna.biz/

Pine City Area
Pine Innovation Center
315 Main Street S., Suite 155
Pine City, MN 55063
320-322-4040
http://www.pinecitychamber.com/pine-innovation-center/

Plaza Verde
Neighborhood Development Center (NDC)
1516 E. Lake Street
Minneapolis, MN 55407
651-291-2480
http://www.ndc-mn.org/what-we-do/business-incubators/

Red Wing Ignite
419 Bush Street
Red Wing, MN 55066
651-327-2115
http://www.redwingignite.org

University Enterprise Laboratories (UEL) - U of M
Facility with lab, office space, and supportive programming for early-stage life science, biotech, agriculture, healthcare, materials science, and analytics companies.
1000 Westgate, Suite 101
St. Paul, MN 55114
612-641-2800 | info@uelmn.org
http://www.uelmn.org

University of Minnesota
Office for Business & Community Economic Development
Business Development training, workshops, meet & greets as well as an annual Supplier Diversity Expo.
2221 University Ave. S.E., Suite 136
Minneapolis, Minnesota 55414
612-624-0530 | bced@umn.edu
https://bced.umn.edu

University of MN Duluth (UMD)
Natural Resources Research Institute (NRRI)
5013 Miller Trunk Highway
Hermantown, MN 55811
218-788-2694 800-234-0054 | nrriinfo@d.umn.edu
https://www.nrri.umn.edu/about/discover-nrri/what-nrri

Valley Technology Park
510 County Road 71
Crookston, MN 56716
218-470-2000
http://www.valleytech.org

West Broadway Business & Area Coalition (WBC)
1011 W. Broadway Ave., Suite #202
Minneapolis, MN 55411
612-353-5178 | info@westbroadway.org
http://westbroadway.org/

MANAGEMENT ASSISTANCE, GENERAL

SCORE

SCORE is a 501(c)(3) nonprofit organization and a resource partner of the U.S. Small Business Administration (SBA). The nation's largest network of volunteer, expert business mentors, is dedicated to helping small businesses get off the ground, grow and achieve their goals.

SCORE provides a wide range of services to established and budding business owners alike, including: Mentoring; Webinars and Courses on Demand; Library of Online Resources; and Local Events.

https://www.score.org/

SCORE Minnesota Chapter Offices

Central Minnesota SCORE
https://centralminnesota.score.org

Main Office
355 5th Ave. S.
St. Cloud, MN 56301
320-240-1332 | central.mn@scorevolunteer.org

Alexandria SCORE
1601 Jefferson Street
Alexandria, MN 56308
320-762-4510

Brainerd SCORE
501 West College Drive
Brainerd, MN 56401
218-855-8151

Park Rapids SCORE
301 Court Ave.
Park Rapids MN 56470
218-732-2259

Twin Ports -Duluth and Superior region
Office: 800-933-0346, x: 8151
Direct: 218-855-8151

Minneapolis SCORE
https://minneapolis.score.org

Main Office
8700 W. 36th Street, Suite 125A
St. Louis Park, MN 55426
952-938-4570 | minneapolis.score@gmail.com

- **Business Plan Center**
  (Live business plans only - mentor referral required)

- **Video Mentoring only**
  (All mentoring scheduled here is done through the Internet via video conferencing)

- **At Large**

Blaine Library / Northtown Library [Walk in only]
711 County Rd 10 N.E.
Blaine, MN, 55434
952-938-4570

Brookdale Library [Walk in only]
6125 Shingle Creek Pkwy
Brooklyn Center, MN, 55430
612-543-5600

Brooklyn Park Library [Walk in only]
8500 W Broadway Ave.
Brooklyn Park, MN, 55443
612-543-6225

Maple Grove Library [Walk in only]
8001 Main Street N.
Maple Grove, MN, 55369
952-938-4570

Minneapolis Central Library
300 Nicollet Mall
Minneapolis, MN, 55401
952-938-4570

Plymouth Library
- 2nd Tuesday of Every Month from 3– 6pm
  [Walk In Only - No Scheduled Appointments]
15700 36th Ave N
Plymouth, MN, 55446
952-938-4570

Ridgedale Library
12601 Ridgedale Drive
Minnetonka, MN, 55305
612-543-8800

Rum River Library [Walk in only]
4201 6th Ave
Anoka, MN, 55303
952-938-4570

Southdale Library - Branch
7001 York Ave S
Edina, MN, 55435
952) 938-4570

South Central Minnesota SCORE
https://southcentralminnesota.score.org

525 Florence Ave.
Owatonna, MN 55060
507-455-3215 | scmnscore@gmail.com

South Metro SCORE
https://southmetro.score.org

350 W. Burnsville Parkway, Suite 425
Burnsville, MN 55337
952-890-7020 | SouthMETRO@SCORE-MN.org

Southeast Minnesota SCORE
https://seminnesota.score.org/

Main Office
220 South Broadway, Suite 100
Rochester, MN 55904
507-200-0760 | sore0406@scorevolunteer.org

Austin Branch
329 Main Street N., Suite 102
Austin, MN 55912
507-269-7252

St. Paul SCORE
https://stpaul.score.org
2345 Rice Street, Suite 207
Roseville, MN 55113
651-632-8937 | stpaul@scorevolunteer.org

Minnesota Small Business Development Centers (Mn SBDCs)
No cost counseling and business consulting.
State Administrative Office
1st National Bank Building
332 Minnesota Street, Suite E200
St. Paul, MN 55101-1351
651-259-7423 877-653-8333
https://mn.gov/deed/business/help/sbdc/

Twin Cities Metro Area Mn SBDC
University of St. Thomas
Terrance Murphy Hall 100
1000 LaSalle Ave.
Minneapolis, MN 55403
651-962-4500
https://business.stthomas.edu/centers-institutes/schulze-school/about-schulze/small-business-dev-center/

Satellite/Outreach Centers:

Metropolitan Economic Development Assoc. (MEDA)
1256 Penn Avenue North
Minneapolis, MN 55411
612-259-6564
https://www.meda.net

Northwest Mn SBDC
University of Minnesota - Northwest MN Foundation
201 3rd Street N.W.
Bemidji, MN 56602
218-755-4255 | nwsbdc@nwmf.org
https://www.nwsbdc.org

Satellite/Outreach Centers:

University of Minnesota Crookston
218-281-8318

North Central Mn SBDC
Central Lakes College
501 W. College Drive
Brainerd, MN 56401
218-855-8140
http://www.clcmn.edu/small-business-development-center/

Satellite/Outreach Centers:

Cass County Economic Development Corporation
303 Minnesota Ave. W.
Walker, MN 56484
218-547-7262 | cass.edc@co.cass.mn.us
https://www.casscountyedc.com

Chisago County HRA/EDA
38871 7th Ave.
North Branch, MN 55056
651-674-5664
http://www.chisagocounty.org

Kanabec County Economic Development Authority
320-209-5031

Todd County Development Corporation
347 Central Ave.
Long Prairie, MN 56347
320-732-2128
http://www.toddcountydevelopment.org/business-resources/technical-assistance

Northeast Mn SBDC
11 E. Superior Street, Suite 210
Duluth, MN 55802
218-726-7298 | info@nesbdc.org

Satellite/Outreach Centers:

Cook County / Grand Marais Economic Development Authority
Grand Marais
218-387-3112

Itasca Economic Development Corporation -Grand Rapids,
218-326-9411

Natural Resources Research Inst. (NRRI) -Hermantown
218-788-2694

Hibbing / Chisholm
218-749-7752

Koochiching Economic Development Association
International Falls
218-283-8585

Quad Cities -Virginia, Eveleth, Gilbert, and Mt. Iron,
Mesabi Range Community & Technical College - Virginia
218-749-7752

West Central Mn SBDC
Concordia College
Grant Center 220
1310 8th Street S.
Moorhead, MN 56562
218-299-3037 | sbdc@cord.edu
https://westcentralmnsbdc.com

Southwest Mn SBDC
Southwest Minnesota State University
1501 State Street – ST 201
Marshall, MN 56258
507-537-7386 | sbdc@smsu.edu
https://www.sbdcassistance.com

South Central Mn SBDC
Mankato State University
424 North Riverfront Drive, Suite 101
Mankato, MN 56001
507-389-8875 | info@myminnesotabusiness.com
https://www.myminnesotabusiness.com

Southeast Mn SBDC
Rochester Community & Technical College
1926 College View Drive S.E.
Rochester, MN 55904
507-285-7536
http://www.rochestersbdc.com/

Satellite/Outreach Centers:

Development Corporation of Austin (DCA)
507-443-9495

Community and Economic Development Associates
Chatfield
507-867-3164

Rice County Small Business Development Center
Faribault
507-334-4381

Owatonna Area Business Development Center
Owatonna
507-451-0517
https://www.owatonna.biz/

Winona -The Garage Cowork Space
507-459-3060

Central Mn SBDC
St. Cloud State University
355 5th Ave. S.
St. Cloud, MN 56301
320-308-4842
https://www.stcloudstate.edu/sbdc/

Other

AURI (Agricultural Utilization Research Institute)
Helps develop new uses for agricultural products through science and technology, partnering with businesses and entrepreneurs.
https://www.auri.org/

Facilities:

Crookston / Marshall / St. Paul / Waseca
218-281-7600

B.E.S.T. (Business & Entrepreneurial Support Team) of Waseca County
508 S. State Street
Waseca, MN 56093
507-833-9281
http://discoverwaseca.com/resources/economic-development/b-e-s-t/

Bunker Labs
National 501(c)(3) not-for-profit organization built by military veteran entrepreneurs to empower other military veterans as leaders in innovation.
400 S. 4th Street #401
Minneapolis, MN 55415
952-212-6320
https://bunkerlabs.org

CEDA (Community & Economic Development Assoc.)
Assist small businesses with start-up, expansion, relocation, business plans, loan analysis, and marketing.
1500 South Highway 52 PO Box 483
Chatfield, MN 55923
507-867-3164
https://www.cedausa.com/

Metropolitan Consortium of Community Developers (MCCD) - Open to Business Program
3137 Chicago Ave.
Minneapolis, MN 55407
612-789-7337 | info@opentobusinessmn.org
https://www.mccdmn.org/open-to-business

Minneapolis, City of
Business Technical Assistance Program (B-TAP)
City of Minneapolis program was created to provide consulting support to businesses located in Minneapolis.
612-673-5095 | btap@minneapolismn.gov
http://www2.minneapolismn.gov/business/B-TAP

St. Paul
Planning & Economic Development (PED)
Business Technical Assistance
City Hall Annex
25 West 4th Street, Suite 1300
St. Paul, MN 55102
651-266-6600
https://www.stpaul.gov/departments/planning-economic-development

Open for Business
https://www.stpaul.gov/businesses/OpenForBusiness

University of Minnesota
Office for Business & Community Economic & Dev.
Business Development Services
Provides management and technical assistance to small businesses to provide educational, legal and accounting resources/tools, workshops, seminars, customized training, and direct coaching support.
2221 University Ave. S.E., Suite 136
Minneapolis, Minnesota 55414
612-624-3704 | bced@umn.edu
https://bced.umn.edu/

University of Minnesota Extension
Retaining businesses in your community
Program is designed to help communities retain and expand their businesses.
https://extension.umn.edu/economic-development/retaining-community-businessesy

Grow North MN
Creates unique programs and events for entrepreneurs, organizations and institutions; resource database and library.
University of Minnesota -Holmes Center for Entrepreneurship
321 19th Ave. S.
Minneapolis, MN 55445
612-625-0027 | hello@grownorthmn.com
https://carlsonschool.umn.edu/grownorth

Minnesota Materials Exchange
Providing a business-reuse network.
200 Oak Street S.E., Suite 350-1
Minneapolis, MN 55455
612-624-4633 800-247-0015
https://mnexchange.org/

Women Entrepreneurs of Minnesota
P.O. Box 16003
Minneapolis, MN 55416
info@wemn.org
https://wemn.org/

MANAGEMENT ASSISTANCE FOR MINORITY BUSINESSES

African Development Center (ADC) of Minnesota
1931 South 5th Street
Minneapolis, MN 55454
612-333-4772 877-232-4775
http://www.adcminnesota.org

ADC Rochester
415 16th Street S.W.
Rochester, MN 55902
507-282-7333 877-232-4775

ADC Willmar
518 Litchfield Ave. S.W.
Willmar, MN 56201
320-262-8545 877-232-4775

African Economic Development Solutions (AEDS)
1821 University Ave. W., Suite S-145
St. Paul, MN 55104
651-646-9411 | info@aeds-mn.org
http://aeds-mn.org/

Asian Economic Development Association (AEDA)
422 University Ave. W., Suite 14
St. Paul, MN 55103
651-222-7798 | info@aeda-mn.org

India Chamber of Commerce
12527 Central Ave. N.E., Suite 189
Minneapolis, MN 55434
612-405-3050 | info@indiachamber.org
http://www.indiachamber.org

Latino Economic Development Center (LEDC)
http://www.ledc-mn.org

Plaza Los Lagos: Minneapolis Office
1510 E. Lake Street, Lower Level
Minneapolis, MN 55407
651-395-4030

East Side Enterprise Center: St. Paul Office
804 Margaret Street
St. Paul, MN 55106
651-621-2758

Metropolitan Economic Development Association (MEDA) / Minority Business Development Agency (MDBA) Business Center
MBDA Business Center is a part of a nationwide network of thirty-nine centers. Operated by MEDA, the MBDA is the only federal agency created specifically to foster the growth of minority owned businesses in America.
1256 Penn Avenue North
Minneapolis, MN 55411
612-332-6332 | info@meda.net
https://www.mbda.gov/businesscenters/minneapolis#10/44.9803/-93.2663

Minnesota American Indian Chamber of Commerce
2345 Rice Street, Suite 200
St. Paul, MN 55113
612-877-2117 | info@maicc.org
https://www.maicc.org

Minnesota Black Chamber of Commerce
401 N. Robert Street, Suite 150
St. Paul, MN 55101
651-224-4320
http://www.minnesotabcc.org

Minnesota Hmong Chamber of Commerce
965 Payne Ave., Suite 200
St. Paul, MN 55130
651-504-5588 | info@hmongchamber.com
https://www.hmongchamber.com

Minnesota Indigenous Business Alliance
P.O. Box 40354
St. Paul, MN 55104
https://www.mniba.org

North Central Minnesota Minority Supplier Development Council (NCMSDC)
111 3rd Ave. S., Suite 240
Minneapolis MN 55401
612-465-8881 | info@mmsdc.org
http://wyww.northcentralmsdc.net

Native American Community Development Institute (NACDI)
1414 E. Franklin Ave.
Minneapolis, MN 55404
612-235-4976 | info@nacdi.org
https://www.nacdi.org

Neighborhood Development Center (NDC)
663 University Ave. W., Suite 200
St. Paul, MN 55104
651-291-2480
http://www.ndc-mn.org

Northside Economic Opportunity Network (NEON)
1007 W. Broadway Ave. N.
Minneapolis, MN 55411
612- 302-1505 | info@neon-mn.org
https://www.neon-mn.org

Quorom
310 East 38th Street, Suite 209
Minneapolis, MN 55409
612-460-8153 | info@twincitiesquorum.com
http://www.twincitiesquorum.com/

Red Lake Nation Planning & Economic Department
P.O. Box 587
Red Lake, MN 56671
218-679-1460
https://www.redlakenation.org/planning-and-economic-development/

Women's Business Centers (WBCs)
WomenVenture
2021 E. Hennepin Ave., Suite 200
Minneapolis, MN 55413
612-224-9540
https://www.womenventure.org

Women's Business Alliance North
Entrepreneur Fund, Inc.
202 W. Superior Street, Suite 311
Duluth, MN 55802
218-623-5747
https://www.entrepreneurfund.org/womens-business-alliance/

Women's Business Alliance Central
Entrepreneur Fund, Inc.
309 1st St NE, Suite 103
Little Falls, MN 56345
218-735-6033
https://www.entrepreneurfund.org/womens-business-alliance/

Women's Business Development Center (WBDC) – Minnesota
Provides WBE (Women's Business Enterprise) Certification to majority-owned women's businesses in Minnesota.
2021 E. Hennepin Ave., Suite 200
Minneapolis, MN 55413
612-259-6584 | wbdc-mn@wbdc.org
https://www.wbdc.org/mn/

Women's Business Enterprise National Council (WBENC)
WBE (Women's Business Enterprise) Certification
https://www.wbenc.org/certification-faqs/

PROCUREMENT / PURCHASING / CERTIFICATION / OTHER ASSISTANCE

FEDERAL CONTACTS

Federal Service Desk
866-606-8220
https://www.fsd.gov

beta.sam.gov
The System for Award Management (SAM) is the Official U.S. Government system that consolidated the capabilities of CCR/FedReg, ORCA, and EPLS.
https://beta.sam.gov/

Federal Procurement Data System (FDPS)
FDPS contains detailed information on contract actions over $25,000.
https://www.fpds.gov/fpdsng_cms/index.php/en/

U.S. Department of Commerce
Minority Business Development Agency (MBDA)
A federal agency created to foster the establishment and growth of minority-owned businesses in America.
1401 Constitution Ave. N.W.
Washington, D.C. 20230
202-482-1940
https://www.mbda.gov

U.S. Department of Labor (DOL)
Office of Small and Disadvantaged Business Utilization (OSDBU)
Administers DOL's responsibility to ensure procurement opportunities for small businesses, small disadvantaged businesses, women-owned small businesses, HUBZone businesses, and businesses owned by service-disabled veterans.
200 Constitution Ave. N.W.
Washington, DC 20210
866-487-2365
https://www.dol.gov/agencies/oasam/business-operations-center/osdbu/programs

U.S. Small Business Administration (SBA)
https://www.sba.gov

8(a) Business Development Program
https://www.sba.gov/contracting/government-contracting-programs/8a-business-development-program

Contracting
https://www.sba.gov/contracting

HUBZone Program
https://www.sba.gov/contracting/government-contracting-programs/hubzone-program

Veterans Affairs, U.S. Department of
Vendor Information Pages
202-303-3260
https://www.va.gov

Office of Small & Disadvantaged Business (OSBDU)
Verification Assistance Program
https://www.vip.vetbiz.va.gov/

STATE CONTACTS

Minnesota Department of Administration
112 Administration Building
50 Sherburne Ave.
St. Paul, MN 55155

Office of State Procurement (OSP)
Customer and Vendor Services Help line
651-296-2600 800-627-3529 (Minnesota Relay)
http://www.mmd.admin.state.mn.us

Vendor Information
https://mn.gov/admin/business/vendor-info/

Vendor Registration
http://www.mmd.admin.state.mn.us/mn02000.htm

Office of Equity in Procurement (OEP)
Office helps ensure greater equity in state contracting and construction. It certifies Minnesota small businesses are targeted groups, economically disadvantaged, or veteran-owned.
651-201-2402 | procurement.equity@state.mn.us
https://mn.gov/admin/business/vendor-info/oep/

Small Business Procurement Program
The Materials Management Division (MMD) operates a program for Targeted Group, Economically Disadvantaged and Veteran-Owned small businesses.

https://mn.gov/admin/business/vendor-info/oep/sbcp/

Minnesota Procurement Technical Assistance Center (MN PTAC)
Provides technical and marketing assistance to all Minnesota businesses interested in selling their products and services to the government on the federal, state, and local levels.
https://mn.gov/admin/business/vendor-info/ptac/

Minnesota Unified Certification Program (Mn/UCP)
Minnesota Department Transportation (MnDOT), Metropolitan Airports Commission (MAC), Metropolitan Council, & the City of Minneapolis. A one-stop shop for certification of Disadvantaged Business Enterprises (DBEs) on U.S. Department of Transportation contracts in Minnesota.
https://mnucp.org

City of Minneapolis

Contract Compliance Division
612-673-3012
http://www2.minneapolismn.gov/civilrights/contract compliance/index.htm

Metropolitan Airports Commission (MAC)
Office of Diversity
Disadvantaged Business Enterprise (DBE)
612-726-8193
https://metrocouncil.org/Transportation/Projects/Light-Rail-Projects/Southwest-LRT/Construction/Jobs-and-Training/Disadvantaged-Business-Enterprises.aspx

Metropolitan Council
Disadvantaged Business Enterprise (DBE) Program
https://metrocouncil.org/About-Us/What-We-Do/Office-of-Equal-Opportunity/Small-Business-Programs/Disadvantaged-Business-Program.aspx

MnDOT -Office of Civil Rights
Disadvantaged Business Enterprise (DBE)
651-366-3071
http://www.dot.state.mn.us/civilrights/dbe.html

REGIONAL / COUNTY / CITY CONTACTS

Women's Business Development Center (WBDC) – Minnesota
2021 E. Hennepin Ave., Suite 200
Minneapolis, MN 55413
612-259-6584 | wbdc-mn@wbdc.org
https://www.wbdc.org/mn/

Metropolitan Council
Office of Diversity
390 Robert Street N.
St. Paul, MN 55101
651-602-1000

Doing Business with the Council
https://metrocouncil.org/About-Us/What-We-Do/Doing Business.aspx

Small Business Programs
https://metrocouncil.org/About-Us/What-We-Do/Doing Business/Small-Business-Programs.aspx

Central Certification Program (CERT)
Small business certification program used by Hennepin & Ramsey Counties and City of St. Paul Owned Business Enterprise (MBE), Women-Owned Business Enterprise (WBE), and Small Business Enterprise (SBE).
c/o Contract and Analysis Services
City Hall/Courthouse 280
15 W. Kellogg Blvd.
Saint Paul, MN 55102
651-266-8900
https://www.stpaul.gov/departments/human-rights-equal-economic-opportunity/contract-compliance-business-development/central

Hennepin County
A-1730 Government Center
300 South Sixth Street
Minneapolis, MN 55487-0175
612-348-3181
https://www.hennepin.us/business/work-with-henn-co/contracting-with-hennepin-county

Ramsey County
Contracts & Vendors
https://www.ramseycounty.us/businesses/doing-business-ramsey-county/contracts-vendors

City of Minneapolis
Procurement
http://www.minneapolismn.gov/finance/procurement/index.htm

City of St. Paul
https://www.stpaulbids.com/lmp/SourcingSupplier/controller.servlet?context.session.key.SupplierGroup=1&context.dataarea=lmp

Anoka County Purchasing
Government Center
2100 3rd Ave., Suite 300
Anoka, MN 55303
763-323-5300
https://www.anokacounty.us/287/Purchasing

Olmsted County Purchasing
2122 Campus Dr. S.E., Suite 200
Rochester, MN 55904
507-328-7085
https://www.co.olmsted.mn.us/finance/Pages/Purchasing.aspx

St. Louis County Purchasing
Richard H. Hansen Transportation and Public Works Complex
4787 Midway Road
Duluth, MN 55811
218-726-2666
https://www.stlouiscountymn.gov/departments-a-z/purchasing/registration-and-solicitations

Stearns County
Procurement Department
705 Courthouse Square, Room 47
St. Cloud, MN 56303-4701
320-656-3607
https://www.stearnscountymn.gov/1114/Procurement

Bloomington
Finance Department - Purchasing Section
1800 W. Old Shakopee Road
Bloomington, MN 55431-3027
952-563-8795
https://www.bloomingtonmn.gov/purchasing

Duluth
Purchasing Department
411 W. 1st Street, Room 100
Duluth, MN 55802
218-730-5340
https://www.duluthmn.gov/purchasing/

Note: This is only a partial listing of city and county offices. Further information can be obtained by contacting individual city and county offices.

MINORITY SUPPLIER ASSISTANCE

Metropolitan Economic Development Association (MEDA)
Provides business development services, business financing and access to market opportunities to support entrepreneurs of color.
1256 Penn Avenue North
Minneapolis, MN 55411
612-332-6332
http://www.meda.net

North Central Minnesota Minority Supplier Development Council (NCMSDC)
111 3rd Ave. S., Suite 240
Minneapolis MN 55401
612-465-8881 | info@mmsdc.org
http://www.northcentralmsdc.net

OTHER

D-U-N-S Number
Dun & Bradstreet (D&B) provides a D-U-N-S Number, a unique nine digit identification number, for each physical location of your business. D-U-N-S Number assignment is FREE for all businesses required to register with the U.S. Federal government for contracts or grants.
http://fedgov.dnb.com/webform

MN-Small Business Innovation Research (SBIR) / Small Business Technology Transfer (STTR)
Program offers free, confidential, one-on-one assistance in business development and technology commercialization to successfully compete in the federal SBIR/STTR programs.
MHTA (MN High Tech Association)
400 South 4th Street, Suite 416
Minneapolis, MN 55415
952-230-4555
https://www.mhta.org/mnsbir/

Enterprise Minnesota
Enterprise Minnesota is an ISO 9001:2008 certified consulting organization that works with medium and smaller manufacturing enterprises to help them compete and grow profitably.
2100 Summer Street N.E., Suite 150
Minneapolis, MN 55413
612-373-2900
https://www.enterpriseminnesota.org/

TAX AND ACCOUNTING ASSISTANCE

Minnesota Association of Public Accountants
PO Box 301
Big Lake, MN 55309
612-366-1983 | admin@mapa-mn.com
https://mapa-mn.com/

Minnesota Society of Certified Public Accountants
1650 W. 82nd Street, Suite 600
Bloomington, MN 55431
952-831-2707 800-331-4288
https://www.mncpa.org

Minnesota Society of Enrolled Agents
https://www.mnsea.org

Prepare + Prosper
2610 University Ave. W., Suite 450
St. Paul, MN 55114
651-287-0187 | contact@prepareandprosper.org
http://prepareandprosper.org

ADDITIONAL RESOURCES

ADA INFORMATION

ADA.gov
Americans with Disabilities Act (ADA) Assistance
Information and technical assistance on the Americans with Disabilities Act.
https://www.ada.gov/

ADA Business Connection
https://www.ada.gov/business.htm

ADA Minnesota

Resource providing Minnesota citizens with disabilities, businesses, communities, government, universities and colleges assistance in implementing the ADA.

530 Robert Street N.
St. Paul, MN 55104
651-603-2015 (Voice) 888-630-9793
http://adaminnesota.org/

COUNTY LICENSING AGENTS

Anoka County
License Bureau / Government Center
2100 3rd Ave., Suite 600
Anoka, MN 55303
763-324-4200
https://www.anokacounty.us/1362/Licenses-Permits

Clay County
Auditor -Clay County Courthouse 2nd Floor
807 11th Street N., 2nd Floor
Moorhead, MN 56560
218-299-5006
https://claycountymn.gov/162/Auditor

Dakota County
1590 Highway 55
Hastings, MN 55033
651-554-6600 952-891-7570
https://www.co.dakota.mn.us/Permits/SLC/Pages/default.aspx

Hennepin County
Government Center -Lower Level, Suite A-025
300 South Sixth Street
Minneapolis, MN 55487
612-348-8240 | License.GC@hennepin.us
https://www.hennepin.us/business#licenses-permits

Olmsted County
Public Health Services
2100 Campus Drive S.E., Suite 100
Rochester, MN 55904
507-328-7500
https://www.co.olmsted.mn.us/applyfor/licenses/Pages/default.aspx

Ramsey County
Property Records & Revenue Department
90 West Plato Blvd.
St. Paul, MN 55107
651-266-2000

Licenses, Permits & Inspections
https://www.ramseycounty.us/business/licenses-permits-inspections

Food & Vending
https://www.ramseycounty.us/businesses/licenses-permits-inspections/licenses-inspections/food-vending

Scott County
Government Center
200 Fourth Ave. W.
Shakopee, MN 55379
952-445-7750
https://www.scottcountymn.gov/334/Licenses-Permits

Sherburne County
Auditor/Treasurer
13880 Business Center Drive N.W.
Elk River, MN 55330
763-765-4351 800-438-0576
https://www.co.sherburne.mn.us/182/Auditor-Treasurer

Stearns County
Environmental Services Administration Center Room 343
705 Courthouse Square
St. Cloud, MN 56303
320-656-3613
https://www.stearnscountymn.gov/1017/Licenses

St. Louis County
Auditor/Treasurer's Office
Miller Hill Mall
1600 Miller Trunk Highway, Ste. E03
Duluth, MN 55802
218-279-2520
https://www.stlouiscountymn.gov/business/permits-licenses-and-records

Washington County
14949 62nd Street N.
Stillwater, MN 55082
651-430-6175
https://www.co.washington.mn.us/index.aspx?NID=1219

CITY LICENSING CONTACTS

Bloomington
City Clerk's Office
1800 W. Old Shakopee Road
Bloomington, MN 55431-3027
952-563-4923
https://www.bloomingtonmn.gov/licensing

Brooklyn Center
6301 Shingle Creek Parkway
Brooklyn Center, MN 55430
763-569-3300
http://www.cityofbrooklyncenter.org/index.aspx?NID=266

Brooklyn Park
5200 85th Ave. N.
Brooklyn Park, MN 55443
763-493-8182
https://www.brooklynpark.org/permits-and-licenses/

Coon Rapids
City Clerk
11155 Robinson Drive
Coon Rapids, MN 55433
763-767-6493
https://www.coonrapidsmn.gov/175/City-Clerk

Duluth
City Clerk's Office
330 City Hall, 411 W. First Street
Duluth, MN 55802
218-730-5923
https://www.duluthmn.gov/licenses-permits/

Eagan
City Clerk Permits
3830 Pilot Knob Road
Eagan, MN 55122
651-675-5034
https://www.cityofeagan.com/city-clerk-permits

Minneapolis
City Hall, Room 107
350 South Fifth Street
Minneapolis, MN 55415-1391
612-673-2080
http://www2.minneapolismn.gov/licensing/index.htm

Plymouth
3400 Plymouth Blvd.
Plymouth, MN 55447-1482
763-509-5080
https://www.plymouthmn.gov/departments/administrative-services-/city-clerk/licensing

Rochester
City Clerk's Office
201 4th Street S.E., Room 135
Rochester, MN 55904
507-328-2900
https://www.rochestermn.gov/departments/city-clerk

St. Cloud
City Clerk
400 Second Street S.
St. Cloud, MN 56301
320-255-7210
http://www.ci.stcloud.mn.us/486/Business-Licensing

St. Paul
Department of Safety & Inspections
375 Jackson Street, Suite 220
St. Paul, MN 55101
651-266-8989
https://www.stpaul.gov/departments/safety-inspections/licenses

*This is only a partial listing of the larger cities business licensing offices.

CO-WORKING / CREATIVE / INCUBATOR SPACES

Brainco
2601 2nd Ave. S., Studio 1
Minneapolis, MN 55408
952-931-0303 | coworking@brainco.org
https://brainco.org

CoCreateX
1137 Burns Ave.
St. Paul, MN 55106
team@cocreatex.com
https://cocreatex.com

Collider Coworking
14 4th Street S.W.
Rochester, MN 55902
507-722-0306 | hello@collider.mn
https://www.collider.mn/

Creators Space
218 7th Street E., Suite 100
St. Paul, MN 55101
651-340-6736 | mailbox@creatorsspace.com
https://www.creatorsspace.com

Finnovation Lab
817 5th Ave. S. #4000
Minneapolis, MN 55404
info@finn-lab.com
https://finn-lab.com

FLOCK
2611 1st Ave. S.
Minneapolis, MN 55408
612-333-2688 | info@flockmpls.com
https://www.flockmpls.com

Forge North
Movement of entrepreneurs, investors, makers, collaborators, and allies from all industries and sectors working together.
612-234-2228 | hello@forgenorth.com
https://forgenorth.com/

Fueled Collective
612-545-5745 | hello@cocomsp.com
https://fueledcollectivemn.com/

Fueled Collective Minneapolis Downtown
Minneapolis Grain Exchange Building
400 S. 4th Street, Suite 401
Minneapolis, MN 55415
612-545-5745
downtownmpls@fueledcollectivemn.com

Fueled Collective Minneapolis Northeast
1400 Van Buren St. N.E., Ste. 200
Minneapolis, MN 55413
612-224-9995 | northeastmpls@fueledcollectivemn.com

Fueled Collective St. Paul Lowertown
213 4th Street E., 4th Floor
St. Paul, MN 55101
651-204-2148 | stp@fueledcollectivemn.com

Garden Fresh Farms Commercial Kitchen and CSA
1065 MN Highway 36 E.
Maplewood, MN 55109
612-886-6631
http://www.gardenfreshfarms.com/home.html

Glen Nelson Center
Osborn370
370 Wabasha St. N.
St. Paul, MN 55102
https://www.glennelson.org/

Grow North MN - University of Minnesota
Creates unique programs and events for entrepreneurs, organizations and institutions; resource database and library.
321 19th Ave. S.
Minneapolis, MN 55445
hello@grownorthmn.com
https://carlsonschool.umn.edu/grownorth

Impact Hub MSP
Coworking, shared and dedicated workspaces, community-led workshops, and facilitate peer-to-peer learning.
825 Washington Ave. S.E.
Minneapolis, MN 55414
651-318-2800 | host.msp@impacthub.net
https://www.impacthubmsp.com/

Industrious Office
https://www.industriousoffice.com

Minneapolis -Downtown
60 South 6th Street, #2800
Minneapolis, MN 55402
651-796-2331 | info@industriousoffice.com

Minneapolis -North Loop
323 Washington Ave. N., 2nd Floor
Minneapolis, MN 55401
651-900-7900

Incubology
Brings technology start-ups together in a shared environment. Dedicated lab and office space. Entrepreneurs from diverse disciplines including biotech, pharma, device, nano and chem.
1 Imation Way
Oakdale, MN 55128
bd@blossom-medical.com
https://www.incubology.com/

Joe Warthesen Food Processing Center -Pilot Plant
University of Minnesota, Department of Food Science and Nutrition
1334 Eckles Ave.
St. Paul, MN 55108
612-624-1290
https://fscn.cfans.umn.edu/research-services/pilot-plant

LaunchPad
102 1st Street W.
Bemidji, MN 56601
218-444-5758 | Launchpad@greaterbemidji.com
https://launchpadbemidji.com/

Lift Bridge Cowork
310 1/2 Main Street S.
Stillwater, MN 55082
651-300-4952
https://www.liftbridgecowork.com/

Lunar Startups
Collaborative space and experience for high-growth entrepreneurs in Osborn370. Provide dedicated space, resources, programming and stewardship to cohort startups.
370 Wabasha St. N.
St. Paul, MN 55102
hello@lunarstartups.org
https://www.lunarstartups.org/

ModernWell
2909 South Wayzata Blvd.
Minneapolis, MN 55405
763-999-7920 | hello@modernwell.co
https://modernwell.co/

MN Foodcrafters
Large shared commercial kitchen.
865 Pierce Butler Route
St. Paul, MN 55104
651-336-7880

New Rules
2015 - 2019 N. Lowry
Minneapolis, MN 55411
612-548-4110
http://www.newrulesmn.com/

Northside Food Business Incubator /
Northside Economic Opportunity Network (NEON)
1007 W. Broadway Ave. N.
Minneapolis, MN 55411
612-302-1505 | info@neon-mn.org
http://www.neon-mn.org/

Red Wing Ignite
419 Bush Street
Red Wing, MN 55066
651-327-2115
http://www.redwingignite.org

STUDIO COWORK
919 Lilac Drive N.
Minneapolis, MN 55422
https://www.studiocowork.com/

The Commons
952-474-1001
https://www.thecommonswp.com

540 Lake Street
Excelsior, MN 55331
915 Mainstreet
Hopkins, MN 55343

14451 MN Hwy. 7
Minnetonka, MN 55345

The Coven
30 N. 1st. Street
Minneapolis, MN 55401
612-259-7383 | hello@thecoven
https://thecoven.com/

The Garage Cowork Space
123 Lafayette Street
Winona, MN 55987
507-474-1955 | hello@thegarargecowork.com
https://www.thegaragecowork.com/

The Reserve
https://reserve.work

4940 W. 77th St.
Edina, MN 55435
952-217-5825

1915 Hwy 36 West
Roseville, MN 55113
612-481-5007

724 Bielenberg Drive
Woodbury, MN 55125
651-735-8866

The Riveter
4388 France Ave. S.
Edina, MN 55410
883-474-8383 |hello@theriveter
https://www.theriveter.co

Third Haus
4420 Drew Ave. South, Suite C
Minneapolis, MN 55410
612-584-9190 | info@thirdhaus.com
https://thirdhaus.com/en/contact

WeWork
877-217-3809
https://www.wework.com/l/minneapolis

Capella Tower
225 South 6th Street
Minneapolis, MN 55402

729 N. Washington Ave, Suite 600.
Minneapolis, MN 55401

workit
635 Fairview Ave. N.
St. Paul, MN 55104
612-770-2520
https://co-workit.com/

NONPROFIT INFORMATION

Minnesota Council of Nonprofits (MCN)
MCN works to inform, promote, connect and strengthen individual nonprofits and the nonprofit sector.
2314 University Ave. W. #20
St. Paul, MN 55114
651-642-1904 800-289-1904
info@minnesotanonprofits.org
https://www.minnesotanonprofits.org

SVP (Social Venture Partners) Minnesota
SVP Minnesota is a 501(c)(3) organization that improves lives by investing time, talent and capital in innovative, early stage social ventures directed at underserved teens in the Twin Cities.
14451 Highway 7, Suite 203
Minnetonka, MN 55435
952-933-5560 | info@svpmn.org
http://www.socialventurepartners.org/minnesota/

University of Minnesota
Office for Business & Community Economic Development
Designed to help nonprofit organizations that serve urban communities build capacity and enhance their performance and effectiveness.
612-624-0530 | bced@umn.edu
http:/bced.umn.edu

OTHER

Forge North
Movement of entrepreneurs, investors, makers, collaborators, and allies from all industries and sectors working together.
612-234-2228 | hello@forgenorth.com
https://forgenorth.com/

Startup Compass
https://forgenorth.com/resource-compass/

Medical Alley Association
Minnesota's and the nation's largest state-based health industry advocacy organization.
4150 Olson Memorial Highway, Suite 430
Golden Valley, MN 55422
952-542-3077 | info@medicalalley.org
https://www.medicalalley.org

Metro Independent Business Alliance (IBA)
Membership organization works to promote locally owned, independent businesses in the Metropolitan area.
P.O. Box 40560
St. Paul, MN 55104
651-387-0738

Buy Local Twin Cities
https://www.buylocaltwincities.com/

Minnestar
A showcase for working technology products made in Minnesota.
https://minnestar.org

Minnebar
An annual technology and software conference held in the Twin Cities. Like other BarCamps, Minnebar is a user-generated conference that is participant-led.
https://minnestar.org/minnebar/

Minnedemo
A showcase for working technology products made in Minnesota.
https://minnestar.org/minnedemo/

DIRECTORY OF LICENSES AND PERMITS

DIRECTORY OF LICENSES AND PERMITS

Expanded state licenses, permits, and registration listings are available on the **Minnesota ELicensing** website at https://mn.gov/elicense/.

REGULATED ACTIVITY	DEPARTMENT	CONTACT
Aboveground Storage Tank Installations		
Aboveground Storage Tanks (see **Tanks**)		
Abstracter		
Abstracter: Company & Individual Proprietor / Individual	Commerce, Minnesota Dept. of	651-539-1599 800-657-3978
Accountants		
Certified Public Accountant (CPA) / CPA Firms Registered Accounting Practitioner (RAP)	Accountancy, Minnesota State Board of	651-296-7938
Acupuncture		
Acupuncture Registration	Chiropractic Examiners, Minnesota Board of	651-201-2850
Acupuncture Practitioner	Medical Practice, Minnesota State Board of	612-617-2130
Adjuster (see **Insurance**)		
Adoption		
Private Child Caring or Placing Agency License (Rule 4)	Human Services, Minnesota Dept. of	651-431-6500
Advertising Devices, Signs		
Sign Contractor Bond	Labor and Industry (DLI), Minnesota Dept. of	651-284-3034
Advertising Device Permit	Transportation, Minnesota Dept. of	651-366-4671
Agent (see **Athlete Agent**)		
Air Emissions/Quality		
Air -Individual Part 70 Operating Permit or State Operating Permit Air -Non-Metallic Mineral Processing General Permit Air -Registration Permits (Options A, B, C, or D)	Pollution Control Agency (MPCA), Minnesota	651-296-6143 800-657-3938
Air -Capped Permits (Option 1/2)	Pollution Control Agency (MPCA), Minnesota	651-282-6143
Feedlot Construction Short-Form Permit Feedlot Interim Permit Feedlot NPDES/SDS Permit (General and Individual) Open Lot Agreement (OLA) State Disposal System Permit	Pollution Control Agency (MPCA), Minnesota	651-282-6300 800-657-3938
Aircraft		
Aircraft Registration	Transportation (MnDOT), Minnesota Dept. of	651-234-7201
Aircraft Dealer's License	Transportation (MnDOT), Minnesota Dept. of	651-234-7232
Airports		
Airport License: -Public -Private -Special Use -Personal-Use	Transportation (MnDOT), Minnesota Dept. of	651-234-7230
Commercial Operators -Aviation	Transportation (MnDOT), Minnesota Dept. of	651-234-7232
Alarm and Communication Contractors		
Power Limited Technician Technology Systems Contractor	Labor and Industry (DLI), Minnesota Dept. of	651-284-5064
Alcohol (see also **Liquor**)		
Permit to Purchase and/or Possess Ethyl Alcohol and/or Distilled Spirits	Public Safety (DPS), Minnesota Dept. of	651-201-7512

REGULATED ACTIVITY	DEPARTMENT	CONTACT
Alcohol and Drug Treatment Providers		
Alcohol & Drug Counselor (ADC) -Temporary Permits	Behavioral Health & Therapy (BBHT),	651-201-2758
Licensed Alcohol and Drug Counselor (LADC)	Minnesota Board of	
Professional Firm Registration -BBHT		
Chemical Dependency Detoxification Programs (Rule 32)	Human Services (DHS), Minnesota Dept. of	651-431-6500
Chemical Dependency Treatment (Non-Detox) Programs (Rule 31)		
All-Terrain Vehicles (ATVs) (see **Motorized Vehicles** and **Utility Vehicles**)		
Alternative Health Care		
Minnesota Doula Registry	Health (MDH), Minnesota Dept. of	651-201-3731
Unlicensed Complementary and Alternative Health Care Practitioners		
Acupuncture Practitioner	Medical Practice, Minnesota State Board of	612-617-2130
Naturopathic Doctor Registry		
Ambulance Service (see **Emergency Medical Services**)		
Ammonia		
Anhydrous Ammonia Storage System Permit	Agriculture (MDA), Minnesota Dept. of	651-201-6275
Animals		
Certificate of Free Sale for Animal Feed	Agriculture (MDA), Minnesota Dept. of	651-201-6212
Livestock Dealer License	Agriculture (MDA), Minnesota Dept. of	651-201-6509
Livestock Dealer's Agent License		
Livestock Market Agency License		
Livestock Meat Packing Company / Agent License		
Poultry, Hatching Eggs and Ratites	Animal Health (BAH), Minnesota Board of	320-231-5170
Poultry Dealer and Poultry Hatchery and Breeding Flock Permits		
Poultry Testing Agent Authorization		
Commercial Dog or Cat Breeder	Animal Health (BAH), Minnesota Board of	651-201-6804
Farmed Cervidae Registration		
Kennel License (Dogs and Cats)		
Feed Foodwaste to Animals License	Animal Health (BAH), Minnesota Board of	651-201-6824
Animal Exhibition Permit	Animal Health (BAH), Minnesota Board of	651-201-6826
Livestock Auction Markets and Community Sales Permit	Animal Health (BAH), Minnesota Board of	651-296-2942
Pet Food Processing Permit		
Registration of a Brand		
Rendering Plant Permit		
Sheep/Goats Scrapie Registration		
Endangered Species Permit	Natural Resources (DNR), Minnesota Dept. of	651-259-5073
Permit to Exhibit Captive Wildlife	Natural Resources (DNR), Minnesota Dept. of	651-772-7906
Apiaries		
Apiary Certificate of Inspection	Agriculture (MDA), Minnesota Dept. of	651-201-6578
Appraiser		
Appraisal Management Company	Commerce, Minnesota Dept. of	651-539-1599
Appraiser Individual: Nonresident / Residential		800-657-3978
Apprenticeship		
Apprenticeship Registration	Labor and Industry (DLI), Minnesota Dept. of	651-284-5090 800-342-5354
Aquaculture		
Aquatic Farm License	Natural Resources (DNR), Minnesota Dept. of	651-297-4935

REGULATED ACTIVITY	DEPARTMENT	CONTACT
Archaeology		
Archaeological Fieldwork	Office of the State Archaeologist, Minnesota	612-725-2411
Architecture		
Architect	Architecture, Engineering, Land Surveying, Landscape Architecture, Geoscience and Interior Design (AELSLAGID), MN Board of	651-757-1515
Asbestos		
Asbestos Contractor License Asbestos Inspector Certificate Asbestos Management Planner Certificate Asbestos Project Designer Certificate Asbestos Site Supervisor Certificate Asbestos Training Course Permit Asbestos Worker Certificate Notification of Asbestos-Related Work and Amendments	Health (MDH), Minnesota Dept. of	651-201-4620
Assessors		
Assessor Certification: Various Classes	Assessors, Minnesota State Board	651-566-6086
Athlete Agent		
Athlete Agent Registration	Commerce, Minnesota Dept. of	651-539-1599
Athletic Trainer		
Athletic Trainer	Medical Practice, Minnesota State Board of	612-617-2130
Attorney		
Lawyer Registration	Lawyer Registration Office, Minnesota Judicial Branch	651-296-2254
Auctioneer		
Auctioneer	Contact local County Auditor office.	
Audiology		
Audiologist License	Health (MDH), Minnesota Dept. of	651-201-3726
Automatic Teller Machines (ATMs)		
Electronic Financial Terminal Authorization (Nonfinancial Institutions) Electronic Financial Terminal Notification (State-Chartered Financial Institutions)	Commerce, Minnesota Dept. of	651-539-1700
Aviation		
Aircraft Registration	Transportation (MnDOT), Minnesota Dept. of	651-234-7201
Aircraft Dealer's License Airport License: Personal-Use Airport Airport License: Private Airport / Public Airport Commercial Aviation Operators License	Transportation (MnDOT), Minnesota Dept. of	651-234-7232
Bail Bond Agent/Agency		
Insurance Agent (Bail Bond)	Commerce, Minnesota Dept. of	651-539-1599 800-657-3978
Bail Bond Agent New Bonding Agency	Judicial Branch, Minnesota	651-297-7650

REGULATED ACTIVITY	DEPARTMENT	CONTACT
Bait		
Exporting Minnow Dealer	Natural Resources (DNR), Minnesota Dept. of	651-297-4935
Minnow Dealer's License		
Minnow Retailer		
Nonresident License to Purchase, Possess and Transport Frogs		
Nonresident Minnow Hauler License		
Resident Frog Dealer (Take, Possess, Transport, Sell)		
Resident License to Purchase, Possess & Transport Frogs		
Banking (see also **ATMs**, **Commercial Mortgage Brokering**, **Credit Unions**, **Currency Exchange**, **Debt Prorating Agency**, **Loans** (Non-Bank Lenders), **Mortgage Originator or Servicer**, **Safe Deposit Company**)		
Electronic Financial Terminal (EFT) / Branch	Commerce, Minnesota Dept. of	651-539-1600
Capital Stock Savings Bank	Commerce, Minnesota Dept. of	651-539-1714
Detached Facility		
Electronic Financial Terminal (EFT)		
Industrial Loan and Thrift		
Interstate Bank Mergers and Branching		
Interstate Trust-Trust Office or Representative Trust Office		
Minnesota Bank or Trust Company Mergers		
Purchase and Assumption Application		
State Bank Charter or Trust Company Charter or Industrial Loan & Thrift Company With Deposit-Taking Powers		
State Bank Trust Authority		
Trust Service Office Authority		
Barbering		
Barbers and Barbershops: Various Classes	Barber Examiners, Minnesota Board of	651-201-2820
Hair Braiding Registration	Cosmetology, Minnesota Board of	651-201-2742
Bed and Breakfast		
Bed and Breakfast Registration (to serve liquor)	Public Safety (DPS), Minnesota Dept. of	651-201-7510
Food, Beverage and Lodging License	Health (MDH), Minnesota Dept. of	651-201-4500
Bingo (see GAMBLING)		
Boat Dealer		
Boat Dealer License	Natural Resources (DNR), Minnesota Dept. of	651-296-2316 800-285-2000
Boats for Hire		
Annual Boat Operating Permit	Labor and Industry (DLI), Minnesota Dept. of	651-284-5544 800-342-5354
Tour Boat Intoxicating Liquor License	Public Safety (DPS), Minnesota Dept. of	651-201-7506
Body Art		
Body Art Establishment	Health (MDH), Minnesota Dept. of	651-201-3770
Body Art Technician Licenses		
Boilers/Boiler Operating Engineer		
Boiler Engineer: Ten Classes	Labor and Industry, (DLI) Minnesota Dept. of	651-284-5031
Boilers and Pressure Vessel Registration	Labor and Industry, (DLI) Minnesota Dept. of	651-284-5137
Boxing		
Boxer License	Office of Combative Sports, Labor and Industry, (DLI) Minnesota Dept. of	651-284-5366
Boxing / MMA Officials/Corner License		
Promoter License (Combative Sports)		

REGULATED ACTIVITY	DEPARTMENT	CONTACT
Brokers (see also **Motor Vehicle Dealer**)		
Food Broker License	Agriculture (MDA), Minnesota Dept. of	651-201-6627
Real Estate Limited Broker	Commerce, Minnesota Dept. of	651-539-1599
Real Estate Salesperson; Real Estate Broker		800-657-3978
Securities Agent, Securities Broker-Dealer	Commerce, Minnesota Dept. of	651-539-1631
Residential Mortgage Loan Originator License	Commerce, Minnesota Dept. of	651-539-1700
Viatical Settlement Broker	Commerce, Minnesota Dept. of	651-539-1748
Brokers License to Represent a Distillery, Winery or Importer / Broker's Employee License	Public Safety (DPS), Minnesota Dept. of	651-201-7500
Motor Vehicle Dealers License	Public Safety (DPS), Minnesota Dept. of	651-201-7800
Note: For the purposes of the motor vehicle dealers license, a "Dealer" includes licensed new motor vehicle dealers, used motor vehicle dealers, motor vehicle brokers, wholesalers, auctioneers, lessors of new or used motor vehicles, scrap metal processors, used vehicle parts dealers, and salvage pools.		
Building Mover		
Building Mover License	Transportation (MnDOT), Minnesota Dept. of	651-366-3680
Building Official		
Accessibility Specialist	Labor and Industry (DLI), Minnesota Dept. of	651-284-5068
Certified Building Official / Limited		
Certified Building Official Limited		
Bullion		
Bullion Product Dealer Dealer/ Dealer Representative	Commerce, Minnesota Dept. of	651-539-1599
Burning		
Open Burning Permit	Natural Resources (DNR), Minnesota Dept. of Contact the local city government, fire department, local forestry office or fire warden.	866-533-2876
Bus Shelters		
Bus Shelter Permit	Transportation (MnDOT), Minnesota Dept. of	651-582-1443
Camps and Campgrounds		
Youth Camp Permit	Health (MDH), Minnesota Dept. of	651-201-4500
Recreational Camping Area License	Health (MDH), Minnesota Dept. of	651-201-4510
Carriers (see also **Courier** and **Motor Carrier**)		
Common Carrier (Plane/Boat/Train) License to Sell Intoxicating or 3.2% Malt Liquor	Public Safety (DPS), Minnesota Dept. of	651-201-7500
Commercial Driver's License (CDL)	Public Safety (DPS), Minnesota Dept. of	651-297-5029
Passenger Carrier Registration (Intrastate)	Transportation (MnDOT), Minnesota Dept. of	651-215-6330
Property Carrier Registration (Intrastate)		
Unified Carrier Registration	Transportation (MnDOT), Minnesota Dept. of	651-366-3680
Limousine Service Permit	Transportation (MnDOT), Minnesota Dept. of	651-366-3700
Special Transportation Certificate (STS)		
Catering		
Food, Beverage and Lodging License	Health (MDH), Minnesota Dept. of	651-201-4505 651-201-4500
Caterer's Permit with Alcohol	Public Safety (DPS), Minnesota Dept. of	651-201-7510
Charitable Organizations		
Charitable Solicitation Registration	Attorney General, Minnesota Office of	651- 757-1496
Charitable Trusts		
Professional Fundraiser Registration		
Check-Cashing Company		
Currency Exchange License / Branch / Registration	Commerce, Minnesota Dept. of	651-539-1700

REGULATED ACTIVITY	DEPARTMENT	CONTACT
Chemical Dependency		
Alcohol & Drug Counselor (ADC) -Temporary Permits	Behavioral Health & Therapy (BBHT),	651-201-2758
Licensed Alcohol and Drug Counselor (LADC)	Minnesota Board of	
Professional Firm Registration		
Chemical Dependency Detoxification Programs (Rule 32)	Human Services (DHS), Minnesota Dept. of	651-431-6500
Programs (Rule 32)		
Chemigation		
Chemigation Permit & Chemigation Substantial Alteration Permit	Agriculture (MDA), Minnesota Dept. of	651-201-6240
Child Care		
Child Care Center License (Rule 3)	Human Services (DHS), Minnesota Dept. of	651-431-6500
Family Child Care and Group Family Child Care License (Rule 2)		
In-home Child Care	Contact County Social Services Dept.	
Child Placement		
Private Child Caring or Placing Agency License Rule (4)	Human Services (DHS), Minnesota Dept. of	651-431-6500
Chiropractic		
Acupuncture Registration	Chiropractic Examiners, Minnesota Board of	651-201-2850
Animal Chiropractic Registration		
Doctor of Chiropractic		
Graduate Preceptor Registration (GPP)		
Independent Examiner Registration		
Professional Firm Registration		
Chlorofluorocarbons (CFCs)		
CFC Recyclers and CFC Recovery Equipment and Technician Certification	U.S. Environmental Protection Agency (EPA)	800-296-1996
Cigarette		
Unfair Cigarette Sales Act (UCSA) Fee	Commerce, Minnesota Dept. of	651-539-1500
Fire Standard Compliant Cigarettes (FSC) Certification	State Fire Marshal, Public Safety (DPS), Minnesota Dept. of	651-201-7203
Cigarette & Tobacco Distributor & Subjobber Licenses	Revenue (DOR), Minnesota Dept. of	651-297-1882
Clubs (Health, Social Referral, Buying Clubs)		
Health, Social Referral, Buying Clubs Registration	Attorney General, Minnesota Office of	651-296-7575
Coin Dealer		
Bullion Product Dealer / Representative	Commerce, Minnesota Dept. of	651-539-1599
Collection Agency		
Collection Agency and Debt Collector	Commerce, Minnesota Dept. of	651-539-1599 800-657-3978
Combative Sports		
Boxer License	Office of Combative Sports,	651-284-5366
Boxing / MMA Officials/Corner License	Labor and Industry (DLI), Minnesota Dept. of	
Mixed Martial Arts (MMA) Combatant License		
Promoter License (Combative Sports)		
Commercial Drivers		
Commercial Driver's License (CDL)	Public Safety (DPS), Minnesota Dept. of	651-297-5029
CDL Hazardous Materials Endorsement / School Bus Driver Endorsement		
Commercial Driver Training		
Commercial Driver Training School License	Public Safety (DPS), Minnesota Dept. of	651-201-7626
Commercial Mortgage Brokering		
Real Estate Broker: -Limited -Nonresident -Resident	Commerce, Minnesota Dept. of	651-539-1599 800-657-3978
Communication Contractors		
Power Limited Technician	Labor and Industry (DLI), Minnesota Dept. of	651-284-5031
Technology Systems Contractor		
Satellite System Contractor (SSC)	Labor and Industry (DLI), Minnesota Dept. of	651-284-5034
Unlicensed Individual -Electrical &Power Limited Reg.	Labor and Industry (DLI), Minnesota Dept. of	651-284-5084

REGULATED ACTIVITY	DEPARTMENT	CONTACT
Complementary Health Care		
Unlicensed Complementary and Alternative Health Care Practitioners	Health (MDH), Minnesota Dept. of	651-201-3731
Composting		
Compost Facility Permits -Source Separated Organic Materials (SSOM) Compost Facility / Solid Waste Compost Facility	Pollution Control Agency (MPCA), Minnesota	651-296-6300 800-657-3864
Contractors		
Elevator Contractor	Labor and Industry (DLI), Minnesota Dept. of	651-284-5031
Technology Systems Contractor		
Residential Building Contractor / Remodeler	Labor and Industry (DLI), Minnesota Dept. of	651-284-5034
Construction Contractor Registration	Labor and Industry (DLI), Minnesota Dept. of	651-284-5074
Corporate Take-Overs		
Corporate Take-Over Offers Registration	Commerce, Minnesota Dept. of	651-539-1629
Cosmetology		
Cosmetology -Individual Licenses / Salons / Schools	Cosmetology, MN Board of	651-201-2742
Cosmetology -Temporary Military Permit		
Hair Braiding Registration		
Eyelash Extension Technician		
Counselors		
Licensed Professional Clinical Counselor (LPCC)	Behavioral Health & Therapy (BBHT),	651-201-2739
Licensed Professional Counselor (LPC)	Minnesota Board of,	
Alcohol & Drug Counselor (ADC) -Temporary Permits	Behavioral Health & Therapy (BBHT),	651-201-2758
Licensed Alcohol and Drug Counselor (LADC)	Minnesota Board of	
Professional Firm Registration -BBHT		
Marriage and Family Therapist	Marriage and Family Therapy, Minnesota Board of	612-617-2220
Courier (see also **Carriers** and **Motor Carriers**)		
Passenger Carrier Registration (Intrastate)	Transportation (MnDOT), Minnesota Dept. of	651-215-6330
Property Carrier Registration (Intrastate)		
Unified Carrier Registration Agreement	Transportation (MnDOT), Minnesota Dept. of	651-366-3680
Limousine Service Permit	Transportation (MnDOT), Minnesota Dept. of	651-366-3700
Crane		
Crane Operator Certification	Labor and Industry (DLI), Minnesota Dept. of	651-284-5050
Credit Services Organization		
Credit Services Organization Registration	Commerce, Minnesota Dept. of	651-539-1570
Credit Unions		
Credit Union Certificate of Organization	Commerce, Minnesota Dept. of	651-539-1709
Currency Exchange		
Currency Exchange License / Branch	Commerce, Minnesota Dept. of	651-539-1570
Currency Echange Registration		
Day Care / Day Services		
Adult Day Services Centers License (Rule 223)	Human Services (DHS), Minnesota Dept. of	651-431-6500
Child Care Center License (Rule 3)		
Adult Foster Care License (Rule 203)	Contact County Social Services or	
Family Adult Day Services	County Human Services Department	
Family Child Care and Group Family Child Care License (Rule 2)		
In-home Child Care		
Debt Collection		
Collection Agency and Debt Collector	Commerce, Minnesota Dept. of	651-539-1599 800-657-3978

REGULATED ACTIVITY	DEPARTMENT	CONTACT
Debt Prorating Agency		
Debt Management Services Provider Company / Branch	Commerce, Minnesota Dept. of	651-539-1700
Debt Settlement Services Provider Company License		651-539-1705
Dentistry		
Dental Assistant / Hygienist / Dental Guest License	Dentistry, Minnesota Board of	612-548-2129
Dental Lab Registration		
Dental Therapist / Advanced Dental Therapist		
Dentist		
Deputy Registrar		
Deputy Registrar Appointment	Public Safety (DPS), Minnesota Dept. of	651-201-7970
Dietitians		
Dietitian License	Dietetics & Nutrition Practice, Minnesota Board of	651-201-2764
Doctors		
Physician (Medical Doctor and Doctor of Osteopathy)	Medical Practice, Minnesota Board of	612-617-2130
Drainage		
Drainage Permit	Transportation (MnDOT), Minnesota Dept. of	651-366-4638
Driver Education / Training		
Driver Education Program	Public Safety (DPS), Minnesota Dept. of	651-201-7626
Commercial Driver Training School License		
Drivers		
Drive-Away / In-transit License	Public Safety (DPS), Minnesota Dept. of	651-201-7800
Overdimensional Load Escort Driver Certificate	Public Safety (DPS), Minnesota Dept. of	651-297-5029
Driver Medical Waivers	Transportation (MnDOT), Minnesota Dept. of	651-366-3700
Driveways		
Access Driveway Permit	Transportation (MnDOT), Minnesota Dept. of	651-366-4668
Drugs (Human and Veterinary)		
Controlled Substance Researcher	Pharmacy, Minnesota Board of	651-201-2825
Drug / Medical Gas Wholesaler License		
Drug Manufacturer License		
Medical Gas Distributor		
Pharmacist License / Pharmacy Intern		
Pharmacy License / Pharmacy Technician		
Electric High Voltage Transmission Lines		
Route Permit	Public Utilities Commission (PUC), Minnesota	651-201-2255
Electricians / Power		
Class A Journeyman Electrician	Labor and Industry (DLI), Minnesota Dept. of	651-284-5031
Electrical Installer Class A & B		
Lineman		
Maintenance Electrician		
Master Electrician Class A		
Power Limited Technician		
Unlicensed Individual -Electrical and Power Limited Registration		
Electrical Contractors	Labor and Industry (DLI), Minnesota Dept. of	651-284-5034
Technology Systems Contractor		
Portable Power Distribution Systems and Temporary Installations		

REGULATED ACTIVITY	DEPARTMENT	CONTACT
Elevators		
Master / Limited Master / Journeyworker Elevator Constructor	Labor and Industry (DLI), Minnesota Dept. of	651-284-5031
Elevator / Limited Elevator Contractor	Labor and Industry (DLI), Minnesota Dept. of	651-284-5034
Emergency Medical Services / EMT		
Education Program Coordinator Emergency Medical Technician (EMT) Registration Emergency Responder Registration	Emergency Medical Services Regulatory Board (EMSRB), Minnesota	651-201-2800
Medical Response Unit Minnesota Ambulance Service License	Emergency Medical Services Regulatory Board (EMSRB), Minnesota	651-201-2804
Employment / Employment Agency		
Employee Leasing Company Registration / Exemption	Commerce, Minnesota Dept. of	651-539-1743
Payroll Card Issuer	Labor and Industry (DLI), Minnesota Dept. of	651-284-5070
Energy Facilities		
Certificate of Need	Public Utilities Commission (PUC), Minnesota	651-201-2236
Site Permit for Large Electric Generating Power Plant Site Permit for Large Wind Energy Conversion Systems	Public Utilities Commission (PUC), Minnesota	651-201-2255
Engineering		
Engineer-In-Training Professional Engineer	Architecture, Engineering, Land Surveying, Landscape Architecture, Geoscience and Interior Design (AELSLAGID), MN Board of	651-296-2388 651-757-1513
Environmental Health Specialist/Sanitarian Registration		
Environmental Health Specialist / Sanitarian Registration License	Health (MDH), Minnesota Dept. of	651-201-4500
Estate Sales		
Estate Sales Conductor	Contact local County Auditor Office	
Explosives		
Explosives License / Explosives Permit Ownership or Possession of an Explosive Device or Incendiary Device Application	State Fire Marshal, Public Safety (DPS), Minnesota Dept. of	612-386-4657
Family Therapy (see **Marriage**)		
Farms		
Minnesota's Corporate Farm Report: Corporataion / LLC / LLLP / Trust-Pension-Investment Fund	Agriculture (MDA), Minnesota Dept. of	651-201-6083
Feed, Commercial		
Certificate of Free Sale for Animal Feed	Agriculture (MDA), Minnesota Dept. of	651-201-6051
Commercial Feed License / Pet and Specialty Pet Foods	Agriculture (MDA), Minnesota Dept. of	651-201-6211
Feedlots		
Feedlot Construction Short-Form Permit Feedlot Interim Permit Feedlot NPDES/SDS Permit (General and Individual) Open Lot Agreement (OLA) Registration (Feedlot Program) State Disposal System Permit	Pollution Control Agency (MPCA), Minnesota	651-296-6300 800-657-3938
Fertilizer		
Bulk Pesticide/Fertilizer Storage Facility or Substantial Alteration Permit	Agriculture (MDA), Minnesota Dept. of	651-201-6274
Agricultural Liming Material License Anhydrous Ammonia Storage System Permit	Agriculture (MDA), Minnesota Dept. of	651-201-6275
Fertilizer License / Specialty Fertilizer Registration Soil and Plant Amendment Registration	Agriculture (MDA), Minnesota Dept. of	651-201-6379

REGULATED ACTIVITY	DEPARTMENT	CONTACT
Financial Counselors/Planners / Investment Adviser		
Financial Counselor or Planner	Commerce, Minnesota Dept. of	651-539-1638
Investment Adviser / Representatives		
Fire Protection (see **Fireworks Display**, **Sprinkler Systems, Tanks**)		
Firearms (see also **Explosives**)		
Firearms Training Certification	Bureau of Criminal Apprehension (BCA), MN, Public Safety (DPS), Minnesota Dept. of	651-793-1076
Federally Licensed Gun Dealers	Bureau of Alcohol, Tobacco and Firearms	404-417-2750
	U.S. National Licensing Center	866-662-2750
Firefighter		
Licensed Firefighter	Firefighter Training & Education, (MBFTE) Minnesota Board of	651-201-7259
Qualified Instructor		
Fireworks Display		
Fireworks Display Operator	State Fire Marshall, Public Safety (DPS), Minnesota Dept. of	612-386-4657
Fireworks Display Permit -Outdoor / Indoor Displays		
Fish / Fishing (see also **Bait**)		
Fish Processing / Smoking Operation Permit	Agriculture (MDA), Minnesota Dept. of	651-201-6027
Endangered Species Permit	Natural Resources (DNR), Minnesota Dept. of	651-259-5090
Fishing Tournament Permit	Natural Resources (DNR), Minnesota Dept. of	651-259-5200
Live Fish Transportation Importation and Stocking Permit		
Rough Fish Removal Permit		
Educational Fishing License Waiver for Students	Natural Resources (DNR), Minnesota Dept. of	651-259-5236
Fisheries Research Permit Application		
Aquatic Farm License	Natural Resources (DNR), Minnesota Dept. of	651-297-4935
Commercial Netting of Fish		
Fish Packer / Vendor License		
International Fish Buyer - Retail / Wholesale		
Lake Superior Fish Buyer - Retail / Wholesale		
Food		
Cottage Food Producer Registration	Agriculture (MDA), Minnesota Dept. of	651-201-6027
Fish Processing / Smoking Operation Permit		
Special Event Food Stand		
Dairy Plant License / Dairy Transfer Station	Agriculture (MDA), Minnesota Dept. of	651-201-6062
Food Broker License		
Milk and Cream Buyer and Tester License		
Non-Resident Frozen Food		
Retail Food Handler / Wholesale Food Handler Licenses		
Wholesale Food Handler		
Wholesale Food Processor/Manufacturer		
Wholesale Food Processor or Manufacturer License USDA		
Livestock Meat Packing Company / Agent License	Agriculture (MDA), Minnesota Dept. of	651-201-6290
Farmstead Cheese Permit	Agriculture (MDA), Minnesota Dept. of	651-201-6300
Minnesota Grown Logo Labeling License	Agriculture (MDA), Minnesota Dept. of	651-201-6510
Wholesale Produce Dealers License	Agriculture (MDA), Minnesota Dept. of	651-201-6620
Food Certificate for Export/Certificate of Free Sale	Agriculture (MDA), Minnesota Dept. of	651-201-6676
Food, Beverage and Lodging License	Health (MDH), Minnesota Dept. of	651-201-4500
Environmental Health Specialist/Sanitarian Registration License		
Minnesota Certified Food Protection Manager (MCFPM)		
Wild Rice Dealer License / Wild Rice Harvest License	Natural Resources (DNR), Minnesota Dept. of	651-355-0147
Forest Products		
Firewood Producer Certification	Agriculture (MDA), Minnesota Dept. of	888-545-6684
Permit to Cut Timber	Natural Resources (DNR), Minnesota Dept. of	651-259-5280
Special Product and Fuelwood Permits		

REGULATED ACTIVITY	DEPARTMENT	CONTACT
Foster Care		
Adult Foster Care License (Rule 203)	Contact County Social Services or	
Child Foster Care License	County Human Services Department	
Franchises		
Franchise Offer or Sale Registration	Commerce, Minnesota Dept. of	651-539-1638
Frogs		
Nonresident License to Purchase, Possess and Transport Frogs	Natural Resources (DNR), Minnesota Dept. of	651-297-4935
Resident Frog Dealer (Take, Possess, Transport, Sell)		
Resident License to Purchase, Possess and Transport Frogs		
Fuels		
Refuse Derived Fuel Processing Permit	Pollution Control Agency (MPCA), Minnesota	651-296-6300
Fuels Distributors License	Revenue (DOR), Minnesota Dept. of	651-296-0889
Special Fuel License		800-657-3938
Fundraising		
Charitable Solicitation / Professional Fundraiser Registration	Attorney General, Minnesota Office of	651-757-1496
Funeral Directors		
Mortuary Science (Mortician) License	Health (MDH), Minnesota Dept. of	651-201-3829
Funeral Establishments		
Crematory License	Health (MDH), Minnesota Dept. of	651-201-3829
Funeral Establishment License		
Fur		
Fur Buyer (Raw) -Nonresident	Natural Resources (DNR), Minnesota Dept. of	651-355-0147
Fur Buyer (Raw) Corporation -Nonresident		
Fur Buyer -Supplemental		
Fur Tanning and Dressing License		
Game and Fur Farm License		
Raw Fur Dealer		
Gambling / Gambling Equipment		
Distributor's License	Gambling Control Board, Minnesota	651-639-1900
Excluded Bingo / Excluded Raffle		
Exempt Permit for Limited Gambling Activities		
Gambling Manager's License		
Manufacturer's License		
Organization License		
Manufacture and/or Distributor of Gambling Devices	Public Safety (DPS), Minnesota Dept. of	651-201-7529
Temporary Possession of a Gambling Device		
Lawful Gambling Tax Permit	Revenue (DOR), Minnesota Dept. of	651-297-1772 800-657-3605
Game Farm		
Game and Fur Farm License	Natural Resources (DNR), Minnesota Dept. of	651-297-4935
Gas Storage Underground		
Underground Storage of Gas or Liquids Using Natural Geologic Formations Permit	Natural Resources (DNR), Minnesota Dept. of	651-296-0322
Gasoline		
Fuels Distributor License	Revenue (DOR), Minnesota Dept. of	651-296-0889
Genetically Engineered Organisms		
Agricultural Based Genetically Engineered Organism Release Permit	Agriculture (MDA), Minnesota Dept. of	651-201-6531
Non-Agricultural Based Genetically Engineered Organism Release Permit	Environmental Quality Board (EQB), MN Minnesota Dept. of Administration	651-201-2477

REGULATED ACTIVITY	DEPARTMENT	CONTACT
Genetics		
Genetic Counselor	Medical Practice, Minnesota Board of	612-617-2130
Geology		
Geologist-in-Training Professional Geologist	Architecture, Engineering, Land Surveying, Landscape Architecture, Geoscience and Interior Design (AELSLAGID), MN Board of	651-757-1518
Ginseng, Buying and Selling		
License to Buy or Sell Wild Ginseng	Natural Resources (DNR), Minnesota Dept. of	651-297-4935
Grain		
Grain Buyer's License Grain Buying and Storing License	Agriculture (MDA), Minnesota Dept. of	651-201-6157
Grocery Stores (see **Food**)		
Group Homes		
Boarding Care Home Supervised Living Facility	Health (MDH), Minnesota Dept. of	651-201-4101
Boarding and Lodging Establishment or Lodging Establishment Providing Special services Registration	Health (MDH), Minnesota Dept. of	651-201-4101
Guides		
Lake Superior Fishing Guide License	Natural Resources (DNR), Minnesota Dept. of	651-297-4935
Bear Hunting Outfitters License Master Bear Hunting Outfitters License	Natural Resources (DNR), Minnesota Dept. of	651-355-0147
Hazardous Waste		
Hazardous Waste Generator License Hazardous Waste Treatment, Storage or Disposal Permit	Pollution Control Agency (MPCA), Minnesota	651-296-6300 800-657-3864
Health Care Facilities		
Birth Center License Boarding Care Home Boarding and Lodging Establishments or Lodging Establishments Providing Special Services Freestanding Outpatient Surgical Centers Hospice Hospital and Critical Access Hospital License Housing with Services (HWS) Establishment Mobile Health Evaluation and Screening Provider Nursing Homes Supervised Living Facility	Health (MDH), Minnesota Dept. of	651-201-4101
Mental Health Center and Clinic Certification (Rule 29)	Human Services (DHS), Minnesota Dept. of	651-431-6500
Health Clubs (see CLUBS)		
Health Maintenance Organizations (HMO)		
Accountable Provider Network (APN) License Community Integrated Service Network License Health Maintenance Organization Certificate of Authority	Health (MDH), Minnesota Dept. of	651-201-5100 800-657-3916
Hearing Aids		
Hearing Instrument Dispenser (HID) Certification / Trainee	Health (MDH), Minnesota Dept. of	651-201-3731
Hemp		
Industrial Hemp Pilot Program Growers / Processors License	Agriculture (MDA), Minnesota Department of	651-201-6123
Herbs		
License to Buy or Sell Wild Ginseng	Natural Resources (DNR), Minnesota Dept. of	651-297-4935

REGULATED ACTIVITY	DEPARTMENT	CONTACT
Home Health Care		
Home Management Registration	Health (MDH), Minnesota Dept. of	651-201-4101
Hospice		
Home Care	Health (MDH), Minnesota Dept. of	651-201-5273
Hospice (see HOME HEALTH CARE)		
Hospitals		
Hospital and Critical Access Hospital License	Health (MDH), Minnesota Dept. of	651-201-4101
Hotels, Motels and Restaurants		
Lodging License	Health (MDH), Minnesota Dept. of	651-201-4500
Minnesota Certified Food Manager Certification (CFPM)		
Food, Beverage and Lodging License	Health (MDH), Minnesota Dept. of	651-201-4505
Bed and Breakfast Registration (to serve wine)	Public Safety (DPS), Minnesota Dept. of	651-201-7507
Hunting Guide (see GUIDES)		
Immigration Services	Review Minn. Stat. § 325E.031	
Insurance		
Insurance Adjusters: Various	Commerce, Minnesota Dept. of	651-539-1599
Insurance Agency:		
Corporate or Partnership Agency		
Individual Proprietorship Agency		
Insurance Agent: Non-resident Producer / Resident Producer		
Managing General Agent		
Reinsurance Intermediary: Resident Brokers and Managers		
Reinsurance Intermediary: Non-resident Resident Brokers and Managers		
Travel Insurance Producer Business Entity License		
Insurance Premium Finance Company	Commerce, Minnesota Dept. of	651-539-1700
Vehicle Protection Product Warrantor Registration	Commerce, Minnesota Dept. of	651-539-1743
Purchasing Groups	Commerce, Minnesota Dept. of	651-539-1745
Third Party Administrator License	Commerce, Minnesota Dept. of	651-539-1748
Utilization Review Organization (URO) Registration		
Viatical Settlement Broker / Investment Agent / Provider		
Interior Designer		
Certified Interior Designer	Architecture, Engineering, Land Surveying, Landscape Architecture, Geoscience and Interior Design (AELSLAGID), MN Board of,	651-757-1515
Interpreter		
Spoken Language Health Care Interpreter Roster	Health (MDH), Minnesota Dept. of	651-201-3731
State Court Interpreter -Spoken Language Certification	Judicial Branch, Minnesota	651-297-5300
Invention Development Services		
Invention Development Service Disclosure	Attorney General, Minnesota Office of	651-296-3353
Investment Adviser / Investing		
Investment Adviser	Commerce, Minnesota Dept. of	651-539-1638
Securities Agent, Securities Broker-Dealer		
MNvest Portal Operator Registration		
Jewelry (see **Precious Metals**)		

REGULATED ACTIVITY	DEPARTMENT	CONTACT
Junk Dealers, Pawnbrokers, and Second Hand Dealers		
May be regulated by both city & county where business is located.		
Kennels (see **Animals**)		
Laboratories		
Environmental Laboratory Accreditation	Health (MDH), Minnesota Dept. of	651-201-5324
Land Surveyor		
Land Surveyor / Land Surveyor-In-Training	Architecture, Engineering, Land Surveying, Landscape Architecture, Geoscience and Interior Design (AELSLAGID), MN Board of,	651-757-1518
Lands (Public)		
Registration of Exploratory Borer	Natural Resources (DNR), Minnesota Dept. of	651-231-8464
Permit for Removal of Stockpiled Iron-Bearing Material	Natural Resources (DNR), Minnesota Dept. of	651-231-8484
Permit to Cut Timber	Natural Resources (DNR), Minnesota Dept. of	651-259-5280
Special Product and Fuelwood Permits		
Easement Across State-Owned Land Managed by the Minnesota Department of Natural Resources (DNR),	Natural Resources (DNR), Minnesota Dept. of	651-259-5404
Lease of State-Owned Land Managed by the DNR		
State Industrial Minerals Lease		
State Iron Ore/Taconite Lease		
State Metallic Minerals Lease		
State Peat Lease		
License to Cross Public Lands and Waters	Natural Resources (DNR), Minnesota Dept. of	651-259-5959
Permit to Mine-Iron Ore and Taconite		
Permit to Mine-Nonferrous and Metallic Minerals		
Permit to Mine Peat		
Resource Management Access Permit	Natural Resources (DNR), Minnesota Dept. of	651-296-6157
Special Events on State Forest Roads Permit		
Landscape		
MnDOT Landscape Specialist Certificate	Transportation (MnDOT), Minnesota Dept. of	651-336-3631
Landscape Architect		
Landscape Architect	Architecture, Engineering, Land Surveying, Landscape Architecture, Geoscience and Interior Design (AELSLAGID), MN Board of,	651-757-1514 651-757-1515
Lawn Service (see **Fertilizer** and **Pesticides**)		
Lawyer		
Lawyer Registration	Lawyer Registration Office, Minnesota Minnesota Judicial Branch	651-296-2254
Lead		
Independent Examination Permit	Health (MDH), Minnesota Dept. of	651-201-4620
Lead Firm Certificate		
Lead Inspector License		
Lead Interim Control Worker		
Lead Project Designer License		
Lead Risk Assessor License		
Lead Sampling Technician		
Lead Supervisor License		
Lead Training Course Permit		
Lead Worker License		
Notification of Lead Hazard Reduction Work and Amendments		
Liming Material		
Agricultural Liming Material License	Agriculture (MDA), Minnesota Dept. of	651-201-6725
Limousine Service (see **Motor Carrier**)		

REGULATED ACTIVITY	DEPARTMENT	CONTACT
Liquor / Alcohol		
Brand Label Registration	Public Safety (DPS), Minnesota Dept. of	651-201-7504
Brew Pub Brand Registration		
Brew Pub Off Sale Intoxicating Liquor License		
Brewer Off Sale Intoxicating Liquor License		
Broker's Employee License		
Brokers License to Represent a Distillery, Winery or Importer		
Certification of an On Sale Brewer's Taproom License and Sunday License		
Common Carrier (Plane/Boat/Train) License to Sell Intoxicating or 3.2% Malt Liquor		
Consumption and Display (Set up) Permit		
Distilled Spirits Importer's License		
Farm Winery License / Farm Winery Branch License		
Importer's Representative's Identification Card		
License to Sell Intoxicating or 3.2% Malt Liquor on a Common Carrier		
Malt Beverage Importer's License		
Micro Distiller / Micro Distillers Cocktail Room		
Micro Distillers Off Sale License		
Sacramental Wine License		
Small Brewer Off Sale Intoxicating Liquor License		
Tour Boat Intoxicating Liquor License		
Wholesaler -Intoxicating Liquor / Malt Beverages / WineBranch License		
Wholesaler / Manufacturer Intoxicating Liquor License		
Wholesaler's / Manufacturer Salesperson's ID Card		
Wholesaler's / Manufacturer Intoxicating Liquor License		
Wine Importer License		
Wine or Malt Beverage Educator On-Sale License		
Bed and Breakfast Registration (to serve wine)	Public Safety (DPS), Minnesota Dept. of	651-201-7507
Brewer Sampling Notice		
Club On Sale Retail Liquor License		
Manufacturer's (Brewer/Malt Liquor/Intoxicating Liquor) Warehouse Permit		
Renewal of Liquor, Wine, or Club License		
Retailers Identification (Buyer's) Card for Liquor & Wine		
County/City On Sale Wine License	Public Safety (DPS), Minnesota Dept. of	651-201-7510
County On Sale Intoxicating Liquor License		
Off Sale Intoxicating Liquor License		
Consumption and Display (Set up) Permit	Public Safety (DPS), Minnesota Dept. of	651-201-7512
Permit to Purchase and/or Possess Ethyl Alcohol and/or Distilled Spirits		
Consumption and Display, Temporary One Day Permit	Public Safety (DPS), Minnesota Dept. of	651-201-7513
Permit for a 1 Day - 4 Day Temporary On-Sale Liquor Permit		
Sacramental Wine License		
Caterer's Permit with Alcohol	Public Safety (DPS), Minnesota Dept. of	651-201-7525
Certification of an On Sale Liquor License, 3.2% Liquor License, or Sunday Liquor License		
Optional 2 A.M. Permit		
Livestock		
Livestock Dealer / Dealer's Agent License	Agriculture (MDA), Minnesota Dept. of	320-634-7354
Livestock Market Agency License		
Livestock Meat Packing Company / Agent License		
Livestock Auction Markets and Community Sales	Animal Health (BHA), Minnesota Board of	651-296-2942
Loans (Non-Bank Lenders)		
Accelerated Mortgage Payment Provider	Commerce, Minnesota Dept. of	651-539-1570
Consumer Small Loan Lender (Payday Lender) / Branch		
Industrial Loan and Thrift Company / Branch License		
Motor Vehicle Sales Finance Company / Branch License		
Regulated Loan Company / Branch License		

REGULATED ACTIVITY	DEPARTMENT	CONTACT
Lobbyists		
Lobbyist Registration	Campaign Finance and Public Disclosure Board, Minnesota	651-539-1187 800-657-3889
Managed Care		
Workers' Compensation Managed Care Org Cert.	Labor and Industry (DLI), Minnesota Dept. of	651-284-5173
Manufactured Homes		
Manufactured Home Park License	Health (MDH), Minnesota Dept. of	651-201-4510
Manufactured Home Dealer License	Labor and Industry (DLI), Minnesota Dept. of	651-284-5034
Manufactured Home Dealer Subagency License		
Manufactured Home Installer		
Manufactured Home Limited Dealer License		
Manufactured Home Manufacturer License		
Manure		
Commercial Animal Waste Technician (CAWT)	Agriculture, Minnesota Dept. of	651-201-6615
Massage (see **Unlicensed and Complimentary Health Care Practitioners** for State compliance information)		
Massage Therapists	Contact local city government offices for any local licensing requirements.	
Marriage		
Marriage and Family Therapist	Marriage and Family Therapy, Minnesota Board of	612-617-2220
Marriage License	Local Registrar of County	
Meat Packing		
Wholesale Food Processor Manufacturer USDA	Agriculture (MDA), Minnesota Dept. of	651-201-6027
Livestock Meat Packing Company / Agent License	Agriculture (MDA), Minnesota Dept. of	651-201-6290
Medical Gas		
Medical Gas Certification Registration	Labor and Industry (DLI), Minnesota Dept. of	651-284-5031
Medical Gas Dispenser	Pharmacy, Minnesota Board of	651-201-2825
Medical Waivers		
Driver Medical Waivers	Transportation (MnDOT), Minnesota Dept. of	651-366-3700
Medicine, Practice of		
Genetic Counselor	Medical Practice, Minnesota State Board of	612-617-2130
Medical Faculty License		
Physician (Doctor of Medicine (M.D.) and Doctor of Osteopathic Medicine (D.O.))		
Physician Assistant Registration		
Professional Firm Registration		
Respiratory Care Practitioner Registration		
Telemedicine Registration		
Podiatrist	Podiatric Medicine, Minnesota Board of	612-617-2200
Mental Health Services		
Mental Health Center and Clinic Certification (Rule 29)	Human Services (DHS), Minnesota Dept. of	651-431-6500
Residential Treatment for Emotionally Disturbed Children License (Rule 5)		
Residential Treatment for Mentally Ill Adults License		
Midwifery		
Traditional Midwife License	Medical Practice, Minnesota State Board of	612-617-2130
Mining and Minerals		
Permit for Removal of Stockpiled Iron-Bearing Materials	Natural Resources (DNR), Minnesota Dept. of	218-231-8484
Registration of Exploratory Borer		
Permit to Mine - Iron Ore and Taconite/ Nonferrous Metallic Minerals/Peat	Natural Resources (DNR), Minnesota Dept. of	651-259-5959
State Iron Ore/Taconite/ Metallic Minerals/Peat Lease		

REGULATED ACTIVITY	DEPARTMENT	CONTACT
Ministers		
Ministers of any religious denomination, before they are authorized to solemnize a civil marriage, shall file a copy of their credentials of license or ordination or, if their religious denomination does not issue credentials, authority from the minister's spiritual assembly, with the local registrar of a county in this state, who shall record the same and give a certificate of filing thereof. The place where the credentials are recorded shall be endorsed upon and recorded with each certificate of civil marriage granted by a minister. See Minn. Stat. § 517.04 - .05 and .18.		
Mixed Martial Arts (MMA)		
Boxing / MMA Officials/Corner License	Office of Combative Sports, Minnesota,	651-284-5366
Mixed Martial Arts (MMA) Combatant License	Labor and Industry (DLI), Minnesota Dept. of	
Promoter License (Combative Sports)		
Mobile Homes (see **Manufactured Homes**)		
Money Transmitting		
Money Transmitter	Commerce, Minnesota Dept. of	651-539-1600
Mortgage Originator or Servicer		
Closing Agent	Commerce, Minnesota Dept. of	651-539-1599
Mortgage Loan Originator License	Commerce, Minnesota Dept. of	651-539-1600
Residential Loan Mortgage Originator License / Exemption		
Morticians		
Mortuary Science (Mortician) License	Health (MDH), Minnesota Dept. of	651-201-3829
Motels (see **Hotels**, **Motels and Restaurants**)		
Motor Carrier		
Motor Carrier Direct Pay Certificate	Revenue (DOR), Minnesota Dept. of	651-296-6181
Building Mover License	Transportation (MnDOT), Minnesota Dept. of	651-215-6330
Driver Medical Waivers		
Household Goods Mover Permit		
Passenger Carrier Registration (Intrastate)		
Property Carrier Registration (Intrastate)		
Moving Buildings Over Highways Permit When Over Legal Size(s) or Over Legal Weight	Transportation (MnDOT), Minnesota Dept. of	651-296-6000
Oversized, Overweight Vehicles: Single Trip Permit, Job Permit, and Annual Permit		
Unified Carrier Registration Agreement	Transportation (MnDOT), Minnesota Dept. of	651-366-3680
Limousine Service Permit	Transportation (MnDOT), Minnesota Dept. of	651-366-3700
Special Transportation Service (STS)		
Motor Vehicle Dealers		
Drive-Away/In-transit License	Public Safety (DPS), Minnesota Dept. of	651-201-7800
Motor Vehicle Dealers License et al.		
Note: A "Dealer" includes licensed new motor vehicle dealers, used motor vehicle dealers, motor vehicle brokers, wholesalers, auctioneers, lessors of new or used motor vehicles, scrap metal processors, used vehicle parts dealers, and salvage pools.		
Motorized Vehicles / Utility Vehicles		
All-terrain Vehicle (ATV) Dealer / Manufacturer License	Natural Resources (DNR), Minnesota Dept. of	651-296-2316
Boat Dealer License		800-285-2000
OHM (Off-highway Motorcycle) Dealer / Manufacturer		
ORV (Off-road Vehicle) Dealer's / Manufacturer License		
Snowmobile Dealer / Manufacturer License		
Nonresidential Services Programs		
Day Training and Habilitation (DT & H) Services for the Developmentally Disabled	Human Services (DHS), Minnesota Dept. of	651-431-6500
Independent Living Assistance for Youth License (245A.22)		
Supported Employment Services (SES) for Persons with Developmental Disabilities		

REGULATED ACTIVITY	DEPARTMENT	CONTACT
Notary Public		
Notary Public Commission	Secretary of State (SOS), Office of the MN	651-296-2803 877-551-6767
Nurseries		
Nursery Stock Dealer / Grower Certificate	Agriculture (MDA), Minnesota Dept. of	651-201-6329
Minnesota Grown Logo Labeling License	Agriculture (MDA), Minnesota Dept. of	651-201-6510
Nursing		
Supplemental Nursing Services Agency Registration	Health (MDH), Minnesota Dept. of	651-201-4101
Nursing Assistant Registry	Health (MDH), Minnesota Dept. of	651-215-8705
Approval of a Nursing Program Approval of Professional (Registered) Nursing Programs APRN (Advanced Practice Registered Nurse) Registry Border State Registry Licensed Practical Nurse (LPN) / Registered Nurse (RN) Professional Nursing Firms Registration Public Health Nurse Registration Certificate	Nursing, Minnesota Board of	612-317-3000
Nursing Home Administrators		
Nursing Home Administrator	Executives for Long Term Services and (BELTSS), Board of	651-201-2730
Nursing Homes		
Nursing Homes	Health (MDH), Minnesota Dept. of	651-201-4101
Nutritionist		
Nutritionist License	Dietetics & Nutrition Practice, Minnesota Board of	651-201-2764
Occupational Therapy		
Occupational Therapy (OT) Practitioner / Occupational Therapy Assistant (OTA)	Occupational Practice Therapy, Minnesota Board of	651-548-2179
Optometry		
Optometrist Professional Firm Registration	Optometry, Minnesota Board of	612-617-2173
Osteopaths (see DOCTORS)		
Pawnbrokers		
Pawnbrokers Code of Conduct	Contact local city or county government offices.	
Payroll		
Payroll Services Registration (Third Party Bulk Filer)	Revenue (DOR), Minnesota Dept. of	651-282-5225 800-657-3605
Payroll Card Issuer	Labor and Industry (DLI), Minnesota Dept. of	651-284-5070 888-342-5354
Peddlers, Transient Merchants		
Peddler, Transient Merchant License	Contact local County and City offices	
Personal Care Assistant		
Personal Care Assistant (PCA) Certification	Human Services (DHS), Minnesota Dept. of	651-431-2700 800-366-5411 651-431-4300
Pesticide		
Golf Course Pesticide Applicator License Pesticide Dealer License	Agriculture (MDA), Minnesota Dept. of	651-201-6137
Bulk Pesticide/Fertilizer Storage Facility or Substantial Alteration Permit	Agriculture (MDA), Minnesota Dept. of	651-201-6274
Structural Pest Control Applicator/Company License	Agriculture (MDA), Minnesota Dept. of	651-201-6379

REGULATED ACTIVITY	DEPARTMENT	CONTACT
Pesticide (continued)		
Pesticides Registration	Agriculture (MDA), Minnesota Dept. of	651-201-6583
Commercial Pesticide Applicator License	Agriculture (MDA), Minnesota Dept. of	651-201-6615
Noncommercial Pesticide Applicator		
Private Pesticide Applicator Certificate		
Application for a Permit to Control: Aquatic Plants, Algae, Algae, Swimmer's Itch, and Leeches	Natural Resources (DNR), Minnesota Dept. of	651-259-5200
Pet Food		
Commercial Feed License (Includes Pet and Specialty Pet Foods)	Agriculture (MDA), Minnesota Dept. of	651-201-6176
Pet Food Processing Permit	Animal Health (BAH), Minnesota Board of	651-296-2942
Petroleum (see **Fuels** and **Storage**)		
Pharmacist / Pharmacy		
Drug / Medical Gas Wholesaler / Medical Gas Distributor	Pharmacy, Minnesota Board of	651-201-2825
Drug Manufacturer		
Pharmacist License		
Pharmacy Preceptor / Intern Technician Registration		
Pharmacy / Pharmacy Technician License		
Professional Firm Registration		
Physical Therapy		
Physical Therapist / Therapist Assistant License	Physical Therapy, Minnesota State Board of	612-627-5406
Physician Assistants		
Physician Assistant (registration)	Medical Practice, Minnesota Board of	612-617-2130
Pipefitter		
Master / Journeyworker High Pressure Pipefitter (HPP)	Labor and Industry (DLI), Minnesota Dept. of	651-284-5031
Unlicensed High Pressure Pipefitter (HPP) Registration		
High Pressure Pipefitter (HPP) Contractor	Labor and Industry (DLI), Minnesota Dept. of	651-284-5034
Pipelines		
Pipeline Routing Permit	Public Utilities Commission, Minnesota	651-201-2255
Plants		
Minnesota Seed Permit		
Screenings Purchase Permit	Agriculture (MDA), Minnesota Dept. of	651-201-6309
Nursery Stock Dealer / Grower Certificate	Agriculture (MDA), Minnesota Dept. of	651-201-6329
Collecting, Labeling and Selling Certain Wildflowers	Agriculture (MDA), Minnesota Dept. of	651-201-6619
Endangered Species Permit	Natural Resources (DNR), Minnesota Dept. of	651-259-5073
Permit to Transport and/or Collect Aquatic Vegetation	Natural Resources (DNR), Minnesota Dept. of	651-259-5092
Application for a Permit to Control: Aquatic Plants, Algae, Swimmer's Itch & Leeches	Natural Resources (DNR), Minnesota Dept. of	651-259-5200
Plumbers		
Backflow Prevention Certification	Labor and Industry (DLI), Minnesota Dept. of	651-284-5031
Certified Pipelayer		
Master / Journeyman Plumber License		
Unlicensed Individual - Plumbing Registration		
Plumbing Contractor / Contractor Bond	Labor and Industry (DLI), Minnesota Dept. of	651-284-5034
Podiatric Medicine, Practice of		
Podiatrist	Podiatric Medicine, Practice of	612-617-2200
Professional Firm Registration		
Police		
Peace Officer License	Peace Officer Standards and Training (POST), Minnesota Board of	651-643-3060

REGULATED ACTIVITY	DEPARTMENT	CONTACT
Pools (Public)		
Certified Pool Operator	Health (MDH), Minnesota Dept. of	651-201-4503
Swimming Pool and Spa Pool Plan Review		
Poultry		
Poultry Dealer Permits	Animal Health (BAH), Minnesota Board of	320-231-5170
Poultry Hatchery & Breeding Flock Permits		
Poultry Import Permits		
Poultry Testing Agent Authorization		
Power Plant Siting		
Site Designation and Certificate of Site Compatibility	Public Utilities Commission (PUC), Minnesota	651-201-2255
Precious Metal		
Bullion Product Dealer / Dealer Representative	Commerce, Minnesota Dept. of	651-539-1599
Precious Metal Dealer License	Regulated by County Auditor	
Note: A Precious Metal Dealer is any person(s) engaged in the business of buying secondhand items containing precious (silver, gold and platinum) metal. Minn. Stat. § 325F.73		
Private Detectives / Protective Agents		
Private Detectives License	Private Detective and Protective Agent Services, Minnesota Board of	651-793-2666
Protective Agent Services License		
Psychology, Practice of		
Licensed Psychologist	Psychology, Minnesota Board of	612-617-2230
Professional Firm Registration		
Racing (Horse)		
Advanced Deposit Wager (ADW) Provider	Racing Commission (MRC), Minnesota	952-496-7950
Racing Class A License (Ownership and Operation)		
Racing Class B License (Racing & Card Club Operation)		
Racing Class C License (Occupational)		
Racing Class D License (County Agricultural Assns.)		
Veterinarian	Veterinary Medicine, Minnesota Board of	651-201-2844
Radiation		
Radioactive Materials Licensing	Health (MDH), Minnesota Dept. of	651-201-4400
Radiologic Technicians Note:		
Note: Contact American Registry of Radiologic Technologists at 651-687-0048. Minnesota is not a licensing state.		
Radio		
Radio Station	Federal Communications Commission	202-418-2700
Radio Monitoring		
Mobile Monitor Permit - Individual / Media / Non-Law Monitoring	Bureau of Criminal Apprehension (BCA), MN	651-793-1054
Radon		
Radon Measurement Professional License	Health (MDH), Minnesota Dept. of	651-201-4601
Radon Mitigation Professional / Company & Sole Proprietor		
Raffles (see **Charitable Organizations** and **Gambling**)		
Real Estate		
Abstracter: Company & Individual Proprietor / Individual	Commerce, Minnesota Dept. of	651-539-1599
Appraiser: Nonresident / Residential		
Appraisal Management Company		
Closing Agent		
Real Estate Broker: Limited Broker / Nonresident / Resident		
Real Estate Company		
Real Estate Salesperson: Nonresident / Resident		
Subdivided Land and Time Shares Registration	Commerce, Minnesota Dept. of	651-539-1638

REGULATED ACTIVITY	DEPARTMENT	CONTACT
Recreational Camping Area (see **Camps & Campgrounds**)		
Recyclers (see **Chloroflurocarbons (CFCs)** and **Motor Vehicle Dealer**)		
Refuse-Derived Fuel Processing		
Refuse Derived Fuel Processing Permit	Pollution Control Agency (MPCA), Minnesota	651-296-6300 800-657-3864
Registrar (see **Deputy Registrar**)		
Rehabilitation Consultants / Counselors		
Qualified Rehabilitation Consultants, QRC Firms, and Registered Rehabilitation Vendors	Labor and Industry (DLI), Minnesota Dept. of	651-284-5083
Rehabilitation Counselor for the Blind	State Services for the Blind (SSB), MN DEED	651-642-0500
Rendering Plant (see **Animals**)		
Research, Drug		
Controlled Substance Researcher	Pharmacy, Minnesota Board of	651-201-2825
Residential Services Programs		
Housing with Services Establishment Registration	Health (MDH), Minnesota Dept. of	651-201-4101
Children's Residential Facilities Residential Treatment for Mentally Ill Adults (Rule 36)	Human Services (DHS), Minnesota Dept. of	651-296-0156
Respiratory Therapist		
Respiratory Care Practitioner Registration	Medical Practice, Minnesota Board of	612-617-2130
Restaurants		
Food, Beverage and Lodging License Minnesota Certied Food Protection Manager (CFPM)	Health (MDH), Minnesota Dept. of	651-201-4505
Bed and Breakfast Registration (to serve liquor)	Public Safety (DPS), Minnesota Dept. of	651-296-6159 651-296-9519
Roads and Highways		
Moving Buildings Over Highways Permit When Over Legal Size(s) or Over Legal Weight Oversized Vehicles: Single Trip Permit, Job Permit, and Annual Permit	Transportation (MnDOT), Minnesota Dept. of	651-296-6000
Access Driveway Permit Construction of Tunnels Under Highways Permit Drainage Permit Miscellaneous Work On Trunk Highway Right of Way Utility Permit on Trunk Highway Right of Way	Transportation (MnDOT), Minnesota Dept. of	651-366-4668
Advertising Device Permit	Transportation (MnDOT), Minnesota Dept. of	651-366-4671
Roofers		
Residential Roofer	Labor and Industry (DLI), Minnesota Dept. of	651-284-5034
Safe Deposit Box Company		
Safe Deposit Box Company	Commerce, Minnesota Dept. of	651-539-1714
Sales and Use Tax		
Tax Identification (ID) Number	Revenue (DOR), Minnesota Dept. of	651-282-5225 800-657-3605
Sales and Use Tax Exempt Status	Revenue (DOR), Minnesota Dept. of	651-296-6181 800-657-3777

REGULATED ACTIVITY	DEPARTMENT	CONTACT
Salons		
Cosmetology -Individual Licenses, Salons and Schools	Cosmetology, Minnesota Board of	651-201-2742
Salvage, Motor Vehicle (see MOTOR VEHICLE DEALER)		
Sand and Gravel		
Air -Non-Metallic Mineral Processing General Permit	Pollution Control Agency (MPCA), Minnesota	651-282-6143 800-657-3938
Sanitarians		
Environmental Health Specialist / Sanitarian Registration License	Health (MDH), Minnesota Dept. of	651-201-4500
Satellite Television Systems (see COMMUNICATION CONTRACTORS)		
Scanners		
Mobile Monitor Permit - Individual / Media / Non-Law Monitoring	Bureau of Criminal Apprehension (BCA), MN	651-793-1054
School Administrator		
School Administrative Licenses	School Administrators (BOSA), Minnesota	651-582-8754
Schools		
Barbers and Barbershops: Various Classes	Barber Examiners, Minnesota Board of	651-201-2820
Cosmetology - Individual Licenses, Salons and Schools Cosmetology School Surety Bond	Cosmetology, Minnesota Board of	651-201-2742
Approval of Practical Nursing Programs Approval of Professional (Registered) Nursing Programs	Nursing, Minnesota Board of	612-317-3000
Degree-Granting Institutional Registration Private Career School License	Office of Higher Education (OHE), Minnesota	651-642-0567 800-657-3866
Commercial Driver Training School License	Public Safety (DPS), Minnesota Dept. of	651-296-3966
Screenings		
Screenings Purchase Permit	Agriculture (MDA), Minnesota Dept. of	651-201-6123
Second Hand Dealers		
May be regulated by both city and county where business is located.		
Securities Sales		
MNvest Portal Operator Registration Securities Broker-Dealers Firm and Agents Securities Offering Registration	Commerce, Minnesota Dept. of	651-539-1638
Security Guards		
Protective Agent Services License	Private Detective and Protective Agent Services, Minnesota Board of	651-793-2666
Security Systems (see **Alarm and Communication Contractors**)		
Seeds		
Minnesota Seed Permit Screenings Purchase Permit	Agriculture (MDA), Minnesota Dept. of	651-201-6531
Shelters (see **Bus Shelters** and **Health Care Facilities**)		
Shooting Preserves		
Commercial Shooting Preserve License Private Shooting Preserve License	Natural Resources (DNR), Minnesota Dept. of	651-297-4935
Signs (see **Advertising Devices**)		

REGULATED ACTIVITY	DEPARTMENT	CONTACT
Social Work		
Social Work Professional Firm Registration	Social Work (BOSW), Minnesota Board of	612-617-2100
Social Worker License (Various Classes)		
Professional Firm Registration		
Soil Science		
Professional Soil Scientist	Architecture, Engineering, Land Surveying, Landscape Architecture, Geoscience and Interior Design (AELSLAGID), MN Board of,	651-757-1513
Soil Scientist-In-Training		
Solid Waste		
Industrial Solid Waste Land Disposal Permit	Pollution Control Agency (MPCA), Minnesota	651-296-6300 800-657-3864
Mixed Municipal Solid Waste Land Disposal Permit		
Municipal Solid Waste Combustor Ash Land Disposal Permit		
Solid Waste Recycling Facility Permit-By-Rule (PBR)		
Solid Waste Storage Permit		
Solid Waste Transfer Facility Permit		
Type II Landfill Operator or Inspector Certificate		
Type III Landfill Operator or Inspector Certificate		
Type IV Waste Disposal Operator or Inspector Certificate	Pollution Control Agency (MPCA), Minnesota	651-757-2599
Type V Waste Disposal Operator or Inspector Certificate		
Special Events on DNR lands		
Special Events Permit	Natural Resources (DNR), Minnesota Dept. of	651-296-6157
Special Transportation Services		
Special Transportation Services (STS) Certificate	Transportation (MnDOT), Minnesota Dept. of	651-366-3700
Speech Pathology		
Speech-Language Pathologist License	Health (MDH), Minnesota Dept. of	651-201-3726
Sprinkler Systems		
Fire Protection Managing Employee Certificate	State Fire Marshall, Public Safety (DPS), Minnesota Dept.	651-201-7207
Fire Protection Sprinkler System Contractor License		
Fire Protection Sprinkler System Designer Contractor License		
Fire Sprinkler Systems Plan Review		
Journeyman Sprinkler Fitter Certification		
Limited Journeyman Sprinkler Fitter Certification		
Multipurpose Potable Water Piping System Contractor/Installer/Journeyman License		
Storage (see also **Warehouses**)		
Underground Storage of Gas or Liquids Using Natural Geologic Formations Permit	Natural Resources (DNR), Minnesota Dept. of	763-425-0322
Student Exchange Organizations		
International Student Exchange Organizations	Secretary of State (SOS), Office of the MN	651-296-2803
Subdivided Lands		
Subdivided Land and Time Shares Registration	Commerce, Minnesota Dept. of	651-539-1638
Surety Bond		
Cosmetology School Surety Bond	Cosmetology Examiners, Minnesota Board	651-201-2742
Mechanical Contractor Bond	Labor and Industry (DLI), Minnesota Dept. of	651-284-5034
Plumbing Contractor Bond		
Sign Contractor Bond		

REGULATED ACTIVITY	DEPARTMENT	CONTACT
Tanks		
Aboveground Storage Tank (AST) Permits (>1M Gallon)	Pollution Control Agency (MPCA), Minnesota	651-296-6300
Aboveground Storage Tank (AST) Registration		800-657-3864
Underground Storage Tank (UST) Contractor / Supervisor Certificate		
Underground Storage Tank (UST) Registration	Pollution Control Agency (MPCA), Minnesota	651-757-2429
Tanning Facilities		
Safety and equipment standards established by Minn. Stat. § 325H.01 et. Seq. For licensing information contact the municipality where the facility is located.		
Taxes		
Unfair Cigarette Sales Act (UCSA) Fee	Commerce, Minnesota Dept. of	651-539-1500
Payroll Services Registration (Third Party Bulk Filer)	Revenue (DOR), Minnesota Dept. of	651-282-5225
Tax Identification (ID) Number (Sales Tax and Use Permit)		800-657-3605
Fuels Distributors License / Special Fuel Dealer	Revenue (DOR), Minnesota Dept. of	651-296-0889
Motor Carrier Direct Pay (MCDP) Certificate	Revenue (DOR), Minnesota Dept. of	651-296-6181
Sales and Use Tax Exempt Status Certificate		
Gambling Tax Permit	Revenue (DOR), Minnesota Dept. of	651-297-1772 800-657-3605
Cigarette & Tobacco Distributor & Subjobber Licenses	Revenue (DOR), Minnesota Dept. of	651-556-5035
Taxidermy		
Taxidermist License	Natural Resources (DNR), Minnesota Dept. of	651-355-0147
Teaching		
Teaching Licenses -Various Types / Special Permissions	Professional Educator Licensing and Standards Board (PELSB)	651-539-4200
School Administrative Licenses	School Administrators, Minnesota Board of	651-999-7387
Telecommunication Service Provider		
Wholesale Transport Registration	Public Utilities Commission (PUC), Minnesota Commerce, Minnesota Dept. of	651-539-1880
Telemarketing		
Telemarketing Sales Rule	Federal Trade Commission (FTC), U.S.	877-382-4357
Television		
Television Station	Federal Communications Commission (FCC), U.S.	202-418-1600 888-225-5322
Timber (see also **Forest Products**)		
Tobacco		
Unfair Cigarette Sales Act (UCSA) Fee	Commerce, Minnesota Dept. of	651-539-1500
Fire Standard Compliant Cigarettes (FSC) Certification	State Fire Marshal, Public Safety (DPS), Minnesota Dept. of	651-201-7203
Cigarette & Tobacco Distributor & Subjobber Licenses	Revenue (DOR), Minnesota Dept. of	651-297-1882
Tow Truck Operators		
Vehicle Owner	Contact local city or county government office	
Trailer Parks		
Manufactured Home Park License	Health (MDH), Minnesota Dept. of	651-201-4510

REGULATED ACTIVITY	DEPARTMENT	CONTACT
Trees		
Tree Care Registry	Agriculture (MDA), Minnesota Dept. of	651-201-6095
Firewood Producer Certification	Agriculture (MDA), Minnesota Dept. of	888-545-6684
Certified Tree Inspector	Natural Resources (DNR), Minnesota Dept. of	651-259-5300
Tunnels		
Construction of Tunnels Under Highways Permit	Transportation (MnDOT), Minnesota Dept. of	651-366-4668
Turtle and Tortoise		
Turtle and Tortoise License	Natural Resources (DNR), Minnesota Dept. of	651-297-4935
Underground Storage Tanks (see TANKS)		
Unlicensed Complimentary and Alternative Health Care Practitioners	Office of Unlicensed Complementary and Alternative Health Care Practice (OCAP), Health (MDH), Minnesota Dept. of	651-201-3706

All unlicensed complementary and alternative health care providers (CAP) must comply with Minn. Stat. Chapter 146A. The Minnesota statute contains a partial list of the types of practices that are included in these statutory requirements. Some of these are massage therapy, aromatherapy, acupressure, healing touch, Qi Gong energy healing, healing practices utilizing food, food supplements, nutrients and the physical forces of heat, cold, water, touch and light, detoxification therapy, herbalism, homeopathy and naturopathy. The statute is designed to cover all unlicensed complementary and alternative healing methods and treatments.

The last section of the law requires each practitioner to provide each client with a client bill of rights prior to service. (Minn. Stat. § 146A.11) A client bill of rights must also be posted in a prominent location in the office. The purpose of the client bill of rights is to give all clients access to relevant information about the complementary and/or alternative service they will receive, and information about how to file a complaint if they are dissatisfied.

There is specific statutory language which must be copied identically from the statute. This language is in quotations. Also, each client must sign a statement showing that s/he received the bill of rights.

REGULATED ACTIVITY	DEPARTMENT	CONTACT
Utilities		
Route Permit for High Voltage Transmission Lines	Public Utilities Commission (PUC), Minnesota	651-296-7124
Site Permit for Large Electric Generating Power Plant		
Site Permit for Large Wind Energy Conversion Systems		
Installation of Utilities and/or Miscellaneous Work on State Rail Bank Property	Transportation (MnDOT), Minnesota Dept. of	651-366-4668
Utility Accommodation on Trunk Highway Right of Way		
Utility Crossings of Public Lands and Waters		
License to Cross Public Lands and Waters	Natural Resources (DNR), Minnesota Dept. of	651-296-0237
Vending Machines		
Retail Food Handler License	Agriculture (MDA), Minnesota Dept. of	651-201-6627
Unfair Cigarette Sales Act (UCSA) Fee	Commerce, Minnesota Dept. of	651-539-1500
Cigarette & Tobacco Distributor & Subjobber Licenses	Revenue (DOR), Minnesota Dept. of	651-556-3035
Veterinary Medicine		
Professional Firm Registration	Veterinary Medicine, Minnesota Board of	651-201-2844
Veterinarian		
Viatical Settlements		
Viatical Settlement Broker / Investment Agent / Provider License	Commerce, Minnesota Dept. of	651-539-1748
Warehouses		
General Merchandise Storage License	Agriculture (MDA), Minnesota Dept. of	651-201-6011
Grain Buy and Store License	Agriculture (MDA), Minnesota Dept. of	
Grain Buyer License		
Manufacturer's (Brewer/Malt Liquor/Intoxicating Liquor) Warehouse Permit	Public Safety (DPS), Minnesota Dept. of	651-284-7507

REGULATED ACTIVITY	DEPARTMENT	CONTACT
Waste		
Compost Facility Permit	Pollution Control Agency (MPCA), Minnesota	651-296-6300
Demolition Debris Disposal Facility Permit-By-Rule		800-657-3864
Demolition Debris Land Disposal Facility Permit		
Feedlot Construction Short-Form Permit		
Feedlot Interim Permit		
Feedlot NPDES/SDS Permit (General and Individual)		
Hazardous Waste Generator License		
Hazardous Waste Treatment, Storage or Disposal Permit		
Industrial Solid Waste Land Disposal Permit		
Mixed Municipal Solid Waste Land Disposal Permit		
Municipal Solid Waste Combustor Ash Land Disposal Permit		
Refuse Derived Fuel Processing Permit		
Registration (Feedlot Program)		
Solid Waste Recycling Facility Permit-By-Rule		
Solid Waste Storage Permit		
Solid Waste Transfer Facility Permit		
State Disposal System Permit		
Subsurface Sewage Treatment Systems License (Designers, Installers, Inspectors, Maintainers) Certificate		
Wastewater-Municipal & Industrial NPDES/SDS Permit		
Type II Landfill Operator or Inspector Certificate	Pollution Control Agency (MPCA), Minnesota	651-757-2072
Source-Separated Organic Materials Transfer Facility Permit-By-Rule (PBR)	Pollution Control Agency (MPCA), Minnesota	651-757-2348
Type III Landfill Operator or Inspector Certificate		800-657-3864
Type IV Waste Disposal Operator or Inspector Certificate	Pollution Control Agency (MPCA), Minnesota	651-757-2599 800-657-3864
Type V Waste Disposal Operator or Inspector Certificate		
Wastewater Operator Certification		
Water Appropriation		
Water Appropriation General Permit -Animal & Livestock Operations	Natural Resources (DNR), Minnesota Dept. of	651-259-5700
Water Appropriation General Permit - Temporary Projects		
Water Appropriation Irrigation Permit		
Water Appropriation Non-Irrigation Permit		
Water Conditioning		
Unlicensed Individual -Water Conditioning Installer	Labor and Industry (DLI), Minnesota Dept. of	651-284-5031
Water Conditioning Installer Master/Journeyman		
Water Conditioning Contractor	Labor and Industry (DLI), Minnesota Dept. of	651-284-5034

REGULATED ACTIVITY	DEPARTMENT	CONTACT
Water Quality		
Lake Service Provider (LSP)	Natural Resources (DNR), Minnesota Dept. of	651-259-5131
Feedlot Construction Short-Form Permit		651-296-6300
Feedlot Interim Permit		800-657-3864
Feedlot NPDES/SDS Permit (General and Individual)		
Feedlot Registration		
Feedlot State Disposal System Permit		
Sanitary Sewer Extension Permit		
State Disposal System Permit		
Wastewater-Municipal & Industrial NPDES/SDS Permit		
Wastewater -SDS Pretreatment General Permit (MNP)		
Industrial Stormwater Multi-Sector General Permit	Pollution Control Agency (MPCA), Minnesota	651-757-2119
NPDES General Permit		800-657-3804
NPDES/SDS Industrial Stormwater General Permit		
Balast Water Permits	Pollution Control Agency (MPCA), Minnesota	651-757-2380
Underground Storage Tank (UST) Registration	Pollution Control Agency (MPCA), Minnesota	651-757-2429
		800-657-3938
Wastewater Operator Certification	Pollution Control Agency (MPCA), Minnesota	651-757-2599
		800-657-3864
Water Supply		
Water Operator Training Approval	Health (MDH), Minnesota Dept. of	651-201-4690
Water Supply System Operator Certificate		
Water Wells and Borings		
Wells and Borings: Bored Geothermal Heat Exchanger Contractor	Health (MDH), Minnesota Dept. of	651-201-4600 888-345-0823
Wells and Borings: Dewatering Well Contractor License		
Wells and Borings: Environmental Well Contractor		
Wells and Borings: Explorer License (Exploratory Borings)		
Wells and Borings: Monitoring Well Contractor License		
Wells and Borings: Screen & Pitless Installer License		
Wells and Borings: Well Contractor License		
Wells and Borings: Well Sealing Contractor License		
Waters (Public)		
Lake Aeration Systems Permit	Natural Resources (DNR), Minnesota Dept. of	651-259-5087
Public Waters Work Permit	Natural Resources (DNR), Minnesota Dept. of	651-259-5700
Dam Safety Permit	Natural Resources (DNR), Minnesota Dept. of	651-259-5715
License to Cross Public Lands and Waters	Natural Resources (DNR), Minnesota Dept. of	651-296-0237
Weighing and Measuring Equipment		
Placing in Service Permit	Commerce, Minnesota Dept. of	651-539-1599
Wild Rice		
Wild Rice Dealer License	Natural Resources (DNR), Minnesota Dept. of	651-355-0147
Wild Rice Harvest License		
Wildlife Exhibit		
Permit to Exhibit Captive Wildlife	Natural Resources (DNR), Minnesota Dept. of	651-772-7906
Workers' Compensation		
Letter of Recognition of a Collective Bargaining Agreement Related to Workers� Compensation	Labor and Industry (DLI), Minnesota Dept. of	651-284-5432
X-Ray Machines (see **Radiation**)		
Limited Scope X-ray Operator & Bone Densitometry Exams	Health (MDH), Minnesota Dept. of	651-201-4545
X-Ray Equipment Operator Test		
X-Ray Equipment Service Provider		